P9-CDC-561

The Southern Colonial Frontier, 1607-1763

W. Stitt Robinson

University of Kansas

HISTORIES OF THE AMERICAN FRONTIER
Ray Allen Billington, General Editor
Howard R. Lamar, Coeditor

UNIVERSITY OF NEW MEXICO PRESS

Albuquerque

Library of Congress Cataloging in Publication Data

Robinson, Walter Stitt.
    The southern colonial frontier, 1607–1763.

    (Histories of the American frontier)
    Bibliography: p. 271
    Includes index.
    1. Southern States—History—Colonial period,
ca. 1600–1775. 2. Frontier and pioneer life—
Southern States. I. Title.
F212.R62   975'.02   78-21432
ISBN 0-8263-0502-4
ISBN 0-8263-0503-2 pbk.

© 1979 by the University of New Mexico Press. All rights reserved.
Manufactured in the United States of America.
Library of Congress Catalog Card Number: 78–21432
International Standard Book Number: 0–8263–0503–2 (Paper)
                              0–8263–0502–4 (Cloth)
First edition.

DEACCESSIONED

The Southern Colonial Frontier, 1607-1763

DEACCESSIONED

TO CONNIE

Foreword

Just fifty years ago—in 1928—Verner W. Crane, then a young associate professor at Brown University, first called attention to the significance of the southern colonial frontier in his groundbreaking monograph, *The Southern Frontier, 1670–1732,* an in-depth study of the Carolina fur trade as an instrument for expansion. In the half-century since that pioneering volume appeared, hundreds of scholars have extended the beachhead that he established; learned articles and monographic studies have dealt with the exploration of the overmountain country, aspects of the movement of peoples into the piedmont and Appalachians, Indian wars and alliances, the sectional conflicts that arrayed tidewater planters against interior farmers, and dozens of other topics related to expansion. Surprisingly, however, no author has undertaken the formidable task of synthesizing and interpreting this vast body of material to provide a single integrated narrative history of the southern frontier.

That is the achievement of Professor W. Stitt Robinson of the University of Kansas in this scholarly book. Relying on the voluminous volume of detailed information entombed in articles in state and national journals, the hundreds of monographs that probe aspects of the subject, and his own extensive research findings, he has produced a volume that blends the masses of information accumulated during the past half-century into a readable narrative rich in interpretative passages and meaningful conclusions. The result is a book that not only sheds light on an important aspect of the American experience, but adds significantly to our knowledge of frontiering and the frontier process.

Professor Robinson's concern, properly, is with the movement of peoples and their institutions from seaboard to interior, and with the impact of that movement on their lives and thought. The first frontier that he describes—the Chesapeake Bay coastal lowlands—is actually a frontier of Europe. In two solid chapters he explores the relationship between the New World environment and the imported Old World cultures, showing both the extent to which pioneers adapted and the degree to which traditionalism stifled innovation. In the succeeding chapters the reader follows the frontiersmen southward and westward as they swarm into the Carolinas, occupy the piedmont uplands, and eventually overrun the rich valleys of the Appalachians to the verge of the Mississippi Valley. Professor Robinson's final chapters appraise the impact of the wars for empire on the South, in terms first of the Spanish thrust northward from the Floridas, then of the French thrust eastward from the interior. He climaxes his narrative by telling us much about the educational and religious changes resulting from the westering experience.

The broad outlines of this story are well known to historians. To it, however, Professor Robinson has added two things: a well-conceived structure that reveals hitherto isolated elements of the story to be meaningfully related, and an abundance of detailed information that allows us to understand southern colonial expansion for the first time. We have known a great deal about the settlement pattern as population spread westward from the Chesapeake Bay lowlands; he adds a virtual mile-by-mile description of that migration, as well as a demographic analysis that tells us much about its nature. We have known that many settlers of the interior were Scots-Irish and Germans from Pennsylvania; he balances our understanding by showing us that a large number of the pioneers were from east of the mountains, and by tracing their course westward parish by parish, county by county. We have known that speculators played a major role in the occupation of the Great Valley; he documents that role by telling us how and where they operated, and by delineating the strength of their influence. Every page brings the reader face to face with fresh information and enlightening interpretations.

The result is a book of sound scholarship that will reward the well-versed historian as well as the first-time reader. Professor Robinson has not written an excitement-packed yarn for the armchair voyager into the past. His treatment of the French and Indian War is not a gory account of wilderness warfare and hair-buying; rather, it shows the inability of the southern colonies—themselves largely isolated from direct attack—to cooperate in defensive measures or in aiding their northern neighbors. The reader learns, too, that a less glamorous conflict—the Cherokee War—occupied the attention of the backwoods south while more romantic heroes were creating legends by battling the French and Indians in the northern forests. The focus of this book is not on the romantic but on what seemed—and was—important to the colonists. This is the stuff of good history, and Professor Robinson has written some very good history indeed.

His volume is one of a multivolume series, "The Histories of the American Frontier," being published by the University of New Mexico Press under the able supervision of its director, Hugh W. Treadwell. This series has a dual role: first, to describe in some fifteen volumes—of which this is one—the advance of the frontier across that portion of the North American continent that we now know as the United States; second, to explore aspects of the pioneering experience that make the story of expansion meaningful to today's society. Within this second category, books are being prepared on the frontier family, the lumber frontier, comparative frontiers, and the expansion of western cultures over the Pacific basin.

Whatever its category, each volume in the series is written by a recognized authority who brings to his task an intimate knowledge of the subject that he covers and a demonstrated skill in narration and interpretation. Each will offer the general reader a sound but readable account of one phase of the frontiering experience, and the specialized student a documented narrative built on fresh information and integrated into the broader story of the nation's growth. It is the hope of the authors and editors that this full account of the most American part of the American past will expand our understanding of an important portion of our national heritage, and thus aid the American people to understand themselves as they face the global problems of the twentieth-century world.

Ray A. Billington

The Huntington Library

Howard R. Lamar

Yale University

Preface

One of the distinguishing characteristics of the late medieval period and the early modern era of European history was the impulse for expansion. Europe entered upon one of its most dynamic periods as explorers and colonizers went forth in all directions, searching for trade and new trade routes, for gold and other precious metals, and for new domains to aggrandize the emerging national states. They traveled also for religious purposes, motivated either by a burning missionary zeal or by the desire to worship as they pleased. Whether religious crusaders, agents of a national state, authorized individual entrepreneurs, or simply adventurers and freebooters, they contributed to the expansionistic spirit of the Age of Exploration and Discovery.

England under the Tudors, having emerged from the nationalizing crucible of the Hundred Years War with France, was well aware of the vigorous Portuguese trade with the East and of the Spanish ventures in the Americas that poured gold into the nation's coffers. She also knew of the efforts of her recent antagonist, France, in exploring and colonizing ventures during the sixteenth century under such leaders as Jacques Cartier.

England's thin claim to North America went back to the voyage of John Cabot in 1497 under the authorization of the Tudor King Henry VII to search out and occupy all lands "which before this time have bene unknowen to all Christians."[1] She continued her probing of unknown areas during the sixteenth century. Martin Frobisher and others sought unsuccessfully a northwest passage to the Orient; Hugh Willoughby and Richard Chancellor searched for a northeast route. Still other Englishmen spread over the Atlantic in more southerly waters. Elizabethan sea dogs led by John Hawkins and Francis Drake challenged the Spanish trade monopoly by seizing Spanish gold and other valuables from ships or colonies wherever found and returning with their booty to tell of "singeing King Philip's beard." Sir Humphrey Gilbert, carrying letters patent of 1578 from Queen Elizabeth I, lost his life in 1583 while attempting to colonize as far north as Newfoundland. In 1584, under almost identical patent provisions, Sir Walter Raleigh, half-brother of Sir Humphrey, was authorized to discover and occupy "such remote, heathen and barbarous lands, countries, and territories, not actually possessed of any Christian Prince, nor inhabited by Christian People."[2]

Raleigh lost no time in preparing for exploratory and colonizing expeditions to the New World. His efforts, however, failed to establish a permanent

English settlement with the "Lost Colony" of 1587 on Roanoke Island. But the contributions of two adventurers on his expeditions, Thomas Hariot and John White, produced a lasting influence on subsequent colonizers and on students of these pioneer efforts. Hariot, mathematician and expert in matters of navigation, accompanied the 1585 expedition and wrote his *Briefe and True Report of the New Found Land of Virginia,* the originals of which have become highly cherished items of Americana. White, an artist on the 1585 expedition and governor of the 1587 one, created valuable paintings of Indians and the American flora and fauna. His drawings were reproduced as engravings in 1590 by Theodore De Bry of Frankfurt along with a reprinting of Hariot's *True Report,* and the contributions of Hariot and White helped draw attention to one of Europe's most challenging frontiers.

America was, indeed, one of the frontiers of Europe in this Age of Exploration and Colonization. The early coastal settlements, separated from the mother country by an ocean, differed from the usual frontier, which was adjacent to established areas over a continuous land mass. Therefore, the first settlements were more isolated than later ones. In influencing the development of American civilization, the European heritage confronted not only the distant and isolated environment but also two new racial groups, the Indian and the Negro. It is the American experience on the southern colonial frontier, from Maryland south to Georgia, that is the focus of this study.

Problems within individual colonies have been considered, where necessary, before those that transcended colonial boundaries. Most often it has seemed desirable to treat the common frontier problems of Maryland and Virginia as a part of the Chesapeake country, and then consider the area of the two Carolinas and Georgia. The scope of the study has necessitated a limited selection of examples to illustrate the general statements that are made. But efforts have been made to draw upon the history of all the southern colonies, from the work of other scholars and from the writer's own original research in both the United States and Great Britain.

In addition to the essential features of government with changes that resulted through years of experience and the variety of economic experiments that contributed to the development of the basic economy, attention is directed to the role of land policy in settling a new country and the contest for territorial control in international wars involving primarily England, France, and Spain. Special emphasis has been given to the influence of the frontier in intercolonial problems, Indian-white relations, and the importance of ethnic groups in cultural history.

The broad range of agreements and disagreements in intercolonial affairs involved frontier problems as one of their most persistent issues. Boundary disputes, Indian trade regulations, and military campaigns led to negotiations among colonial leaders, either through their own initiative or by instructions from the crown. These negotiations, whether successful or not, were a part of the vital experience in efforts for unified actions that eventually resulted in the collective action of the American colonies in the American Revolution.

Indian affairs, consistently a critical factor, at times determined the very existence of pioneer settlements. The space devoted to Indian relations in colonial records is much greater than the limited attention given by some modern writers would indicate. There have been eloquent pleas for the ethnohistorical approach that would provide a more thorough history of the Indians and reflect the Indian point of view. Certainly more complete and better balanced histories of Indian tribes are needed for an analysis of Indian-white relations. Within the space limits of this study, however, it has been possible to include only limited material on the history of various tribes. Efforts have been made to give a judicious and fair appraisal of the Indian without attempting to write from what might be called the Indian view.

Cultural history of the southern colonies stands as one of the areas still in need of further research, including the old established regions as well as new frontier settlements. Primary attention in this study has been given to two of the most important areas of cultural endeavor—religion and education. They involve particularly the role of various European ethnic groups, including their interaction with each other as well as their contact with the Indian and the Negro.

The term *frontier* is used in three ways, and its meaning in each case will, I hope, be clear from the context. First, there are occasional references to the *frontier line of settlement,* which refers to expanding areas of limited population, containing approximately from two to six persons per square mile. Second, the term may designate a *frontier colony* or a *frontier county*—that is, a geographic setting near unoccupied regions, usually endowed with available land and other natural resources capable of prosperous development. We think of such frontiers as pointing west, but in colonial days they might extend in other directions—to the north, south, or even to the east. Third, the struggle of individuals for survival and for improvement of their own position in society, as well as the modification of their institutions in the geographic setting described above, is called *the frontier experience.*

Quotations in the text have been transcribed literally, with only minor changes in form for the purpose of readability. Raised letters, for example, have been uniformly lowered. Words which used *v* where we use a *u*, or *f* where we use *s*, are reproduced here in the modern form. The thorn (*y*) has been replaced by *th*, giving *the* instead of *ye;* the ampersand (*&*) has been transcribed as *and.*

Since the Gregorian reforms of the calendar were not adopted by the British until 1752, it has been necessary to distinguish between Old Style and New Style. The day of the month from original sources has been retained as Old Style, and both years have been included from January 1 to March 25.

Space does not permit recognition of all the individuals who have contributed to the completion of this volume. For assistance in making research materials available, however, I would like to express my appreciation to the staffs of the following institutions: Library of Congress in Washington, D.C.; Clements Library, Ann Arbor, Michigan; the Newberry Library, Chicago; in Maryland, the Hall of Records at Annapolis and the Maryland Historical Society in Baltimore; in Virginia, the Virginia State Library and Virginia Historical Society in Richmond, and the library of the University of Virginia in Charlottesville; in North Carolina, the Division of Archives and History at Raleigh, the Library of the University of North Carolina at Chapel Hill, and the Library of Duke University at Durham; in South Carolina, the South Carolina Department of Archives and History and the South Caroliniana Library in Columbia, and the South Carolina Historical Society in Charleston; in Georgia, the Georgia Department of Archives and History in Atlanta and the Library of the University of Georgia at Athens; and in Kansas, the Library of the University of Kansas. In my research abroad, excellent cooperation was provided in London by the British Public Record Office, British Museum, Lambeth Palace Library, and the Society for the Propagation of the Gospel in Foreign Parts; in Belfast, the Public Record Office of Northern Ireland; and in Edinburgh, the National Library of Scotland, the Scottish Record Office, and the Library of the University of Edinburgh.

I would also like to express my gratitude for financial assistance through research grants from the Social Science Research Council, the American Philosophical Society, and the General Research Fund of the University of Kansas which has also provided sabbatical leaves.

A special word of thanks is extended to editors for their many helpful suggestions and queries: Ray Allen Billington of the Huntington Library as General Editor of the Series, Howard R. Lamar of Yale University as Coeditor, and David V. Holtby of the editorial staff of the University of New Mexico Press.

University of Kansas   W. Stitt Robinson
Lawrence, Kansas
January 1979

Contents

List of Illustrations

List of Maps

1

The Chesapeake's First Frontier: Virginia, 1607–32

During the dawning years of the seventeenth century, English commercial enterprise, which since the days of Henry VII had sparked the exploration of distant North America, was ready to undertake the more ambitious task of colonization. Merchants in London and from outports such as Plymouth and Bristol petitioned for the right to establish colonies in America in the area generally known as Virginia, a name fashioned by Sir Walter Raleigh to glorify his virgin queen. In response, two companies were incorporated by the charter of 1606, the Virginia Company of London and the Plymouth Company.[1] The London Company was authorized to settle a tract of land 100 miles square in the southern part of the area extending from the thirty-fourth to the forty-first degrees north latitude, or from the Cape Fear River in present North Carolina to modern New York City. Within this area the company launched English colonization of North America in 1607 with the first permanent English settlement at Jamestown, part of the Chesapeake's first frontier.

Colonists found a variety of terrain on the southern colonial frontier from Maryland south through Georgia. Jamestown was part of the coastal plain or tidewater, a flat or slightly rolling area often low and swampy near the serried coastline, ranging in width from about fifty to over two hundred miles. The coastal plain extended westward to the fall line, an imaginary line along the falls or rapids of the rivers where small-ship navigability ended. Near the western edge of the tidewater was a strip approximately fifty miles wide through the Carolinas and Georgia known as the pine barren section. Its sandy soil and twisted, scraggy pine trees provided opportunities for forest products, such as naval stores, but at the same time the area posed unfamiliar challenges to the agricultural pioneer. The tidewater rivers and their valleys, with richer soil than the ridges, were particularly important for agriculture and became preferred avenues of migration; the fall line became historically significant as the location of clusters of settlements that later became commercial centers and towns or cities.

West of the fall line was the piedmont. Its hilly, undulating surface reached toward the mountains in a series of ridges and valleys noted for their natural beauty as well as for the geographical features that differentiated it from the

1

coastal plain. Having a higher elevation and somewhat cooler climate, the piedmont contained a soil that was less sandy than the coastal plain and in some places boasted a limestone base. The mountain barriers to the westward-moving pioneer were parts of the Appalachian Highland, including the Blue Ridge Mountains of Virginia, with the forest-covered ranges, and the Great Smoky Mountains in North Carolina. Lying between the Blue Ridge on the east and the top of the Allegheny Mountains to the west was a vast system of parallel ridges and valleys extending from New York into northern Alabama from northeast to southwest. The valleys were a favorite route for immigrants in the eighteenth century. Few English colonials except hunters, land speculators, and soldiers ventured beyond the Allegheny and Cumberland mountains before 1763 and from there into the Ohio and Mississippi valleys.

Over this varied terrain the colonists encountered many Native American groups. Their presence provided a challenge as persistent for the newcomers to America as adjustment to a new physical environment. The Indians' social and political organizations—village, band, tribe, nation, and confederacy—had evolved prior to the arrival of Europeans. Though classified by race as of Mongoloid stock, they exhibited variations in size, color of skin, shape of head, and other physical characteristics. Early colonists also noted variations in dress, skin painting, hair styles, and body adornments indicative of differences in culture among the native groups.

One of the most useful and most scientific ways of classifying Indians is by language. For the area north of Mexico, inhabited by more than a million Native Americans when the Europeans arrived, one estimate suggests as many as 300 different languages. A widely accepted classification contains seven major phyla, or language superstocks, for all of America north of Mexico. Two of these cover most of the Southeast and extend to other areas: (1) the Macro-Algonquian phylum including the Algonquian family, with the Powhatan Confederacy and the Shawnee, and the Muskhogean family, consisting of such groups as the Creeks, Chickasaw, and Choctaw; (2) the Macro-Siouan phylum with the Siouan family and the Iroquoian family, including the Cherokee, Tuscarora, and the Five Nations in New York of Seneca, Cayuga, Onondaga, Mohawk, and Oneida. Within these general classifications there were also dialects which posed additional problems of communication for colonists, particularly for traders and missionaries who had more frequent contact with local groups.[2]

A second classification that has been widely accepted is the division of Indians into culture areas based upon geographical and natural influences determined by environmental and ecological factors. No classification is entirely satisfactory, a situation further complicated for the southeastern United States by the limited archaeological work that has thus far been completed. But these natural areas do provide meaningful designations for

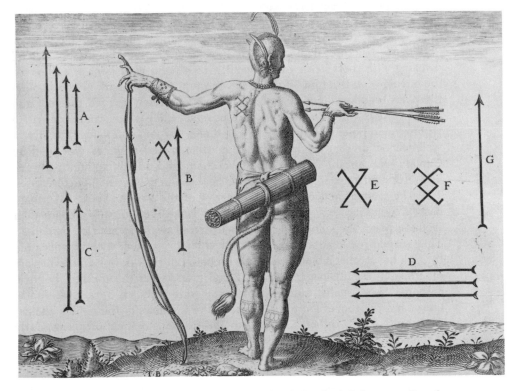

Marks of the chief men in early Virginia (present-day North Carolina). Indians near Roanoke Island in the 1580s identified themselves with marks painted on their backs relating them to a leader or a particular village. Figure A, for example, was the mark of Wingina, chief of Roanoke; figures C and D belonged to chiefs of the village of Secota. (Engraving of John White's watercolor by Theodore De Bry published in 1590. This photograph reproduced from the German edition, *Wunderbarliche, Doch Warhafftige Erklärung, von der Gelengenheit und Sitten der Wilden in Virginia*, Frankfurt, Germany, 1590.)

such common influences as climate, terrain, vegetation, and fauna. The plentiful supply of trees, for example, provided the material for the huts and houses constructed by the natives; and the presence of animals—particularly the beaver, and, even more important in some areas, the deer—not only provided material for clothing and essential food but also determined many of the trade relationships with whites. A recent description of culture areas divides the United States east of the Mississippi River into the Eastern Woodlands, from Virginia north into Canada, and Southeast, from Virginia south through Florida.[3] These two divisions differed with respect to climate, animals, and other influences, but they shared certain factors, such as the abundance of trees, that shaped the life-style of the natives.

The Indians the Jamestown settlers first encountered were those of the Chesapeake region, and their life-style reflected their adaptation to their surroundings. Using wood from the forests, the Indians constructed houses or huts such as the Algonquian wigwam, including both the circular or "beehive" structure with a domed roof, and the rectangular or "arbor" dwelling with roofs like a tunnel vault. Green poles were bent or arched for the circular constructions of the dome or vault. Strips of bark or roots bound the poles together, and either bark or mats of rushes covered the roof and sides.[4] Houses were usually clustered in small villages, sometimes palisaded with wooden poles or stakes, and located near gardens and fields. They had a well-defined division of labor between women and men; as described by Captain John Smith, "The men bestowe their times in fishing, hunting, wars, and such manlike exercises, scorning to be seene in any woman like exercises. . . . The women and children do the rest of the worke. They make mats, baskets, pots, morters; pound their corne, make their bread, prepare their victuals, plant their corne, gather their corne, beare al kind of burdens."[5] Their social organization was a matrilineal kinship system with identification through the mother's bloodline and with both political power and ownership of property usually passing to the blood relatives of the mother. Political authority was usually exercised by males with only an occasional Indian queen, but the succession to power passed to the heirs of the mother such as from brother to brother and then to the sisters and their offspring. Early Virginians were to witness the helm of political power pass from brother to brother.

The colonists in early Chesapeake settlements had contact first with sedentary Algonquian tribes. In tidewater Virginia the Indians were a part of the Powhatan Confederacy. Named for its leader, the confederacy consisted of about thirty different tribes, six of which had come under Powhatan's jurisdiction by heredity, the other having submitted to his rule through conquest prior to the settlement of Jamestown. While the term *confederacy* has most often been used for the followers of Powhatan, the term *empire* is more appropriate to the organization he was fashioning in the early seventeenth century.[6] Powhatan extended his control by using relatives in key political positions, by exacting tribute from subordinate groups, and by striking forcefully at recalcitrant villages and shifting them to areas more easily supervised. West of the Powhatans in the piedmont area of Virginia were other tribal groups that were usually designated under two confederacies, the Monacan along the James River and the Manahoac near the headwaters of the Rappahannock. Their culture was not as highly developed as the Powhatans, and for many years they have been classified as Siouan linguistic stock, although recent studies have suggested their possible identification with an old dialect of Algonquian.[7] Colonists in early Maryland found primarily Algonquian-speaking natives, including several small groups that were known on the Eastern Shore as Nanticoke, and on the Western Shore as Piscataway. Near the Pennsylvania boundary along the Susquehanna River lived the other group of Maryland Indians who played an important part in Indian-white relations, the Susquehannock.

The town of Secota. The Indian town of Secota, located probably on the north bank of Pamlico River in present Beaufort County, North Carolina, was visited by the colonists sent out by Sir Walter Raleigh in the 1580s. John White's drawing shows a tobacco plot (*E*) and three fields of corn (*F*, *G*, *H*) at different levels of maturity; huts or houses built from poles of trees and including roofs like a tunnel vault; areas where they met for feasts, prayers, and other ceremonies. (Engraving of John White's watercolor by Theodore De Bry, published in *Wunderbarliche*. . . , Frankfurt, Germany, 1590.)

How the Indians built their boats. The Indians near Roanoke Island displayed their ingenuity in building their boats without the metal tools to which they were later introduced. They used fire to fell the tree, burn off the top and boughs, and finally to char the trunk, which was then scraped with shells until the boat was ready for launching in the water. (Engraving of John White's watercolor by Theodore De Bry, published in *Wunderbarliche. . .* , Frankfurt, Germany, 1590.)

Indians played a number of roles in the lives of the newcomers to America. They provided valuable assistance sometimes and at other times threats to survival; they were sources of vital foods yet at times the inflictors of starvation; they supplied valuable skins and furs but also presented a challenge to white hunters and trappers; they were often valuable military allies but on other occasions they were bitter antagonists in the international struggle for America among European powers. The Indians were also objects of crusades for religious conversion and education, and they occupied valuable lands for which titles became controversial. Today we are still debating moral and legal issues raised by the dispossession of the Indian.

Defining the status of land and providing for government were paramount problems for the Chesapeake's first frontier settlement. Following traditions of earlier grants, King James I claimed land in America primarily on the basis of the prior right of discovery and the absence of subjects of any other

Christian prince. Landholding was based in part on vestiges of the feudal system that continued to exist even though constantly being challenged in the age of expansion and colonization. The land was held not "in fee simple" with absolute ownership, a concept that was not a part of English law at the time; it was granted "in free and common soccage," with the holder a tenant of the king, to whom he owed fealty and the payment of a quitrent.[8] In England the quitrent, generally accepted as a fixed rent paid to a feudal superior in lieu of rendering service, was an obligation established by custom. In America, however, it was often viewed more as a tax upon land that had previously carried no such feudal obligation but had been carved out of the wilderness by the sweat and toil of the colonists. Therefore, resistance to the quitrent increased, and it persisted as a point of conflict for officials of government in the southern colonies throughout the period of this study.

The charter of 1606 provided for strong control by the crown over the colonies that were planned by both the London and Plymouth companies. This was achieved through the establishment of the council for Virginia that was appointed by the king. It was to be resident in England and was to answer to the king through the Privy Council for supervision of both companies. In addition, each company was to have a council in America with its initial membership determined by the council for Virginia and with a president selected by the local group. One of these, the London Company, succeeded in starting Jamestown as an important but precarious beginning on the southern colonial frontier.

With preliminary organizations completed for the first expedition of the London Company, three ships, the *Sarah Constant,* the *Godspeed,* and the *Discovery,* sailed in December 1606 and arrived the following spring in Chesapeake Bay with 104 or 105 colonists. After examining various locations, the leaders selected a site that was a reasonable distance from the sea, convenient for western exploration, and could be fortified against hostile Europeans. The area was also low and marshy, however, so malarial conditions and other diseases plagued the first few years of settlement. Despite the abundance of fruits and berries, fish in the many streams, and wild game including deer, bear, and an occasional buffalo, the early settlers had great difficulty in obtaining adequate supplies. They were unfamiliar with the natural resources of America despite the earlier reports such as Thomas Hariot's *Briefe and True Report . . . of Virginia.*[9] They devoted too much attention to the search for trade products and precious metals, particularly gold, to satisfy the major interest of the company.

The cultural baggage of Old World ideas also militated against satisfactory adjustment to New World challenges. The "gentlemen" that came were by English tradition not supposed to engage in manual labor; some even brought footmen, who were a part of the early colony's labor force. Others from sixteenth and early seventeenth century England were influenced by the decreased demands upon their time with the spreading out of employment such as work arrrangements by the year rather than the day, or by the restrictions upon types of work for each person by specialized tasks only. Still others, accustomed to England's small pastures and farms, had traditionally devoted only a little time to cultivation of their small plots and were used to being idle for substantial periods of time. Some settlers viewed the colonial venture as a military expedition, and English tradition did not expect military venturers to produce crops and supplies.[10]

The composition of the early shiploads of settlers contributed directly to the problem. Too many "gentlemen" came on early expeditions and failed to contribute their fair share of labor, either because they were accustomed to privilege or because they lacked skills and experience. Those gentlemen who were willing to exert themselves were of limited usefulness; one contemporary noted that "the axes so oft blistered their tender fingers, that commonly every third blow had a lowd oath to drowne the eccho."[11] Among the first group of settlers, for example, we know the names of 67, and 29 of them were listed as "gentlemen." When more settlers and provisions arrived in 1608, among the 73 (out of 120) immigrants whose names we know, "gentlemen" exceeded laborers by 28 to 21. Among the other occupations listed were preacher, carpenter, blacksmith, barber, tailor, drummer, apothecary, and perfumer.[12] In addition to the excess of "gentlemen," then, there was a striking lack of agricultural workers, and a conspicuous absence of the jack-of-all-trades types who were the American frontiersmen of later years.

The settlers who did come were in effect servants of the company, which owned the product of their labor and operated the colony during the first few years with a common storehouse. Too much reliance was placed upon replacement supplies from England that did not always arrive, and negotiations with neighboring Indians were only partially successful in filling the serious shortages that resulted. George Percy describes vividly the difficulties of September 1607:

> Our men were destroyed with cruell diseases, as Swellings, Flixes, Burning Fevers, and by warres, and some departed suddenly, but for the most part they died of meere famine. There were never Englishmen left in a forreigne Countrey in such miserie as wee were in this new discovered Virginia. Wee watched every three nights, lying on the bare cold ground, what weather soever came, [and] warded all the next day, which brought our men to bee most feeble wretches. Our food was but a small Can of Barlie sod in water, to five men a day, our drinke cold water taken out of the River, which was at a floud verie salt, at a low tide full of slime and filth, which was the destruction of many of our men. Thus we lived for the space of five moneths in this miserable distresse, not having five able men to man our Bulwarkes upon any occasion. If it had not please God to have put a terrour in the Savages

hearts, we had all perished by those vild and cruell Pagans, being in that weake estate as we were; our men night and day groaning in every corner of the Fort most pittifull to heare. If there were any conscience in men, it would make their harts to bleed to heare the pitifull murmurings and outcries of our sick men without reliefe, every night and day, for the space of sixe weekes, some departing out of the World, many time three or foure in a night; in the morning, their bodies trailed out of the Cabines like Dogges to be buried. In this sort did I see the mortalitie of divers of our people.

It pleased God, after a while, to send those people which were our mortal enemies to releeve us with victuals, as Bread, Corne, Fish, and Flesh in great plentie, which was the setting up of our feeble men, otherwise, wee had all perished. Also we were frequented by divers Kings in the Countrie, bringing us store of provision to our great comfort.[13]

Even worse was yet to come. In 1608 fire destroyed the colony's fort and storehouse. Capain John Smith was able to impose some discipline by demanding more work from all colonists and by ruthless negotiations with the Indians, but his departure in 1609 (because of wounds from a gunpowder explosion) was followed by extreme deprivation of supplies and unwillingness on the part of the Indians to trade. So severe was the "starving winter" of 1609 that the colonists temporarily abandoned Jamestown and boarded ship in June 1610, but with the arrival of new supplies they turned back to continue the colony.

There were some signs of new hope in the enlarged and expanded program that was inaugurated in England in 1609. A new charter was sought from the king to make possible reforms in governmental organization both in England and in Virginia; and a broader base for financial support was laid by inviting the public to subscribe to a joint-stock fund. By the charter of 1609 the new organization was incorporated as the Treasurer and Company of Adventurers and Planters of the City of London for the First Colony in Virginia. In England the head of the reorganized company was designated as treasurer, and the major change in control was the transfer of authority over the colony from the crown to the company, with the powers of government in the hands of the treasurer and council. This council in England, which continued for some time to be called the council for Virginia, had its jurisdiction limited to the activities of the London Company; its membership came entirely from the company; and its members were in effect selected by the leading promoters of the company. One major governmental change occurred in the colony when the president and council were eliminated in favor of a strong governor to be advised by a council. The former provision for title to an area of land 100 miles square was changed to give title to "all that space and circuit of land" lying 200 miles north and 200 miles south of Point Comfort

James Fort, Jamestown, Virginia. Reproduction of the James Fort first built at Jamestown in 1607. Located about one mile from the original site, the Fort is 420 feet long facing James River, and 300 feet on the other two sides. The buildings are reproduced of wattle and daub of the type frequently used in the seventeenth century. (Photography courtesy of the Jamestown-Yorktown Foundation, Virginia.)

from the sea coast "up into the land, throughout from sea to sea, west and northwest," plus islands within 100 miles of the coast. While the description "up into the land . . . west and northwest" was vague, it nonetheless served as a lure to Virginians for western expansion in the years ahead.

Promises of land to those who subscribed to the joint-stock undertaking also improved the colony's prospects, although no immediate grants were made to individuals by the charters of 1606, 1609, or the third one in 1612.[14] Already tried successfully by English ventures in the East Indian trade, the joint-stock approach invited individuals to invest money in colonial efforts by ownership of shares, and it also encouraged individual participation in colonization by assigning the value of one share of stock to each person who agreed to go to the new colony. Each share of stock was valued for Virginia at £12 10s. Those who invested their money and remained in England were designated *adventurers*, while the term *planter* was applied to one who went to the colony, with his personal adventure evaluated at one unit of investment at the same rate of £12 10s. Each planter could obtain additional shares by purchase. While resembling in a limited way the corporate shares of stock of more recent times, the joint-stock holdings differed in having a definite time limit or terminable date and in usually being organized for a specific undertaking. Both adventurer and planter were promised a proportionate share of any dividend distributed, whether in land or in money. The joint-stock arrangement was originally set to continue seven years from its inception in 1609. During this period monetary dividends might be declared, and at the end of the period the land suitable for cultivation was to be divided, with at least 100 acres to be given for each share of stock.

In the absence of private title to land in the early years of the Virginia colony, the company relied upon a corporate form of management, pooling community effort to clear the land, construct buildings, develop agriculture, and engage in trade with the Indians. This was not an experiment based on any theory of communism like that later expounded by Karl Marx and Friedrich Engels, for the joint-stock claims were limited in time. Most of the settlers were more in a position of contract laborers performing service for the company, and plans were devised for monetary dividends even before 1616, the end of the seven-year period, if the colony prospered. But the colony did not make significant improvement; the same problems that were evident from its beginning persisted.

Sir Francis West, Lord Delaware (De la Warr), held the commission of governor from 1610 until his death in 1618. Since he spent much of his time in England because of his health, deputy or lieutenant governors actually handled administrative details in the colony, including Sir Thomas Gates and Sir Thomas Dale. Dale proceeded to expand in 1611 the legal regulations set forth the previous year by Gates, resulting in their publication in 1612 in England as *Lawes and Orders, Divine, Politique, and Martial for the Colony of Virginia*. Providing for both civil and military regulations, these laws, sometimes referred to as Dale's Laws, set forth stern measures for many capital crimes, including such offenses as profaning God's name or ridiculing colonial officials. They also delineated military requirements, including guard duty and defense, and they imposed martial law upon the settlers. This last provision, however, applied only to military affairs; it did not mean complete subjection to martial rule, as often interpreted.

Judging from Dale's code of laws and other records, the colonists lived by a more religious and orderly schedule than we might expect in these early chaotic times. Living in homes with gardens assigned to them, the settlers obtained food regularly from the public supply magazine but were free to obtain additional provisions through work in their own plots when not called upon to assist in cultivating crops such as corn and flax in the common gardens. In the seasons requiring labor in cultivation and harvesting, individual workers were called to duty by drum for a four-hour stretch beginning at 6:00 A.M. Religious services intervened at 10:00 A.M., followed by the issuing of supplies from the common storehouse and by periods of leisure. The beat of the drum at 2:00 P.M. signaled the start of another two-hour work session, which ended with a second religious service at 4:00 P.M. Each day, then, included not only two work periods but two worship services; on Sundays there were more intensive meetings.[15] This system appears efficient, but one is struck by the limited number of hours devoted to work by the group—only six hours during the most urgent seasons of cultivation. In addition to whatever explanation is offered for this limited exertion—poor health, hunger, low energy, lack of skills, or the influence of Old World attitudes toward work—the lack of private incentive from individual landholding was surely also a factor.

Colonial officials initiated modifications to the common landholding prior to the promised distribution of land in 1616. Sir Thomas Dale inaugurated private use of land under a tenant-farm policy in 1614, providing for the allotment of three acres of "cleare ground" to settlers whose seven-year indentures were expiring. In effect, they became tenants of the company and were obligated to render only one month's service to the colony at some period other than planting and harvesting time and to contribute annually to the common magazine two barrels and a half of corn on the ear. By 1616, eighty-one colonists out of the total population in Virginia of 351 were a part of the new tenant-farm policy.

These 351 hardy settlers were scattered along the James River. Jamestown had continued from 1607; Kecoughtan (named Elizabeth City after 1619) at the tip of the peninsula facing the entrance to the Chesapeake Bay had its start in 1610; and Henrico established in 1611 at the falls of the James provided the western extreme of the settlement. Between Henrico and Jamestown along the river, Bermuda (later Charles City) was added in 1613 and contained about 68 percent of the settlers upstream beyond Jamestown in 1616. One report in that last year stated, even though somewhat exaggerated, that "They sow and reape their Corne in sufficient proportion without want or impeachment; their Kine multiply already to some hundreds, their Swine to many thousands, their Goates and Poultry in great numbers, every man hath house and ground to his owne use."[16]

The tenant-farm policy temporarily improved supplies, yet problems still beset the company in the tenth year of its operation with only 351 persons alive in the colony and limited funds in the treasury. There had been few new subscribers; some of the earlier subscribers had defaulted on their second or third payments; and the use of lotteries had failed to provide adequate money. The end of joint ownership of land with the declaration of land dividends was to occur in 1616, but the company lacked the necessary funds to defray the administrative costs for the transfer. Furthermore, many believed insufficient acreage had been cleared of trees and surveyed. The arbitrary conduct of the Deputy Governor Samuel Argall, who arrived in Virginia in May 1617, contributed further to the delay in carrying out the plan for land distribution.

The adventurers were told in 1616 that "this course of sending a Governor with Commissioners and a Survayor, with Men, Ships, and sundry provisions" would be expensive, and plans were announced for a preliminary or "first Divident" of fifty acres with the expressed hope that a later division would bring at least 200 acres for every share.[17] The preliminary division, though, required more money, and shareholders were asked to subscribe another £12 10s. to help pay for the administrative cost. A fifty acre grant would be made for each additional subscription. This provision for obtaining land by "treasury right" lapsed in 1624, but it reappeared in 1699 and became an important financial arrangement in the eighteenth century. Planters in the colony were also to receive a fifty acre grant for their personal adventure, and even new adventurers were invited to buy shares at the usual £12 10s. and were promised fifty acres with the privileges of the old adventurers. Response to these offers was poor and the company's woes persisted.

To overcome their financial problems and to encourage further colonization, the officials of the company experimented with solutions through the use of their most positive asset in these early years—the abundance of land. Continuing an earlier precedent, they made grants of land in return for service to the company. The council of Virginia, for example, awarded to Sir Thomas Dale land valued at 700 pounds sterling; to Sir Thomas Smith for his noteworthy efforts as treasurer or chief official of the company, 2000 acres; and to Captain Daniel Tucker for aiding the colony with his pinnace and for his service as vice-admiral, fifteen shares of land.[18]

A further stimulus to colonization and to agricultural production was the company's encouragement of private or voluntary associations, organized on a joint-stock basis, to establish settlements beginning in 1617. These "societies of adventurers" were, at their own expense, to send to Virginia tenants, servants, and supplies. The associates exercised certain governmental powers over the settlement, being authorized until a formal government could be established to issue orders and ordinances consistent with the laws of England. Their holdings, designated particular plantations or hundreds, were not to be located within five miles of the four boroughs officially recognized in 1618, and they were to be ten miles from other settlements unless on opposite sides of an important river.[19] These provisions, designed to foster expansion and at the same time to avoid conflict among plantations, instead tended to disperse the colony and complicated efforts to maintain adequate protection from the threat of hostile natives.

There were three general types of particular plantations. The first of these represented the voluntary pooling of land and resources by several adventurers of the company, since few had adequate land or financial support to go it alone. The company granted a patent to contiguous areas of land in proportion to the number of shares of stock possessed by the group. An excellent example of this type was the Society of Smith's Hundred. Organized in 1617 and named for Sir Thomas Smith, treasurer of the company, its name was changed to Southampton Hundred after Smith's shares were sold to the Earl of Southampton in 1620. The original grant included 80,000 acres and was located on the north side of the James River in the area between Tanks Weyanoke and the Chickahominy River. The associates spent £6000 and settled at least 300 colonists within their boundaries, and there they experimented with the production of iron, herding cattle, and the cultivation of tobacco and corn. Sir George Yeardley, who as governor had a general concern for the welfare of the whole colony and a financial interest in the hundred as well, noted in 1619 that the area was "destitute of cowes" and with unfavorable weather conditions for tobacco, "our cheifest care must be for corne."[20]

In the second type of particular plantation, an adventurer combined with persons outside the company to obtain a grant. The title usually resided in the original adventurer, and the nature of government and special privileges was similar to Smith's Hundred. Captain Samuel Argall in settling Argall's Town used one of the first of this kind. Argall and his associates transported twenty-four colonists for which they received 2400 acres just north of Jamestown. While settlements made at Paspahegh Country and Argall's Town were recognized as legal and separate entities in 1619, they were later absorbed in the area designated as the governor's land.

The third type of grant involved new adventurers who bought stock in the company to organize a particular plantation. An example was the private grant to Christopher Lawne, who with associates transported 100 settlers in 1619 and established Lawne's Plantation on the south side of the James River downstream from Hog Island in the Warrasqueoc area. Lawne soon died and his associates obtained a renewal of the patent in 1620 with the name changed to the Isle of Wight.

Forty-four grants were made for particular plantations in the four years following the election of Sir Edwin Sandys as treasurer in 1619. The company made six others before this time under Sir Thomas Smith. Not all of the projected plantations, however, were ever located, and few were settled to the extent planned by the company. Historical records are scarce for these projects and much of their story remains incomplete.[21]

Migration was stimulated by all three types of particular plantations, and further impetus to change was the company's reorganization of its administration begun in 1618. Sir Thomas Smith was still in control as treasurer and participated in the reform, but the major contribution came from Sir Edwin Sandys, who succeeded to the position of treasurer in the spring of 1619. Rules and by-laws largely prepared in 1618 were formally adopted and restated in the "Orders and Constitutions" in June 1619. A particularly significant change instituted in 1618 was "the greate Charter" containing a uniform land policy.[22]

This charter outlined plans for distribution of the land dividend and included provisions for the headright system. One hundred acres were promised "upon the first division" to all adventurers for each paid-up share of stock at £12 10s., another 100 acres "upon A Second Division" after the first allotment had been settled. Ancient planters—those who had arrived in the colony prior to the departure of Sir Thomas Dale in 1616—were to receive similar grants if they had come at their own expense. These foregoing grants were to be free of quitrent. Ancient planters who came to the colony at the company's expense would receive the same amount of land after a seven-year term of "Service to the Company on the common Land" but would be required to pay a quitrent of one shilling for every fifty acres.

For settlers arriving after the departure of Dale in 1616 or those migrating during the seven-year period from 1618 to 1625, separate regulations applied. If "transported thither at the Companies charges," the colonist was to serve as a half-share tenant for seven years with no promise of a land grant. Any colonist paying his own expense was to receive as a headright fifty acres on the first division and the same amount on the second. This provision for the fifty-acre headright was set up for a seven-year period, but it continued as the essential key to Virginia's land policy for the remainder of the century.[23] Three features were fundamental to this important innovation in land policy. First of all, it used the valuable land resources of the New World as a stimulus to settlement and was an intriguing lure to the landless European. Second, it rewarded the individual settler who could provide his own way to the colony as well as benefited the enterprising promoter who organized and financed the transportation of immigrants by awarding to him a headright grant for each settler. Some of these settlers became indentured servants for three to seven years, and in some colonies they received land after completing their period of indenture. Third, the headright system provided that the amount of land granted should relate directly to the number of people who actually immigrated. Large areas of land were granted only if an appropriate number of newcomers could occupy and develop them. This last principle was often violated during the seventeenth century and eventually abandoned in Virginia in the eighteenth.

For a period from 1619 to 1623, only one-third of the people who purchased a share in the company and thereby received a bill of adventure came to Virginia and took up their claim. Another third sent over agents, or in some cases heirs, to benefit by the grants, while the remaining one-third disposed of their shares to others.[24] About one-seventh of the population of over 1200 in 1624 obtained land from the company;[25] the other settlers continued as indentured servants or tenant farmers working out their maintenance or transportation either for the company or for private individuals who financed their trip.

The image of the American frontiersmen conjures up the isolated settler, living at considerable distance from others and eschewing the influence of group organization. But isolation of individuals or of single family units was not the usual pattern of settlement in early Virginia. Instead, colonists preferred communities as a way to overcome difficulties in a new and strange country, including threats from either the Spanish or Indians. Moreover, the experience of several years of common ownership of land and a common storehouse contributed to the grouping of settlements. As the communal

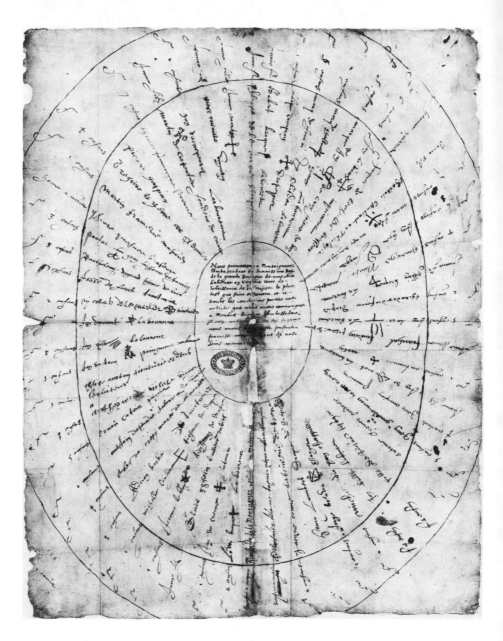

Round Robin Petition from Walloon emigrants to go to Virginia, July 1621. Petition or declaration by Walloon and French emigrants expressing their desire to go to Virginia in 1621. The round robin signatures were arranged in a circle to disguise the order in which they were made and to discourage recriminations against the leaders of the group. (Reproduced by permission of the Public Record Office, London. Document C O 1/1, No. 54A.)

organization gave way to individual title to land and to trade, provision was made for the concentration of settlement in four boroughs. Argall introduced them as early as 1617; they were continued under "the greate Charter" of 1618 as James City, Charles City, Henrico, and Kecoughtan. These four settlements were not county administrative units but were simply population centers; in relation administratively to particular plantations they were of equal but not superior status.

This relationship was evident as the instructions to Sir George Yeardley provided equal number in the representative assembly called in 1619, an important precedent for future government and a step that both transmitted the English tradition of representative government and recognized the local needs of the young and struggling colony. Creation of the Assembly was designed to eliminate the stern measures initiated under "Dale's Laws" and to solicit greater participation by colonists in law making by the election of officials. This move was expected to enhance individual morale, but it was also hoped that the body could forge greater unity of purpose for the settlements.

The councilors selected by the company and the burgesses elected by the freemen met together as the Assembly on July 30. The burgesses had twenty-two representatives, two from each of the eleven districts: James City, Charles City, Henrico, Kecoughtan, Martin's Brandon, Smith's Hundred, Martin's Hundred, Argall's Town, Flowerdew Hundred, Lawne's Plantation, and Warde's Plantation. Representatives for Warde's Plantation were challenged as members of the Assembly because of settlement without authority of the company; however, after examination they were permitted to take their seats with admonition to obtain the necessary permission by the next Assembly. Delegates from Martin's Brandon were denied seats primarily because Martin was unwilling to give up provisions in his patent exempting his settlement "from all services of the Colonie excepte onely in case of warre against a forren or domesticall enemie."[26]

The short session from July 30 through August 4 in a hot summer in Jamestown considered many measures that provide insight into the problems of a frontier community. Attention was given to distribution of land to individuals, protection of the land rights of ancient planters, encouragement of additional settlement, and cultivation of grants already made. The morals of the colony were safeguarded in restrictive measures on idleness, drunkenness, swearing, and gaming at dice and cards. Church attendance was required and taxes were to be imposed for clothing apparel to avoid excesses in dress. Stealing a neighbor's boat or canoe was declared a felony, and restitution was ordered for theft of canoes or other items from the Indians. Throughout the session, the problem of Indian affairs recurred. Some delegates questioned the wisdom of having plantations ten miles apart in view of uncertain relations with the Indians, and caution was urged in employing the natives as laborers in the settlements. Colonists, on the other hand, were exhorted to continue the education and conversion of the Indians by bringing in "the native's children to be educated by them in true religion and civile course of life." Neither dogs of the English nor arms and ammunition were to be sold to the Indians; trading ventures required permission of the governor. In other provisions for improving the economy, tradesmen were urged to work hard and specific encouragement was given to the production of mulberry trees, flax, hemp, vines, and cattle.[27]

This legislation with its encouragement of a variety of crops and products characterizes the economic activities of the early years of Virginia. The colonists, as ordered by the trade-oriented company officials, engaged in fruitless searches for precious metals during the first few years. They also obtained items such as sassafras and clapboards as possible profit-making products for ships returning to England. Their experiments included different crops, both indigenous and imported, as well as wine, silk, glass, and the mining of iron ore. English grain, including wheat, barley, oats, and rye, was planted by early Virginians at the same time they were becoming familiar with maize or Indian corn,[28] and in fact both were sometimes planted in the same field. Governor Samuel Argall noted in 1617 that fields exhausted from the growth of Indian corn would grow English grain. Governor Yeardley during his first year in the colony reported that two crops were obtained from the same field within one year: a harvest of English grain in the spring or early summer followed by a crop of Indian corn in the fall along with some volunteer grain growing from seeds dropped from the harvesting of the first crop. The first Assembly in 1619 encouraged grain and corn production and required that every householder provide "one spare barrell of corne, to be delivered out yearly, either upon sale or exchange as need shall require."[29] The colonists soon preferred Indian corn to English grain and, therefore, gave greater attention to its cultivation. In this way their harvesting experience and their initiative in adjusting to the economic potential of their frontier area were readily apparent in their corp plantings.

Encouragement was also given to viniculture for the production of wine. Virginia Company officials attempted to supplement the native vines by bringing both vines and vignerons in 1610, and the Assembly in 1619 required that each householder should plant and cultivate "ten vines untill they have attained to the art and experience of dressing a Vineyard either by their owne industry or by the Instruction of some Vigneron."[30] Some 10,000 vines were reported on the land designated for a college in 1621.

The production of silk and the growth of mulberry trees for silkworms attracted more interest than viniculture, but early reports of the abundance of both mulberry trees and silkworms were misleading. As it turned out, many of the so-called silkworms were only caterpillars of no use to the silk industry,

Church Tower, Jamestown, Virginia. Church Tower in Jamestown, Virginia, built in 1639. The first representative legislative assembly in the American colonies met on the site of this Church Tower in a wooden church in 1619. (Photograph courtesy of the Jamestown-Yorktown Foundation, Virginia.)

and it became necessary to import both silkworms and "silkworm seeds" from England and the continent. Ralph Hamor noted in 1614 that silkworms had emerged from the cocoons by the thousands, but in 1621 the Virginia Company sent over additional worms from the king's supply in England and from France, Italy, and Spain. Governor Francis Wyatt in the same year received instructions "Not to permit any, but the council and the heads of hundreds, to wear gold in the clothes, or to wear silk till they make it themselves."[31]

Other crops were promoted with less success. The council of the Virginia Company in London instructed Dale to experiment with flax and hemp in 1611. The first Virginia Assembly in 1619 ordered every householder to "plante and dresse" 100 flax plants indigenous to America, and all colonists with seed were to experiment with both hemp and English flax.

The establishment of glass furnaces near Jamestown was one of the most intriguing efforts to promote manufacturing. Founded to provide the colonists glass beads needed for the Indian trade and the glass used by English manufacturers, the intermittent efforts of 1608 and 1609 were renewed in the early 1620s. Several Italians were brought to the colony and directed first by Captain William Norton and after his death by George Sandys, brother of Sir Edwin Sandys and treasurer of the company. The effort, however, had to be abandoned after the unhappy Italians, who wished to return to Europe, caused serious damage to the furnace when one "crackt it with a crow of iron" with the results that it "flew in peeces."[32] The impetuous Italians, a damaging windstorm, Indian attacks, and the problem of getting proper sand all contributed to the abandonment of the venture.

Iron ore was obtained during the first three or four years in early Virginia, and by the 1620s Southampton Hundred took money—including funds for Indian education—and established the iron works on Falling Creek. With assistance also from the company, a total of four to five thousand pounds was expended on the project. This effort continued during the 1620s, but it was soon overshadowed by interest in tobacco production, a crop that pushed aside many economic activities dictated by company officials without knowledge of frontier areas.

Tobacco emerged as the prime product in the Chesapeake economy, despite the opposition of King James I to that "black stinking fume." In his well-known *Counterblast to Tobacco* issued anonymously, King James opposed the increasing use of tobacco introduced from America by early explorers and colonizers like Christopher Columbus and Sir Francis Drake and encouraged in Elizabethan England by Sir Walter Raleigh. King James' objections have become the familiar complaint that the use of tobacco is "a custome loathsome to the Eye, hateful to the Nose, harmful to the Brain, dangerous to the Lungs." He also employed more gentle appeals, asserting that the use of tobacco was "against all humanity," for the husband was not

Glass House, Jamestown, Virginia. A reproduction of the Glass House of 1608 at Jamestown. Glassmaking was one of the first industries attempted in the colony of Virginia. (Photograph courtesy of the Jamestown-Yorktown Foundation, Virginia.)

"ashamed to reduce thereby his delicate, wholesome, and clean-complexion'd Wife to that extremity, that either she must also corrupt her sweet Breath therewith, or else resolve to live in a perpetual stinking torment."[33]

The king's criticisms did not stop experiments in Virginia by John Rolfe to improve the taste and commercial potential of the Indian tobacco plant known as *Nicotiana rustica*. Using seed probably from the West Indies, Rolfe planted in 1612 *Nicotiana tabacum* that proved to be superior both in taste and size, it being a plant of six to nine feet in height as contrasted to the two or three feet for Indian tobacco. Thomas Lambert further improved tobacco in 1619 by introducing a better process of curing—hanging the leaves for greater exposure to the sun and air instead of sweating the tobacco in piles covered lightly by hay or grass.

There is some uncertainty about the origin and classification of the two types of tobacco known during the colonial period as Oronoco and sweet-scented. Both may have descended from the *Nicotiana tabacum* of John Rolfe and developed different characteristics because of the nature of soil.

Tobacco: *Nicotiana rustica* (figure 2) and *Nicotiana tabacum* (figure 1). (Photograph of illustration at end of volume by [De Villeneuve], *Traité Complet de la Culture, Fabrication et Vente du Tabac*, Paris, 1791.)

Whatever the origin, sweet-scented had a smaller round leaf, a finer texture, and a milder taste than Oronoco. Thriving best on sandy soil, it grew mainly in Virginia along the lower waters of the York and James rivers; as settlements expanded, it spread along the Rappahannock and the south banks of the Potomac. Oronoco was better suited to the rich and strong lands of upper river valleys and the "back settlements" of Virgina and later in most of Maryland. In these areas Oronoco with its sharp bite produced a large and coarse leaf shaped "like a fox's ear." The improved variety of tobacco, mostly sweet-scented, contributed to an impressive increase in tobacco exports for the early years of Virginia. A Virginia export of 20,000 pounds for the market in England in 1617 rose to 60,000 pounds by 1622 and to 500,000 by 1628.[34]

Colonists moved to new areas to claim more land for themselves and to escape from the soil depletion characteristic of tobacco production. Drawing heavily on the nitrogen and potash of the soil, the tobacco crop usually left no portion of the plant for soil re-enrichment and instead contributed to "toxicity, harmful soil fungi, root rots, and micro-organisms."[35] After growing three or four crops in the same field without rotations, the planter then abandoned the exhausted area and turned to virgin soil that was cleared by workers during the winter when their labors were not needed for the routine of seeding, transplanting, topping, suckering, stripping or cutting, and curing. The more fertile new ground was preferred where trees had been removed with the stumps often still remaining, and in these fields plants were cultivated mainly by hoeing. Plows were little used for tobacco until near the end of the colonial period when the "old fields" were again planted for tobacco. The acres abandoned during the seventeenth century were frequently reclaimed for the growing of wheat and other grain. The colonists' continual need for new lands brought them into conflict with the Indians holding prior claim to the area and complicated Indian policy and Indian-white relations.

From the founding of the Virginia colony, Indian policy received considerable attention from both officials of the London Company and local authorities in Virginia who were usually better informed on details of Indian affairs. Security was a primary concern, and the council in London initially recommended alliances with the tribes nearest English settlements and agreements to wage war on the enemies of their tribes. In effect, this meant an alliance with the Powhatan and possible war with the Monacan or Manahoac. The Powhatan, consisting of about thirty different tribes at the time of the settlement of Jamestown, had an estimated population of between 8500 and 9000 living in the tidewater area from the Potomac River to the James and including the Eastern Shore.[36] The Monacan included more than five tribes and lived along the James River near the fall line; their chief town, Rasawek, was located at the junction of the James and Rivanna rivers in present Fluvanna County. The Manahoac, consisting of perhaps twelve tribes, occupied the land about the headwaters of the Rappahannock. An estimate of the combined population of these two groups suggests a total equal to the Powhatan.[37]

The proposed alliance with the Powhatan as planned by the English involved a coronation of their chief with a copper crown and the presentation of other gifts. Acceptance of the crown was to be interpreted as acknowledgment of a superior English title to the land. But the shrewd chief refused to kneel when accepting the crown, and he continued to thwart efforts of the English to subjugate his tribes. The colonists then considered the possibility of making all Indians tributary to the English. References were made to experience of the Spanish with tributaries, but the instructions displayed only a vague knowledge of Spanish policy.

Actually the Spanish employed an elaborate system for tribute from the Indians under the *encomienda* in the sixteenth century. In Mexico the system represented only a modification of the tribute system that the Spanish found in use by the Aztec. In other areas there were variations in the nature of the *encomienda* because of the differences in the number of Indians. The theory of the *encomienda* provided for the commendation of Indians to certain Spaniards, known as *encomenderos*, who were entitled to either tribute or labor, sometimes both. In return, the Indians were to receive both protection and religious instruction. As the system worked out for the Spanish, only service was performed in the Caribbean islands where the number of Indians was small, while on the mainland both service and tribute were rendered to the *encomenderos*.[38]

The council of the Virginia Company recommended tributary status as early as 1609. Such a status would not be entirely new for Virginia Indians because Powhatan had imposed a tribute system upon his followers, collecting from local "werowances," or chiefs, products like corn, beans, deer, turkey, skins, beads, and copper. As suggested by the council, if Powhatan could not be made prisoner, he should be made a tributary. The same status should be imposed on all tribes in the areas, and from every tribal leader should come "so many measures of Corne at every Harvest, soe many basketts of Dye so many dozens of skins so many of his people to worke weekely," all proportioned according to the extent of the territory and population of the tribe.[39]

The instructions for imposing a tributary system also provided for a significant reversal in policy by advocating the destruction of Powhatan's power by alliances with his enemies and with natives at a greater distance from the colony. If friendly agreements were to be made, the council instructed in 1609, "doe it with those that are farthest from you and enemies unto those amonge whom you dwell," for there would be the least opportunity for conflict. The perpetual enemies of Powhatan, the Monacan and the Manahoac, were then suggested as possible allies.[40]

Before Sir Thomas Gates arrived with instructions in 1610, Captain John Smith on his own initiative negotiated an agreement with Powhatan for the sale of land near the falls of the James River. A conflict over authority in the colony prevented approval of the purchase, but the provisions are significant for an analysis of the evolution of Indian policy. The proposed treaty stated that the English would defend Powhatan and his followers from the Monacan on the conditions that they resign to Smith on behalf of the English

> the fort and houses and all that countries for a proportion of copper. That all stealing offenders should bee sent him, there to receive their punishment. That every house as a custome should pay him a bushell of corne for an inch square of copper, and a proportion of *Pocones* as a yearely tribute to King *James* for their protection, as a dutie: what else they could spare, to barter at their best discration.[41]

Powhatan retained a suspicious and cautious approach to negotiations with the English, but he did finally enter into what was known as the "married peace," resulting from the marriage of his daughter Pocahontas to the Englishman John Rolfe in 1614. Details of the peace, if such were formulated, are not known.

The impact of the agreement was evident in the action of the Chickahominy tribe, which had remained independent and had refused to submit to Powhatan. Fearing that Powhatan might be free to conquer them, the Chickahominy offered to submit to the authority of the English on the condition that they could retain their laws and form of government. The English agreed and concluded a peace with the tribe containing the following provisions: that the Indians should be called Englishmen and be true subjects of King James; that they should always be ready to furnish 300 men against the Spanish or other enemies; and that every fighting man, at harvest time, should bring two bushels of corn to the English as a tribute and receive in return as many hatchets.[42] These provisions were not carefully observed, but are significant in view of the colony's later policy for promoting trade, for increasing the number of tributaries, and for using tributary tribes as a defense against hostile neighbors.

During the remainder of Powhatan's rule, amicable relations existed between his followers and the colony of Virginia. There was an increase in the informal trade that had existed from earliest contacts of Indians and whites, involving in some instances simply the exchange of beads, trinkets, cooking utensils, hatchets, pickaxes, and other small items for such products as Indian corn, fish, turkey, skins, and furs. Early traders included the bold and audacious John Smith who on his canoe explorations of the Chesapeake streams turned his contacts into opportunities for obtaining vital supplies for the fledgling colony, particularly Indian corn that helped sustain the starving colonists who had not yet adjusted to the challenges of a new country.

The colonists soon recognized the value of furs and skins, both for use in the colony and for trade to England and the continent of Europe. Captain Christopher Newport reported on the excellence of furs in Virginia in 1607. Beaver were reported in most of the streams, and colonists visiting Powhatan claimed to have seen 4000 deerskins in his possession. A list of commodities to be sent from Virginia emphasized beaver and otter skins and identified other potential products: sassafras, bay berries, wine, walnut oil, lumber, pitch, tar, and sturgeon. A second list extended the number of furs and skins in 1620 and assigned them the following prices: beaver, seven shillings each; sable, eight to twenty shillings per pair; lucern, two to ten shillings each; marten, four shillings for the best; wildcat, eighteen pence; fox skins, six pence; and muskrat, two shillings a dozen.[43] The full potential of this trade, however, was not realized until there was greater stability in the colony with an increased population.

Meanwhile, the efforts of the colonists for education and conversion of the Indians continued. The plans for Christian missions had been proposed during the initial steps for establishing the colony. King James I recognized the religious motive in the proposed settlement of Virginia and expressed hope for favorable results in the charter of 1606. Numerous other expressions reflected similar concern of those interested in the colony; in 1609, for example, in *A True and Sincere Declaration of the Purpose and Ends of the Plantation*, the company stated that its first aim was "to preach and baptize into Christian Religion, and by propagation of the Gospell, to recover out of the armes of the Divell, a number of poore and miserable soules, wrapt up unto death, in almost invincible ignorance."[44] The council in London issued an order to Sir Thomas Gates in May 1609, instructing him to endeavor with all diligence to convert the natives "to the knowledge and worship of the true god." Toward this end, a number of Indian children were to be procured and instructed in the English language and manners. Furthermore, if convenient, the colony was to remove from the natives their Iniocasockes, or priests, and detain them as prisoners because the priests so "poyson and infecte" the minds of the Indians that it impeded the proselyting of the colony.[45]

The first significant effort by the colony to civilize and Christianize the Indians was to bring boys into the colony. The author of *The New Life of Virginia* reiterated the instructions to Gates by suggesting in 1612 that the colonists "Take their children and traine them up with gentlenesse, teach them our English tongue, and the principles of religion."[46] The colony required each town, city borough, and plantation to begin this work in 1619. The native children most apt in wit and the "graces of nature" were to be selected and instructed in the fundamentals of literature in preparation for a proposed college. Once educated they were then to return to their people and serve as missionaries in converting and teaching others of their race. The colonists also hoped to promote friendly relations with the Indians by training their offspring. Difficulties in this effort were noted by Sir George Yeardley, however, who reported Indians were averse to any agreement that took away their sons.

Governor Yeardley attempted to overcome objections by the natives to separation of their families by inviting whole families to live with the English. They were to be furnished a house, the necessary land for support, and some of the English cattle. In this way, the Indian children would be educated as well as taught the domestic economy of the colony. The company sanctioned the plan but warned the governor to limit the number brought in and to keep a strict guard to prevent treacherous uprisings among those living within the English bounds. Apparently Yeardley carried out his proposal and the Indian chief Opechancanough, eventual successor to Powhatan, provided certain families for each community.

The third—and by far the most elaborate—plan was the establishment of a college to educate the Indians. Promotional tracts were issued in England by the London Company to arouse interest, and pleas by interested persons such as Alexander Whitaker, "the Apostle to Virginia," were published. Even more important in attracting attention was the visit of Pocahontas as Lady Rebecca and several other Indians to England in 1616. The flurry of interest in Indian missions led to numerous contributions: collections from churches authorized by King James I brought in £1500; other contributions included money by direct gift or through wills, communion sets for the college, and books.

The company formulated detailed plans for the use of these donations. The initial fund of £1500—of which £800 was in cash and the remainder represented by general stock of the company that, in its precarious financial position, had borrowed it—was to be used as an endowment and to be invested in the development of 10,000 acres of land set aside at Henrico by the London Company for a "University and College." Tenants were sent over to cultivate the college land; designated as "tenants at halves," they were to receive one half of the proceeds from their labor, the other half to be used for construction of the college and for support of its tutors and students. One hundred tenants were sent over in 1619 for the college land surveyed at Henrico. However, dissatisfaction with the poor returns from the land led Sir Edwin Sandys to engage George Thorpe as deputy of the college land in 1620. Thorpe, a member of the council of the London Company and a councilor of the governor of Virginia, was responsible, first of all, for supervising the investments in the college land, but his influence and character extended beyond these activities. He advocated a humanitarian and just policy in dealing with the Indians. This "worthy religious Gentleman" punished severely anyone under his authority who harmed the natives. To gain favor with Opechancanough, Thorpe provided a house for him built in English fashion and equipped the door with lock and key. The native chief was so fascinated by this that he locked and unlocked the door a "hundred times a day," thinking "no device in all the world was comparable to it."[47]

Other plans for a college involved selection of officers. Patrick Copland, who became the projector of the first English free-school in North America, was named president-elect, and Richard Downes, trained as a scholar in England, came to the colony to work in the college in 1619. From all these plans and preparation many significant results were expected for the future. Then suddenly the benevolent purposes and hopeful anticipations were shattered by the catastrophe that in a few hours leveled the labor of so many years—the massacre of 1622.

Powhatan had died in 1618. His rule had passed in matrilineal descent to his brother Opitchapan, but the brother was feeble and never a good warrior; consequently, he was soon overshadowed by the more courageous Opechan-canough, another brother of Powhatan and implacable foe of the English. While appearing friendly to the colony, he denounced to his followers the encroachment upon Indian lands of tobacco fields spreading over areas formerly growing berries or Indian corn and threatening the plentiful supply of game the natives had enjoyed. He also denounced the trading practices of the English. But most important of all, he was convinced that the continued increase of the number of whites jeopardized the Indian way of life and the importance of the Powhatan Confederacy. Consequently, he skillfully organized the concerted action that burst upon the unsuspecting colonists on the morning of Good Friday, March 22, 1621/2. A contemporary account by a colonist dramatizes the element of surprise by the Indians:

> as in other dayes before, they came unarmed into our houses, without Bowes or arrowes, or other weapons, with Deere, Turkies, Fish, Furres, and other provisions, to sell, and trucke with us, for glasse, beades, and other trifles: yea in some places, sate downe at Breakfast with our People at their tables, whom immediately with their owne tooles and weapons, either laid downe, or standing in their houses, they basely and barbarously murthered, not sparing either age or sexe, man, woman or childe.[48]

Within a few hours, at least 347 of the 1240 settlers, including six members of the council, had been slain. The settlements above the Appomattox River were almost exterminated, and elsewhere the number killed was very great. Even George Thorpe, who had diligently worked as a missionary among the natives, did not escape the blow of the Indian's tomahawk. His corpse, like others, was mutilated in a manner "unbefitting to be heard by any civil eare."[49] The dispersal of the settlements contributed to the devastation, although Jamestown and vicinity were partly spared by the warning of Chanco, a convert to Christianity.

Opechancanough began militant opposition to English settlements in 1622, a course he pursued with great persistence and courage for over two decades until his death. His reaction to the English contrasted sharply with that of two other leading members of the confederacy, Powhatan himself and Pocahontas, his daughter. After social contact and assimilation, Pocahontas had married John Rolfe and visited England where she was received as an Indian princess. Her son, Thomas Rolfe, was to serve later as a colonial official after the death of his father in 1622. Powhatan, influenced by the marriage of his daughter, tolerated the English encroachments but remained wary of their advances and kept an independent political status. To continue this independence, Opechancanough apparently was convinced that an aggressive attack was the best action.

The success of the 1622 assaults led the council in Virginia to decide that it was mandatory "to quitt many of our Plantacons, and to unite more neerely together in fewer places" for defense.[50] Most of the cattle were brought to the Jamestown area, and the remaining people were concentrated in Jamestown and the plantations just across the river.

When word of the attack reached the members of the company in England, they immediately issued orders for a war of extermination. The previous friendly policy was dramatically reversed to one of revenge. The council in London sent the following instruction to Governor Francis Wyatt in August following the massacre:

> Wee cannot but with much griefe proceed to the condempnation of theire bodies, the saving of whose Soules, we have so zealously affected . . . we conceive no meanes so prop[er], nor expedient, as to maintaine continually certaine bands of men of able bodies, and inured to the Cuntrie; of stout minds, and active hands, that may from time to time . . . pursue and follow them, surprisinge them in their habitations, intercepting them in theire hunting, burninge theire Townes, demolishing theire Temples, destroyinge theire Canoes, plucking upp theire weares, carrying away their Corne, and depriving them of whatsoever may yeeld them succor or relief.[51]

Before either instructions or supplies could be received from England, the colony, greatly stunned and able to arm only about 180 men—eighty of whom could do little more than "carrie burthens"—initiated vigorous coordinated attacks led by George Sandys, Yeardley, Captain William Powell, and Captain John West. Near the end of the year, the governor and council wrote to England that "more Indians had been killed during this fall and winter than during the whole history of the Colony."[52] George Sandys added a more poignant commentary when he noted that the massacre and a general sickness had cost the colony "few lesse than 500, and not manie of the rest that have not knockt at the doores of death, yet with our small and weake forces wee have Chased the Indian from their aboade, burnt their houses, taken their Corne and slayne not a few."[53]

In England, news of the massacre sparked investigation of the Virginia

Company, and along with it the Bermuda Company, by the commission headed by Sir William Jones. The investigation prompted the Privy Council to request a writ of *quo warranto*, and the court of King's Bench annulled the charter of the company in May 1624. The massacre and ensuing inquiry were not solely responsible for ending the company's control and making Virginia a royal colony. Other factors that contributed in varying degrees of importance were the failure of the colony to thrive economically, the poor financial condition of the company, political differences between Sir Edwin Sandys and the king, internal dissensions between the Sandys faction and the Smith-Warwick group, and the staggering death rate of almost three out of four persons from 1619 to 1624.

During the decade following the massacre, improving the security of the colony shaped relations with the Indians and affected the daily life of the settlers. A systematic plan of devastating attacks was followed during times of hostility, and the governor appointed commanders of the several plantations and authorized them to levy from their respective places as many men as could be safely spared. Other precautionary measures were taken. To impress upon the colonists the continued necessity for utmost vigilance, the governor and legislature proclaimed that March 22, the anniversary date of the massacre, be solemnized annually as a holy day. The Assembly also ordered that all dwelling houses be palisaded for defense against the Indians, that no person leave the settlement without an armed accompanying party, and that no men work in the fields without their arms or a sentinel to guard them. Commanders of every plantation were admonished to maintain a sufficient supply of powder and ammunition to keep the guns of all colonists repaired. No powder was to be used unnecessarily in the shooting of guns at drinking parties or other forms of entertainment, and a careful watch was to be kept at night. These measures were re-enacted several times, and it is evident that the colonists did not always adhere to these restrictions. Yet conditions in the colony were stabilized sufficiently for a significant increase in population during the decade.

Royal officials provided for a count of the colonists in the Muster list of 1624/5 as the Virginia Company was dissolved.[54] Analysis of population and demographic patterns from this inventory of persons provides detailed information on the social structure and organization of frontier society. The Muster list is a house-to-house survey enabling researchers to assess changes in the population make up of the colony from its first all-male expedition in 1607 with the addition of other shiploads of immigrants, including the well-known group of ninety young white maidens in 1619 and the first black immigrants in the same year of twenty or more Negroes. In general, the colony was still a predominantly white male society, born in Europe, and relatively young. From the total population of the Muster list of 1218 people, males predominated with a count of 934 or 76.7 percent, while females accounted for 22.1 percent with 270. The remaining 1.2 percent cannot be identified by sex. The youthful nature of the society is reflected in the figure that 76.1 percent of those identified by age fell below thirty; women were distinctly younger and included none over age thirty-nine, while only sixty-three men were in their forties or older.[55]

The newness of the colony and the lack of stability in reproduction of population are reflected in the fact that 89.1 percent of those on the Muster were born in Britain or on the continent of Europe. At least seventy-eight children can be identified as native sons and daughters of Virginia, possibly twenty-one more; but even with the addition of these twenty-one, only 8.2 percent of the white population would be American born.[56]

The low number of births is an indicator of the limited role of the family in social organization. Only 334 members of the colony were married, just 30.7 percent of those eligible for matrimony if the age of eligibility began at fifteen. Only 483 persons of the total of 1218, or 40 percent, even had relatives in the colony.[57] The majority of relationships, then, were found within the nuclear family of husband, wife, and children, and this unit was far more important in social organization than the extended family with grandparents or other relatives.

The number of children per family was also small if, indeed, there were any children at all. A total of 102 couples or 61.1 percent of the families had no offspring, while one-child families were common. Excluding the 102 childless couples from the total of 189, there remains sixty-two couples with only one child, seventeen with two, six with three, and two with four.[58] Virginia was still many years away from the larger families of the eighteenth century such as Patrick Henry with seventeen children.

Frontier communities have often been noted for the very high percentage of women who were married, particularly in a predominantly male population; but this pattern does not fully prevail in Virginia of the 1620s. There were forty-three women age twenty or over who were not married at the time of the Muster, thirty-nine of them having been in the colony for three years or more and four having been widowed for at least a year. One factor contributing to the number of unmarried women was that thirty-four of the above forty-three women were indentured sevants, and English social custom tended to discourage marriage until the period of indenture was over. While the tradition was influential, it by no means dictated the choices of all colonists in a new country, for there were twenty-four servants among the 334 who were married. One of the couples was black and by the time of the Muster had a child.[59]

The racial mix and social structure of the colony may also be observed at this early stage. Included in the 507 listed as servants in 1625 were twenty-two of the twenty-three blacks in the colony (identification of the remaining one cannot be established) and one of the two Indians present in the Muster. It is interesting that any Indians were included as members of the colony at that time. Since they were not listed as being imported by ship, apparently they were part of that small group identified in the colonial period as individual Indians living either as freemen, servants, or slaves within the colony without tribal ties. In that status, they differed from larger groups known as "foreign Indians" at a greater distance from the colony, or from those retaining tribal connections who later accepted the status of tributary.

The total number of servants was spread among approximately one-third of the households, a category of social organization larger than the family and designating individuals associated for the use of the same property and supplies. The average number in each household out of the total list of 309 was only 3.9 persons, but over half of the servants belonged to fourteen households, one household having as many as forty servants and another having thirty-six.[60]

Following the Muster, the population more than doubled and by 1628 or 1630 had reached 3000. The twenty-seven settlements of 1625 were concentrated along the James River, dotting the northern and southern banks from Chesapeake Bay to the fall line. Virginians across the bay on the Eastern Shore clustered to the south. The increase by the end of the decade filled in the area between the James and York rivers in primarily a north-south pattern of migration as well as additions to the Eastern Shore in movement mainly from west to east. This expansion occurred on the eve of dramatic increases that were to occur in Virginia as well as in the new colony of Maryland whose founding was already being considered in England.

2

Expansion in the Chesapeake:
Virginia and Maryland, 1632–60

When the colony of Maryland was carved from the lands originally granted Virginia, its pioneers duplicated the experience of their neighbors with two major differences in frontier living. First of all, the new arrivals benefited greatly from the hard lessons learned by the Virginians in the choice of settlement sites, in negotiating with Indians for land and trade, and in applying the techniques and skills essential for adjustment to a new physical environment. At the same time, by colonizing under a proprietary charter rather than a company grant, the Maryland settlers were burdened by a greater number of vestiges of the feudal system that gradually withered away under the influence of the American experience and the new environment.

George Calvert, the first Lord Baltimore, had been a member of the Virginia Company and his continued interest in America led him to obtain a proprietary grant to Avalon in 1623, a tract in southeastern Newfoundland. Failing in his efforts to establish a settlement in this northern area, he visited Virginia and by 1632, the year of his death, had arranged for a patent from King Charles I for the territory just north of the Potomac despite opposition from Virginians. The bounds of the grant issued to Cecilius Calvert, the second Lord Baltimore, were for a line west from Delaware Bay along the fortieth parallel to the "first fountaine" of the Potomac River, then south and east along the Potomac River to its mouth and across the bay by "a straight line" to Watkin's Point and the Atlantic.[1]

Within this area the first settlement sponsored by the Calverts began with the arrival of over 200 colonists on the *Ark* and *Dove* in March 1634. Greatly impressed with the physical surroundings of the area, Jesuit Father Andrew White of the expedition noted that Chesapeake Bay was "the most delightful water I ever saw." For the Potomac River he added,

> This is the sweetest and greatest river I have seene, so that the Thames is but a little finger to it. There are noe marshes or swampes about it, but solid firme ground, with great variety of woode, not choaked up with undershrubs, but commonly so farre distant from each other as a coach and fower horses may travale without molestation.[1]

The absence of malarial infested swamps provided a definite advantage over Jamestown.

Landing first on St. Clement's Island (now Blakiston), Governor Leonard Calvert and others went at once to the town of the Indians to seek another advantage for the colonists—friendly relations with the natives nearest them. The Indians in the area of early settlement were the Piscataway (later indentified as Conoy), including the Piscataway village on the creek of the same name where the chief had his residence. Of Algonquian linguistic stock, the Piscataway and their neighboring allies included approximately 2000 members in the early seventeenth century. Noting their body paint, beardless faces, and decorative beads, Father White added descriptions of their dress and their houses:

> Their apparell is deere skins and other furrs, which they weare loose like mantles, under which all their women, and those which are come to mans stature, weare Perizomata [girdles] of skins, which keep them decently covered from all offence of sharpe eies. All the rest are naked, and sometimes the men of the younger sort weare nothing at all. . . .
>
> Their houses are built in an halfe ovall forme 20 foot long, and 9 or 10 foot high with a place open in the top, halfe a yard square, whereby they admit the light, and let forth the smoke, for they build their fire, after the manner of ancient halls of England, in the middle of the house, about which they lie to sleep upon mats, spread on a low scaffold hafe a yard from ground.[3]

Two other major groups in Maryland had similar customs in dress and housing. The Nanticoke, known as "Tidewater people," inhabited the Eastern Shore along with other smaller tribes or villages also of Algonquian linguistic stock and had an estimated population in the early seventeenth century of 2700. The Susquehannock, who lived to the north along the river of the same name near the present Pennsylvania border, were Iroquoian linguistic stock. They were a large tribe of possible 5000 in the early seventeenth century and made occasional raids upon the Piscataway[4] to "waste and spoile them and their country."

The friction between these groups made the tasks of Governor Calvert easier. At the town of the Piscataway he was met at the water's edge by 500 bowmen. Negotiations proceeded easily to the purchase of some thirty miles "for axes, hoes, cloth and hatchets."[5] The governor then moved the colony nine or ten leagues downstream where the first settlement was established at St. Mary's. Located on a high, dry area with a more healthy climate than Jamestown, the early Marylanders benefited further by having access to both the cleared fields and the houses that the Indians turned over to them. With these favorable conditions supporting them, the colonists would soon confront the complexities of the proprietary charter and the proprietary plans for land distribution, governmental institutions, and court systems.

Lord Baltimore's charter to establish a colony on the American frontier

Conjectural drawing of the town of St. Mary's, Maryland, 1634. Drawing by Cary Carson depicting the town of St. Mary's drawn from research completed in 1972. The town, described by Leonard Calvert in 1634, was located one-half mile from St. Mary's River and enclosed within a palisade of 120 square miles. (Photograph courtesy of the Division of Historical and Cultural Affairs, St. Mary's City Commission.)

reflected the special and exclusive privileges that existed for late medieval English frontiers. Some modifications were even made between the time of the grant of 1623 for Avalon in Newfoundland and the one for Maryland in 1632. The form of tenure was changed from *in capite*, or knight service, for the Avalon grant to free and common soccage, which minimized obligations to the rendering of two Indian arrows annually and to taking the oath of allegiance. In both the Avalon and Maryland grants, however, Lord Baltimore had shrewdly stipulated his powers over his frontier settlement were to be that which the Bishop of Durham had exercised "at any time heretofore."[6] This meant the proprietor was to have near absolute power over the colony: official writs were to carry the name of the proprietor, final authority for legislative and court decisions rested with him, and lands were to be bestowed in the name of the proprietor, not the king, and under terms agreeable to Lord Baltimore. There were the general restrictions that the laws of the colony should not run counter to the laws of England, and that legislation should be enacted only after some consultation with the freemen of the colony.[7] But, in general, the near absolute powers for new colonies in America were designed to serve the same purpose of security for seventeenth century settlements as they had for the fourteenth century. While in part effective, the American experience and changing political factions in England gradually modified the medieval heritage.

Land was important on both the medieval and seventeenth-century frontiers. The policy for grants in Maryland reflects more influence of feudalism than in Virginia, but the basic goals of land policy in both colonies were essentially the same: to use the lure of the land as an impetus to settlement and to employ the headright system as the essential feature of land grants during most of the seventeenth century. The "Conditions of Plantations" for the first adventurers in 1633 provided that for every five men between the ages of sixteen and fifty transported to Maryland for settlement, 2000 acres of land would be granted with an annual rent of 400 pounds of "good wheat." If fewer than five men came, the adventurer received 100 acres for adults (including women and servants) and fifty acres for children under sixteen. Conditions for later adventurers changed several times prior to 1660; less generous provisions for land were introduced, and ten persons were required by 1635 for 2000 acres and twenty persons by 1642 for the same amount. The quitrent by 1635 was also stated in terms of shillings—that is, twenty shillings for 1000 acres to be paid in "the Comodities of the Country," the same as the familiar two shillings for 100 acres required in Virginia.[8]

The "Conditions of Plantations" also provided for the creation of manors from the grants of 1000 to 3000 acres with a special name to be given the manor by the adventurer. Each manorial lord was also authorized to hold court leet and court baron—institutions in which he exercised private jurisdiction—and to profit from the fines imposed.[9] Court baron handled civil cases with fines not exceeding forty shillings, while court leet dealt with criminal acts within the manorial bounds. About sixty manors were actually established in seventeenth-century Maryland in addition to the ones set up for the proprietary family. The extent to which courts leet and baron were conducted cannot be definitely determined, but it is certain they existed and that the prerogative to manorial lords was exercised. Extant records refer to a court baron on St. Gabriel's Manor in 1656, and to both court leet and court baron on St. Clement's Manor for five court sessions from 1659 to 1672.[10] Situated on an island in the Potomac in St. Mary's County, St. Clement's Manor goes back to the original grant in 1639 to Thomas Gerard, who was prominent in the colony as surgeon, planter, and political official.

Reading these rare documents vividly reveals the vestiges of feudalism in colonial Maryland. The manorial court record has anachronistic references to the "essoines"—those excused from court—the "resiants"—residents of the manor but neither freeholder nor leaseholder—the steward, and the bailiff. But the nature of the cases before the courts also reflects the everyday problems of a frontier community. In 1659, offenders were fined "for marking one of the Lord of the Manors hoggs," and several Indians were hauled into court and fined for "breakinge into the Lord of the Mannors orchard," and for stealing "hoggs flesh," a shirt, and a canoe. One Samuell Harris was charged with breaking "the peace with a stick" and for "bloudshed comitted," while a complex case of domestic difficulty of two manorial tenants was carried over to the next meeting of the county court.[11] This latter agency, the county court, eventually proved to be the most significant judicial body of the colony, although other administrative units were important during the early years.

Both the manor and the hundred were tried under the frontier conditions of Maryland as smaller administrative bodies, while the county was evolving as the most significant unit of local government in response to the particular demands of the southern locale and its patterns of settlement. Kent Island, located off the Eastern Shore and originally occupied by Virginians, was established as a hundred and was at first referred to as a part of St. Mary's County. This designation came at a time when villages were so new that there was little distinction between provincial and local government. St. Mary's County, in effect, referred to the government of the colony that followed the precedent of the Palatinate or Bishopric of Durham, which had been organized as a county. Maryland, however, gave a more vital role than other English colonies to the hundred with its constable having powers comparable to the same office in England. The hundred at first served as the key unit in military organization and in the imposition of taxes. In judicial matters the constable represented the hundred at the county court. But the office was soon overshadowed by a local "Conservator of the Peace," or justice of the peace, who served as one of the commissioners of the county, and from whom one person was designated the chief commissioner or chief magistrate. The hundred also initially served as the unit for representation for the colonial legislature in the original charter. By the decades of the 1640s and 1650s the county had emerged in Maryland as the basic agency of local administration and assumed duties comparable to the county court in Virginia in the vital areas of representative government, military organization, taxation, judicial matters, and certain other civil affairs like the maintenance of roads and the care of orphans. County commissioners had both judicial and administrative tasks, and apparently a significant number served in Virginia and Maryland as county commissioners and members of the lower house of the colonial legislatures.

Virginia had created the county system in 1634 to respond to its increase in population. Four thousand nine hundred settlers lived along the James River below the falls and in the lower part of Accomack on the Eastern Shore. The Virginia Assembly divided the colony into eight divisions: Henrico with a population of 419; Charles City with 511; James City, 886; Warwick, 811; Warrasqueoc, 522; Elizabeth City, 854; Charles River, 510; and Accomack, 396. Called "shires" in the act of the Assembly,[12] the divisions quickly became known as counties and provided governmental functions similar to their English counterpart. Below the county, individuals appointed by the commanders of the plantations were mainly responsible for the exercise of government, and they were recognized by colonial officials as the "local magistrate and militia officer," an office suggestive of the later position of justice of the peace.[13]

The Virginia act creating eight counties also provided that lieutenants were to be appointed and sheriffs were to be elected with essentially the same duties as the office in England. The position of lieutenant, however, was apparently little used, for the head of the county court seems to have commanded the militia during most of the seventeenth century. The office of sheriff took over from the provost marshal as police officer, and the sheriff in Virginia as well as in Maryland resembled in many ways the corresponding office in England. Yet it was not identical, although there is evidence of much borrowing from England in most of these early institutions. Comparison of the office of sheriff in England and the Chesapeake colonies of Virginia and Maryland confirms the greater number of similarities, but it also suggests areas of differences that developed in the colonies. For example, the sheriff in Virginia and Maryland had greater responsibility in financial matters and collected poll taxes as well as either royal or proprietary revenues such as the quitrent. He had less authority in judicial duties since all of the courts of the sheriff in England were not reproduced in pioneer America. The sheriff in the Chesapeake did not inherit the social position of the English official, but he did gain influence by the more democratic nature of his office, by its more

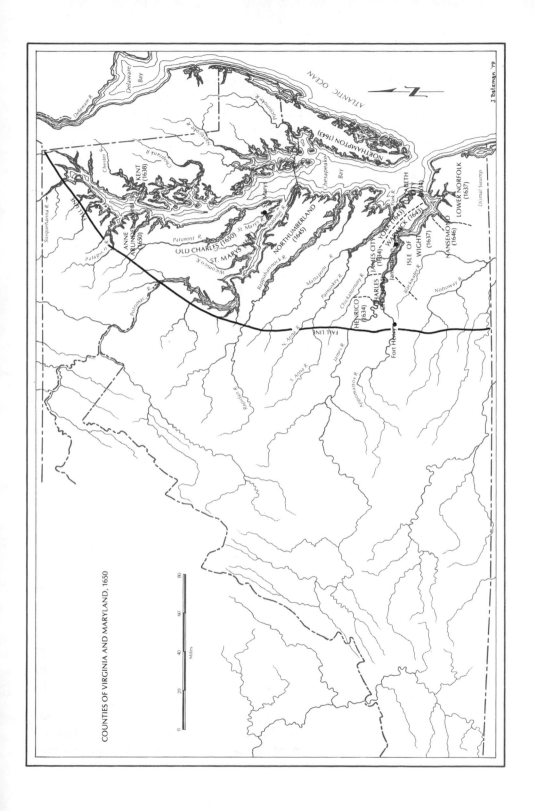

COUNTIES OF VIRGINIA AND MARYLAND, 1650

KENT (1638)

ANNE ARUNDEL (1650)

OLD CHARLES (1650)

ST. MARYS

NORTHUMBERLAND (1645)

NORTHAMPTON (1643)

LOWER NORFOLK (1637)

NANSEMOND (1646)

ISLE OF WIGHT (1637)

ELIZABETH (1634)

WARWICK (1643)

YORK (1643)

JAMES CITY (1634)

CHARLES (1634)

HENRICO (1634)

FALL LINE

Fort Henry

ATLANTIC OCEAN

Chesapeake Bay

Delaware Bay

Dismal Swamp

Delaware R.

Susquehanna R.

Chester R.

Choptank R.

Nanticoke R.

Potomac R.

Patuxent R.

St. Mary's R.

Wicomico R.

Rappahannock R.

Mattaponi R.

Pamunkey R.

Chickahominy R.

N. Anna R.

S. Anna R.

James R.

Appomattox R.

Rocky R.

Blackwater R.

Nottoway R.

Rapidan R.

Patapsco R.

J. Bateman '79

local association rather than royal or provincial, and by the increasing importance of the county in both colonies as the seventeenth century progressed.[14] The strongest factor at work shaping these institutions was the particular American situation nurturing their growth. The colonists responded to immediate problems with what seemed at the time reasonable solutions without always being aware of the extent to which they resembled earlier institutions.

Early immigrants to Maryland came from a variety of national and social backgrounds and were soon to contribute to the evolution of governmental agencies and policies. Prior to the founding of Maryland, Virginians had occupied Kent Island as a trading post under the direction of William Claiborne, who had come to Virginia in 1621 and had taken an active leadership role as surveyor, fur trader, Indian fighter, council member, and secretary of the colony. Claiborne attempted unsuccessfully in a bitter controversy to keep the island out of Maryland jurisdiction. Over 200 English immigrants made up the first settlement at St. Mary's, and both Catholics and Protestants were represented in the colony that had been designed by the Calvert family as a haven for those who felt oppressed by English anti-Catholic measures. As it turned out, most of the twenty or more gentlemen on the first expedition were Catholic, while most of the artisans and laborers were Protestant, resulting in the well-known provision for toleration of all Christians in the act of 1649.[15] The Jesuit missionaries in the early settlements sought a separate political status and proposed to obtain their own territory by land purchases from the Indians. Lord Baltimore, however, vigorously defended his title to the land and succeeded in preventing the Jesuits from establishing autonomous settlements and from acquiring their own title to the land.

Puritan migration to early Maryland included a substantial number of immigrants from Virginia who sought the toleration of different religious commitments. The migration originated from the several settlements of Puritans located along the Nansemond and Elizabeth rivers in Virginia in the 1630s and 1640s. Having come primarily from southern and southwestern England with additional ones from London and Belfast, they decided by 1642 to attempt a more formal church organization by obtaining three ministers from New England. Sir William Berkeley, who arrived in Virginia in February 1641/2 to begin his service as governor, had a strong commitment to the Anglican Church and discouraged the efforts of the Puritans. The Virginia Assembly responded with legislation in March 1642/3 requiring conformity to the Church of England by ministers;[16] two of the Puritan clergy then returned to New England. Congregations of Puritans, nonetheless, stayed on in Virginia until 1648 when some 400 to 600 under the leadership of Richard Bennett moved to Maryland upon the invitation of Governor William Stone, who as a Protestant had just succeeded a Catholic governor.

Locating on the Severn River, they established the settlement of Providence in the area of present Annapolis and later became a part of Anne Arundel County. The area became the focal point of the bitter fight between the Puritans and the supporters of the proprietor at the battle of the Severn in 1655.

While the conflict was primarily one in which the Puritans and other antagonists to the proprietor such as William Claiborne took advantage of the turbulence arising from the civil war in England that overthrew the monarchy in the 1640s and 1650s, it also reflects the tense situation in Maryland where new and isolated settlements asserted their independent position. The Puritans with their largest concentration along the Severn River had established community settlements many miles from the colonial seat at St. Mary's and selected their own local official. Although sending a representative to the Assembly, they were attempting to manage their own affairs, both religious and secular, with a control over others resembling the efforts of their Puritan counterparts in the Massachusetts Bay Colony. When Lord Baltimore ordered his appointed governor, William Stone, to reestablish proprietary authority over the Puritans, a military showdown came on March 25, 1655, on the Severn with the Puritans led by William Fuller, designated governor by opponents of the proprietor. Aided by two ships in the river, the Puritan forces decisively defeated Stone and his followers. A hundred or so fighters were on each side, although the exact number of participants has never been determined. The victorious forces condemned ten men to death, but finally executed only four excluding Stone. They went on to raid and plunder the Jesuit settlements, disrupting their Indian missionary work, and they continued their free course of action until Lord Baltimore was able to regain control of his colony in 1658.[17]

The largest number of new settlers in Maryland continued to come from England and Ireland, but there were other newcomers. Quakers were attracted by the policy of toleration. From along the Delaware River, there came a few Dutch who left New Netherland and a few Swedes from the small settlement of New Sweden; Protestant French Huguenots came to America to escape restrictions imposed upon them in Catholic France. Some of these immigrants sought out Maryland; others ended up in areas of boundary disputes with the colony of Pennsylvania that were not resolved until the eighteenth century.

The location of expanding settlements and the patterns of migration were influenced by several factors. Initially the colonists planted wheat, corn, and other food crops, but within a few years their major efforts turned to tobacco as a commercial crop. Because tobacco growers wanted to locate where ships could pick up their crops, the Chesapeake Bay dictated the major areas of expansion in Maryland and Virginia. Land grants by the proprietors often determined the thrust of settlement in both the small grants to individuals as well as with the larger grants of over sixty manors. Another factor was the limited presence of Indians in Maryland and the agreements or treaties that were worked out for the possession of neighboring territories. Religious commitments and the policy of religious toleration also contributed to the motives for migration, particularly for such groups as the Puritans, Quakers, and French Huguenots.

These factors are reflected in the creation of counties to meet the needs of the expanding population from the original colony at St. Mary's of over 200.[18] Settlements along St. Mary's River spread to both sides of the Potomac River and farther north along both banks of the Patuxent River. Until January 1637/8 when the first county of St. Mary's was noted with the appointment of a sheriff, government was apparently provided without county organization by Governor Leonard Calvert, brother of the second Lord Baltimore. The Isle of Kent, designated at first as a hundred, achieved the status of a county in 1642 and gradually added settlers to the Virginians who were originally there. The county of St. Mary's was the focal point of settlements west of the Chesapeake, as was Kent for settlements on the Eastern Shore. The recognition by a law of April 29, 1650, of Anne Arundel County had its background in the migration of Puritan families during the 1640s, as previously noted, from Nansemond River in Virginia to the western shore of the Chesapeake near present Annapolis. A few months later on November 21, 1650, a division known as Charles County, or Old Charles, was established on the south side of the Patuxent by order of the governor with approval of the council. It came into existence to accommodate the settlers brought over by Robert Brookes, who apparently by promise of Lord Baltimore was made commander of the county. The bounds of this temporary county ran along the Patuxent from Susquehanna Point, or present Cedar Point, southward to a boundary in the vicinity of the present Three Notch Road. By 1654, however, Robert Brookes had been relieved as commander, and the area of Old Charles became a part of the new county designated during the summer of 1654 as Calvert in honor of the proprietary family. Sandwiched between St. Mary's on the south and Anne Arundel to the north, Calvert County stretched along both shores of the Patuxent River, extending from the "Pynehill River" on the south to "herring Creeke" on the north. Through Puritan influence the name was changed in October of 1654 to Patuxent but restored to that of Calvert in 1658. Charles County of today, or the new Charles, dates from April 13, 1658, and was created to provide for the settlements that fanned out westward from St. Mary's along Nanjemoy and Port Tobacco creeks. Encompassing the expansion along the northern banks of the Potomac, the new county was a more convenient administrative center for the area than was the original settlement at St. Mary's. Agreement with the Indians for white settlers to refrain from colonizing along Matawoman Creek temporarily checked westward expansion along the Potomac. In the bay area to the north, the scattered

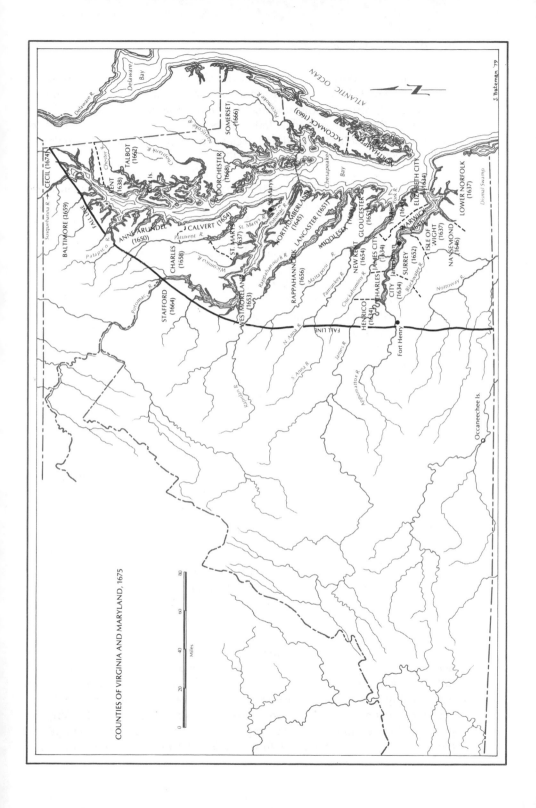

COUNTIES OF VIRGINIA AND MARYLAND, 1675

CECIL (1674)
BALTIMORE (1659)
KENT (1638)
TALBOT (1662)
SOMERSET (1666)
DORCHESTER (1668)
ANNE ARUNDEL (1650)
CALVERT (1654)
ST. MARYS (1637)
CHARLES (1658)
NORTHUMBERLAND (1645)
LANCASTER (1651)
ACCOMACK (1663)
NORTHAMPTON
WESTMORELAND (1653)
RAPPAHANNOCK (1656)
MIDDLESEX
GLOUCESTER (1651)
STAFFORD (1664)
NEW KENT (1654)
YORK
ELIZABETH CITY (1634)
LOWER NORFOLK (1637)
HENRICO (1634)
CHARLES CITY (1634)
JAMES CITY (1634)
WARWICK (1634)
SURREY (1652)
ISLE OF WIGHT (1637)
NANSEMOND (1646)

ATLANTIC OCEAN

Delaware Bay
Delaware R.
Susquehanna R.
FALL LINE
Patapsco R.
Chester R.
Sassafras R.
Kent Is.
Choptank R.
Potomac R.
Nanticoke R.
Wicomico R.
Patuxent R.
St. Marys R.
Piscataway R.
Chesapeake Bay
Rappahannock R.
Mattaponi R.
Pamunkey R.
Chickahominy R.
James R.
York R.
Back River
Nottoway R.
Dismal Swamp
Potomac R.
FALL LINE
Rapidan R.
N. Anna R.
S. Anna R.
Appomattox R.
Fort Henry
Occaneechee Is.

Miles
0   20   40   60   80

J. Bateman '79

settlements along both sides of the Chesapeake on the Patapsco and Sassafras rivers occasioned the creation of the additional county of Baltimore, apparently in 1659, although the documents for the founding are not extant. A treaty with the Susquehannock Indians opened this area for limited settlements. Thus by 1660 Maryland had organized six counties with a population of about 7000 or 8000 English colonists.[19]

The increase of population and the creation of governmental organizations were closely related to the economic activities of the colonists. While Maryland did not in its first years of settlement emphasize the growing of tobacco, the plant quickly emerged as the most significant crop in Maryland as was already true for Virginia. The nature of Chesapeake Bay was an important factor in making the two colonies producers of tobacco in sufficient quantity for international markets. Containing 150 rivers, creeks, and smaller streams, the Chesapeake has an estimated shoreline with its tidewater tributaries of about 4612 miles.[20] From private wharves along these many streams, tobacco was consigned to merchants mainly from the London area during the seventeenth century, and they acted as agents for the planter selling his crop in England and purchasing items requested by the colonials. While some tobacco producers in the early years were cut off from navigable streams and had to arrange with other planters for use of their wharves, this practice became more common in the eighteenth century as the frontier line moved westward into the piedmont. But even in some instances in the seventeenth century, small boats were used to convey tobacco along the smaller streams, and occasionally the tobacco planter had to resort either to the use of carts for transporting hogsheads or to the rolling of hogsheads by pulling with horses or pushing by hand. The direct participation by both large and small planters in the marketing of tobacco minimized the need for commercial centers or towns in the colonial Chesapeake.

The increase of tobacco production led to numerous regulations to protect the valuable export trade by assuring a quality product and to guarantee a satisfactory market price. Inspection had begun in Virginia as early as 1619; in the magazine or general storehouse in Jamestown tobacco was to be burned if condemned by the magazine custodian. By 1632 and 1633 provision was made for five, and later seven, stores or warehouses in Virginia where tobacco was to be inspected. The repeal of these measures in 1641 returned inspection to the control of the plantation commander and later to the county lieutenant.[21] Maryland provided for "Bad Tobacco" to be burned in 1640 and instructed the three "viewers" to condemn all "ground leafes Second Crops leafs notably brused or worm eaten or leaves house burnt sun burnt frot bitten wheather beaten in the house sooty wett."[22] Other restrictions for Virginia probibited the tending of second crops or slips of tobacco and even regulated the number of leaves per plant to be tended. No more than fourteen leaves were to be grown and not over nine were to be gathered.[23] Both Maryland and Virginia stipulated control over packing of tobacco, and both outlawed the inclusion of ground leaves with other leaves of better quality.[24]

Other steps were taken to provide both price control and crop control. Virginia experimented with limiting the number of plants to 3000 per worker or even 2000 or 1500 plants per person, including women and children. Attempts were also made to limit the time of planting or replanting, and to require all tobacco "struck" before the end of November.[25] These measures were difficult, if not impossible, to enforce, particularly the requirements for the counting of plants and the counting of leaves.

While concerned with the nature of the tobacco crop, colonial officials devoted some attention to other products in both old and new settlements. During these early decades in both Virginia and Maryland, all areas are so much a part of frontier conditions that they are relevant to this study. A Virginia proclamation in 1628 had directed "that such a reasonable proportion of tobacco shall be planted, only, as may be cultivated without injury to a plentiful crop of corn."[26] Continuing these earlier concerns for balancing grain production with that of tobacco, Virginia's enthusiasm for grain went so far as to have the Assembly strive for wheat exports. In March 1657/8, 10,000 pounds of Virginia tobacco were offered to any person who produced in one year 500 pounds sterling of "English wheate" for export.[27] No evidence has been found to show that this ambitious goal was achieved by any of the colonists. Little more was achieved in encouraging wine production by bringing over Greek vignerons and by the Assembly offering a bounty of 10,000 pounds of Virginia tobacco for any colonists making "two tunne of wine" in one year from grapes grown in Virginia. The difficulty of the situation is exemplified in that the vignerons themselves turned to tobacco planting for adequate support. Flax and hops were also included without significant results in the "premium" of 10,000 pounds of tobacco for production to the value of 200 pounds sterling.[28]

The encouragement to silk production deserves a special note even though these efforts also failed. Following the Indian attack of 1622, the Virginia Assembly continued an earlier requirement that every freeman was to grow mulberry trees, and again in 1638 the Assembly expressed an interest in the revival of silk production. Edward Digges during the 1650s brought to Virginia at least two experienced Armenian silk producers, the best known one named George,[29] and by 1654 eight pounds of silk had been produced. Publication of the pamphlet, *The Reformed Virginian Silk-Worm*,[30] aroused further interest by predicting greater achievements in the industry if the silkworms were permitted to feed in the open where they would eat upon the mulberry as well as upon other trees. Likewise, the Assembly again encouraged the industry by providing 4000 pounds of tobacco for George the Armenian to "stay in the country," and by requiring holders of 100 acres "in fee" to plant and care for ten mulberry trees within the next two years.[31] This encouragement gave an impetus to silk production for the next few years, but not enough to overcome the competition from tobacco.

There was also an important place for livestock in the Chesapeake's frontier settlements. The term *livestock* meant horses, cattle, hogs, goats, and sheep, although in seventeenth century records the term *cattle* is similarly used. Taking the modern definition of cattle, we note that those brought to early Virginia and Maryland came mainly from England and Ireland. They represented, as suggested by Lord Ernle for English cattle, "the haphazard union of nobody's son with everybody's daughter";[32] black, white, and red cattle in the British Isles became mixtures of color and breed in the colonies.

After persevering despite inadequate supplies and Indian attacks of the 1620s, Virginia could count only 500 cattle, 526 tame swine, about 300 goats and kids, one horse and one mare. Horses obviously did not play as important a role in the early Chesapeake as on later American frontiers. Virginia continued to experiment with ways to preserve the cattle essential for increasing its supply. In March 1629/30, the Assembly prohibited the killing of female cattle unless they were "past breedinge, or are likely to dye by some infirmity."[33] A further restriction was added in 1633 probibiting the export from Virginia of "cowes, heifers, or female catle."[34] These measures along with the expansion of settlements and the growth of population contributed to the increase in livestock, as reported in 1649 for Virginia, of 20,000 cattle, 3000 sheep, and 5000 goats.

Protection was also provided for hogs, even for the wild ones that had multiplied from the original stock that came primarily from the British Isles with possible additions from either the West Indies or northern colonies. Killing "wild swyne" without permission of the governor was probibited in Virginia in 1632, but at the same time killing deer or other wild beasts was permitted because this hunting would keep the colonists "trained in the use of theire armes" and would keep the Indians at a safe distance. To eliminate wolves, colonists were permitted to kill one wild hog for their own use for every wolf head brought in to the commander of their area.[35] Killing a tame hog of another colonist was declared a felony in March 1642/3, but this classification was repealed in 1647 and payment of a tobacco fine or two years of labor service was substituted. In January 1639/40, a special requirement was passed about keeping hogs in pens. Tame hogs were to be retained in pens during the night and to be cared for by "keepers" during the day, or else the owner was liable for any damage they might do.[36]

Fencing in stock was not the general policy on the Chesapeake frontier, but fencing the crops was widespread. The enclosure movement in England dating from the twelfth century provided the precedent of fencing in either crops or pastures, but the choice in the Chesapeake area seems to have been a case of the most expedient response to the small number of acres being

cultivated. Fencing the fields, therefore, became law in both Virginia and
Maryland of the seventeenth century. As early as 1626 the order to "rail, pale,
or fence" cultivated lands was issued by the General Court in Virginia for all
settlers in areas where there were cattle ranges. Again in February 1631/2
and in September 1632, the Assembly required the enclosing of planted
ground with "sufficient fences" or else the planters would suffer damage to
their crops at "theire oune perill."[37] Ten years later a similar enactment for a
"sufficient fence" for "cleared ground" reiterated the responsibility of the
owner of the land and made him liable in case any damage was done by
killing or by "doggs sett upon" trespassing hogs and cattle.[38] In 1646 a
"sufficient fence was four and a half feet high and "substantiall close downe
to the bottome," the appraisal of its sufficiency being made by two men
designated by a commissioner.[39] Maryland in 1640 and 1654 enacted measures incorporating Virginia's definition of size and provision for personal
liability.[40] The concern for the sufficiency of the fence led eventually to the
common description of "pig-tight, horse-high, and bull-strong."

The colonists turned to the material at hand and used the abundant wood
supply to construct the Virginia or worm fence. The early Virginians and
Marylanders split the rails and were able to put together the now familiar
zigzag fence without having to use the precious nails for which even houses
had been burned to preserve. Furthermore, the fence could be moved from
fields abandoned because of soil exhaustion to new ground under cultivation
and fulfill the legal requirements for sufficient fences.

Turning out the livestock necessitated some form of identification that
would serve the same purpose that branding with a hot iron has done in more
recent times; the technique resorted to was marking the ears. An unlimited
combination of slits, crops, underbits, overbits, swallow forks, and so forth
were used and recorded in the county records where their entry was required.
The marking was a proof of ownership that also curtailed thievery by
colonists and by Indians.

Both Indians relations and the control of cattle were related to the
construction in the 1630s of a palisade in Virginia running between the James
and York rivers. The project had been discussed several times before. As far
back as 1611, Sir Thomas Dale in a letter to the Earl of Salisbury had
recommended the construction of a fortified settlement at Chiskiack on the
York River. In 1623 Governor Francis Wyatt and his council, remembering
the devastating Indian attacks of the previous year, wrote of the plan for
securing the forest by running a pale between Martin's Hundred on the James
and Chiskiack on the York.[41] Again in 1624 this suggestion was made to the
royal commissioners sent over by the king to determine the most suitable
places for fortification.

To construct the palisade, the Assembly offered land and tax exemption as inducements to settlement between Queen's Creek and Archer's Hope Creek. In February 1632/3, a fortieth part of the men in the "compasse of the forest" between the two creeks and Chesapeake Bay were ordered to meet at Dr. John Pott's plantation to erect houses to secure the neck of land commonly known as the "Peninsula."[42] With this encouragement by the Assembly, a palisade six miles in length was completed, running from Queen's Creek to Archer's Hope Creek and passing through Middle Plantation, later Williamsburg. Houses were constructed at convenient distances, and men were assigned to patrol the line of defense during times of imminent danger. By setting off a little less than 300,000 acres of land, the palisade provided defense for the new plantations between the York and James and served as a restraining barrier for the cattle of the colony.

Virginia increased in poplation from about 4900 in 1634 to about 15,000 by 1648. The expansion of settlements shifted northward above the James and York rivers to the Rappahannock, where there was available fertile land near the water ways needed for transport of tobacco to market. Prior to the arrival of Governor William Berkeley, the area north of the York River and along the Rappahannock had been opened by the Assembly, but contingent upon adequate security being provided to exposed settlements. Restrictions were continued for the area of the Rappahannock by the Assembly of March 1642/3, and settlement was, in effect, postponed until permitted by a later Assembly. These restrictions were not finally removed until 1648 and 1649 because of the fears resulting from the Indian massacre of 1644.

The second attack by the Indians came on April 18, 1644, and was led by the same implacable foe who had directed the first assault, Opechancanough, still leader of the former Powhatan Confederation. This second major effort to eliminate the English from Virginia was probably a response to continued encroachments upon Indian lands, including grants made by Governor John Harvey from 1636 to 1639. According to a contemporary account sent to London and printed in 1649, some of the Indians confessed that Opechancanough had been informed by colonists of the civil war in England. The Indian chief, perhaps seizing the civil strife as an occasion to attack, moved to exterminate the colony by surprise attacks and by starvation.[43] The exact influence of this information cannot be determined, although it is certain that needed supplies from England were not available because of the English civil war.

Characterized by the familiar tactics of Indian warfare, the attack of 1644 inflicted a total loss of 400 to 500.[44] The sections suffering most were the inadequately defended settlements newly established along the upper waters of the Pamunkey and York rivers. In retaliation, expeditions similar to the ones following the first massacre were ordered. With Captain William Claiborne as commander-in-chief of the campaigns, the colony was divided into sections, each county being responsible for campaigns against the Indians dwelling nearest to it. For the march against the Pamunkey Indians on the river of the same name, 300 men were chosen from the lower counties and supplies were furnished by public levies. To meet the expenses of the campaigns conducted by the three counties of Isle of Wight, Lower Norfolk, and Upper Norfolk, the Assembly required every fifteen tithable persons to furnish and completely maintain one soldier during the campaign. Soldiers wounded in action were to be maintained by the counties from which they were sent.[45] These campaigns indicate the systematic procedure adopted in the prosecution of the war, but additional aid was needed and sought both from other colonies and from England. Appeals to the Dutch on the Hudson, the Swedes on the Delaware, and the English apparently met with no success. Governor Berkeley was persuaded by the Assembly to return to England during the summer of 1644 in search of assistance.

While Berkeley was away, the Assembly in February 1644/5 took additional, innovative measures to fortify the outlying regions of the frontier line. Blockhouses or forts were established at strategic points: Fort Charles at the falls of the James River, Fort Royal at Pamunkey, Fort James on the ridge of Chickahominy on the north side of the James, and in the next year, Fort Henry at the falls of the Appomattox River.[46] The maintenance of these forts involved considerable expense, more than the officials of the colony wished to draw from the public treasury.[47] Therefore, they decided to grant these forts with adjoining lands to individuals who would accept the responsibility for their upkeep as well as the maintenance of an adequate force for defense. Fort Henry, located at present-day Petersburg, was granted to Captain Abraham Wood with 600 acres of land plus all houses, edifices, boats, and ammunition belonging to the fort. Wood was required to maintain and keep ten persons continuously at the fort for three years. During this time he was exempted from all public taxes for himself and the ten persons. Upon similiar terms Lt. Thomas Rolfe, son of Pocahontas and John Rolfe, received Fort James and 400 acres of land and Capt. Roger Marshall occupied Fort Royal and 600 acres. Since there was no arable land adjoining Fort Charles at present-day Richmond, additional benefits were made for its maintenance.[48] The forts served as the first line of defense against further possible attacks by the natives. Being the center of the varied activities of the frontier, they were also the starting point for attacks upon the Indians and for parties exploring new areas, and they became the center of trade for the outlying regions.

Governor Berkeley returned to Virginia in June 1645, but without significant aid because of civil war in England. Berkeley, however, soon broke the Indian resistance by leading in person "a Party of Horse" that captured near Pamunkey the aged Opechancanough, now so feeble that he had to be "carried about by his Men" and "his Eye-lids . . . so heavy, that he could not see, but as they were lifted up by his Servants."[49] Taken as prisoner to Jamestown, he was treacherously shot by a guard wishing to avenge the injuries the wily old chief had inflicted upon the colony.

The successor to Opechancanough, Necotowance, had become "King of the

Indians," but the tribes were unable to "connect the links in the federative chain" that had formerly united their operations.[50] Faced by a force that seemed insuperable, Necotowance signed a treaty of submission whereby he and his followers became tributaries of the English in 1646. He acknowledged that he held his kingdom from the crown, and he agreed that his successors would be appointed or confirmed by the king's representative in the colony. The Assembly then promised to protect the Indian king and his subjects from their enemies, in return for which Necotowance was to deliver twenty beaver skins annually "att the goeing away of Geese."[51]

The peace of 1646 was very important for Indian-white relations in Virginia. It imposed upon the largest group of Indians close to the colony the status of tributary, and it also represented a decision relative to alliances. Prior to that time the colony had wavered back and forth on the principle of becoming allies of the Powhatan Confederacy or of allying against it with more distant tribes; the peace confirmed the former principle.

Of equal, if not even greater, importance was another part of the treaty that provided for a boundary line between the Indians and the English. The Indians were free to inhabit and hunt on the north side of the York River without interruption from the English; however, settlements were permitted in the lower reaches of that river if Necotowance was first informed by the governor and council. The natives agreed to abandon the land from the fall line to Kecoughtan between the York and James rivers. Any Indian found in the area was subject to death unless he was a messenger sent by Necotowance to the English. Englishmen trespassing on the Indians' hunting ground were guilty of a felony. In order to distinguish Indian messengers, the colony provided coats of striped material, to be obtained at the various forts before entering the colony.[52]

The boundary line was a historic change in Indian policy. It foreshadowed the more intricate system of reservations found in later American history. It implied a recognition of the Indian's right of occupation of the land, although it did not go so far as to acknowledge the sovereign right of the Indian, for European powers, as a general rule, made no such recognition. Additionally, it demonstrated the efforts of colonial leaders to preserve on assigned lands the Indians who were willing to live peaceably.

The provision of the peace regulating English locations on the north side of the York River posed the problem of fulfilling the requirement for "seating" the land within three years. For those with grants in the area, the time for actual occupation or improvement by buildings began from the date at which the area was opened for settlement. Individuals who had to vacate their lands in exposed areas during the attacks of 1644 were first given an extension for reseating of one year in 1647, and at the expiration of the period the extension was renewed for three years before the lands would "be accompted or adjudged soe deserted."[53]

A more delicate problem confronted Governor Berkeley and the Assembly by the settlers between the Rappahannock and Potomac rivers in "straying plantations." The colonists first were ordered to withdraw south of the York River within one year because of the small number of settlements and their inadequate protection. Authorization was then made for the erecting of a fort protected by forty men at the head of the Rappahannock River. But the continued population build-up and the demand for more land soon prompted reversal of the restrictive policy; the Assembly designated the peninsula between the Rappahannock and Potomac as Northumberland County with the privilege of electing burgesses in 1647. At the further insistence of the burgesses, the governor and council in the same session acquiesced in removing the restriction on settlement north of the York and Rappahannock rivers, to be effective September 1, 1649. Until the effective date, patents and surveys could be made in anticipation of removal of the barrier. The law making it a felony to go north of the York River was thereby repealed.[54]

Following these legislative actions, the flood gates were thus opened and the land-hungry Virginians—both native and recent immigrants—spread out over the newly opened areas. Like streams that wind their way along the terrain of lowest elevation, the newcomers searched out the most desirable locations, settling the fertile valleys and areas accessible to water routes. The four great rivers of Virginia—the Potomac, Rappahannock, York, and James—carried colonists north and west. Other settlers went either east and north along the Eastern Shore or south and west below the James River. The appearance of new counties recorded much of this expansion.[55] South of the James River, Surry County was carved out of James City County in 1652. Gloucester County was formed about 1651 from a part of the area north of the York River to the Piankatank River, while Lancaster was created about the same time just to the north spanning both sides of the Rappahannock River near Chesapeake Bay. The rapid colonization along the south bank of the Potomac River added the county of Westmoreland in 1653 with bounds west of Northumberland County out to the falls of the Potomac. Two other counties were added as migrations moved inland along the rivers, New Kent County in 1654 from the "upper part" of York County, and Rappahannock County in 1656 from the western area of Lancaster County. The creation of these new counties kept pace with expanding population and provided county courts that were more conveniently located for the new areas.

The degree of social mobilty present during the early years of Maryland history is revealed in an examination of two groups, the gentry and indentured servants. The frontier conditions of the whole colony presented opportunities for social betterment that were to decline in the established settlements in subsequent years. Despite the heavy feudal heritage that existed for proprietary Maryland, a significant degree of upward mobility in social position emerged. Part of this may be attributed to the opportunities concomitant with the departure from England where class lines were more rigidly drawn, although by no means completely stratified or immobile. Part of the change came from the initiative of individuals in the new colony where the opportunities to acquire land or to hold political offices were open to a broader segment of society.

Analysis of the early gentry as listed in the records of the Provincial Court during the four decades following 1637 identifies as many as 300 men with the rank of gentlemen. The majority of these (275 or 83 percent) were so identified from their first entry in the record and most likely from their first appearance in the colony, while the remainder (55 or 17 percent) achieved the status after reaching the colony by rising from a lower rank. But for the 330 who had the rank of gentlemen, one study concludes that 225 (82 percent) of them did not qualify as real gentlemen in England but apparently took advantage of the fluid situation or "shipboard mobility" to claim for themselves a higher rank in the new country.[56] This is probably an exaggerated estimate of the number who climbed the social ladder in transit across the ocean because a substantial number of gentry were attracted to Maryland by association with the Calvert family or because they aspired to be part of a stratified society. Whatever the exact number that made the leap, they were joined by others in the rank of gentlemen who elevated themselves by the acquisition of land in early Maryland, or more often by securing public office such as provincial posts, county commissioners, county sheriffs, county surveyors, militia officers, or ship captains. In England, the gentry traditionally held these appointments, but the expanding number of counties in Maryland was an opportunity for the nongentry group to gain these positions and thereby aid in their own vertical mobility.

The prospects of indentured servants' achieving a higher status in Chesapeake society presents equally intriguing questions. After serving their tenure of three to seven years to compensate primarily for transportation costs to the New World, what fortune awaited them? How did they adapt after providing their labor during these years when their contribution as workers was sometimes more highly cherished in Chesapeake society than land itself? Did they survive? Were they able to become landowners themselves as the provision for freedom's dues specifically provided in Maryland? Did they become eligible for public office? And were they able to rise above a position that has sometimes been equated as little better than slavery itself?

A study of 275 indentured servants who came to Maryland before 1642 provides evidence to delineate the career of 158 of them as freemen. The fate of the 117 (over 40 percent) not recorded as freemen is not fully known. The deaths of fourteen of them are recorded; others may have suffered the same end; still others may have gone to other colonies either as freemen or as refugees from servitude. Not all of the 158 ex-indentured servants in Maryland became landholders and participated in the exercise of governmental affairs, but enough did to exemplify the opportunities that were available in this early frontier society. Approximately 50 percent (seventy-nine or eighty-one—there is a problem of precise identification) are known to have become landholders in Maryland. Only thirteen to fifteen of the 158 freemen were without land after living in Maryland for over ten years. Some of the 158 migrated to other colonies, and at least eleven of the twenty-five going to Virginia took up land there. Most of those holding land in Maryland acquired from fifty to 400 acres, although fourteen surpassed 1000 acres and one acquired over 4000.[57]

Opportunities for these former indentured servants extended also to participation in governmental affairs at various levels. Many of the 158 identified as freemen served as jurors; twenty-two of them also served the province in other offices, several occupying more than one position. Sixteen served as justices of the peace, seven as sheriffs, four as militia officers, twelve in the legislature as burgesses, and two on the council. The social mobility for former indentured servants is exemplified in the new frontier county of Charles, created in 1658. Four of its six county court justices named in the first year were former servants, and four more ex-indentures were added to the court during the next three years. Three of these justices also served in the Maryland Assembly as representatives of Charles County.[58] The greater opportunity, therefore, appeared in the newer counties, but the social and economic development of the entire colony was fluid enough in the early decades for some governmental positions to be open to former indentured servants in all counties.[59]

3

Western Exploration and Conflict in
Virginia and Maryland:
Bacon's Rebellion and the Glorious Revolution

The passing years of the seventeenth century and the increase of population in the Chesapeake colonies stirred new interests in western exploration and the fur trade. In the last half of the seventeenth century, the decline in the number of Indians and the depletion of the fur-bearing animals of the coastal area meant that expeditions were lured westward in search of the valuable fur and skin trade.[1] The motivation for going west was a complex mixture of self-interest of the explorers and traders and of intercolonial competition and international struggles—the latter persisting throughout the period of this study and involving the Dutch, Spanish, and French.

Interest in Western Europe in furs and skins was evident in the later Middle Ages and intensified following the early settlements in America. The finer furs such as sable, ermine, and fox were used to adorn the robes of royalty and of the lords and ladies of the nobility. The soft, short underlayer of hair of the beaver was superbly suited for the manufacture of the stylish beaver hats; "Upon his heed a Fluandryssh bever hat" noted Chaucer about his merchant in *The Canterbury Tales*.[2] King Charles I said in a royal proclamation in 1638 that "the wearing of beaver hats" had "of late times become much in use, especially by those of sort and quality."[3]

Before contacts with the supplies of America, the British imported furs through the Hanseatic League in Germany and from Russia, particularly after the glowing report from Richard Chancellor in 1553 of the "fine furres as Sables, Martens . . . Bevers, Foxes, Minkes, Ermines . . . and Hartes" of Russia.[4] The Dutch entered the fur trade in the sixteenth century and eventually became important middlemen for fur from Russia for other parts of Western Europe. Their control of New Netherlands allowed them to pursue a similar role in seventeenth-century America. The demand for luxurious furs continued with the settlement of early America, yet there also developed the need for skins and furs to sell to a broader segment of society, a demand met through the deerskin trade of the southern colonies.

In contrast to the fur trade of New England, on the southern colonial frontier deerskin was widely used and even exported to meet the demands of the British and European markets. The Indians, of course, made clothing from deerskins before the arrival of Europeans, and the first paintings made by John White in the 1580s depict their costumes. Colonials soon came to wear deerskin when made into hunting jackets, leggins, moccasins, and—for those who preferred primitive dress—the breech cloth. Other utilitarian purposes included ammunition carriers, thongs for the farmer, and supplies of the hunter including the strap for the coon or fox horn. Raccoon was the second most popular pelt on the southern colonial frontier, and frequently the striped skin became a picturesque cap. The beaver, while not as abundant as in New England, was still trapped in the seventeenth century, and its value was such that twenty beaver skins were designated as Indian tribute to the colony of Virginia by the treaty of 1646.

The nature of the Indian trade changed as the journey lengthened and as more resources were needed to venture into this tempting but uncertain business. Trade between Indians and whites until the mid-seventeenth century had been conducted by short overland trips of a few miles to Indian villages, by short water routes that took white traders by small boat or canoe to the Indian habitats, or at white villages or trading sites that the natives frequented to exhange their skins and furs for the products upon which they were becoming increasingly dependent. The Indians wanted beads, cooking utensils, clothing apparel, pickaxes, and shovels, and they were particularly eager to get firearms and ammunition as well as intoxicating beverages.

The decline in the number of Indians and the depletion of the fur-bearing animals of the coastal area forced the traders and explorers west. The Virginia Assembly in 1643 set a precedent for the encouragement of western exploration by issuing a charter to Walter Chiles, Walter Austin, Richard Hooe, Joseph Johnson, and other possible associates "to undertake the discovery of a new river or unknowne land bearing west southerly" from Appomattox River.[5] Reward for their venture was to be receipt of the full profits of trade with the Indians for a period of fourteen years. The expedition was probably hindered by the Indian attack of 1644, but soon afterwards the forts established along the fall line of the rivers stirred interest in westward expansion.

Fort Henry, located at present-day Petersburg, was the starting point for an important expedition in 1650. Under the leadership of Abraham Wood, commander of the fort, and Edward Bland, an English merchant, the small group of adventurers started to the southwest with Indian guides. With their destination probably the Tuscarora villages, the party crossed the Blackwater, Nottoway, and Meherrin rivers, reaching after a five-day journey the falls of the Roanoke River near present Clarksville, Virginia. Then they decided to turn back after examining the area.[6] Further exploration was abandoned because they feared the plots being fomented by the natives. They sensed the hostility of the Occaneechee, a small tribe of Siouan stock occupying the island of the same name in present-day Mecklenburg County, Virginia. The Occaneechee regarded warily any expedition that might endanger their profitable position as middlemen in the Indian trade. Several other ventures were authorized during the 1650s, but few seem to have produced significant results.

New impetus given to exploration of the West resulted in the crossing of the Allegheny Mountains during the 1670s. Although several colonials displayed both interest and initiative in exploration and trade, the real source of renewed interest in the West was in England. The English conquest of the Dutch in 1664, the organization of the Hudson's Bay Company in the 1670s, and the continuation of competition with France stimulated English interest in the fur trade. In London many leading nobles took an active interest in trading enterprises, and through these efforts the city became increasingly important as a center for the fur trade.

During the years 1669 and 1670 John Lederer, a German physician, made three journeys into the unexploited lands to the west. His second expedition, it is certain, was supported by Virginia Governor William Berkeley, who was the "American agent" of English nobles interested in western enterprises; he probably supported the other two expeditions as well. Lederer started on the first venture in March 1669, with three Indians from a Chickahominy village at the falls of the Pamunkey. Gradually he worked his way across the piedmont passing near present Charlottesville, Virginia, to the summit of the Blue Ridge. After wandering in the snow in search of a passage through the mountains, he returned home along the same route. His second expedition, consisting of a party of twenty-five Englishmen and Indians, began from the falls of the James in May 1670. After going through Manakin Town, the party went due west overland breaking trail to present Buckingham County. There the party split when most of them wanted to turn back; Lederer, accompanied by a single Indian guide, struck off to the southwest. His route is uncertain, though a course west across the Staunton River to Occaneechee Island is suggested by recent research. He continued south to the Sara (Cheraw) Indian town on the upper waters of the Yadkin River in North Carolina, on to the Waxhaw village along the North and South Carolina line, and then to the town of the Catawba Indians at Ushery near present Fort Mill, South Carolina, before turning back. On his third venture, Lederer with a party of fourteen left the falls of the Rappahannock River in August 1670, and travelled westward along the north fork of the river to the heights of the Blue Ridge. There the party gazed across the Shenandoah Valley to the Alleghenies; but the travelers were so weary and "the cold so intense" that they "drank the Kings Health in Brandy, gave the Mountain His name" and then returned home.[7]

Lederer's expeditions sparked interest in additional exploration. Under the auspices of Abraham Wood another small company of adventurers set out from Fort Henry in September 1671. Leaders of the expedition were Captain Thomas Batts, Robert Fallam, and Thomas Wood, who receive credit for making "the first recorded passage of the Appalachian Mountains." Hoping to discover waters flowing into the "South Sea," the party turned westward, crossed and recrossed the Staunton River, and then lingered for a few days in Roanoke Valley at the Totero town. Then they pushed on to the west and on September 13, 1671, reached New River, which flows westward and ultimately empties into the Ohio and Mississippi rivers. Thinking they had reached the tidal water of the western sea, the party turned back where New River breaks through the mountains in present Giles County, Virginia, near the West Virginia line.[8]

Two years later the trail to Tennessee was opened by an expedition again sponsored by Abraham Wood. Led by James Needham and Gabriel Arthur, the group in April 1673 journeyed to the southwest, crossed the Roanoke River at Occaneechee Island, and continued to the waters of the upper Yadkin. There the party turned directly to the west, climbed the North Carolina mountains to the summit of the Blue Ridge, and descended the western slope to a Cherokee Indian village on one of the eastern tributaries of the Tennessee River.[9] Needham, on a return trip to the Cherokee village from Fort Henry, was killed by a traitorous Occaneechee. Arthur, however, remained with the Cherokee to learn their language. After barely escaping the same fate of his colleague, Arthur survived other hazards on expeditions with the Cherokee to West Florida, South Carolina, and the Shawnee country of Ohio. To these two men, noted for their daring adventure, goes credit for opening the Cherokee trade with Virginia, and for extending English influence over the powerful Indian tribes of the Southeast.

The key figure among explorers and Indian traders during the third quarter of the seventeenth century was Abraham Wood. Called the "Frontenac of Virginia," he was so active in frontier exploits that it has been suggested that the "history of westward expansion during the period is almost a biography of this remarkable man."[10] Biographical facts are limited, but enough is known to trace his meteoric rise in the political, economic, and social affairs of Virginia. He is presumed to be the same person as the Abraham or Abrahm Wood who came to Virginia in 1620 as an indentured servant and was listed as serving on Captain Samuel Mathews' plantation across the river from Jamestown in January 1623/4 and February 1624/5. He served as justice of the peace and as burgess from Henrico during part of the 1640s and from Charles City during part of the 1650s before he became a member of the council in 1658, serving at least twenty-two years on this body. Appointed captain of the militia in 1646—the same year he was given command of Fort Henry—he rose to the rank of major general in the militia and had an active career as Indian negotiator and Indian fighter in addition to his vigorous promotion of western exploration. His holdings of valuable lands, one of the

Cherokee Indian using blowgun. The blowgun, made from a hallowed cane seven to nine feet long, was a dart-shooting weapon used by the Cherokee and other eastern tribes to shoot birds, squirrels, rabbits, and other small game. The Indians were accurate with the blowgun up to sixty feet. (Photograph courtesy of the Oconaluftee Indian Village, Cherokee, North Carolina.)

major keys to social standing in seventeenth-century Virginia, exceeded 6000 acres.

His successor and preeminent colonial financier was William Byrd I. Falling heir to the estate of Thomas Stegg, his uncle, Byrd at the age of eighteen came into possession of some 1800 acres of land along the falls of the James River in the area of present Richmond in 1670. Byrd's inheritance included a position of social prominence and the potential of political influence. By 1676 Byrd was captain in the militia of Henrico County; then he became escheator of the county and its representative as a burgess, and still later a member of the council.[11] From his strategic position at the falls of the James, Byrd's economic interests were Indian trade and commerce with

Cherokee Indian making darts for blowgun. The darts were slender splints of hard wood about ten to twenty inches long and wrapped at one end with thistledown, cotton, animal hair, or some soft material to provide an air seal in the hollowed cane. The darts were propelled by blowing with the mouth. (Photograph courtesy of the Oconaluftee Indian Village, Cherokee, North Carolina.)

frontiersmen. As early as 1671 he was active in western ventures, for the journal of Robert Fallam noted in September upon arrival among the Tutelo that "We immediately had the news of Mr. Byrd and his great company's Discoveries three miles from the Tetera's [Totero] Town."[12]

The experiences of William Byrd I with the Indian trade in the 1670s and 1680s provide further insights into business on the frontier. He extended the trading path to tribes beyond the Chesapeake area, making contacts with tribes as distant as the Catawba in Carolina and the Cherokee in the mountains. Byrd's trading expeditions or caravans were either financed solely by him or in partnership with others. Byrd's son, William II, noted that some caravans had as many as 100 horses and fifteen or sixteen persons. Horses in the caravans could carry pack loads of trading goods of 150 to 200 pounds and with adequate forage could complete twenty miles each day;[13] dangers, however, were frequent. William Byrd I, for example, reported the death of five members of one caravan from Indian attacks some thirty miles west of Occaneechee Island, and two years later he lamented the "ill Successe" of his traders where two were killed some 400 miles away and others lost all of their horses.[14]

Marketing abroad brought additional challenges that tested the acumen of the trading entrepreneur. Byrd experienced economic success when the price and supply of furs and skins was right, when ships were available to transport merchandise, and when goods for trading with Indians were adequate. Byrd's letters, however, reveal problems with all of these at some time. Since ships were not always at his command, Byrd invested in shares or part ownership of different ships in an effort to aid both his tobacco and Indian trade. He felt himself at a disadvantage without up-to-date reports on current prices for the fur and skin trade and explained to his agent in England the difficulty of getting market prices only about once a year, stating that by "being in the darke, I have been a Considerable looser within this twelfe moneth."[15] He struggled also with the supply of appropriate furs and skins, noting, for example, the inadequate number of beaver skins one year; on another occasion he stated that there were too many raccoons being forced upon him and he intended to purchase additional ones only as competition of the trade demanded. The nature and quality of trade goods continually concerned Byrd, and time and again he instructed and admonished his agents on this. The color of many duffels, or coarse woolen cloth, was too light; what was needed was a darker blue. Beads in greater quantity were essential for the trade, and small white beads were much preferred to the large white ones previously sent. Complaints of reduced sales were made because kettles had holes in them, the Indian hoes were too small, and the dogs of the gunlocks did not hold properly.[16] These deficiencies in products concerned Byrd both because of the loss of sales by the refusal of the Indians to buy, and by competition from other traders.

His greatest challenge came perhaps during the early years of his trading ventures when he faced loss of his business. Operating with a license from the governor, Byrd's position was jeopardized when the Assembly under Governor William Berkeley's influence restricted the number who could continue in the trade. By act of March 7, 1675/6, county courts, consisting of justices of the peace appointed by the governor, were authorized to appoint commissions of five men to conduct trade for each county. All late Indian traders in particular were "utterly barred and exluded,"[17] including both William Byrd I and young Nathaniel Bacon, Jr., who had arrived in the colony only two years before. The restriction was made, in part at least, in an effort to improve Indian-white relations, but Indian hostility was the spark setting off Bacon's Rebellion.

Nathaniel Bacon, Jr., only twenty-seven years of age when he arrived in Virginia in 1674, emerged as the leader of the conflict which bears his name. Nephew of Nathaniel Bacon, Sr., of the Virginia council and a cousin by marriage to Governor Berkeley, he parlayed these connections and his Cambridge education in England to gain a seat on the council himself. His father provided him with sufficient funds to purchase a tobacco plantation along the James River in a frontier area near the holdings of William Byrd I. Bacon, therefore, had already extended his economic activities to the Indian trade when both he and Byrd came under the exclusion of the county court in 1676. That action was one of the initial steps leading to Bacon's challenge to the governor.[18]

Berkeley, then almost seventy years of age, had been appointed governor of Virginia in 1641 and had served during most of the period in this position except when removed from office during 1652 to 1659 by the English civil war. His effective service and widespread support during his early years as governor led the councilors and burgesses of Virginia to invite him to return to this position even before Charles II restored royal authority in England in 1660. Berkeley had been the conqueror of Opechancanough, had initiated the tributary system among Virginia Indians, and had been a vigorous supporter of western explorations that brought contact with more distant Indian tribes. Berkeley recognized his decline in vigor and his diminished ability to confront the challenge of defense of the colony even before the renewal of Indian agitation in the 1670s. Referring as early as 1667 to "my very old age," he initiated overtures to return to England and by 1676 he urged his replacement, stating that *"I am not able to support my selfe at this Age six months longer."*[19]

Trouble, however, had already started on the frontier with the Doeg and Susquehannock Indians in Maryland. Berkeley had to remain at the helm of government in Virginia and both his Indian policy and plans for defense were critical factors in the conflict that erupted. The Doeg took part in the first bloodshed in July 1675, and that set off raids and counterraids along the Chesapeake frontier. The Doeg, in trade with Thomas Mathews of Stafford County in Virginia, accused him of failing to make adequate payments. They sought compensation by taking some of his hogs; the raiders, however, were foiled in their attempt and some were slain. In retaliation, they later returned and killed one of Mathews' workers. Before dying, the man told Sunday morning churchgoers that the Doeg were the assailants. This news spurred Colonel George Mason and Captain George Brent to lead thirty Stafford militia into Maryland and attack not only the Doeg, but, by mistake, the Susquehannock, who had been forced south along the Potomac at Piscataway Creek by their long-standing enemies, the Seneca of the Five Nations.

Maryland at first protested the march of Virginians into her territory. But as Indian depredations continued, Maryland sent 250 troops in September under Major Thomas Truman to join the Virginia militia commanded by Colonel John Washington and Major Isaac Allerton from the Northern Neck. Authorized to make "a full and thorough inquisition" of the troubles,[20] they omitted the search for information and charged the Susquehannock with the murders. Five Susquehannock chiefs, invited by Major Truman to confer on the matter, came expecting to negotiate but were wretchedly murdered on September 26, with Truman apparently being primarily responsible for the order to kill the chiefs.

The enraged Susquehannock eluded the Maryland and Virginia militia and crossed the Potomac early in January 1675/6. As they moved southward along the Virginia frontier, they plundered and murdered the whites, killing thirty-six colonists within the month at the falls of the Rappahannock River in the area of Sittenburne Parish. The raids threatened all of Virginia by upsetting the equilibrium of Indian-white relations and by stirring up the tributary Indians, who provided a first line of defense from hostile intruders.

Settlements in the area of the attack were reduced from seventy-one to eleven within two weeks. Along the falls of the James in the present area of Richmond, the Indians killed three men on William Byrd's plantation at Belvidere and murdered an overseer of Nathaniel Bacon, Jr. Mrs. Bacon, in a letter to her sister about the hardships suffered, wrote: "I pray God keep the worst Enemy I have from ever being in such a sad condition."[21]

When Berkeley received word of these attacks, he immediately prepared to send an expedition against the invaders. Sir Henry Chicheley, selected to lead the march, was instructed to pursue the natives until the security of the colony was again restored. But just as all plans for the expedition were completed, the governor ordered that it should be abandoned. Chicheley's commission was revoked and his forces ordered to disband. Settlers in exposed areas on the frontier were instructed by the governor to cooperate in defense by having ten men in each settlement, and the matter of defending the colony was presented to the Assembly in March.

The exact reason Berkeley disbanded Chicheley's expedition is not known. He may have been influenced by the Susquehannock's offer of peace or by a conviction of the difficulty in locating them. Other possible factors prompting Berkeley's action were the age of the governor, who was described by Francis Nicholson as being "old and infirm";[22] the concern of the governor for profits in the fur trade; the conviction that the Indians had been severely wronged; fear that the campaign would set off a general war that would be as devastating and expensive as current reports indicated for King Philip's War in New England; and a conviction that the tributary Indians would suffer from the difficulty of distinguishing between friendly and hostile Indians. Berkeley had been solicitous in protecting the friendly tribes after the 1646 treaty, and he undoubtedly felt responsible to provide the protection explicit in the agreement.

Whatever motivation was most influential, Berkeley's opponents claimed he was mainly interested in preserving his lucrative fur trade with the Indians. Bacon accused him of monopolizing the trade with the natives and of granting licenses only to those traders who gave the governor one-third of their furs. He also attributed the governor's action to the desire to protect his "tender eye of Interest";[23] and his followers murmured that the chief executive preferred to let the colony suffer in order "that no bullets would pierce bever skins."[24] "These traders at the head of the rivers buy and sell our blood," Bacon added in his "Manifesto Concerning the Present Troubles in Virginia."[25] The inhabitants of James City County, alarmed by the sale of arms to the Indians by "diverse covetous" persons, complained that such quantities of arms and ammunition had been traded that the "Indians have bin therewith better pvided then ourselves."[26]

No evidence conclusively shows that Berkeley benefited personally from the control of the trade, either by issuing licenses or by initiating the commissions of five men appointed by county courts. Bacon also had a stake in the Indian trade and could have been motivated by the desire to preserve and expand his economic interests. For the most part, however, he seemed more bent on warring against Indians, whether friendly or hostile. The motive of the Indian trade cannot, therefore, be considered the primary factor for the actions of either Berkeley or Bacon, but it should not be completely dismissed as a possible contributing influence in the complex of motivations.

In lieu of an authorized expedition such as Chicheley's against the raiding tribes, Governor Berkeley took steps to secure the frontier areas by influencing the Assembly, beginning on March 7, 1675/6, to cut off the supply of arms and ammunition to tributary Indians except as issued to those employed by the colony, and to adopt for the colony primarily a defensive rather than an offensive policy. Action was to be taken against Indians known to have committed depredations and on all suspected Indians who failed to provide hostages or other securities for their good behavior. Since their "retirements are not easily discovered to us . . . . a flying army may not be so usefull." Therefore, 500 troops were to be drawn from other parts of the colony and stationed in forts along eight rivers—the Potomac, Rappahannock, Mattapony, Pamunkey, James, Appomattox, Blackwater, and Nansemond —with one other fort on the Eastern Shore. Additionally, friendly Indians were to be hired to defend against the enemy.[27]

The frontiersmen living close to the Indians were deeply concerned about the security of both their families and their homes and objected to the forts as a passive defense; furthermore, they resented the taxes imposed to build these outposts. They were, therefore, ready for an active leader when Bacon visited a group of volunteer fighters near the junction of the Appomattox and James rivers. James Crews of Turkey Island and William Byrd I, both friends of Bacon, helped persuade

> Mr. Bacon to goe over and see the Soldiers on the other side James river and to take a quantity of Rum with them to give the men to drinke, which they did, and (as Crews etc. had before laid the Plot with the Soldiers) they all at once in field shouted and cry'd out, a Bacon! a Bacon! a Bacon! w'ch taking Fire with his ambition and Spirit of Faction and Popularity, easily prevail'd on him to Resolve to head them, His Friends endeavoring to fix him the Faster to his Resolves by telling him that they would also goe along with him to take Revenge upon the Indians, and drink Damnation to their Soules to be true to him, and if hee could not obtain a Commission they would assist him as well and as much as if he had one; to which Bacon agreed.[28]

After Bacon's acceptance of leadership and Berkeley's refusal to give him a commission, the governor came to Henrico to challenge his action. But Bacon had left and led his force of frontiersmen to Occaneechee Island. Some of the erring Susquehannock were camped nearby, and the friendly Occaneechee Indians, having reported their location to the colony, volunteered to attack the Susquehannock and successfully carried out the assault with the aid of Bacon's followers.

For reasons that are not entirely clear, Bacon then turned on the Occaneechee, who were considered friendly Indians although not a tributary tribe. They were middlemen in trade and apprehensive of an English threat to their position. Was Bacon motivated by his greed for their beaver skins valued at £1000? Did he attack, as some reports suggested, because the Occanneechee refused to provide supplies to his followers? Was his major purpose to obtain slaves from the prisoners taken from the Susquehannock? Or did Bacon seek to become a hero warrior and failed to make a distinction, as did later frontiersmen, between friendly and hostile Indians? Whatever influence was most important, Bacon caught the natives by surprise and annihilated most of the tribe. This was the first group of friendly Indians that Bacon defeated in his short but turbulent career in Virginia.

The events in Bacon's Rebellion moved swiftly. Suspended from the council by Berkeley, Bacon nevertheless was elected by Henrico County to the Assembly that met in June 1676 and passed legislation that has been commonly referred to as "Bacon's Laws."[29] Bacon came to Jamestown, was arrested by order of Berkeley, but was pardoned and permitted to resume his seat on the council rather than sit as a burgess. Berkeley also promised Bacon a commission but delayed in granting it; Bacon went home to the falls of the James and then returned to Jamestown, supported by followers, to force Berkeley to grant the commission in late June. After ineffective campaigns against the Indians, Bacon returned to Jamestown on July 29 when he learned Berkeley was attempting to raise an armed force in Gloucester County against him. Berkeley failed to muster support and sought refuge on the Eastern Shore in Accomack County. Bacon dispatched an expedition by boat against Berkeley, and meanwhile he led in person another campaign against the Indians into the Great Dragon Swamp along the upper Piankatank River. His major search was for the Pamunkey Indians, who although tributaries were suspected of providing hostile Indians with supplies and even direct assistance in attacks upon the colony. Bacon was partially successful in his attacks upon the Pamunkey and returned with exaggerated accounts of his expedition, his second victory against Indians in league with the colony.

Bacon returned to learn of the failure of his expedition to the Eastern Shore. Berkeley had captured the insurgents and then moved on to Jamestown on September 8 in an effort to resume control over the mainland. Besieged by Bacon's forces and unable to influence his followers to fight vigorously, Berkeley again abandoned Jamestown and Bacon re-entered the city on September 19 and destroyed it by fire. Bacon had, therefore, reasserted his authority in the colony when he became fatally ill and died of dysentery on October 26, 1676. Bacon's death enabled Berkeley to resume control of the colony and he proceeded to wreak vengeance by hanging many who had opposed his authority. A total of twenty-three persons died by hanging for the rebellion, fourteen being condemned under martial law. The remaining nine were given the death sentence in the civil action of the governor and council with the participation of the three commissioners—Francis Moryson, Colonel Herbert Jeffreys, and Sir John Berry—who had been dispatched from England along with royal troops. The soldiers were not needed, but the commissioners investigated in detail the background and causes of the rebellion and submitted a report critical of the governor. Berkeley was relieved of his duties and departed on May 5, 1677, for England to answer complaints about his rule in Virginia, but he died before having an opportunity to confer with King Charles II.

What of this colorful and dramatic episode in Virginia's history? Was it primarily a conflict over protection of the frontier from Indian attack? Or was it more a movement for political reform led by the "Torchbearer of the Revolution" against an aging and tyrannical governor?[30] Was it a sectional conflict reflecting the grievances of an exposed and unprotected frontier, or was it more a class conflict that pitted the have-nots against the privileged and aristocratic groups headed by the royal governor? A review of contemporary accounts and later interpretations of the rebellion suggests that the concern over the protection of the frontier loomed larger in significance than a widespread movement for political reform, although both elements were present in the conflict. Furthermore, it appears much more a sectional conflict focusing on an unprotected frontier than an upheaval along class lines.

History cannot be simplified to yield "the cause" or "one cause." Many influences contributed to unrest and to criticism either directly of Berkeley or, in some cases, opposition to the regime that Berkeley represented. The third Anglo-Dutch War of 1674 increased concern over adequate protection of Virginia on the one hand, and at the same time it prompted criticism of taxes designed to strengthen coastal and frontier forts against the Dutch. Twofold criticism emerged in response to the proprietary grant of King Charles II in February 1672/3 of all of Virginia for thirty-one years to Lord Arlington and to Lord Thomas Culpeper, son of one of the original patentees of the Northern Neck in 1649. Berkeley joined other Virginians in protesting this brazen disregard of the interests of the colonists; still others resented the taxes required to pay the expenses of sending agents to protest this grant. The Navigation Acts of the 1660s and early 1670s imposing mercantilistic restraints upon the shipping and trade of the colony also stirred resentment, and again Berkeley was on the side of the colonists in opposing these measures. Other local factors combining to agitate the colonial scene were the depressed price of tobacco, the devastation wrought by recent storms and epidemics, and the aggressiveness of the frontiersmen in Indian-white relations.

What of Bacon's role as a "reformer" and of "Bacon's Laws" of the June Assembly of 1676? There were a number of democratic reforms included in the so-called Bacon's Laws that were declared invalid by the king but were later re-enacted in similar language. Bacon, however, does not appear to have wielded much influence in the Assembly except for two or three laws that pertained to Indian wars and pardons for his followers. He was not in Jamestown most of the time the Assembly was in session from June 5 to June 25, and many of his followers seemed more concerned about commissions to fight Indians.

The democratic reforms that were passed reflected two levels of dissatisfaction with the dominance of "the political and social hierarchy." At the provincial level, prominent planters objected to "the inner provincial clique" surrounding Berkeley and tied to him by patronage. At the county level, criticism was voiced by "ordinary settlers" against the privileges and special powers of leading families in local government.[31] The later re-enactment of the laws of the June Assembly declared invalid by the king indicated the persistence of reform sentiment.

Numerous measures curbing the special privileges of the provincial leaders were all re-enacted. One act prohibited the holding of any office, civil or military, to immigrants without at least three years residence. While applying to both the local and provincial level, it would exclude men such as Bacon or special friends of the governor from office. In other acts, council members were denied their former right to vote with county courts, and they along with their families lost their exemption from paying levies; but they were at least provided some additional salary because of the change. Other measures curtailed the governor's influence by authorizing the county court, rather than the governor, to select its own collectors and for its justices to sign probates.

Other restrictions aimed at county or local leaders were re-enacted the following year. Sheriffs were to hold office no more than "one yeare successively"; no person was to hold two of the offices of sheriff, clerk of the court, surveyor, or escheator. To eliminate abuses in the county levies, representatives were to be elected in each parish to vote with the justices of the peace in levies and other laws.[32]

Many of these measures advanced the cause of liberty and gave greater voice to the people particularly in the administration of local government; however, to draw close parallels between Bacon's Rebellion and the American Revolution with Bacon as the "Torchbearer" seems unwarranted. Bacon, on the occasion of his conversation in September 1676 with John Goode of Henrico, suggested Virginia as well as Maryland and Carolina should "cast off their governors." But Goode put the emphasis more correctly when he told Bacon that his "followers do not think themselves engaged against the King's authority, but merely against the Indians."[33]

As to the nature of the rebellion—whether more a sectional or a class conflict—there is limited evidence about the social and economic status of those who participated.[34] There were large landholders on both sides of the conflict, with Bacon having support from wealthy and influential citizens like William Drummond, Richard Lawrence, William Kendall, Giles Brent, Thomas Goodrich, and Giles Bland, most of whom had significant landholdings in frontier areas. William Byrd I also gave support to Bacon, at least during the initial period of the controversy. Both sides also had numerous followers with more modest landholdings and from all levels of society. The preeminence of frontier security as the most critical issue and the aggressive support given Bacon from the frontier area emphasize the sectional nature of the conflict.

The disturbances in Virginia during Bacon's Rebellion stimulated protests in Maryland. Some actions were similar to those in Virginia, while others reflected the particular situation in Maryland. Charles Calvert, the third Lord

Baltimore, asserted the authority of the proprietor in absolute terms. His actions, however, were not consistent with the mood of the times, for in England Parliament was asserting its increased authority in prelude to the Glorious Revolution of 1688–89. In the colonies the complaints against Calvert included the protests by frontier counties of inadequate protection against Indian attack; the change in 1670 of the right to vote from all freemen to only those with either a fifty acre freehold or personal property valued at £40; the limiting of seats in the Assembly to only two of the four representatives elected; bribing members of the Assembly with the proffer of offices; excessive taxation; nepotism; and favoritism to Catholics. One revolt originated in Charles County in Maryland and represented the westerly settlements across the Potomac from Stafford County, Virginia.[35] While unsuccessful at the time of Bacon's Rebellion in challenging the proprietor, protests would prove more effective in a few years.

With Bacon dead and Berkeley having returned to England, Governor Herbert Jeffreys of Virginia turned his attention to protection of the frontier. In a treaty at Middle Plantation (Williamsburg) in June 1677, he renewed the tributary status with the Indians in Virginia and continued the essential provisions of mutual protection and the payment by each tribe of the "accustomed rent of twentie beaver skinns." In an effort to encourage the intercolonial nature of agreements started by Lord Baltimore, the king and council, after examining the treaty, requested Jeffreys to include other neighboring colonies if possible. Consequently, an additional article was later inserted to the treaty stating that "all Indians and English in the Province of Maryland are inclined in these Articles of peace."[36]

The task of protecting the frontier was less formidable for Virginia and Maryland with the Indians subdued after the assaults during Bacon's Rebellion. Nonetheless, the problem of security continued and resulted in significant innovative experiments in both colonies. These colonies continued to rely primarily upon their militia and the use of forts or garrisons, but they also introduced experiments with special groups or forces that served as rangers. The Maryland Assembly had considered a plan for rangers as early as March of 1647/8,[37] but there is no evidence to indicate that it was adopted that early. Continuing to depend upon forts and militia, the Maryland council in 1662, in response to the news of frontier murders, had ordered militia companies to use scouts "to scour the heads of the Rivers."[38] Three years later in 1665, orders had again been issued for "ranging in the woods" in Anne Arundel and Baltimore counties, or "even to the utmost bounds of the Province upon the Susquehanna River."[39]

Maryland and Virginia were leaders among the thirteen colonies in the testing of possible solutions for security as influenced by military demands and economic necessities. Several similar alternatives were, therefore, attempted both before and after Bacon's Rebellion. In the aftermath of raids against the Susquehannock, the Maryland council in November 1675 authorized a party of thirty fighting men "to Range the woods about Pascattoway & the Susquahannough ffort" and to recover horses lost in the recent expedition. Within the same month it ordered ranging or scouting by twenty men on horses between the Patapsco and Potomac rivers.[40] The following year the Assembly authorized for defense of the colony the use of horse troops as a part of the regular militia, but required in view of their good pay that they provide their own "good, serviceable horse" and supply their own provisions when out ranging. Maryland, therefore, provided officially for a modification of the English militia system to meet the special needs of the American experience.[41] This beginning, dictated by both expediency and economics, has been viewed by some writers as the initial precedent for the creation of the Rangers as a separate American military force with special missions as evident in the twentieth century.[42] In those early years, however, the separation of these forces from other regular units was not consistently sustained. While Maryland usually preferred to depend upon its ranging forces without aid from Indians, Virginia more often included friendly Indians as a part of her frontier security.

Following the renewal of the tributary agreements in 1677, Virginia provided in 1679 for four "houses for stores or garrisons" to be erected at the head of the Potomac, Rappahannock, Mattapony, and the James rivers with provisions that the areas south of the James and on the Eastern Shore might make similar arrangements.[43] A man with horse, arms, and provisions was to be supplied by every forty tithables in the colony, and four Indians from the friendly tribes were to serve at each garrison. For the garrison along the Potomac where there were no tributaries on the Virginia side, scouts from the Matteoman Indians in Maryland were to be obtained. As early as this 1679 measure, Virginia also authorized "ranging and marches" that foreshadowed the turn entirely to the more economical use of rangers in 1682. The temporary storehouses were abandoned in 1682, and eighty light horsemen were provided from the four frontier counties along the great rivers that were most in need of protection—Stafford, Rappahannock, New Kent, and Henrico. These rangers were to scout at least every fourteen days for "the discovery of the enemy."[44] The number of scouting expeditions increased to once each week two years later.[45]

The concern with security along the Virginia and Maryland frontier during this period was occasioned by raids of the Five Nations from New York that were encouraged by the French. According to one report, the French urged the Indians "if they meete with a hogg, Kill him; if a Dog, Kill him; if an Indian, Kill him; if a Englishman, Kill him."[46] Another dubious statement even suggested that the French priests by "pious frauds" taught the Indians that "the Virgin Mary was a French woman, Our Saviour born in France, and the English the Jewes that crucify'd him."[47] To counteract French activity and restore peaceful relations, several delegates went from Virginia and Maryland to treat with the Five Nations along with the New York governor. Colonel Henry Coursey of Maryland represented both colonies in 1677; Colonel William Kendall and Colonel Southey Littleton journeyed to New York in 1679; and Lord Howard of Effingham, governor of Virginia, went in person to Albany for negotiation of a peace of 1684. The confirmation of peace improved order on the frontier, and Virginia abandoned the use of rangers to curtail expenses of the colony in 1686. This suspending of rangers proved temporary. The uprising in Maryland in 1689 in response to the Glorious Revolution and the concern for frontier protection after the outbreak of the long Anglo-French struggle—that started the same year with King William's War—led to reappointment of rangers.

The Glorious Revolution removed the Catholic King James II from the throne of England after the birth of a son in 1688 who would have succeeded him as a Catholic rather than his older daughter, Mary, who was a Protestant and married to William of Orange of Holland. Harboring a number of complaints such as James' belief in the divine right of kings, his attempts to dominate Parliament, and his attacks upon the Anglican Church, Parliament challenged the king and invited William and Mary to ascend the throne of England in this bloodless but important transition to a constitutional monarchy.

News of the change set off three major uprisings in the thirteen colonies. Massachusetts imprisoned Sir Edmund Andros who as head of the Dominion of New England had initiated an arbitrary rule of most of the northern colonies; New York forced the flight of Francis Nicholson as assistant to Andros. Maryland successfully challenged the rule of its proprietor.

In this crisis wild rumors circulated of extreme dangers on the Maryland-Virginia frontier; reacting to these, settlers—particularly in Maryland—abandoned their homes in isolated areas and assembled with others for mutual protection. The rumors posited a twin assault from hostile Indians and French Catholics. Ten thousand Seneca Indians were reported at the head of the Patuxent River, and 9000 more were alleged to be at the mouth of the same river and at Mattapany.[48] Such fear was aroused that a messenger was dispatched to seek help from Virginia. However, investigation of the false rumors by Colonel Henry Darnall of the Maryland council temporarily succeeded in quieting frontier settlers and in recalling the messenger. The Maryland council on March 26, 1689, commended the work of Darnall but expressed concern that some of the rumors came from Virginia settlers where their design "to come over was purely for love of the plunder."[49]

Across the Potomac, Virginia was rocked by its own disturbances—"Parson Waugh's Tumult."[50] John Waugh, the erratic Anglican parson who had come in 1667 to the frontier county of Stafford only three years after its creation, attempted to take advantage of the increased tension over Protestant-Catholic relations to further his own economic and political aspirations. Extending his actions beyond the conventional duties of men of the cloth, Waugh got into difficulty with Virginia and Maryland officials by marrying runaway couples from Maryland, and he engaged in a series of unsuccessful legal battles over title to land with William Fitzhugh. Having come to Stafford County in the early 1670s, Fitzhugh quickly became one of its leaders as lawyer, planter, burgess, justice of the peace, and militia officer.[51] Waugh joined with George Mason I and Martin Scarlet to exert political influence in a group sometimes called Whigs (from an extension of England's political alignments) against a Tory organization led by Protestant Fitzhugh and his Catholic law partner, George Brent. Contested elections for burgesses from Stafford usually resulted in Fitzhugh and his friends prevailing over the increasingly frustrated Waugh and his associates.

The incomplete news of the Glorious Revolution in England and the rumors of papist-Indian threats gave Waugh his opportunity to turn his pulpit into a volcano of tirades against George Brent and the Catholics and to send forth a stream of urgent appeals for Stafford citizens to arm themselves for their own protection in the absence of authorized government. So vehement were 'Waugh's attacks that one contemporary reported in March 1689 that "the Stafford men were wholly intent to kill robb and burne what Capt Brent had."[52] Brent took refuge with his law partner Fitzhugh. Disturbances continued and in June about 200 rioters challenged the sheriff and freed three persons who had been arrested following accusations that they had started the false rumors of the papist-Indian plots. Further violence was prevented when Colonel Nicholas Spencer, secretary of the colony, and two other members of the Virginia council took the initiative by acting for the whole council. They asserted the authority of the new king and queen, William and Mary; they arrested Waugh and some of his associates, restraining Waugh from further preaching; and they succeeded in maintaining control over the Stafford militia by removing Waugh's friends. These actions defused the potential for a frontier explosion on the Virginia side of the Potomac; across the river, though, long-standing complaints against proprietary rule erupted into political disputes.

A delay in official recognition of William and Mary increased the uncertainty of governing authority in Maryland. The proclamation of Virginia recognizing the new sovereigns came on April 26, 1689; Maryland, however, had difficulties with its announcement. Lord Balitmore later stated that his messenger with the proclamation died en route and that he sent a second notice as early as February 1688/9. No record of the second notice has survived, if, indeed, it was ever sent. In this vacuum of power, John Coode, formerly a preacher in England and long a severe critic of proprietary prerogatives, joined with several other leaders in challenging the rule of the proprietor. They formed themselves into a Protestant Association and compiled a list of complaints against proprietary government.[53] Once organized, they armed and moved successfully through the most populous counties—St. Mary's, Calvert, and Charles. They occupied the colonial capital at St. Mary's and forced the submission of Lord Baltimore's council by August 1689. Government then continued under a special legislature called by the Protestant Association. Officially proclaiming William and Mary as sovereigns, the government under the control of the Association continued with uncertainties and with divisive factions for approximately two years. In 1691 Maryland received a royal governor and continued until 1715 as a royal colony.

Meanwhile, William of Orange as King of England brought the nation into the first of a series of four Anglo-French Wars in 1689. The War of the League of Augsburg in Europe against the territorial aspirations of King Louis XIV of France was known in the colonies as King William's War. While the New England and New York frontiers suffered several French and Indian raids, the southern colonial frontier remained calm. French exploring and colonizing efforts were beginning to rim the southern English settlements, but they were still remote and not well established. Following the travels of Père Jacques Marquette and Louis Joliet as far south as the Arkansas River in 1673, Robert Cavelier de la Salle succeeded in reaching the mouth of the Mississippi River in 1682 but his efforts to establish a colony soon thereafter proved disastrous. Henri Tonty, who had accompanied La Salle, did establish a seigniory at the mouth of the Arkansas River and an Illinois colony that continued during the 1690s as a French settlement. Jean Couture, a native of France and identified as a *coureur de bois* by La Salle, assisted Tonty in the administration of these settlements. But Couture himself deserted the French during King William's War and journeyed to Carolina to join the English, mainly from the lure of trade profits. Spain, the other potential antagonist on the southern frontier, was an ally of the English as a member of the League of Augsburg in Europe and refrained from initiating attacks from her Florida settlements.

Virginia did, nonetheless, experience minor modifications of its defense system and returned to the use of rangers and augmented their number.[54] Along the Potomac frontier, for example, the signal for immediate danger was "fireing three Guns at Convenient Distance." The rangers were also instructed to keep order among frontier settlers and to be particularly diligent in preventing unnecessary disturbances at night. Francis Nicholson, newly appointed royal governor of Virginia, arrived in the colony in May 1690 and immediately turned his attention to defense. He went first to the upper reaches of the rivers in exposed areas and concluded that some of the places called "forts" did not deserve the name. Examining the militia, he was disturbed by the inadequate supply of arms that he attributed to poverty;

he hoped to improve them by appeals to the king. He noted the exposure of "out-plantations" along the Virginia frontier and warned against permitting the establishment of others at that time. Aware that security in Virginia depended upon a strongly defended Maryland, Nicholson visited the capital of Maryland at St. Mary's and later went in person along some 100 miles of outer settlements on the Maryland side where he observed the location of white families and conferred with friendly Indians in the area.[55] Nicholson was convinced that security of the frontier was far from adequate; but fortunately for the Chesapeake colonies, it was not tested by the French and their Indian allies in King William's War.

4

The Carolina Coastal Frontier to 1700

Hunters, explorers, traders, and occasional fugitives from justice were among the first Englishmen in the seventeenth century to penetrate the area south of Virginia that was later to take the name of Carolina in honor of King Charles I of England. The territory was originally included in the Virginia charter of 1606, and John Pory of the Virginia legislature visited what is now a part of North Carolina in 1622. He observed that the Albemarle area along the Chowan River was "a very fruitful and pleasant Country, yielding two harvests in a yeere."[1] Sir Robert Heath received a grant from the king to this "Province of Carolana" in 1629, but neither he nor subsequent claimants were able to establish a successful settlement. Edward Bland, companion of Abraham Wood in their expedition of 1650, also visited Carolina and recorded an optimistic view in his 1651 edition of *The Discovery of New Brittaine*. In that country between latitude of thirty-five to thirty-seven degrees, Bland stated that "Tobacco will grow larger and more in quantity. Sugar Canes are supposed naturally to be there, or at least if implanted will undoubtedly flourish." There is also, Bland noted, "great store of fish . . . plenty of Salt," and the Indians have tobacco pipes "tipt with Silver" and copper plates that they wear around their necks. The land yields "two Crops of Indian Corne yearely, whereas Virginia hath but one."[2] Bland, impressed by the potential of the area, obtained authorization from Virginia to settle there, but his death in 1653 cut short the attempt.

These early optimistic statements about the northern part of Carolina belie the important role geography played in isolating early settlements and contributing to an eventual division into the now familiar North and South. A glance at a map of the Atlantic coast also fails to reveal the true state of the North Carolina shore. Rimmed by a series of sand reefs that today are major attractions for tourists, the coast line along Cape Hatteras became "the grave yard of the Atlantic" in the seventeenth century. The hazardous sailing in these waters contributed to its isolation, and additionally five shallow sounds within the sand reefs—the largest of which were Albemarle Sound to the north of Roanoke Island and Pamlico Sound to the south—prevented anchorage by sea vessels. The series of rivers—the Chowan, Roanoke, Tar, and Neuse—that flowed southeasterly into these sounds did not provide the same inviting waterways for early settlements that existed in Virginia. Only the Cape Fear River, emptying into the Atlantic Ocean at present Wilmington, provided a suitable port of entrance and became the target of several early colonizing groups.

The coast of South Carolina also featured a large number of bays and inlets that were less extensive than Albemarle or Pamlico sounds in North Carolina, but they played a more prominent role in early settlements of the coastal plain that became known as the low country. It included such areas as Winyah Bay, Bull Bay, St. Helena Sound, Port Royal Sound, and the harbor for the site of the major urban settlement of Charles Town. The coast line's image of green timber was broken by meandering and sluggish streams that produced, near the coast, wet and swampy lands that would later take on an important agricultural significance with the production of rice. Inland several streams originated in North Carolina in the piedmont section and continued, often with changed names, through South Carolina and the coastal plain to the Atlantic. The Yadkin River in North Carolina, for example, became the Peedee River in South Carolina. The Catawba River in North Carolina flowed into the Wateree River in South Carolina and joined with the streams of the Congaree and Saluda to form the Santee. To the south the Savannah River eventually became the dividing line between South Carolina and Georgia. It was strategically located for early trade and settlement routes. The flat and low lands at the mouth of these rivers in the coastal plain were little above sea level. Still today while standing on the banks of these streams, one can get that strange sensation that comes from observing the rush of water upstream from the coast line at high tide. Rice planters were to face the challenge of controlling this flow for the benefit of their crops.

The number of Indians inhabiting the coastal and inland areas of both North and South Carolina at the time of white contacts in the seventeenth century cannot be determined in exact figures. For North Carolina the total estimate is 30,000, but the tribes of first contact near the coast were small in number and familiar in appearance to Europeans from the John White drawings and engravings done on the expeditions sent out by Sir Walter Raleigh to Roanoke Island in the 1580s. Indians from the three major linguistic stocks of Algonquian, Iroquoian, and Siouan with different dialects within stocks were found in the Carolinas. For cultural divisions there was greater similarity in the general classification of Eastern Woodland and Southeastern, yet some minor variations existed among different groups.

Most of the smaller tribes first encountered near Albemarle Sound were of Algonquian linguistic stock. The Chowanoc were located along Chowan River, and a small tribe or tribal confederation of the Weapemeoc inhabited the area north of Albemarle Sound consisting of the Pasquotank, Perquiman, Poteskeet, and Yeopim. Estimates of their number vary from about 200 to 1000 for the seventeenth century. Immediately south of the sound were other

Algonquians who were known as the Machapunga or Mattamuskeet, the Hatteras near the cape of the same name, the Bay or Bear River tribes who had been frequent visitors to Roanoke Island, and the Pamlico along the river and sound of the same name. Estimates of their population for the seventeenth century vary from about 300 to 450. Farther south were two other small groups of the Neusiok or Neuse River Indians and the Coree near the sound that perpetuates their name. Both were most likely of Iroquoian linguistic stock and numbered in the seventeenth century no more than 200. The Cape Fear Indians had frequent contacts, most of them hostile, during early settlements in the 1660s. They numbered only about 200 and later moved to South Carolina in the eighteenth century.[3] For many years they have been classified as of Siouan linguistic stock, but recently anthropologists have questioned this classification.[4]

In South Carolina near the coastline and north of the present site of Charleston, there were in the mid-seventeenth century such small tribes as the Waccamaw, Winyaw, and Sewee. Farther inland were the Santee, Peedee, Congaree, and Wateree; still farther into the piedmont were the Sugeree, Waxhaw, and the Cheraw (or Sara). South of present Charleston and extending to the Savannah River were the Cusabo, a loose confederation involved in many early contacts and including such tribes as the St. Helena, Combahee, Edisto, Stono, and Kiawah. The total population of these many small tribes has not been accurately determined for the seventeenth century.[5] Another small but fierce group, the Westo Indians, were living inland from the coast along the Savannah River at the time of Carolina settlement in the seventeenth century. Involved both in trade and war for a few years, they still have not been positively identified as Yuchi or Cherokee, or possibly some other Iroquoian, Siouan, or Algonquian linguistic family.[6]

Three larger groups—the Tuscarora, Catawba, and Cherokee—were to play a prominent role in Indian-white relations of Carolina and other colonies in the eighteenth century. The Tuscarora, classified as Iroquoian stock and closely related to the Five Nations or Iroquois Confederacy of New York, occupied the inner part of the coastal plain and their villages dotted the middle reaches of the Pamlico, Tar, Neuse, and Roanoke rivers. Numbering 4800 to 5600 at the turn of the eighteenth century, they later came into conflict with the colonists in the bitter Tuscarora War.[7] The Catawba, estimated to have 4600 people in 1682, were the largest eastern Siouan tribe and lived along the Catawba River near the present boundary of North and South Carolina.[8] In Indian-white relations, they were friends of the English colonists though several times attacking them. Their contacts were primarily with the colony of South Carolina where some of the tribe still survive today on a state reservation. Farther west in the Appalachian Mountains along the eastern border of Tennessee and the western portions of North Carolina, South Carolina, and Georgia was the important tribe or nation of Cherokee.

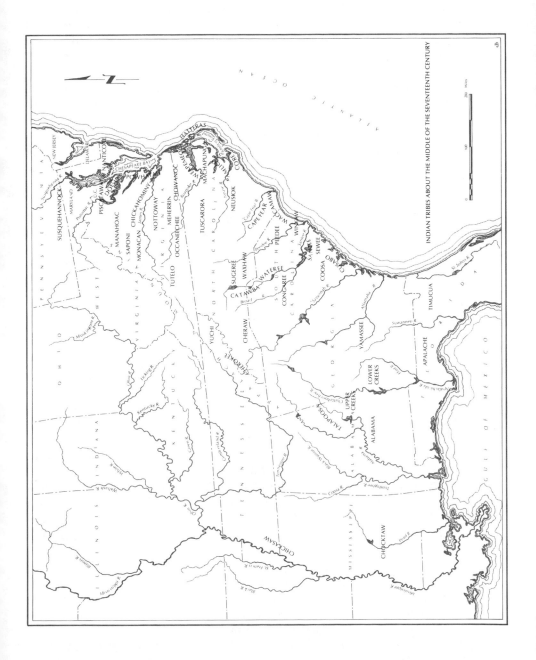

INDIAN TRIBES ABOUT THE MIDDLE OF THE SEVENTEENTH CENTURY

Of Iroquoian linguistic stock and having a population of about 20,000 in 1729, the Cherokee were consistently at the center of the stage of Indian-white relations as friend or foe, and as a participant in Indian trade as white population increased.

Several attempts to colonize the Carolina coast ended in disaster before the first permanent settlement was planted. As early as 1660 a number of New England adventurers failed in efforts to settle on the Cape Fear River and in abandoning the place left a disparaging notice attached to a tree as a warning to any who might follow them to the inhospitable land.[10] Another group of settlers organized in Barbados under the leadership of Peter Colleton and Thomas Modyford had dispatched Captain William Hilton on two exploratory missions during the summer of 1663. As recorded in his favorable account of the area for his second voyage, Hilton made peace with the Indians and purchased the "River and land of Cape-Fair" from Indian chiefs in the area. In 1664 these adventurers started a settlement at "Charles Town" at the mouth of the Cape Fear River.[11] This was the first of three Charles Towns that were started in either North or South Carolina before the third succeeded and became the Charleston we know today. Proposals by the Barbadian adventurers to purchase additional land and establish an autonomous "County or Corporation" were discouraged by the Carolina proprietors.

The eight proprietors receiving the Carolina grant included members experienced in American colonization and influential in royal circles. The major initiative for the project started with Sir John Colleton, a successful Barbadian planter, who then solicited assistance from others including George Monck, Duke of Albemarle and a leader in the restoration of Charles II to the throne, and from the Berkeley brothers: Sir William Berkeley, governor of Virginia, and his elder brother, Lord John Berkeley, active in the administration of naval affairs and a close friend of the royal family. Other proprietors included Sir Anthony Ashley Cooper, later the Earl of Shaftesbury and formerly a Barbadian planter; Edward Hyde, Earl of Clarendon and the king's first minister; Sir George Carteret, vice chamberlain of the royal household and treasurer of the navy; and William Craven, Earl of Craven, a wealthy former soldier of the king.

The Carolina proprietary grant of 1663 from King Charles II included territory between 31° and 36° north latitude.[12] These limits were enlarged in 1665 by moving the line northward one-half degree (or 30 minutes) to include early settlers from Virginia in the area of Albemarle Sound and two degrees to the south as a challenge to the Spanish.

The Spanish occupation of Florida began with their destruction of the French Huguenot settlement under Jean Ribault, who had founded Fort Caroline in 1564 on the St. Johns River after an earlier attempt two years before had failed. Responding to this territorial and religious challenge by "heretics," King Philip II of Spain dispatched Don Pedro Menéndez de Avilés with a strong force in 1565. Menéndez established the Spanish settlement at St. Augustine and then in an overland attack on Fort Caroline ruthlessly wiped out the French, boasting in his report to the king that "I had Juan Ribao and all the rest put to the knife." He justified his action by adding that he considered it "necessary to the service of God and of your Majesty."[13]

The Spanish established control over the area by the dual approach of military forts or presidios and the adaptation of the Spanish mission station to the purpose of converting Indians in dispersed settlements, teaching them agriculture, and at the same time holding them under Spanish influence. Jesuit missionaries labored with these tasks until 1572 and were followed by the more successful Franciscans in 1573. Presidios and mission stations pushed along the coast of the Gulf of Mexico beyond the Apalachicola River, and the Franciscans were as far west as Apalache in 1633. Major missionary work persisted in the 1660s and 1670s around the mission of San Luis in the area of present Tallahassee where Fort San Marcos had been constructed along the St. Marks River soon after 1658. Even more intensive were the forts and missions dotting the sea islands and coasts as far north as present South Carolina with one Jesuit mission possibly reaching the Chesapeake country in 1570. Spain's most effective expansion came from the work of missionaries who learned the language of the Indians and exercised control through Christian conversion with only limited support from military personnel. Obtaining enough missionaries was difficult for between 1615 and 1646 only forty-three Franciscans were licensed by the king of Spain for Florida; the authorized number of missionaries in Florida was increased to sixty in 1646 and a few years later to seventy, but only about forty persons were available for duty. Yet as limited as the numbers were for both missionaries and Spanish soldiers, they exercised control in behalf of Spain over more than 25,000 Indians and posed a major threat to English colonizing efforts.[14]

Virginians drifting into the Albemarle Sound area in the 1660s began purchasing land from the Indians. They formed a small settlement at about the same time the eight proprietors initiated efforts to implement control of their colonial grant. The first land sale on record for North Carolina—though not the first transaction—was made to George Durant by the Yeopim Indians in 1662, a year before the proprietary grant.[15] Other purchases soon followed and reached such an extent that Virginia officials imposed restrictions on further sales. The proprietary grant of 1663 recognized these purchases by a saving clause in the proprietary charters that allowed them to stand as valid even though they were not obtained from the proprietor. The proprietors had an initial interest in developing the northern part of their grant and issued instructions for its administration to Sir William Berkeley, one of the eight proprietors who was then serving as royal governor of Virginia. The instructions also recognized the purchase of land from the Indians and suggested that if no other means were available for support of the governor of the area, he could have the sole trade of furs for three years or some shorter period if other provisions were made.[16] Berkeley, by authorization of these instructions, appointed William Drummond as governor of the Albemarle settlements.

Anticipating an economy that would complement the products of the West Indies, the proprietors stated that "the land in Carolina will produce wines of all sorts silks, reasons of all sorts, currants figs, ollives, oyle, capers and tobacco as good as that of Virrgines."[17] The land policy was spelled out in instructions for the colony and particularly in the "Concessions and Agreement" of 1665, which in addition to the settlement of Albemarle had provisions for two other settlements to the south: Cape Fear of Clarendon, and Port Royal or Craven south of Cape Romania, both of these planned for the present area of South Carolina. The "Concessions" stipulated land grants for Albemarle that were less generous than the going rate of fifty acre headrights in Virginia, if one considers the decreasing amounts provided for each year beyond January 1665/6. For those arriving before this date, 80 acres were to be granted to each freeman and an equal amount for his wife and each manservant with specified arms and victuals; 40 acres were to go to other servants including women, children, and slaves over fourteen years of age. On the decreasing scale provided, for the third year beginning January 1667, grants were halved from 80 and 40 to only 40 and 20 acres.[18] The half penny per acre rent also exceeded the usual quitrent in Virginia of two shillings per 100 acres. Protests to the proprietors for equal treatment with Virginia brought an adjustment to the same rate, but only until the plans of the proprietors for the colony were revised and restated in 1669.

Meanwhile, another group of Barbadian planters with associates in both England and the New World were organized under the leadership of John Yeamans, a Barbadian planter and friend of John Colleton, one of the Carolina proprietors. Their goal was also the Cape Fear. The General Concessions and Agreements of 1665 provided for the three projected settlements (Cape Fear, Albemarle, and Port Royal) to have separate governments with a governor, council, and elected assembly for each. Ill advisedly, however, the variable amounts of land available for the three areas differed considerably; compare, for example, the stipulations for Albemarle and Port Royal. As noted above, the provisions for Albemarle of 80 acres for freemen, wife, and manservant and 40 acres for other servants, were reduced for the third year to 40 and 20. For comparable time and situation in Port Royal, the amounts were 150 acres and 75 acres reduced to 60 and 30.[19] Albemarle settlers naturally resented the higher figure for Port Royal.

Yeamans and his supporters sent an expedition to the mouth of the Cape Fear in the fall of 1665. Despite losing supplies in a shipwreck, the newcomers joined those already at the Cape Fear and engaged in the construction of houses and the tilling of fields of corn, tobacco, indigo, and potatoes. From this settlement, Lieutenant Colonel Robert Sandford conducted an exploratory expedition along the Carolina coast as far south as the proposed additional settlement at Port Royal during the summer of 1666. His vivid report,[20] not published until 1885, relates several contacts with Indians who were friendly despite their probable knowledge of the Cape Fear settlement and despite the earlier work of Spanish missionaries whose religious efforts were still evident in the area. At Port Royal the friendly Indian leader agreed to permit Sandford to take a native "propper young fellowe" back to the English settlement; in return Dr. Henry Woodward, a young English surgeon, was welcomed to remain among the Indians to learn their customs and language. Staying with them for four years, Woodward gained valuable knowledge about the Indians and the Spaniards that was to contribute to the prominent role that he later played as agent for the proprietors.

Despite this auspicious beginning, the Cape Fear settlement of "Charles Town" languished and was abandoned in 1667. Settlers on the Cape Fear resented the more generous land grants proposed for Port Royal; they opposed the payment of quitrents on poor sandy and swampy land as well as the requirement for seating one person per 100 acres; and they were disturbed at the changes in land titles occasioned by the issuing of the Concessions after some settlers had already taken up claims. Growing hostility of the once friendly Indians, disputes between agents in England and the Barbadian leaders, and the consequent neglect by Barbados of adequate supplies sounded the death knell of the settlement. One official remorsefully noted in his letter to John Colleton "that all that came from us made it their business soe to exclaime against the Country as they had rendered it unfitt for a Christian habitation; which hindered the coming of the people and supplys to us soe as the rude Rable of our Inhabitants were dayly redy to mutany against mee for keeping them there soe long."[21]

As the decade of the 1660s came to a close, the credit side of the colonizing ledger looked poor, indeed. "Charles Town" on the Cape Fear had been abandoned; Port Royal had only been explored, not colonized. Only the settlement around Albemarle Sound continued, consisting of a few hundred colonists located largely north of the sound along the Chowan River. Their economic and political life matured slowly in the decade prior to the major effort of the proprietors in promoting the southern half of their grant during the 1670s. This gradual growth contrasted sharply with the more concerted effort of the proprietors in promoting the early beginnings of South Carolina.

Much of the responsibility for pressing forward the interests of the Carolina proprietors fell upon the shoulders of Sir Anthony Ashley Cooper, then only forty-six years of age. Death, political exile, old age, or indifference had curtailed the activity of most of the other proprietors. With assistance that has never been fully determined from John Locke as his physician and associate, Ashley drew up the Fundamental Constitutions of Carolina to provide a revised scheme for colonization and to endeavor to pump new life into the Carolina venture. This document, apparently influenced by James Harrington's *Oceana* of 1656, provided for the transfer of parts of a feudal society to America with its elaborate social and political structure, and has, according to some recent scholars, been more "derided than understood."[22] Part of the Constitutions was actually put into operation, and efforts by the proprietors were made for several years to implement other portions.

Landholding was the key to social organization with two-fifths of the land to go to the proprietors and others of the "hereditary nobility" and the remaining three-fifths to lords of the manor and freeholders. Proprietors were to hold the prime position with a seigniory of 12,000 acres in each of the eight counties of the colony; then the landgraves with four baronies each totalling 48,000 acres; next the caciques, a term derived from the Spanish appellation for Indian chiefs, with 24,000 acres; the lords of the manor with 3000 to 12,000 acres; the freeholders with 50 acres; and finally the highly unrealistic provision for leet men and leet women whose position of attachment to the land and subjection to the jurisdiction of their lords resembled serfdom of the Middle Ages.[23]

The Fundamental Constitutions for the frontier community of Carolina resulted in establishment of the Palatine Court and the designation of at least twenty-six landgraves and thirteen caciques in 1671.[24] Some of those so designated came to Carolina and retained the title of nobility for more than one generation, although in most cases the title did not survive beyond the first generation if retained that long. Some seigniories, baronies, and manors were designated, although they do not appear to have involved the actual political and judicial control that had been experienced earlier in Maryland. They concerned mainly the granting of land and the pursuit of agricultural and industrial ventures.

The basic tenet of the proprietary land policy was not reflected in full detail in the Fundamental Constitutions but was found in other instructions to the governors where the familiar headright grant constituted the formula for the distribution of land as well as an important facet of the promotional schemes for colonists. The proprietors followed the earlier policy of variable and declining amounts of land offered for the 1670s and 1680s, ranging from 150 acres down to 50.[25]

Under the guiding hand of the Earl of Shaftesbury, the completion of plans for a new settlement around the area of Port Royal provided for Sir John Yeamans in Barbados either to serve as governor or to designate a suitable person as leader. Joseph West was placed in command of the fleet that proceeded from England, and Yeamans designated William Sayle, then of

Bermuda, as governor of the colonists. Describing Sayle as "a man of no great sufficiency yet the ablest I could meet with,"[26] Yeamans added that as a Bermudian he might augment the list of settlers with some of his fellow islanders. After examining various parts of the Carolina coast from Bull Bay to St. Helena Sound and Port Royal Sound, the settlers decided upon the Ashley River and settled first on the western bank above Town Creek at a place they called Albemarle Point. The proprietors soon changed the name to Charles Town in honor of the king. By 1680 this area became Old Charles Town when the proprietors ordered a change of the main seat of government and the main port city to be Charles Town at Oyster Point at the junction of the Ashley and the Cooper rivers. Described as "a Key to open and shutt this settlemt into safety or danger,"[27] Charles Town in its new location became the most important urban center of the southern colonies and was known after 1783 as Charleston.

The first settlers arriving in 1670 were mainly English with a sprinkling of Scots and Irish. The majority of the group were apparently in the status of servant, although it is difficult to determine the exact number since individuals may have been listed as servants and thereby obtained an allotment of land for the master when imported and a second allotment for themselves when their status of servant was declared at an end, usually after a year or two. An incomplete breakdown of the ninety-three passengers arriving on the *Carolina* in 1670 shows seventeen masters, sixty-two servants, and thirteen free persons without servants; but it is impossible to determine how many were actually bound to indentured servitude. By January of 1671/2 the total number of colonists was listed as 406, including 278 men capable of bearing arms, 69 women, and an additional 59 persons under the age of sixteen.[28] A few Negro slaves were also imported with the earliest settlers, three coming in with the first group in 1669. Under the land policy of the time, equal allotments of 150 acres were authorized for Negroes.

Interaction among different races—red, white, and black—was a critical theme in Carolina history, particularly in South Carolina with the variety of Indian groups present before white colonization and with the increasing number of blacks in the low country as the colony expanded in population. The first racial interaction of major concern was with the Indian. By the time of the settlement of Carolina, the English had more knowledge of the natives and more experience in formulating Indian policy. Virginia had suffered two devastating attacks. Indians such as Pocahontas had been taken to England for visits, and after some of the initial contacts along the Carolina coasts by early expeditions of the 1660s, a few had been taken to Barbados for visits among the English settlements there. Early provisions for the government of Carolina, therefore, contained some guidelines for Indian policy; but even with the experience that the English had by that date, the problem was so complex that efforts by trial and error continued.

The Fundamental Constitutions of 1669 and instructions to governors contained some directions for policy. Proprietary governmental agencies were to deal with Indian treaties and were authorized to make peace or war. While recognizing that the Indians would "be utterly strangers to Christianity" and admonishing that this afforded "no right to expel or use them ill,"[29] the document contained no specific provisions encouraging their education or conversion to Christianity. One of the most restrictive provisions of the Fundamental Constitutions was the order that "No person whatever, shall hold or claim any land in Carolina, by purchase or gift, or otherwise from the natives or any other whatsoever; but merely from and under the Lords Proprietors, upon pain or forfeiture of all his estate, moveable or immoveable, and perpetual banishment."[30] This last restriction on landholding clearly implied the sovereign right of the proprietors and did not at that time provide for the purchase of the Indian's right of occupation. Separate instructions, however, provided an explicit provision for protecting the Indians' occupation of the land. By instructions of July 1669, efforts were made to provide a buffer area for the English colony in its infancy. The proprietors prohibited the occupation of land within two and one-half miles of Indian towns on the same side of a river, and enough land for a barony was to be left around the house or town of every Indian cacique or chief. Gifts to the Indians were authorized, and storekeeper Joseph West was instructed to use the Indian trade for skins to fill shortages of clothes or rugs.[31]

The early settlers encountered other problems not completely covered by official instructions. The first expedition under Governor William Sayle in March 1670 confronted an issue that had vexed early Virginians—the question of Indian allies. The cacique of Kiawah urged the colonists to settle along the Ashley River and to ally with them against the fierce Westo, who lived along the Savannah River but raided as far north as the Ashley.[32] Should the Carolinians ally with the coastal tribes nearest to them against the aggressive Westo, or should they join with the more distant Westo to provide security from the tribes closest to their settlements? The colonists experimented with both solutions to the problem.

Threats from the Spanish in Florida added to the complexity of the issue of allies. These threats drew the small coastal tribes closer to the English; consequently, it was possible to form a league with the "Empr and all those Petty Cassekas" in the area between the English and Spanish.[33] Several instructions were also issued to provide amicable relations with the small coastal tribes. These included the prohibition of strangers trading with the Indians, maintaining a fair value of beads in trade, restrictions on the enslavement of natives, and provision for satisfaction when any of the English inflicted damage and injuries upon them.

Raids by the Coosa and other "Southerne Indians," however, led to forceful retaliation by the colonists and initiation of a limited tributary system by which the Coosa were required "to pay a dear skin monthly as an acknowledgment or else to loose our amitie."[34] The tribute system for Indians was not new, of course, and had existed among the Powhatan in Virginia; but apparently it was less extensively used in Carolina, for Maurice Mathews reported in 1671 that among the coastal tribes "I finde noe tributaries."[35] The system did continue, however, and about 1676 the proprietors issued instructions for officials to render an account of tribute or payment made to any of the colonists or officers from the Indians.

Two major facets of Indian policy in the southern part of Carolina dominated Indian affairs from its beginning in 1670 to the mid-1680s. The first of these involved relations with the coastal tribes who became known as settlement Indians and came under the jurisdiction of the colony. By treaty they conveyed land in response to negotiations in behalf of the proprietors. The "first recorded purchase of Indian lands in South Carolina" on March 10, 1675, ceded to the proprietors the land "of great and the lesser Cassoe lying on the River of Kyewaha, the River of Stono and the freshes of the River of Edistoh" in exchange for "a valuable parcell of cloth, hatchetts, Beads and other goods and manufactures."[36] More extensive grants were added to this in the 1680s through the negotiations of Maurice Mathews for the proprietors with some of the declining tribes such as the Stono, Edisto, and Kusso. In addition to specific deeds from each of these tribes, Mathews obtained a general one that included the whole area from the coast to the Appalachian Mountains. This granting of such extensive lands, much of which was neither actually occupied nor even used frequently by the tribes for hunting, reflects the problem of different concepts of land ownership of the Indian and white and of the difficulty encountered by the Europeans in assessing, even when willing to do so, the land rights of the aborigines. The concept of collective ownership by Indian tribes did not stipulate the specific title and boundaries to which the English were accustomed. More than one Indian tribe sometimes claimed the same area. The attempts to purchase were, of course, initiated by the English and represented their effort to resolve both the moral and legal aspects of the problem as well as the one of expediency. The results, however, usually failed to provide adequate compensation to the Indians, whichever concept was recognized.

The second fact of Indian policy concerned the Westo Indians, a tribe along the Savannah River who terrified the small coastal tribes. Their fighting spirit, aided by firearms from Virginia, established them as a formidable bulwark against tribes to the south and southwest, including those under Spanish influence. Henry Woodward, who had lived among the Indians as early as 1666 to learn their language, was authorized as agent of Shaftesbury in 1674 to begin trade with Indians in the interior and to weigh the advantages of a peace with the Westo rather than a pact with the Kasihta of the Lower Creeks. His "Westoe Voiage" confirmed the former, so he opened trade with the Westo and initiated the alliance that has been designated "the cornerstone of the South Carolina Indian System" to 1680.[37] This "cornerstone," however, was built on a foundation of self-interest, and it failed to provide a solid base for an Indian policy acceptable to both the proprietors and the officials in the colony representing the local planter-merchants. A bifurcation of control of the Indian trade arose from the efforts of Shaftesbury to settle a plantation at Edisto entirely separate from the Ashley River settlement under the governor and council. The efforts for the Edisto settlement were abortive. But in 1677 another arrangement for division of control began when five of the proprietors set up a monopoly over the Carolina trade that was to extend for seven years and to include trade with the Spanish, Westo, Kasihta, and other Indians beyond Port Royal or at equal distance as the Westo and Kasihta.[38] Trade with the smaller tribes along the coast was left open to the colonists.

This Indian trade, whether with the more distant tribes or the small coastal tribes, quickly developed into one of the most important economic activities of the last quarter of the seventeenth century in Carolina. Most of the English trade goods were similar to the ones noted previously for the Chesapeake traffic. The first expedition sent out by the proprietors carried beads, shirts, scissors, hatchets, hoes, and knives. Other products soon added were various types of clothing and cloth, blankets, axes, brass kettles, rum, guns, and ammunition. In exchange for these products the English obtained skins and furs, primarily deerskins, although furs of small animals and some beaver skins were included. Part of the beaver apparently made its way into the trade from Indians farther north such as the Iroquois, who at times found this outlet more profitable when restrictions were imposed in northern English colonies or in Canada.

Exchange of trade goods during the early years of the Carolina colony were often made either in Charles Town and other white villages or at times in the Indian villages themselves. Access to these trade locations was good and permitted individual settlers and the Indians to frequent them. For more distant tribes and trading sites, the two usual methods of transport were by caravans of packhorses and by Indian burdener.

Caravans of twenty or thirty packhorses were most common for a small group of individual traders with each one owning some six or seven horses and often employing an assistant packhorseman. A contingent of 100 or more was sometimes dispatched by a larger group of traders seeking security or operating as an organized company. The horses were usually obtained from the Indians or were sometimes bred by Indian traders who gradually began to take up residence with Indian tribes. Deerskins were placed into packs of approximately fifty pounds with each horse carrying three packs.

As an alternate method of transportation, Indian burdeners were used more regularly in trade with the tribes closest to Charles Town and during the earliest years of Indian-white contacts. Each burdener carried a pack of twenty-five or thirty skins with a weight of fifty or sixty pounds. The burdener either agreed voluntarily to the task for the supplies promised him or he may have been coerced in this labor as an Indian slave. Henry Woodward, for example, on one of his most distant trade ventures, returned from along the Chattahoochee River with 150 burdeners carrying skins.[39] Apparently these were volunteer burdeners for there is no evidence that they were enslaved. The problem of Indian slavery, however, became a critical one and contributed to the continued dispute between the proprietors and the local officials in Charles Town over the control of trade and the role of the Westo.

The proprietors attempted to create a monopoly for themselves over long-distance Indian trade. They thought the colonists would be satisfied with traffic with the small coastal tribes nearby, concluding that "noe man hath reason to complaine."[40] But the proprietors reasoned incorrectly, and tension between the two groups intensified following the murders of Englishmen attributed to the Westo. The colonists were further embittered when the Westo turned over the friendly Cusabo tribesmen as slaves. Finally, the colonists' jealousy of proprietary monopoly brought about three Westo Wars. In these assaults they destroyed the tribe as well as the proprietary monopoly and cast a shadow over Woodward's activities. Little is known about the details of these wars. It is certain that in the second Westo War the local officials in the colony engaged in bold Indian diplomacy by soliciting the assistance of Indians then living on the Savannah, including the Shawnee of Algonquian linguistic stock. Through the aid of the Shawnee, the Westo were defeated without great effort from the English. As noted by one writer, "There was not much Blood shed, or Money spilt; for 4 or 500 [pounds] paid the Charge of the War, and other publick Expences."[41] The few remaining Westo, less than fifty, left the area and mingled with the Creek Confederacy, while the Shawnee until the early eighteenth century filled the vacuum created and were referred to by Governor John Archdale in 1695 as "good friends and useful neighbors of the English."[42]

The role of Henry Woodward in the whole Westo affair was not entirely clear. Government officials in the colony accused him of encouraging the Westo raids on the Cusabo for slaves, and he was fined £100 for high crimes and misdemeanors. The proprietors at first condemned his actions, but after his journey to England they pardoned him and expressed confidence in his loyalty, prudence, and conduct in 1682. They issued him a special commission to explore and search for mines, for a passage over the Appalachian Mountains, and for sites in the interior suitable for planting towns. Woodward was obviously exerting his efforts more directly for the proprietors and was subject to just criticism by local officials who continued to oppose the proprietors' attempts to monopolize part of the Indian trade. The net result of all of his endeavors and his skill in negotiating with the Indians were, nonetheless, of positive value to Carolina trade and expansion.

To foster expansion of the colony, population increase was encouraged. Several European groups responded and immigrated to what is now South Carolina. While the newcomers usually intermingled with established colonists, there were some settlements consisting mainly of one national group such as the unsuccessful venture of Lord Cardross and the Scottish Covenanters. Started in 1684 at Port Royal and designated Stuart's Town, the settlement initially sparked controversy because Lord Cardross claimed a separate jurisdiction or coordinate status with the Charles Town government and attempted to exercise full control over areas contiguous to Port Royal. His meddling in colonial affairs eventually led to encouraging the Yamassee Indians in their raids upon the Spanish Timucua Indians, but the advice was ill-advised and led to collapse of the settlement. The Timucua Indians, a group of several tribes of the same linguistic classification living along the eastern portions of the peninsula of Florida, ranged as far north as the St. Johns River and St. Augustine where the Spanish extended both their civil and spiritual authority over the natives. In retaliation for the attacks on Indians under Spanish tutelage, Governor Juan M. Cabrera of Florida dispatched troops of Spanish and Indians in 1686. They overpowered Stuart's Town which had been weakened by illness; the surviving Scots made their way to Charles Town.

Although this Scottish settlement failed, other immigrant groups contributed to the healthy growth of the southern part of Carolina during the 1680s. The population of slightly over 1000 persons in 1680 doubled within two years mainly due to immigration. The new Charles Town at Oyster Point was described in 1682 by immigrant Thomas Newe as "The Town which two years since had but 3 or 4 houses, hath now about a hundred houses in it, all which are wholy built of wood, tho here is excellent Brick made."[43] Some of the immigrants came from England and were mainly dissenters, escaping the efforts to make them conform to the Established Church or fearing the consequence if James II as Catholic succeeded to the throne. A few came from Ireland; still others were transported from the West Indies, particularly Barbados, by Thomas Colleton. One other distinct group, although not always the most numerous, were the French Huguenots whose presence in South Carolina made a distinct impact upon life in the colony.

The Edict of Nantes of 1598 had provided some protection for the French Protestants in a Catholic country by affording a degree of autonomy in religious, political, and civil rights. But even before the revocation of the Edict by Louis XIV in 1685, persecution existed; some Huguenots sought refuge in other countries—including England—and others came as "individual adventurers" to South Carolina. The largest early contingent of some forty-five Huguenots landed in South Carolina in April 1680 under the leadership of René Petit and Jacob Guerard, who each received a manor of 4000 acres for their efforts. Still others followed and the tempo increased after revocation of the Edict in 1685. The total number coming during the proprietary period is impossible to determine exactly, but it never comprised more than one-tenth to one-sixth of the white population. One count for

March 1698/9 found 438 Huguenots in South Carolina: 195 in Charles Town, 31 in Goose Creek, 101 on the eastern branch of the Cooper River, and 111 on the Santee River.[44]

The social processes of interaction and of assimilation for the Huguenots are illustrated by the religious organizations present in the frontier beyond the established settlement of Charles Town. National pride was reflected in the "Prayer of the Charleston Child" referring to the two Huguenot families of Porchers and Hugers (sounds like Eugee):

> I thank God on bended knee
> I'm half Porcher and half Huger.[45]

Six churches can be identified for the Huguenots, five of them established prior to 1706—Charles Town, Goose Creek, Orange Quarter, Jamestown or French Santee, and St. John's Berkeley—and the sixth one not set up until 1763 at New Bordeaux. Assimilation for the French Protestant was very rapid; the Huguenot churches outside Charles Town were either anglicized by request—at Jamestown—or included in the organization for the Anglican Church in 1706—at Goose Creek, Orange Quarter, and St. John's Berkeley. The Charles Town church retained its separate organization as it still does in the twentieth century. The Orange Quarter or French Quarter was designated in 1706 as the parish of St. Dennis. A provision of 1708 stipulated that the French of St. Dennis would pay charges and parochial duties as long as the service was in the French language; but if the service were later performed in English, the church of St. Dennis would then be a "chappel of ease" for the parish church of nearby St. Thomas.[46] The largest concentration of Huguenots outside Charles Town was on the Santee River some sixty miles to the north where 100 French families lived with 60 English settlers in 1706. Despite the French being a majority of the community, the settlement requested establishment of the Anglican parish of St. James on the Santee River in 1706, and the church was authorized to use the French language in its services as long as they "shall think fit and convenient."[47]

The Huguenots were a distinct cultural group and made significant contributions to South Carolina society, but they also merged more quickly with the dominant English culture than other immigrants such as the Germans. Their impact upon the colony, though, was as much economic as it was cultural. They arrived skilled in both agriculture and manual trades, and they were ambitious to improve their own economic position. Originally scheduled to turn their hand to the production of silk, wine from vineyards, and oil from olives, they experimented with these for some years, particularly silk and wine; but in the eighteenth century they turned more to the production of rice and indigo, and after the Revolution to cotton.

These immigrant groups centered in the three counties laid out in 1682 but with boundaries spelled out more specifically in 1685. Berkeley County contained Charles Town and extended from Seewee Bay to Stono Creek; Craven County stretched to the northeast along the coast; and Colleton to the southeast ran to the Combahee River. A fourth county, Granville, was subsequently authorized for the area from Combahee south to the Savannah River. Friction developed among the counties based in part upon political rivalry and in part upon the diversity of ethnic and cultural backgrounds.

The political rivalry tended to pit the newer or more sparsely settled areas against the populous region around Charles Town. This conflict merged with the incipient struggle between the people and the proprietors. The counties were designated as election districts, and the twenty delegates authorized in 1683 were to be divided equally between Berkeley and Colleton counties; Craven was not yet settled and Granville was still a part of Colleton. Berkeley County, being more populous, objected to Colleton having half of the representatives and proceeded to conduct the elections of all delegates in Charles Town rather than in the two separate polling places, one in each county, ordered by the proprietors. Because of the manner of the election, the proprietors ordered the dissolution of the Parliament and criticized Governor Joseph Morton for not exercising a stronger hand in government.

The Parliament had been authorized by the Fundamental Constitutions and was to include the proprietors or the deputies, landgraves, caciques, and from each precinct a freeholder owning at least 500 acres of land elected by freeholders with at least fifty acres. Besides Parliament there was a Grand Council consisting of the proprietors and their counselors with the exclusive right to propose legislation for consideration by the Parliament.[48] Morton's failure to exercise the tight control the proprietors expected over these agencies led to his replacement as governor in 1684.

Relative to the conduct of the election in Charles Town, the proprietors accepted the accusation from Carolina that it was the "dealers in Indians who are the chief sticklers in it." These "dealers," the proprietors continued, boasted that they could with "a bole of punch get who they would chosen" to Parliament and then to the Grand Council. By such control they obtained the passage by the South Carolina Parliament of acts prohibiting the sale of arms to the Indians and required an oath of all men over twelve years of age to abide by this prohibition. Yet the Indian "dealers" flaunted the restrictions and engaged in the trade to their private gain and without penalty. Furthermore, the proprietors charged that by control of Parliament and the Grand Council they "made warrs and peace with the Indians as it best suted their private advantage in trade."[49]

The election dispute, however, aroused opposition to proprietary rule. These objections were voiced by spokesmen of the people, who were sometime designated the popular party from the comparison of the protest to the contest in England between the country and popular groups.[50] Although the proprietors' dismissal of the delegates could be considered as protecting

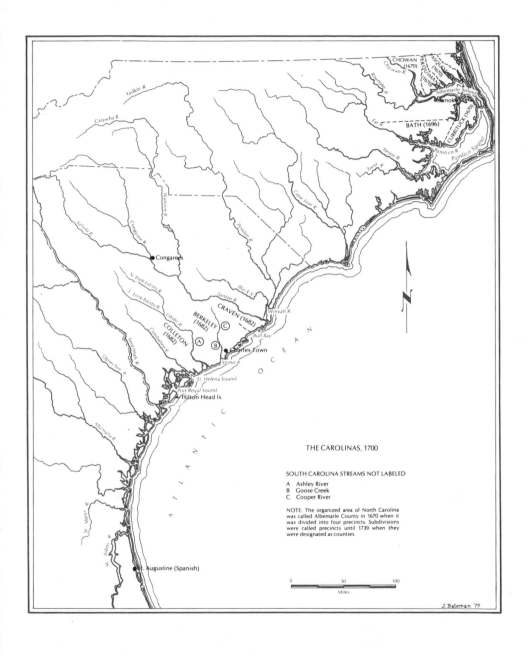

CHOWAN (1670)
Chowan R.
PASQUATANK (1670)
PERQUIMANS (1670)
Roanoke R.
Albemarle Sound
Roanoke
CURRITUCK (1670)
Tar R.
BATH (1696)
Pamlico Sound
Neuse R.
Trent R.
Pamlico R.
Pamlico Sound

Yadkin R.
Catawba R.

Cape Fear R.

Waterce R.

Pee Dee R.

Saluda R.
Congaree R.

● Congarees

Black R.
Santee R.
N. Fork Edisto R.
S. Fork Edisto R.
Edisto R.
Winyah R.
CRAVEN (1682)
BERKELEY (1682)
Combahee R.
COLLETON (1682)
Ⓒ
Ⓐ
Ⓑ
Bull Bay
●Charles Town
Savannah R.
Stono R.

Ogeechee R.
St. Helena Sound
Port Royal Sound
✦Hilton Head Is.

Altamaha R.

N

A T L A N T I C   O C E A N

St. Mary's R.
St. Johns R.
●St. Augustine (Spanish)

THE CAROLINAS, 1700

SOUTH CAROLINA STREAMS NOT LABELED

A   Ashley River
B   Goose Creek
C   Cooper River

NOTE: The organized area of North Carolina
was called Albemarle County in 1670 when it
was divided into four precincts. Subdivisions
were called precincts until 1739 when they
were designated as counties.

0   50   100
Miles

J. Bateman '79

the basic rights of the people, the protest was directed toward the arbitrary actions of the proprietors. Representatives of the people had not been consulted, and the popular party appealed to the royal charter that required assent of the people to the laws. Edward McGrady has suggested that the proprietors intended "to govern the old settlers by the new."[51] The distribution of delegates lends credence to this suggestion because new, less populated areas received more delegates in proportion to their population than did Berkeley County, a reverse situation from the usual frontier experience.

Colonel Philip Ludwell, having served as the political administrator of the northern part of Carolina, was appointed in 1691 over all of Carolina with instructions for the election of twenty delegates. Five were allotted to Albemarle County in the north; five each were provided for Berkeley, Colleton, and Craven counties in the south. If the travel distance was too great for the Albemarle delegates, Ludwell was to designate a deputy for the north and to use a new formula for delegates: seven each from Berkeley and Colleton and six from the portion of Craven falling south and west of the Cape Fear River. Recognizing the political imbalance that still existed, Ludwell followed the new formula for delegates only from the south but met with strong criticism from Berkeley County with 75 percent of the population who were mostly Anglican in contrast to Colleton with mainly Presbyterian and Lutheran dissenters, and Craven with a predominance of Huguenots. Religious differences, therefore, added to the strain that existed between old and new settlements, and Anglican-dissenter friction would continue as a factor in South Carolina politics.[52]

The differences that eventually led to the formal political separation of the two Carolinas were also apparent in the social and economic development of the two areas. South Carolina received special attention from the proprietors. They had definite plans for an orderly settlement and an expansion of towns that would expedite both trade and defense. The economy, in the scheme of the proprietors, would be money crops—cotton, sugar, viniculture, indigo, and ginger—while other products like Indian corn, potatoes, and beans were for subsistence. Cold, dry weather hampered harvests the first year or two of the settlement on the Ashley River, and the high expectations for a variety of crops were tempered by second thoughts about the feasibility of growing cotton, sugar cane, and ginger. Optimism continued for other crops of tobacco, hemp, and flax; frequent experiments with viniculture for wine and the use of mulberry trees were undertaken as well. One correspondent, Joseph Dalton, advocated experiments with dates and almonds. Enthusiasm for tobacco, however, was dampened by the flood of the market of the Virginia leaf during the 1680s. One experiment with silkworms came to a disappointing end when some forty-five French Huguenots, en route to Carolina, had their silkworm eggs "hatch'd at Sea"; before the end of the voyage, "the Worms for want of Provision were untimely lost and destroyed."[53] Other colonists planted a variety of fruits, olive trees, indigo, and such English grains as wheat, oats, rye, and barley. Rice was started sometime during the 1680s or 1690s and would gain a significant place in the economy in the eighteenth century.

The original economic plans went unrealized, but endeavors that had not received much attention in the initial proposals emerged as the most significant part of the undertakings of the colonists. Indian corn proved "hearty and profitable" and was grown more extensively than English grain. Native forests provided turpentine, tar, pitch, and lumber. The natural yields of field and forest proved so beneficial that the number of cattle, hogs, and to a lesser extent sheep had surged upward so rapidly during that seven years before 1682 that Thomas Ashe noted their "many thousand Head" were "rather to be admired than believed."[52] Samuel Wilson observed for the same year that there were "perticular Planters that have already seven or eight hundred head" of cattle.[55] Barrelled beef and pork sent mainly to the West Indies and England and to a lesser extent to the other English colonies north of Carolina became one of the most important trade products.

The most important part of commerce, however, during the late seventeenth century was the Indian trade. Extending both to small coastal tribes and to larger groups to the west and southwest, it involved primarily traffic in deerskins and proved to be the most profitable area of commerce from 1690 to 1705. By 1700, for example, an average of 54,000 deerskins were being exported annually from the southern part of Carolina to England.[56] Trade in Indian slaves also continued, primarily to the West Indies, and at the same time a substantial number were retained within the colony.

In the southern part of Carolina, more Indian slaves were found than in any other mainland colony. Yet this slavery was soon superseded by Negro slavery because increased numbers were available from the activity of the Royal African Company of which at least four of the Carolina proprietors were members. After 1698 the English Parliament extended the opportunities of the African trade to independent traders as well. The prevalence of Negro slavery in South Carolina is reflected in the status breakdown of the 7150 residents in 1703 (see Table 1). The number of slaves present in 1703 underscores the extent to which planters and merchants were developing a stratified society in the colonial period.

Yet it was a society significantly different from the one anticipated by the proprietors. Originally they had designated, as previously noted, twenty-six landgraves and thirteen caciques with large land grants. One of the first ships arriving carried some seventeen masters with a number of servants in 1670. Large landholding continued, but mainly because the local settlers fanned out in search of the most desirable land. The proprietors' rigid plans for control

TABLE 1
Status Distribution[57]

Free		Slave	
Freemen	1460	Negro men	1500
Free women	940	Negro women	900
White men servants	110	Indian men	100
White women servants	90	Indian women	150
White children	1200	Negro children	600
Total	3800	Indian children	100
		Total	3350

and for orderly settlement were modified by this spontaneous initiative; as a result, the proprietors witnessed "the erosion of their brand of feudalism by the South Carolina environment." This "erosion" was evident in the fact that the proprietors were willing to sell baronies for as little as £20 annually by 1690, and by 1698 they were willing to bestow the title of landgrave or cacique upon any settler who would occupy the land.[58] Furthermore, the proprietors were no longer able to restrict settlement to a thirty to fifty mile radius from Charles Town. Aggressive land seekers moved beyond these limits, but a society more highly regimented than North Carolina emerged because of the influence of the proprietors, the growth of Charles Town as a port, and the suitability of the terrain for plantations that supported the economy and style of life of the land-hungry planters.

Albemarle to the north grew slowly in its remote location, with settlements confined largely north of Albemarle Sound along the Chowan River. In 1676 the proprietors criticized the colonists for not moving farther south along the Pamlico and Neuse rivers and for not establishing communication with the settlement on the Ashley River. They went on to recommend to the officials of Albemarle the settlement of three port towns as centers for shipping and also out of "Concerne very much to have some very good Towns in your Plantations for other wise you will not longe continue civillized or ever bee considerable or secure."[59]

Albemarle, however, remained in scattered seatings with no major nucleated settlement during the seventeenth century. Figures on its population vary and do not provide an entirely reliable view of the extent of settlement. One report in the late 1670s stated that "Tythables that is of working hands consist of about 1400 persons, a third part whereof at least being Indians, Negroe and women."[60] Not until the early 1690s did settlement move south of Albemarle Sound with French colonists from Virginia locating on Pamlico River in search of more land, better range for cattle, and a degree of isolation for religious purposes. The population remained small, though, and the official list of tithables in North Carolina submitted to the General Court in the colony in 1694 listed only 787

Old rice barn along the Peedee River, South Carolina. (Photograph by the author.)

individuals. A rent-roll for the same date indicated 4000. With movement south of Albemarle Sound, the county of Bath was created in 1696 on an authorization extended two years earlier by the proprietors, and the new county extended over the whole area from Albemarle Sound to the Cape Fear. Edward Randolph's estimate of "60 or 70 scattered families" for North Carolina's population in 1696 seems much too low in view of other estimates from 3000 to 5000.[61]

Randolph's assertion that the scattered families in North Carolina were "under no regular government"[62] also fails to give an accurate view of the colony. While there was, indeed, more than the normal amount of confusion and inefficiency in Albemarle, a structure of government did function with varying degrees of success. Beginning with William Drummond, a Scottish merchant, in 1664, the governors were commissioned by the proprietors and were assisted by a council of six to twelve men that assumed executive, legislative, and judicial functions as in Virginia. Legislative functions commenced as early as 1665, if not before.

The number of elected representatives increased when Albemarle seated five delegates each from its new divisions known as precincts in 1670. Extending from east to west along the northern side of Albemarle Sound were the precincts of Currituck, Pasquotank, Perquimans, and Chowan. Pasquotank had the largest and most regular pattern of settlement, while Chowan on the western edge was the most sparsely settled. The representatives sat as one body with the governor and council in the General Assembly or Grand Assembly until 1691 when the legislative members changed to a bicameral body and the lower house became the House of Commons.

In 1691 Ludwell received instructions to unite the administration of the two Carolinas, if feasible; he interpreted the project as impracticable and proceeded with the alternate provision of appointing a deputy for Albemarle. Ludwell, therefore, started the appointment of deputies for the northern part of Carolina. This continued until 1710 when Edward Hyde became governor of North Carolina as distinct from the southern part of Carolina.

North Carolina, for the most part, remained an area of small farms. There were a few large landholders or planters, including those granted land by Governor Berkeley in 1663 as their reward for bringing as many as thirty immigrants to the area. But the largest group was small farmers who owned about fifty acres or occasionally over 200 and had come as free immigrants or had served for a time as indentured servants. In either case, land was usually provided them by headright of at least fifty acres, and if indentured servants, they usually received land during the seventeenth century as freedom's dues. Some indentured servants continued to provide labor, most of them voluntary but a few involuntary; and this supply was augmented by slave labor, consisting of a small group of Indian slaves and a steadily increasing number of Negro slaves. A few free Negroes were also present by the end of the seventeenth century.

The small farms of North Carolina produced a variety of indigenous products because few agricultural projects were sponsored by the proprietors or large entrepreneurs in England. External trade was also limited by the lack of good ports in Albemarle and Pamlico sounds. North Carolina was described as having a limited number of small plantations and producing some 800 hogsheads of tobacco, Indian corn, and cattle in 1677. By 1707 Robert Holden in a report to the Board of Trade stated that North Carolina "in which I have been in and lived some time . . . has barrd Inlets into It; which spoyles the trade of it and none but small vessells from New England and Bermoodas trades there, the soyle is more lusty than South Carolina."[63] North Carolina, according to Holden, produced tobacco, grains such as Indian corn and English wheat, beef and pork, tar and pitch, furs and skins from beaver, otter, fox, deer, and wild cat, and certain drugs.

During the seventeenth century, tobacco became the leading staple for the colony as it had in Virginia; corn ranked a close second. Because of the limited port facilities, which were emphasized by Holden, the North Carolinians shipped most of their tobacco to Virginia or by way of Virginia's ports. But the Virginia Act of 1679 prohibited this commerce as "prejudiciall" to Virginians.[64] The North Carolinians continued to send tobacco either secretly through Virginia ports or on ships such as the New England ones that penetrated the hazardous coastline for the golden weed.

The growth of Indian corn contributed to the raising of both cattle and hogs, which played an important role for early North Carolinians. The animals, though, were forced to rely in part upon food that could be obtained from natural products, although contemporary accounts for North Carolina conflict as to the sufficiency of this source. In either case, cattle raising was primarily a subsistence factor in seventeenth-century North Carolina.

Indian trade, which was the most important item of commerce in South Carolina, did not occupy such a prominent posisiton in North Carolina's economy during the seventeenth century. As the century came to a close, the thrust for a vigorous era of expansion came from Charles Town rather than Albemarle. Its beginning was evident in the last decade of the century. Starting from Charles Town, James Moore crossed the Appalachian Mountains as early as 1690 and made contact with the Cherokee. Thomas Welch in 1698 moved through the Chickasaw country in present Mississippi and crossed the Mississippi River to the Quapaw town at the mouth of the Arkansas River. Jean Couture, having deserted an early French settlement in the Illinois country, stimulated interest in English expansion and accepted the offer in 1700 of Joseph Blake, ardent expansionist and deputy governor of South Carolina, for a Carolina expedition to the Mississippi. The surge of activity evident in these expeditions led to a re-examination of Carolina expansion as it related to Indian policy, Indian wars, and the continuation of the international conflict among English, French, and Spanish.

5

Indian Policy and Carolina Expansion, 1700–1720

Anglo-French rivalry for the control of North America intensified on the southern frontier at the beginning of the eighteenth century. The potential of the threat from the Spanish in Florida had, of course, existed from the earliest English penetration. With the passing of Spain as an ally of the English in King William's War, the threat was again renewed. France also finally succeeded in colonizing the Mobile Bay and lower Mississippi area before the turn of the century. Pierre le Moyne d'Iberville, assisted by his brother, Jean Baptiste le Moyne de Bienville, established a French settlement on Biloxi Bay near the mouth of the Mississippi River in 1699 and built Fort Maurepas. Later abandoning the location, Iberville selected a site on the Mobile River where in 1702 the first capital of French Louisiana was located with the construction of Fort St. Louis at the present site of Mobile, Alabama.

In Europe, Charles II of Spain died in 1700 leaving no heir, and immediately the continent was plunged into great turmoil over the question of whether Louis XIV's grandson, Philip Anjou, or Archduke Charles of Austria would be his successor. The candidacy of Philip threatened the balance of power in Europe with the possible increase of French influence through a closer association with Spain. Louis XIV supported his grandson for the throne of Spain as provided in the will of Charles II and set off the War of Spanish Succession. It was known in the American colonies as Queen Anne's War (1702–13).

The contest was mainly between the English and French, even on the southern frontier, but the position of the Spanish in Florida placed them in the center of the plans and attacks of both the English and French. Iberville in 1702 submitted to the French ministry an elaborate plan for the conquest of Carolina and other English colonies to the north with the cooperation of the Spanish in Florida and with the extension of French influence over Indians in the Southeast. Before his proposal could be implemented—if indeed it was practicable—the Anglo-Spanish raids and counter-raids of 1701 and early 1702 led Governor James Moore of South Carolina to attack St. Augustine in late October, with hopes of taking the settlement before it could "be Strengthened with French forses."[1] An English expedition of some 500 whites and 300 Indians overcame the town but was unable after eight weeks of siege to capture the Spanish fort without more powerful naval support. After this failure, Moore was replaced as governor of South Carolina by Sir Nathaniel Johnson; however, he was given the opportunity to lead another expedition aimed at the Apalache Indians. The Apalache were of Musk-hogean linguistic stock and occupied the northern part of present Florida between the Apalachicola and Aucilla rivers with major towns near present Tallahassee and St. Marks. Responding favorably to Spanish missionaries, they had Franciscan missions in at least eight of their major towns and had an estimated population in the late seventeenth century of about 5000.[2] Their geographical location led both the Spanish and French to attempt to use them in undermining English influence over the Lower Creeks.

The maneuvers of the international struggle and the advances to the west and southwest in Indian trade and diplomacy led to contact with Indian tribes not previously encountered. Three large groups were central in Indian relations of the eighteenth century: the Creeks, Chickasaw, and Choctaw. The Creek or Muskogee Confederation were of Muskhogean linguistic classification and in the early eighteenth century consisted of the Lower Creeks and Upper Creeks in parts of present Georgia and Alabama. The Lower Creeks had migrated around 1690 from the Chattahoochee River to Ochese Creek on the upper Ocmulgee to be closer to the English trade. The Upper Creeks inhabited mainly the Coosa and Tallapoosa rivers and together with the Lower Creeks could muster some 3500 warriors in the eighteenth century. Both divisions of the Creek nation were frequent targets of negotiations by competing European powers. More numerous were the Choctaw of Muskhogean linguistic stock with about 5000 warriors and a total population between 15,000 and 20,000. Located west of the Creeks, primarily in the area extending from the upper waters of the Pearl River to the Tombigbee River, the Choctaws were usually pro-French in international diplomacy. In contrast, the Chickasaw tribe was more consistently pro-English but smaller in number with a population estimated from 3000 to 3500 for the beginning of the eighteenth century.[3] They were also of Muskhogean linguistic stock and lived in the northern part of present Mississippi along the upper waters of the Tombigbee and Yazoo rivers.

James Moore sought financial assistance from the South Carolina Assembly for the expedition he had been promised against the Apalache, but without success. Therefore, he assembled a force of 1050 (50 Carolinians and 1000 Indians) with plans to finance the campaign with booty and slaves. The raid of 1704 was a striking success for Moore's forces against the Apalache Indians, who were aided by Spanish friars and soldiers. Several hundred slaves were taken, and an additional 1300 free Indians (300 men, 1000 women and children) were moved near Savannah Town in Carolina across the river from present Augusta, Georgia. Moore reported that "Apalatchia is now reduced to so feeble and low a condition that it can neither support St. Augustine with provisions, nor distrust, endamage or frighten us."[4] The raid left a void in native population in the area around present-day Tallahassee, Florida.

Other attacks continued during Queen Anne's War. A combined French and Spanish assault upon Charles Town in 1706 was successfully repelled by the English. Additional English raids continued against the Timucuan missions and Apalache until an anonymous report of 1710, probably by Thomas Nairne, stated that "there remains not now, so much as one Villeage with ten Houses in it, in all Florida, that is subject to the Spaniards; nor have they any houses or cattle left, but such as they can protect by the Guns of their Castle of St. Augustine."[5]

A leading factor in the diplomatic negotiations with the Indians was trade. In terms of geography the Spanish and French usually had an easier access by river routes from Florida and the Gulf of Mexico to such Indian groups as the Lower Creeks, Alabama, Tallapoosa, and Choctaw. More often the English had to dispatch traders and their caravans over longer land routes, but they gained in advantage with the quantity and quality of their trade goods. This superiority was emphasized by a South Carolina Indian agent in the early eighteenth century when he claimed that "the English trade for Cloathe alwayes atracts and maintains the obedience and friendship of the Indians, they Effect them most who sell best cheap."[6]

As Indian trade expanded in the eighteenth century, the variety of goods available increased, and efforts were made to standardize the value of these goods in relation to the skins and furs that were being traded. One schedule set forth by the Commissioners of the Indian Trade in South Carolina in 1716 exemplifies the variety of goods and equates their value in buckskins for trade (Table 2). Two years later, another schedule repeated many of these items and added others with their value being equated in pounds of heavy dressed deerskins rather than in the number of skins (Table 3).

In addition to the traditional beads, cloth, hatchets, axes, guns, ammunition, and rum, these lists demonstrate the more specialized demands of the Indians for such clothing as coats, laced hats, petticoats, and girdles. They also reflect the natives' interest in paint with the inclusion of vermilion and red lead. While no price for Indian slaves was included, this traffic did continue and the commissioners on one occasion evaluated adult Indian slaves at 200 deerskins.

The reference to heavy dressed deerskins in Table 3 calls attention to the sharp difference that existed in the trade between dressed skins (light or heavy) and raw skins. Light dressed skins were usually about one pound in weight, while heavy approximated two or more. Raw skins were less useful than dressed skins and approximately half as valuable. Two pounds or more of heavy raw deerskins were assigned a value of only one pound of heavy dressed. Trade from the Cherokee country in October 1716 indicates dressed skins dominated exchange: the traders returned with 2087 dressed skins, 89 raw ones, and 36 beaver.[9] The following year another delivery from the Cherokee yielded 901 dressed skins, 56 raw ones, and 30 beaver.[10]

TABLE 2
Indian Trade Schedule[7]

Goods	Buckskins
A Gun	30
A Yard Strouds	7
A Duffield Blanket	14
A Yard Half Thicks	3
A Hatchet	2
A narrow Hoe	2
A broad Hoe	4
Fifty Bullets	1
A Butcher's Knife	1
A pair Cizars	1
Three Strings Beads	1
Eighteen Flints	1
An Ax	4
A Pistol	20
A Cutlash	8
A Shirt	4
A Steel	1
A Calico Petticoat	12
A red Girdle	2
A laced Hatt	8
A Clasp Knife	1
A Yard Cadis	1
Rum, mixed with 1/3 Water; per bottle	1
Salt, Gunpowder, Kettles, Looking Glasses	As you can

A general description of the process of dressing skins by Indians on the southern frontier can apply to many of the tribes in the area. Skins were first put in water for a few hours or left overnight, and they were then placed on a smooth surface, usually a log or some similar object. Unless fur or hair was to remain on the dressed skins in their full natural length, it was removed by scraping with a hard, sharp instrument such as a shell or animal bone. After trade for metal objects began with the whites, the scraping was often done by a metal knife inserted in a wooden handle. Different techniques existed to treat skins. Indians of the Southeast applied a mixture of corn meal and eggs with a small amount of water that was worked into the skins by beating. Some records noted the practice simply of beating young ears of corn into the skins, which apparently served the same purpose that the Plains Indians of the West accomplished with the mixture of cooked brains, liver grease, and yucca plants or oak bark. The skins were then stretched on a wooden frame where they were scraped or rubbed further as needed. When removed from the frame, the skins were worked back and forth over a smooth log or stake to make them more soft and pliable. Before trading, some Indians smoked the skins by hanging them over a pit fire for a few hours.[11]

In the South Carolina Indian trade, skins made their way to Charles Town

TABLE 3
Value of Goods[8]

Goods	Pounds of Skins
A Gun	16
A Pound of Powder	1
Four Pounds Bullets or Shot	1
A Pound red Lead	2
Fifty Flints	1
Two Knives	1
One Pound Beads	3
Twenty-four Pipes	1
A broad Hoe	3
A Hatchet	2
A Pound Vermilion	16
A Yard double striped, yard-wide Cloth	3
A double striped Cloth Coat, Tinsey laced	16
A Half Thicks or Plains Coat, gartering laced	14
A Ditto, not laced	12
A Yard Strouds	4
A Yard Plains or Half Thicks	2
A laced Hat	3
A plain Hat	2
A white Duffield Blanket	8
A blew or red Ditto, two Yards	7
A course Linnen Shirt	3
A Gallon Rum	4
A Pound Vermilion, [and] two Pounds red Lead, mixed	20
Brass Kettles, per Pound	2½
A Yard course flowered Calicoe	4
Three Yards broad scarlet Caddice	1

mainly by overland routes by pack-horse or Indian burdener. As an example of compensation for burdeners, South Carolina officials in 1716 stipulated the following payment for twenty-one Indians who had brought beaver skins from the Cherokee and were to take goods back on their return trip: one and one-half yards of blue duffels for match-coats and one-quarter of a yard of strouds for flaps for each burdener.[12] Some traders allegedly abused burdeners by paying inadequate wages and by imposing a load of seventy pounds or more for a trip of 300 to 500 miles overland.

For the first two decades of the eighteenth century several major trade routes were used for this traffic. Traders moved overland 145 miles from Charles Town northwest to the Congarees, an Indian town near present Columbia, South Carolina, that served as the focus for two inland trails. One route moved northwestward by the Wateree River to the Catawba where it connected with the Occaneechee Path from Virginia. The other trail cut to the west along the Saluda River, moved through Ninety-Six, and on 158 miles to the nearest Cherokee village.

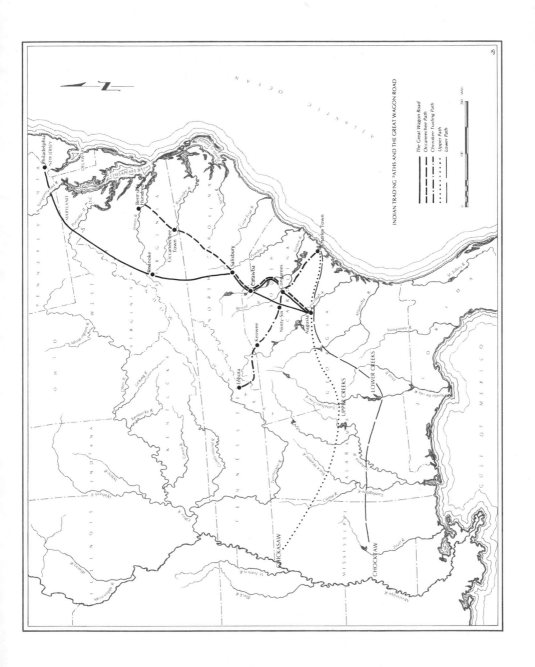

INDIAN TRADING PATHS AND THE GREAT WAGON ROAD

The Great Wagon Road
Occaneechee Path
Cherokee Trading Path
Upper Path
Lower Path

The other most important focal point of trade routes was Savannah Town along the falls of the Savannah River where Augusta, Georgia, is now located. Overland 140 miles from Charles Town, it served as the entrepôt for trade that moved along two routes: by the Lower Path to Creek towns on the Ocmulgee and Chattahoochee rivers and on to the Choctaw, and by the Upper Path to the other Creek towns on the Coosa and Tallapoosa rivers and farther west to the Chickasaw tribe.

For the overland route from Charles Town to Savannah Town, it was possible to substitute water travel by canoe or periago, a boat usually propelled by oars with seven or eight slaves, either Indian or Negro; occasionally sails were used. Although traveling a greater distance, the periago's asset was that it could transport 500 to 700 skins. The craft cost from sixteen to thirty-five pounds, Carolina currency, during the early eighteenth century; care was needed in traversing the waters of the Savannah River, and at times boats were required to anchor in mid-stream before proper docks and storehouses were completed at Savannah Town.[13]

The men who braved the hardships of frontier travel and risked the hazards of the traffic in Indian country were a mixed group. A few of the leading traders had unusual ability, were mostly self-educated, and succeeded in acquiring landed property as well as rendering public service. John Musgrove, for example, served in the Commons House of South Carolina and Theophilus Hastings was a militia officer. Yet most of the traders were illiterate, poor, unscrupulous, and irresponsible with money. Resembling the well-known French *coureurs de bois,* some lived with the Indians and married Indian women, a step that often increased their influence among the tribes with whom they traded. For the first two decades of the eighteenth century, as many as 200 of these white traders were estimated serving at one time as factors of Carolina merchants.[14]

A more articulate, competent group familiar with the Indian country and Indian trade were the men who may be identified as expansionists. South Carolina had elaborate ideas for western expansion as well as plans that foreshadowed both provincial and imperial efforts to spread English hegemony to the Mississippi. One of the first instances of the influence of these expansionists was the enactment by the South Carolina Assembly of an act for regulation of the Indian trade in 1707.[15] This was done after considerable controversy with the governor, Sir Nathaniel Johnson, about the extent of control to be exercised by the legislature, particularly the Commons House. The act required traders to get licenses for all transactions except for settlement Indians and provided for commissioners and for the appointment of an Indian agent who was to spend at least ten months each year executing his duties among the Indians. While proposing to muster the persuasive powers of trade for Indian allegiance, the act also put rigid restrictions upon traders from other colonies such as Virginia, an aspect provoking a crisis in intercolonial relations that is considered in the following chapter.

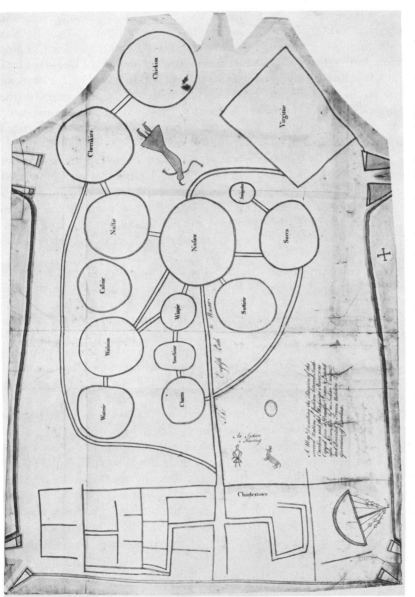

Map of Indian tribes painted on a deerskin. A copy of a map painted on a deerskin by an Indian cacique and presented to Francis Nicholson as governor of South Carolina in 1725. The map sketches the trade routes from South Carolina and Virginia to the Catawba (Nasaw) with connecting trails to other tribes. The left portion of the map includes the Indian's drawing of the streets of Charles Town with a ship in the lower left corner. (Reproduced by permission of the Public Record Office, London. Document C O 700 / NAC / GGN64.)

Thomas Nairne, who along with Thomas Welch had advised the South Carolina Commons House on legislation, was appointed Indian agent by the 1707 act, despite strong friction that existed between him and Governor Johnson over such matters as Johnson's opposition to dissenters in the Assembly and Nairne's favoring the centering of control over Indian affairs in the legislature. An intriguing figure who displayed great zeal for Carolina expansion, Nairne had an elaborate scheme for the conquest of Louisiana by a force of a few English and hundreds of Indians (500 Indians in eighty canoes, 1000 by land). He proposed to maintain the friendship of Indians in the Mississippi Valley by a number of factories for trade; moreover, he advocated English colonization along the South Carolina frontier and suggested expansion in the area once occupied by the Apalache Indians in Florida before their defeat by Carolina a few years earlier. These proposals were not altogether realistic, and the opportunity for Nairne to work for their implementation was limited by a temporary imprisonment because of his clash with Governor Johnson. The ideas were also in advance of the general thinking of officials both in the province and in England, but they foreshadow parts of later British policy for winning the West from the Spanish and French.[16]

After Nairne's imprisonment in 1708, the vigorous policy of the Carolinians languished until 1711 when the English again moved to undo the work of Bienville in preserving peace between the Chickasaw and Choctaw. The pro-French Choctaw were the object of the raids conducted by Thomas Welch with Chickasaw assistance, and by Captain Theophilus Hastings with assistance of the Creeks. The Choctaw suffered some loss of life and property, but most of them retreated to safety. Bienville continued his ingenious countermoves against the English by bringing the Alabama Indians back under the sway of the French as Queen Anne's War ended with the Treaty of Utrecht in 1713. While major changes in America were made at Utrecht relative to territory in the North, the control over Indians was left unresolved except for French agreement not to interfere with the Iroquois in New York.

South Carolina continued trying to eliminate the French after the official end of the war, and these efforts were pushed by the expansionist Price Hughes, a newcomer from Wales and a friend of Nairne. Described as a man with "a particular fancy of rambling among the Indians," Hughes was active in diplomacy among Indians of the Southeast and in 1713 devised a plan for colonization of fellow Welshmen west of the mountains—the first specific proposal of the eighteenth century for British settlement west of the Appalachians. Hughes wanted to recruit only impoverished Welshmen, and he advocated extensive support by Queen Anne and the English government. In return, he proposed "Annarea" as the name of the province in honor of the queen. The new settlement would concentrate in an area like Natchez or on the Yazoo River, and Hughes expected to challenge the French by extending

English control over the land, the Indians, and the Mississippi River.[18] Even though not succeeding in his elaborate scheme, Hughes injected new vigor into the English initiative. He contributed to the establishment of new English trading factories; he improved relations with the Chickasaw and even won over part of the pro-French Choctaw; and he extended his activity with tribes from the Illinois country to the mouth of the Mississippi. His bold moves resulted in his being held prisoner for three days by Bienville at Mobile, where he directly challenged the French claim to the area. After his release and visit to Pensacola, he was killed while traveling alone near the mouth of the Alabama River by pro-French Tohome Indians who had suffered from slave raiding by Carolina traders. Hughes, an ingenious and courageous man, was truly "an authentic prophet of Anglo-American westward expansion."[19]

Relations with Indians in North Carolina, generally peaceful during the seventeenth century, worsened in the eighteenth and erupted in the devastating assaults of the Tuscarora War. The Tuscarora Indians, a branch of the Iroquoian linguistic stock, lived along the Roanoke, Tar, Pamlico, and Neuse rivers. They were kinsmen of the Five Nations or Iroquois in New York and maintained contact with the northern confederacy. Estimated at 5000 in the early eighteenth century, they were North Carolina's most formidable tribe east of the mountain Cherokee.[20]

Several causes have been suggested for the Tuscarora revolt. Some contemporaries attributed the conflict to the influence of the Cary Rebellion, a disturbance primarily over the status of the Anglican Church and the rights of Quakers that eventually prompted Thomas Cary as governor to lead an unsuccessful assault upon the forces of his gubernatorial successor appointed by the proprietors. Although Cary apparently had negotiated with some of the Indians in search of support for his cause, there is no evidence of a direct relationship between that skirmish and the Tuscarora uprising. Some emphasis has been given to the malpractices of white traders among the Indians who cheated and defrauded the natives and who were guilty of enslaving the Indians by conquest or kidnapping. Baron de Graffenried, leader of Swiss and Palatine immigrants, noted with acid pen that the "poor Indians" were "insulted in many ways by a few rough Carolinians, more barbarous and inhuman than the Savages themselves." He also emphasized the "slanders and insinuations of *A few Rioters*" who convinced the Indians that his purpose was to eject them from their homes and move them toward the mountains. De Graffenried did attempt to maintain just relations by purchasing the lands around New Bern from the Indians, even though he claimed to have "already paid double their worth to the Surveyor Lawson."[21]

But it was this very encroachment upon Tuscarora land that was the most important cause in bringing on the revolt. The area of present Carteret

County was entered in 1708 and thus penetrated toward Tuscarora settlements. De Graffenried had received in 1709 from the proprietors a warrant for 10,000 acres of land and Lewis Michel for 3500 for settling the Swiss; John Lawson was authorized to make the survey. New Bern was started in 1710 with over 400 Swiss and Palatine settlers having moved in by that date. The following year as De Graffenried and Lawson were making their way up the Neuse to view the "Upper Country" and to explore to the mountains, both were taken prisoner and Lawson was killed. De Graffenried was later released or escaped, but was told while still detained as a prisoner of how "especially embittered" the Indians were against the encroaching white settlers on the Pamlico, Neuse, and Trent rivers and on Cor Sound.[22] Plans were also revealed for an attack by the Tuscarora assisted by the Mattamuskeet, Pamlico, Neuse, and other Indians.

The opening assault of the Tuscarora War came on September 22, 1711, and spread terror and devastation along the Neuse and Pamlico rivers. Brutality characterized the attack. Even though reports of these events were usually made by whites and may reflect bias and exaggeration, the threat of Indian wars was a powerful psychological force in the life of the pioneer. News of an Indian raid produced a fear that is difficult to gauge, but the unusually vivid reports of the Tuscarora War illustrate the extremes of violence: "Women were laid on their house-floors and great stakes run up through their bodies. Others big with child, the infants were ripped out and hung upon trees." Dead bodies were left in bizarre fashion with one woman "set upon her knees, and her hands lifted up as if she was at prayers, leaning against a chair in the chimney corner."[23] Over two hundred whites were killed, outlying settlements were completely destroyed, and towns such as Bath and New Bern suffered greatly with De Graffenried's colonists subjected to severe physical and spiritual hardships. Trade was disrupted, livestock destroyed, and the instability of the colony that already existed was intensified. Fortunately, the Albemarle Sound area was spared the devastation through the cooperation of Tom Blunt, a friendly Tuscarora village chief, sometimes called "King," who maintained neutrality for some of the Tuscarora bands.

The threat to North Carolina by this Tuscarora outbreak and the subsequent challenges to South Carolina presented critical problems in intercolonial relations. To what extent did fronter problems such as Indian trade or Indian war stimulate intercolonial cooperation? To what extent did they breed intercolonial jealousies and enhance suspicion and mutual denunciation? Was particularism more evident in colonies with or without Indians on their borders? These questions can be profitably examined for several conflicts on the southern colonial frontier.

Cooperation during the Tuscarora War was best between the two Carolinas. The South Carolina legislature provided £4000 and dispatched an expedition of 30 whites and 500 Indians, the best support coming from the Yamassee while many of the settlement Indians abandoned the fight.[24] John Barnwell, sometimes referred to as "Tuscarora Jack," was in command and defeated the hostile natives in two battles near New Bern in January 1711/2. He also established Fort Barnwell on the Neuse River, which provided additional protection for German Palatines in the area. With the aid of North Carolina militia, Barnwell assaulted Hancock's Town at Cotechney where De Graffenried had been held prisoner.[25] Because of the pleas of white prisoners in the fort for their own safety and difficulties such as lack of supplies and the uncertain attitude of Blunt's Tuscarora force, Barnwell came to terms with the Indians. This action later brought forth sharp criticism from Governor Edward Hyde of North Carolina and from Governor Alexander Spotswood of Virginia, and the latter complained that peace had been made "upon very odd and unaccountable conditions which no body expected to last long."[26]

News of the Tuscarora uprising led Virginia to take steps to secure her own colony and to consider the possibility of intercolonial aid to the distressed Carolinians. The support projected by Virginia never materialized. The mustering of militia, including full strength for the counties of Isle of Wight, Surry, and Prince George, was designed to hold Virginia tributaries out of the conflict and to influence those Tuscarora not yet in the conflict either to remain neutral or to join Virginia and Carolina in the fight. The first appeal from the Neuse River inhabitants of North Carolina for aid was considered by Virginia with the decision that the provision for neutrality of Blunt's Tuscarora towns was adequate. The failure of these Tuscarora to fulfill provisions of the treaty[27] led Governor Spotswood and the council of Virginia to send 100 white soldiers and an equal number of Virginia tributary Indians to North Carolina in April 1712. The Virginians expected that expenses from their quitrents would be reimbursed by the proprietors of Carolina; however, in a meeting with Governor Hyde of North Carolina, Spotswood was unable to arrange satisfactory conditions for the use of Virginia forces. The representatives of the Carolina proprietors would not agree to repay the expense of the expedition and would not furnish without charge the essential provisions or means of transportation for the troops. Furthermore, Spotswood asserted that if provisions were taken from Virginia for the expedition, they would be "liable to a duty of ten percent" by the Carolina Assembly. Arguments over these points, combined with the fact that Barnwell had accepted a truce or peace with the Tuscarora without the participation of Governor Hyde, led Spotswood to cancel the proposed march. The Virginia council approved his action.[28]

The Tuscarora went on the warpath again in the fall of 1712, and North Carolina again appealed to Virginia and South Carolina for assistance. Spotswood was pessimistic about the value of the Virginia militia and about the possibility of getting the Virginia Assembly to provide revenue to support its own needs as well as the needs of North Carolina. He did prevail upon the Virginia Assembly to furnish enough "Duffells" for 300 soliders and to provide an additional £1000 to be used for relief in whatever manner the Virginia governor deemed proper. North Carolina was expected to pay for both. Again conditions agreeable to both colonies could not be worked out. Spotswood complained about the action of Thomas Pollock, acting governor, in sending two representatives to coordinate the transfer rather than appearing in person; and he was particularly critical of North Carolina's inability or unwillingness to provide supplies for troops that might come from the Old Dominion. Virginia officials were not enthusiastic about North Carolina's plan that the £1000 be used to hold a Virginia force in reserve pending the outcome of the assistance from South Carolina. These plans came to naught except for the clothes that were delivered and some four barrels of powder sent from Virginia.[29] The efforts, nonetheless, are noteworthy for they represent negotiations between a royal colony and a proprietary colony without mandates issued from England. But Virginia displayed no great generosity in its meticulous demands that every assistance be reimbursed. The crux of the failure seemed to be North Carolina's inability to contribute more substantially to its own protection, rather than any deepseated suspicion or rivalry between the two colonies.

South Carolina under the same proprietary rule again provided the force that rescued her northern sister from the throes of the raiding Tuscarora. Colonel James Moore led the second South Carolina expedition, consisting of thirty-three whites and 1000 Indians, recruited this time more from the Catawba, Creek, and Cherokee tribes rather than from the unreliable settlement Indians.[30] With aid from Pollock as acting governor of North Carolina, the climax of the campaign came with the capture and burning of Fort Nohoroco on Contentnea Creek in March 1712/3. The action of the combined Carolina forces matched the brutality of the first Tuscarora assault. The 1000 casualties of the enemy, the burning of Indians in the fort, the taking of 192 scalps, and the selling into slavery of many of 392 prisoners accent the extremes to which fighting could go on the colonial frontier.[31] The assaults drove the Tuscarora, except those under Blunt, to abandon North Carolina and to join the Iroquois in New York. The move increased the confederacy of Five Nations to Six Nations. North Carolina was, therefore, relieved from this major Indian threat; the colony had suffered major losses and now had excessive bills of credit issued during the war emergency, but it was free of serious factions of government and had recouped sufficiently to return to South Carolina the critical assistance that was soon needed in the Yamassee War.

The Yamassee, it will be recalled, had at the time of the settlement of Charles Town in 1670 been living along the present Georgia coast extending

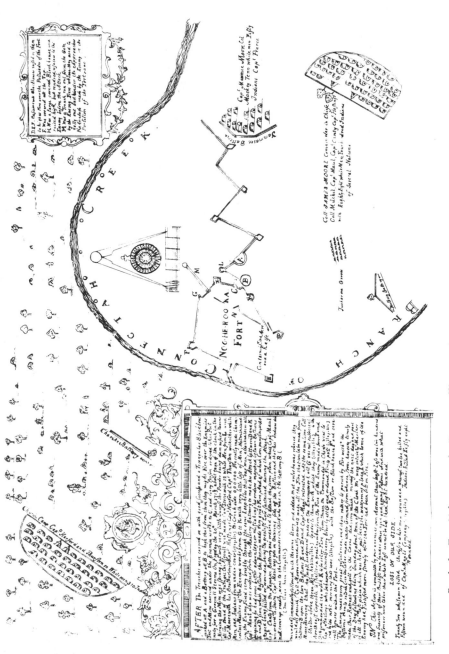

Battle for Fort Nohoroco in the Tuscarora War, March 1712/13. Map of Colonel James Moore's expedition against the Tuscarora Indians and the capture of Fort Nohoroco (Nooherooka) on Contentnea (Connectah) Creek. Fort Nohoroco was described in size as being one and one-half acres. (Photograph courtesy of the Department of Cultural Resources, Division of Archives and History, Raleigh, North Carolina. Document N. 70.10.167.)

into Florida near St. Augustine where they had been the object of Spanish missions for many years. But dissatisfied with Spanish policy and Spanish attempts to transport tribal members as workers to the West Indies, they moved during the winter of 1684–85 closer to English jurisdiction in an area along the coast on the islands of St. Helena and Hilton's Head. From there the Yamassee moved to the mainland during the latter part of the seventeenth century, and a number of white settlers received grants on these and adjacent islands, including Thomas Nairne and John Barnwell. An increase in the number of cattle raisers in Colleton County during the 1690s meant the grazing lands south of the Combahee River were coveted, and colonists began to penetrate the area of Granville County along with white farmers who received substantial grants in the frontier area. The recognition of the value of the Yamassee as a buffer had led the colony in 1707 to reserve a large area for the ten towns of the Yamassee with the prohibition that within these bounds no land be surveyed and no settlement be made of "any stock of horses, hogs, neat cattle or any other stock whatsoever."[32] Except for the islands along the coast, the Yamassee country was to extend from the Combahee River south and southwest to Port Royal and Savannah rivers, and inland or northwest to a line along the heads of the Combahee and Savannah. The island of Coosawhatchie along Port Royal River, then occupied by the Yamassee, was included with the Indian bounds.

These explicit boundaries notwithstanding, some white settlers continued to penetrate the Indian country. In 1711 the Yamassee complained of the settlements and stated that they were "damnified by the Stock of the white Men."[33] Because of this complaint, the Indian commissioner ordered prosecution of both the surveyor and nine persons guilty of violating the boundary. Another concern of the Yamassee probably stemmed from increased activity along the coast, including the provision for establishing Beaufort Town in 1711, and the creation of the parish of St. Helena as coterminous with Granville County that contained the Yamassee country.

The perennial threat of white encroachment was, therefore, a factor in the uprising of the Yamassee, but it was less critical than the angry complaints that were hurled against Carolina traders and their trading practices. This resentment was largely responsible for the Yamassee War, one often described as unique in origins.[34] While that claim probably overemphasizes the differences with other Indian wars, contemporary accounts emphasized the malpractices of traders, most of whom were not licensed as required by the commissioners.[35] Traders were accused of beating Indian men and women, even to death, ravishing Indian women, taking supplies such as corn and poultry without adequate compensation, coercing Indians to serve as burdeners for very little pay, and running up huge debts for which the Indians were held responsible.[36] The Creeks apparently suggested to the Yamassee they avenge their grievances by attacking South Carolina. Both the Spanish in

Florida and the French along the Mississippi no doubt heartily approved of the Indian assault on the English, but no evidence has been found to show they had a direct hand in promoting it.

Charles Town received warning of a pending attack three days before the first major blow fell on April 15, 1715, at Pocotaligo, where only three colonists survived and Thomas Nairne fell victim to Indian torture. The attack spread until hostility against colonial traders and exposed settlements involved the Creeks, Choctaw, Yuchi, Apalache, Catawba, some smaller tribes, and even the Cherokee.

The major events of the war may conveniently be divided into three phases. The first involved the furious attack of the opening assault in April and the quick countermove by Governor Charles Craven in proclaiming martial law and in calling up the militia in Colleton County. He then moved in person with these troops, with the assistance of settlement or tributrary Indians, to a successful attack in June on the Yamassee along the headwaters of Combahee River. A circle of garrisons around Charles Town was set up by the Assembly at a radius of about thirty miles. The second period of the war opened with the attack of the Cheraw and other Indians north of Charles Town about the same time that Craven was defeating the Yamassee. Having returned to Charles Town, Craven was ready by July, with the cooperation of North Carolina forces under Colonel Maurice Moore, to march against the enemies to the north. He had moved only beyond the Santee when forced back by a surprise attack from the south as the Apalache and their cohorts broke through the ring of garrisons and penetrated within a dozen miles of Charles Town. Charles Town was spared, but nearby plantations were damaged before the raiders retreated. The very existence of the colony of South Carolina, however, continued to hang in the balance with the mass of Indians still opposed, the Cherokee hostile, and the Creeks threatening to attack. The major break in the war came with the switch of the Chreokee to the Carolina side largely through the influence of the expedition of Maurice Moore, brother of General James Moore, with some 300 soldiers into the Cherokee country. The Lower Cherokee were more in favor of assistance to Carolina than were the Middle Towns, but the nation turned its back on Creek appeals at the dramatic point of diplomatic decision on January 27, 1715/6, when Creek representatives were slain at Tugaloo by the Cherokee. The last phase of the war was, therefore, under way with Cherokee assistance turning the tide against the Creeks and leading to the migration of the Lower Creeks from the Ochese area back to their former lands on the Chattahoochee River. The Yamassee were driven from the Carolina frontier and sought refuge in Spanish Florida. Gradually, stability returned to South Carolina with the smaller tribes coming to terms with the colony and the Creeks agreeing to a peace in 1717.[37]

Thus passed the gravest threat of the colonial period for South Carolina, and one that had necessitated urgent appeals for assistance from England and from neighboring colonies. The home government sent arms and ammunition, but no fighting men to wage land campaigns. The proprietors faltered in their responsibility by doing little more than turning over quitrents to the colony. North Carolina, even though weak and still recovering from the Tuscarora War, returned the vital assistance it had received by sending troops under Colonel Maurice Moore. Arms were purchased in Boston, although not under as favorable terms as anticipated, and the governors of New York and New Jersey endeavored to get northern Indians, particularly the Seneca, to war against their inveterate Indian enemies to the south to relieve Carolina.

An intriguing phase of intercolonial relations concerned Governor Spotswood of Virginia. When first called upon for assistance, Spotswood and the council dispatched 160 muskets with ammunition from the Virginia magazine. Spotswood then urged the governors of Maryland, Pennsylvania, and New York to prevent their Indians from joining the conspiracy of the Southern Indians. Upon request for troop assistance, Virginia made an agreement with Arthur Middleton to equip and dispatch 300 Virginia volunteers to Charles Town but under terms that appeared too severe for the South Carolina Assembly. Carolina was to pay thirty shillings per month in Carolina money for each man sent, and a slave was to be returned to Virginia to labor for the benefit of the volunteer. Carolina was also to supply food and clothing for the expedition upon its arrival in Charles Town. Some 118 troops plus a second group of about 50 were sent from Virginia, the latter group taking 30 tributary Indians from the Nottoway and Meherrin tribes. These troops rendered assistance in warding off the assault of the Apalache in July 1715. But the effort of South Carolina to get further aid from Virginia failed. The South Carolina Assembly balked at sending slaves, who would have to be women; instead negotiations were conducted with Virginia for a payment of fifty shillings Carolina currency in place of the slave. But Virginia refused the new terms, and Spotswood was sharply critical of South Carolina for not providing supplies and the slaves and for not permitting the Virginia volunteers to serve as a unit under Virginia officers. Neither colony, therefore, was satisfied with the attempt at intercolonial aid. One South Carolinian, referring to the debtors and indentured servants sent by Virginia, stated with exaggeration that most men on the expedition were "the most ignorant creeping naked people th[a]t ever was seen for such a number together, and I verily believe many of them did not know how to load a gun some of them did confess they never did fire one."[38] Spotswood had a final comment that the troops sent by Virginia constituted the first example of intercolonial cooperation of this kind, but, he lamented, "I'm afraid the great discouragements this hath met with will make it the last."[39]

Dire threats to the existence of one colony usually encouraged intercolonial assistance, but intercolonial rivalry and jealousy tugged in the opposite direction. The existence of this rivalry and jealousy prevented development of better relations between the two colonies. Bitter feelings lingered from South Carolina's exclusion of Virginia traders in 1707 despite counterorders from crown officials. Furthermore, jurisdiction over certain Indian tribes was critical, for jurisdiction meant not only control of trade and its profits, but also the availability of these natives to provide frontier security. The prospect of Virginia regaining influence over the Cherokee and Catawba alarmed the South Carolinians, and therefore the negotiations that Virginians conducted with the Catawba Indians during the Yamassee War, including the sale of arms and ammunition, aroused vehement protests from South Carolina. For Virginia and South Carolina in the final analysis, the contest over Indian trade and over the dominant influence upon major tribes contributed more to conflict than to mutual cooperation. Therefore, the generalization that "Particularism was strongest in colonies with no Indian frontier"[40] is not applicable to the squabbles between these two colonies; instead the antagonisms in this case stemmed primarily from competition over the Indian frontier.

The impact of the Yamassee War resulted in several important changes on the southern colonial frontier. It led to South Carolina's modification of its defense policy and to an important shifting of Indian tribes in their location. It intensified the Spanish and French threats from the south and southwest, and it produced a crisis in colonial administration in the crusade to eliminate proprietary control.

To provide for a system of frontier defense that would prove less vulnerable than the turncoat tribes near the colony, South Carolina placed more stress upon frontier posts and rangers that would also provide a mobile screening unit. Several positions were authorized that provided a crescent of defense starting in the interior and extending along the southwestern perimeter of the colony. Near the present site of Columbia and below the junction of the Broad and Saluda rivers, a fort promised in 1716 by Colonel James Moore to the Catawba tribe was built in 1718. It served for both protection and trade until discontinued in 1722. To the southwest along the Savannah River was Fort Moore, located in 1716 at Savannah Town, just opposite and slightly downstream from the later position of Augusta, Georgia. Construction of additional forts was urged in reports to British officials such as the blueprint for British western policy submitted by John Barnwell and Joseph Boone to the Board of Trade in 1720.[41] These recommendations prompted construction in 1721 of the Altamaha Fort, or Fort King George, on the northern branch of the Altamaha River, and the authorization in 1723 of another fort along the Savannah River across from the abandoned Palachacola Old Town as an intermediate point between Fort Moore and Beaufort Fort. These provisions constituted a part of the new western policy enunciated and implemented during the 1720s.

More than stationary forts and their garrison were needed to secure the

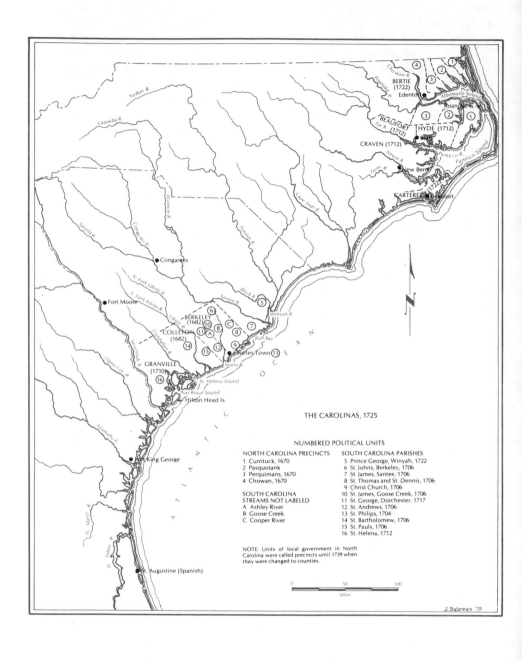

THE CAROLINAS, 1725

NUMBERED POLITICAL UNITS

NORTH CAROLINA PRECINCTS
1 Currituck, 1670
2 Pasquotank
3 Perquimans, 1670
4 Chowan, 1670

SOUTH CAROLINA
STREAMS NOT LABELED
A Ashley River
B Goose Creek
C Cooper River

SOUTH CAROLINA PARISHES
5 Prince George, Winyah, 1722
6 St. Johns, Berkeley, 1706
7 St. James, Santee, 1706
8 St. Thomas and St. Dennis, 1706
9 Christ Church, 1706
10 St. James, Goose Creek, 1706
11 St. George, Dorchester, 1717
12 St. Andrews, 1706
13 St. Philips, 1704
14 St. Bartholomew, 1706
15 St. Pauls, 1706
16 St. Helena, 1712

NOTE: Units of local government in North
Carolina were called precincts until 1739 when
they were changed to counties.

0   50   100
Miles

J. Bateman '79

frontier, and the Assembly turned to rangers who could provide roving units similar to ones Virginia and Maryland had initiated in the 1680s. Providing originally for rangers in 1716, the Assembly continued them in an act in 1717 that designated three groups in addition to the garrisons. One company was assigned to the Old Palachacola Town on the Savannah River with a captain, lieutenant, and twenty-eight privates; another company called the "western rangers" patrolled Rawling's plantation on Edisto Bluff with a captain and five privates; and the third group known as the "northern rangers" had a captain and nine privates. In addition to the provision for recruitment, pay, and care of both the garrison and ranger troops, a bounty of thirty pounds current money was authorized to any person, whether or not in public service, for "every entire scalp of a male Indian enemy he shall kill."[42] The whole scalp had to be presented to discourage unscrupulous individuals from cutting it into several pieces in an effort to collect more than one bounty.

Other changes occurred in the supervision of Indian affairs, particularly Indian trade. The system of Indian commissioners regulating Indian trade by licensing agents continued, but in the aftermath of the Yamassee War the colony wanted to improve administration of the trade and adopted by act of June 30, 1716, the provisions for a public monopoly.[43] This measure had been urged in previous years by planters in the lower house but successfully resisted until this time by the merchants of the upper house. Approval of the monopoly came because of the desperate state of the colony and the despair over the failure of earlier trade and diplomacy to hold the allegiance of the Indians. The measure was also aided by the potential threat of a Virginia revival of trade with Indians to the southwest, particularly the Catawba and Cherokee.

The public monopoly provided for the trade to be handled by the commissioners named in the act under direction from the Commons House. Only three "factories" were authorized and were to be located at Fort Moore, Congaree, and Winyah. This limitation proved unsatisfactory to the Indians because of the distance it forced them to travel and of their preference for traders in their own town. Theophilus Hastings, factor in the Cherokee country, stated to the Commissioners of the Indian Trade in 1716 that "the Charikees utterly dislike coming down to the Garrisons, to deal, and will not agree to that Proposal, on any Account, (except for Rum)."[44] Therefore, additional factories were authorized and set up in Indian towns. There was also considerable quibbling by Carolinians about prices being too high for the Indians and about the possibility of driving them into the arms of the French and Spanish, or at least into the trading posts of the Virginians—both undesirable for Carolinians.

The public monopoly was an issue clouded by conflicting interests, and one focus of discontent was the repeal of the act by the proprietors in July 1718, largely through the urging of London merchants. Although South Carolinians pointed to the repeal as one of their grievances in efforts to rid the colony of proprietary control, they tried to ignore the action and to continue monopoly trade. The local merchants with assistance from influential Londoners, however, persisted in their pressure and succeeded in having the act repealed by the Assembly on March 20, 1718/9. The public monopoly was then replaced by a compromise including a combined public and private trade.[45]

While the mixed public and private trade was in effect, the traffic of the public corporation continued but not at the level of the monopoly period. The annual value of trade was limited; its locations were confined primarily to Fort Moore, Congaree, and Palachacola; and the number of factors was curtailed to three. Private traders with a license from the commissioners resumed trade, although they could not traffic within twenty miles of the public factories and they had to pay a 10 percent tax. With defense still the primary concern of the regulation, proceeds from the trade were used to cover the expense of the military garrisons and the administration of Indian affairs. Revenue in excess of expenses was to be used to strengthen the public trading centers with "stone or brick" forts. The mixed public and private trade, however, proved to be temporary, for there was a complete return to private trade in 1721.[46] Monopolies and semi-public trading ventures were difficult to sustain in colonial America.

The second impact of the war brought important shifting of Indian tribes. The Yamassee moved to the area of St. Augustine under Spanish hegemony and abandoned their lands south of the Combahee, which were then granted for white settlement. The Lower Creeks, who had migrated around 1690 to Ochese Creek on the upper Ocmulgee, moved their place of habitation about 1716 to the Chattahoochee River where their towns were spread from Coweta near the falls southward for about fifty miles. Lower Creeks combined with Upper Creeks along the Tallapoosa River and the forks of the Alabama River in the Creek Confederation, and in the years following the Yamassee War the confederation followed a neutral course between Franco-Spanish and English parties. Architect of the wilderness balance of power was "Emperor" Old Brims, who by action and by word was committed to the maxim "not to espouse any of the quarrels which the French, English and Spaniards have with one another."[47] There were, to be sure, many factions in a confederacy as large and complex as the Creek nation, but Old Brims stood fast on his position of neutrality in the face of Spanish urging and promoted peace with the English in 1717. The negotiations were initiated by the expedition of supplies and men led by Theophilus Hastings and John Musgrove into the Creek country in the summer of 1717 and finalized with the subsequent journey of some eleven Creek chiefs to Charles Town. Although the text of the treaty is lost, apparently there was agreement for revival of Carolina trade and, according to some later reports, prohibition of English settlement south of the Savannah River. Revival of trade with the Creeks placed the

Carolinians in an ambivalent position in view of the renewal of the Creek-Cherokee feud during the Yamassee War. While advocating peace and a vigorous trade with both nations, one Carolinian noted that it was difficult to "assist them in cutting one another's throats without offending either. This is the game we intend to play if possible."[48] For the two other major tribes in the Southeast, the Chickasaw continued on friendly terms with Carolina and gave protection to her traders, but the Choctaw had joined the conspiracy and had come even more strongly under French influence at Mobile and on the Mississippi.

Both Spain and France extended their influence as a result of the Yamassee War and posed an increasing threat to English ambitions to the south and southwest. Spain welcomed the Yamassee to the area of St. Augustine. Some of the scattered remnants of the Apalache Indians had located in the area of Pensacola while others had found refuge with the Creeks. In 1717 the Spanish made a bid for stronger influence by sending seven chiefs of the Apalache and Creek tribes to Mexico to be received by the viceroy as representatives of the king of Spain. Spain set up the presidio of San Marcos in Apalache in 1718, which served as a Spanish stronghold reaching toward Pensacola. It did not, however, attract as many Apalache Indians to the area as the Spanish anticipated. Meanwhile, France loomed as an even stronger contender in the Southeast as she resumed influence over the Choctaw and other Mississippi tribes, and particularly as she set up in 1717 the Alabama Fort, or Fort Toulouse, at the junction of the Coosa and Tallapoosa rivers. Here was the most advanced French penetration toward English settlements, and here stood the French challenge to the English. French commercial and colonization schemes also created additional concern for Englishmen interested in western expansion.

The English enjoyed a temporary advantage as the course of European diplomacy brought a confrontation of France and Spain and resulted in the seizure of Pensacola by the French. England and France were both members of the alliance designed to curtail territorial ambitions in Italy of the Spanish rulers, King Philip V and Queen Elizabeth Farnese. This alignment led to a Franco-Spanish conflict on the American scene from 1719 to 1721 and permitted France, for many years eager to control Pensacola, to occupy the city. The Treaty of Madrid in 1721 returned France to its Spanish alliance and forced her to relinquish control of Pensacola.[49] Despite the temporary easing of international tension for the English, American colonists such as Governor Alexander Spotswood and John Barnwell of South Carolina emphasized the primary threat of French encirclement with secondary assistance from the Spanish. The urgency of these communications encouraged the Board of Trade to consider seriously the problem and to formulate new facets of its policy for American expansion during the decade of the 1720s.

One remaining effect of the Yamassee War should be noted. The devastation of the conflict in South Carolina coupled with the threat of the Franco-Spanish challenge on the western frontier served to raise questions about the political status of the Carolina colonies. The crux of the issue was the challenge to proprietary control of the Carolinas. Criticism of the proprietors was voiced before the Yamassee crisis, but their lethargic action in providing relief to the colony intensified dissatisfaction and contributed to South Carolina's transition to a royal colony in 1719, even though North Carolina's status was not changed until 1729. Several proposals to the British ministry for overcoming the French and Spanish threat, such as those of John Barnwell, were also critical of the proprietors for the lack of vigor in supporting western expansion. There were, of course, many other grievances against the proprietors, some of which were even more vital to the final decision to remove the Carolinas from their jurisdiction.[50] For example, a series of vetoes imposed upon legislation of the Assembly stirred antagonism in 1718 as the proprietors denied the Commons House the right to designate the treasurer of the province and refused the change of the election of Assemblymen from two voting places to each parish. The proprietors also turned back the plan for handling the Indian trade by public monopoly, and frustrated the efforts of the colonists to bring in more white settlers to establish them on the abandoned Yamassee lands. This last problem stirred violent criticism because the proprietors, who had previously approved the granting of land free of rent for four years, nullified legislation that offered 300 to 400 acres for new settlers arriving from Europe. Instead of encouraging white settlers for the Yamassee lands, the proprietors ordered that 12,000 acres be surveyed for each of them. A combination of these grievances helped topple proprietary rule in South Carolina and led to the transition and experiments that followed with a royal governor.

6

Governor Alexander Spotswood and the Virginia Frontier

By the beginning of the eighteenth century, westward migration in colonial Virginia had reached the fall line; a few hearty settlers had penetrated into the piedmont section. Like scrawny fingers these new lines of settlement reached out into the piedmont along the river valleys where the settlers adjusted to the greater distance from commerce along Virginia's rivers and braved such frontier hazards as primitive conditions and occasional raids of hostile Indians. In the interest of better Indian-white relations, efforts were made to restrain the advance of the 1690s by preventing white settlements south of the James River beyond the boundary line established in 1665.[1] But the pressures for expansion continued and the desire for more land persisted as one of the dominant themes of the period, involving leading political figures and eventually reaching the office of the governor.

Meanwhile, the Assembly decided in 1699 to move the colonial capital from Jamestown to Middle Plantation—renamed Williamsburg in honor of the king. The presence of neighboring Indians at various events in the new capital city was a reminder that the froniter was near at hand. In 1700, for example, friendly Indians mingled with great crowds including visitors from New York and Pennsylvania at the graduation exercises of the College of William and Mary, which was already established before the move of the capital. Two years later, Governor Francis Nicholson made special arrangements for a group of Indians to attend the ceremonies at Williamsburg announcing the death of King William III and proclaiming the coronation of Queen Anne. Around forty natives and two queens were present; official orders were read, orations delivered, military formations conducted, and fireworks displayed. The governor arranged a rifle match that culminated in an exhibition of skillful shooting by two Indians with both rifles and bows. As viewed by the Swiss traveler, Francis Louis Michel, the presence of the aborigines added color to the occasion. Some had a narrow spangle in the nose, others a "tuft of strange feathers under their ears." In the evening the young queen danced for the governor and his associates. Wearing "nice clothes of a French pattern," she entered the hall, the gentlemen removed their hats, and the queen bowed. Then she "danced so wonderfully, yea barbarously, that everyone was astonished and laughed."[2]

Neighboring Maryland had also recently moved its capital. The move came with the accession of Francis Nicholson as royal governor in 1694 succeeding Lionel Copley, who had served since 1691 when the government of Maryland was taken out of the hands of the Calvert family, even though the family was permitted to retain its land rights and revenue privileges. The move in part reflected the advance of settlement northward along Chesapeake Bay and in part was influenced by the ascendant Protestants who favored a new location for the capital over Catholic St. Mary's, the urgent pleading of citizens of St. Mary's notwithstanding. Anne Arundel was designated a port town, and the Assembly in the spring of 1695 gave the new capital the name of Annapolis.[3]

At the turn of the century the American colonies were enjoying an interim of peace in the intercolonial wars resulting from European conflicts. But the uncertain peace lasted for only five years from the end of King William's War in 1697 until the succession quarrels in Europe brought war in 1702. On the eve of conflict both Virginia and Maryland gave some attention to the matter of defense, with Virginia the more concerned because of the greater exposure of its outer settlements.

The inadequacies of Virginia's defense were discussed in reports to the Board of Trade by both Governor Francis Nicholson, then of Virginia, and Colonel Robert Quary, who had been in Virginia while the Assembly was in session.[4] Referring to the militia of "undisciplined and unskillful officers and soldiers," both stressed the need of arms and ammunition. Out of a potential of 8000 men for the militia, it was doubtful that more than one-fourth this number could be effectively mustered, and without naval aid it would not be possible to prevent enemy landings along the rivers leading into Chesapeake Bay. Nicholson further reviewed the state of the militia in the various counties, emphasizing that most were "indifferently armed" and that the "uppermost Countys on the several Rivers . . . have the most Militia in them, yet they are very long and the Inhabitants, especially in the upper parts of them, live very stragling." In face of a possible attack from the French and Indians, Nicholson concluded that "our Frontiers by land are but in a very bad condition."[5]

Virginia had continued to authorize rangers for the frontier areas to 1698. In 1701 Governor Nicholson and his council issued other orders to secure the colony. Each county was to provide a list of arms and ammunition and to prohibit their being sent out of the colony. The mustering of the militia and its more intensive training was ordered to provide a defense along the coast against possible French expeditions from the West Indies as well as security for the interior of the colony, the former being the more critical at the time.[6] For "the better strengthening the frontiers," the Virginia Assembly in 1701 proposed settlements "in cohabitations upon the said land frontiers" by inducing "societyes of men" to make the settlement with at least twenty

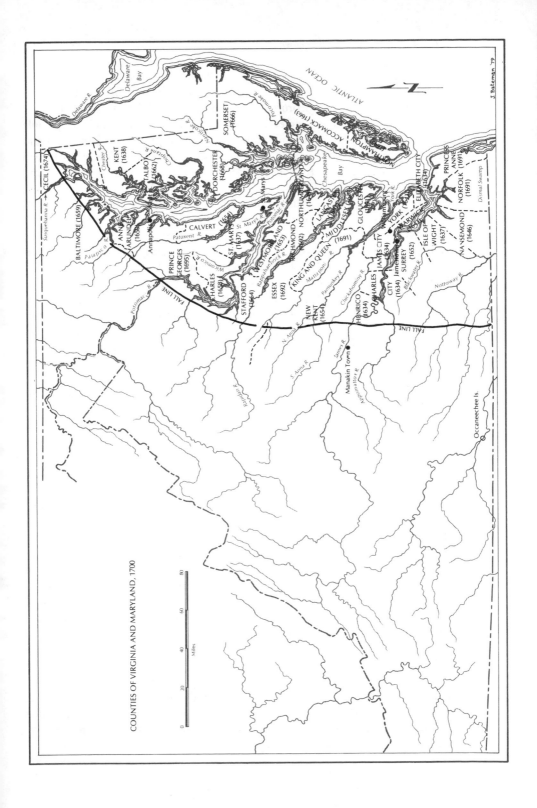

COUNTIES OF VIRGINIA AND MARYLAND, 1700

J. Bateman '79

ATLANTIC OCEAN

Delaware Bay

Delaware R.

Susquehanna R.

CECIL (1674)

BALTIMORE (1659)

Chester R.

KENT (1638)

SOMERSET (1666)

Choptank R.

TALBOT (1662)

DORCHESTER (1668)

Pocomoke R.

Nanticoke R.

NORTHAMPTON (1634)

ACCOMACK (1663)

PRINCESS ANNE (1691)

Chesapeake Bay

ANNE ARUNDEL (1650)

Patapsco R.

Annapolis

St. Mary's R.

CALVERT (1654)

Patuxent R.

ST. MARY'S (1637)

WESTMORELAND (1653)

NORTHUMBERLAND (1648)

LANCASTER (1651)

GLOUCESTER (1651)

YORK (1634)

ELIZABETH CITY (1634)

NORFOLK (1691)

FALL LINE

PRINCE GEORGES (1695)

Wicomico R.

CHARLES (1658)

Potomac R.

STAFFORD (1664)

ESSEX (1692)

Rappahannock R.

RICHMOND (1692)

KING AND QUEEN (1691)

MIDDLESEX (1669)

Mattaponi R.

Pamunkey R.

WARWICK

Back R.

ISLE OF WIGHT (1637)

NANSEMOND (1646)

Dismal Swamp

N. Anna R.

NEW KENT (1654)

Chickahominy R.

JAMES CITY (1634)

Jamestown

CHARLES CITY (1634)

SURREY (1652)

Blackwater R.

HENRICO (1634)

S. Anna R.

Nottoway R.

Rivanna R.

James R.

Manakin Town

Appomattox R.

Occaneechee Is.

FALL LINE

COUNTIES OF VIRGINIA AND MARYLAND, 1700

Miles

0   20   40   60   80

"fighting men" in each one. Land from ten to thirty thousand acres was to be provided each settlement, and with some public support each was to construct a fort for added protection.[7] Despite the elaborate plans, this act was not implemented by "societyes of men." A number of French Huguenots had already arrived, and the subsequent immigrant groups of Scots-Irish and Germans took up settlement under other conditions. These proposed "societyes" were similar to New England towns and to subsequent "stations" on the Kentucky frontier.[8]

Maryland had also continued rangers along her frontier during the 1690s, providing for small groups of an officer and three troopers to relieve each other weekly, and to range alternately beyond the settlements and into the frontier plantations.[9] Maryland's frontier was in general less exposed than that of Virginia, but the removal of the Piscataway Indians led to an extended discussion between the governor and the Assembly over the role of the Indians in providing protection for a portion of the Maryland settlements.

Both Maryland and Virginia managed to exaggerate their own difficulties when faced with the order from crown officials to render assistance to New York in the protection of her frontiers in Queen Anne's War. The Board of Trade recommended aid for New York in the form of both soldiers and money, suggesting that Virginia pay £900 and Maryland £650. A request to Virginia for money for a fort in New York and for a quota of troops, if necessary, met with strong opposition from the Virginia Assembly, particularly the House of Burgesses. The crown suggested that Virginia give aid since her "own Security is so much concerned." But Virginia refused. Opponents of the aid contended that New York simply wanted a fort in order to monopolize Indian trade, and they concluded that Virginia was "in more want of assistance" herself than being "capable of affording it to others."[10] This was done despite the strong urging of Governor Francis Nicholson, who even volunteered to contribute privately to the expenditures of the governor of New York, but the governor's bills apparently were later cancelled by crown officials. Maryland's initial response to the request for aid was not as negative as that of Virginia, for provision was made to provide £300 as half of the money requested. But delays over how the money should be paid, whether by bills on a London firm or some other means, and the example of Virginia's avoidance led Maryland likewise to render no assistance to New York.[11] Colonial particularism ruled supreme.

With the military events of Queen Anne's War centered either to the north in French and Indian attacks in New York and New England or to the south with Spanish forays against Charles Town, the frontier of both Virginia and Maryland remained relatively inactive with the major disturbance coming with privateers along the coast or in Chesapeake Bay. Both colonies relied mainly upon their militia, and minimum efforts were made to improve its efficiency. There was considerable discussion in Maryland about the merits of storing arms and ammunition among the counties. While this seemed desirable for quick arming in case of attack, the Assembly on more than one occasion voted to retain them in a central magazine because of the greater economy and because of inefficient, if not corrupt, administration of the supply by the local county commanders. Maryland also decided to abandon the few rangers that had been used during the 1690s and to discontinue the line of three forts that had been built in the three counties along the advanced area of settlement—in Charles, Anne Arundel, and Baltimore.[12] The reliance upon the militia in Maryland did accent, however, the difficulties private citizens had in equipping themselves with arms and ammunition as foot soldiers or with a horse for mounted troops. Several formulas were suggested to alleviate the problem by having from two to six taxables equip one "footman," and from three to nine taxables maintain a trooper with horse. The colony's security was assured more by the peaceable state of the small Indian tribes within its bounds and the distance from larger hostile tribes and the French. Treaties were reaffirmed with Indians within the bounds of the colony, encouraging continued harmony and the assurance of the Indian's rights to the areas reserved for them. As a precaution, certain designated individuals were authorized to muster an adequate number of men in case of Indian attacks or other frontier disturbances.[13]

Virginia added special groups of immigrants on her frontier that became the vanguard of white settlement and contributed to the protection of the colony. Several years before the Virginia Assembly proposed that "societyes of men" live on the frontier in 1701, steps were taken to bring French Huguenots to America. Dr. Daniel Coxe, English physician, had contacted a group of Huguenots in England under the leadership of Marquis de la Muce and Charles de Sailly. Coxe proposed to establish a group on his lands in Apalache on the Gulf of Mexico, but when denied this by the Board of Trade, his alternative was to colonize on his lands in present Norfolk County, Virginia. King William III approved the venture, awarded the prospective settlers British citizenship, and provided assistance in transportation as well as instructed the colony in Virginia to assist them. William Byrd I, keenly interested in promoting colonization, particularly on lands near his possessions at the falls of the James River, intervened; the band of Huguenot settlers that arrived in Virginia on July 23, 1700, were offered lands above the falls of the James rather than in Norfolk County. The latter area, partly at Byrd's urging, was considered too swampy and furthermore still in dispute with the colony of North Carolina. The Huguenots, therefore, made their way with difficulty about twenty-five miles beyond the falls of the James to Manakin Town, an area formerly occupied by the Monacan (Manakin) Indians, who one hundred years earlier had been powerful antagonists of the Powhatan Confederation. Only a few huts and stones used by the Monacan remained as evidence of previous human occupation.[14]

Some 391 persons had started from Jamestown for the new settlement, but only about 250 were residing in the area a year later in 1701. The major portion of those not remaining apparently settled in other parts of the colony since the death rate was relatively low. Much assistance had to be given the new immigrants, and Governor Francis Nicholson finally appealed for private contributions when the Assembly would provide no further aid. Additional Huguenots arrived, but the council opposed sending other large groups beyond the limits of settlement so they were scattered over areas already established. One group settled at the head of the York River in King William County and retained for a time its separate identity.

The Manakin settlement made substantial economic progress and provided a church within the first year of its settlement despite power struggles among some of the leaders. The report of Michel, on his second visit there in 1701, probably paints too favorable a picture of their settlement because of his close relationship to the group:

> Conditions here differ in every respect from those of other places. Things that are grown are there in such abundance that many Englishmen come a distance of 30 miles to get fruit, which they mostly exchange for cattle. Gardens are filled there with all kinds of fruit. . . . The cattle are fat because of the abundant pasture. The soil is not sandy, as it is generally in Virginia, but it is a heavy, rich soil. Each person takes 50 paces in width, the length extends as far as one cares to make it or is willing to work it. . . . There are more than 60 [French] families there. They all live along the river.[15]

By 1704 the request by the French for additional land and the application by other colonists for nearby grants led the Assembly to set aside 10,000 acres for the settlement and to have William Byrd survey a total of 133 acres for each family. By 1705 a second act of naturalization was implemented, and citizenship in Virginia was bestowed upon those at Manakin Town and on the York River who had not already taken the oath.[16]

Naturalizing the alien was an important step in the process of assimilation but not the only one involved. Even before coming to America, many of the Huguenots in England had become members of the Anglican Church, the official established body in both England and Virginia. Claude Philipe de Richebourg and Benjamin de Joux were ministers with the two major groups that came to Manakin Town, the latter an ordained Anglican. Virginia permitted the Huguenots "virtual autonomy" in religion; they chose the Anglican Church but conducted the service in French. In 1712, part of the group migrated to a settlement on the Trent River in North Carolina and part under Richebourg continuing to the Santee River settlement in South Carolina. Some 214 settlers in 1714 remained at Manakin, which constituted King William Parish. The French language continued to be used. By 1728 the settlement sought a minister who was fluent in both French and English, and by the middle of the century one-half to two-thirds of the sermons were delivered in English. A parochial library was brought to Manakin Town about 1711 and contained some forty books, but all were in English or Latin, none in French.[17] The acculturation process was at work, proceeding gradually because of the isolation of the frontier and the permissive policy of Virginia.

As a frontier settlement, Manakin Town was not subjected to serious threats from either the Indians or the Catholic French. The location of the town, however, contributed to frontier defense. By 1705 instructions provided for the establishment of an infantry company, which in 1710 was made by the new lieutenant governor, Alexander Spotswood, a troop of dragoons.

Spotswood had just assumed the position of lieutenant governor and was to devote major attention and interest to western expansion and frontier defense. Introduced during his first year as governor to the potential of iron mines in Virginia by William Byrd II, Spotswood was soon to combine this economic interest with the desire for additional frontier settlements by placing in 1714 forty German-Swiss miners (including men, women, and children) on his own holdings of 1287 acres at a spot named Germanna, located on the south bank of Rapidan River some twelve miles above the Rappahannock. The immigrants had been invited by Baron de Graffenried to America; Spotswood hit upon the scheme to bring them from England and to use them for both the public interest and his own private schemes. The Board of Trade cautioned against the development of the iron works because of the mercantile argument that it would compete with English industry, but Spotswood had proceeded with the project and suggested the possibility of a supply of silver ore. When Spotswood was also challenged on the land title that belonged to him but was made out in the name of the clerk of the council, he explained in defense that this had been "the constant practice of former Governors."[18]

These challenges notwithstanding, Spotswood had initiated an important plan for protection of the frontier. When the Tuscarora Indians failed to comply with an agreement for securing the area around the Rappahannock River, Spotswood substituted the Germanna project. There a fort was constructed, two cannons provided, and the settlers served at times as rangers. The Assembly provided "Exemption of all Taxes for seven Years"[19] and organized the special parish of St. George, then in Essex County.

A vivid view of life on this frontier outpost was recorded by the Huguenot John Fontaine in his visit there with two companions in November 1715:

> We walked about the town which is palisaded with stakes stuck in the ground, and laid close the one to the other, and of substance to bear out a musket-shot. There are but nine families, and they have nine houses, built all in a line; and before every house, about twenty feet distant from it, they have small sheds built for their hogs and hens, so that the hog-sties and houses make a street. The place that it is paled in is a

pentagon, very regularly laid out; and in the very centre there is a blockhouse, made with five sides, which answer to the five sides of the great inclosure; there are loop-holes through it, from which you may see all the inside of the inclosure. This was intended for a retreat for the people, in case they were not able to defend the palisadoes, if attacked by the Indians.

They made use of this block-house for divine service. They go to prayers constantly once a day, and have two sermons on Sunday. We went to hear them perform their service, which was done in their own language, which we did not understand; but they seemed to be very devout, and sang the psalms very well.[20]

The Germanna settlers apparently had begun the search for iron or silver ore before they decided to take up by 1717 their own land in Fauquier County. Additional Germans from the Palatine were brought in as indentured servants by Spotswood to replace them. Spotswood continued his promotion of iron mines and iron production until his death in 1740, and he was called "the Tubal-cain of Virginia" by William Byrd II.[21]

Spotswood's interest in western expansion both from a public and private point of view was, indeed, unusual. With tenacity he approached the whole complex of problems that focused on the frontier: Indian trade, Indian allies in the international rivalry with France and Spain, frontier defense, western expansion, and land policy. On the southern colonial frontier, he and James Glen of South Carolina tower above other colonial officials in their concern for frontier problems. Spotswood's role, therefore, merits a more detailed consideration than is possible for other colonial officials in Virginia and Maryland.

Competition for Indian trade to the southwest between Virginia and South Carolina had existed before Spotswood's arrival, and the continuation of the conflict militated against intercolonial cooperation in times of crisis. South Carolina claimed jurisdiction over such Indians as the Catawba and Cherokee, and by 1707 the colony had restricted Virginia traders either by asserting jurisdiction or by restricting passage through territory claimed by Carolina. Protests were made by Virginia for the seizure of goods from a number of traders, including Robert Hix and David Crawley in 1707.[22] The chief executive of Carolina attempted to justify his actions by citing the act of 1663 that ordered all goods imported into any colony to be registered within twenty-four hours. Additional restrictions were then imposed by South Carolina by ordering Virginia traders to come to Charles Town to pay a fee of £8 annually and to leave a bond of £100. President Edmund Jenings, acting governor of Virginia, protested these additional restrictions to crown officials and stated that the Indians involved were not even in Carolina territory, that the long trip to Charles Town would ruin the Virginia trade, and that South

Carolina's action was motivated by the "private interest of engrossing that trade."[23]

In response to protests from Virginia, the crown in September 1709 issued an order in council forbidding South Carolina to levy duties upon the goods of Virginians trading with the western Indians. The governor of Carolina was also commanded to return the bond extorted from the Virginians, but the order was ignored. A South Carolina act of 1711 reimposed the restrictions of 1707,[24] and Governor Spotswood then complained to the Board of Trade. The wheels of imperial government were again set in motion, and in January 1712/3 a second order in council was issued commanding the repeal of the Carolina act of 1711.[25] Apparently some violations of the second order continued during these turbulent times on the frontier, for Spotswood again complained in March 1714/5. This conflict over trade clearly dampened the enthusiasm of Virginia for intercolonial assistance during the Yamassee attack upon South Carolina.

Meanwhile, Spotswood was busy with projects for solving many of the other problems on Virginia's frontier. The revived system of rangers had proved "unpopular, expensive, and ineffective."[26] Therefore, Spotswood hoped to economize and improve upon the defense of the colony by the use of tributary Indians, and he convinced the Assembly that this should be done. Spotswood listed the total number of tributaries in 1712 as approximately 700, which included an estimated 250 fighting men. The three main tribes from the tributaries involved in the governor's plans were the Saponi, the Nottoway, and the Tuscarora. The first of these, the Saponi, had been included as tributaries in the peace of 1677 but had subsequently moved south of Virginia. By 1708 they were back in the colony and sought the protection afforded them as tributaries. They were again given this status, and along with members of three tribes of their Siouan kinsmen they agreed to Spotswood's new treaty in 1714. The second major group to participate in the plan was the Nottoway Indians, who lived as tributaries along the river of the same name and were hard pressed by advancing white settlement. The third tribe, the Tuscarora, had just been defeated in the Tuscarora War in North Carolina, and efforts by Spotswood were successful in getting an accord in Virginia with the leaders of the estimated 1500 natives, who were afraid to return to North Carolina to be "knock'd in the head by the English."[27]

The three treaties of February 27, 1713/4, with these tribes provided for new reservations that also fit the defense plan of Virginia. The Saponi were to be located on the south side of the James River "above the inhabitants" with hunting rights between the James and Roanoke rivers. The Nottoway were to be seated on a tract of land between the Appomattox and Roanoke rivers with hunting rights similar to the Saponi. The Tuscarora were allotted land between the James and Rappahannock rivers with hunting permitted on all unpatented land between the same two streams. The last group was purposely to be moved north of the James to sever connection with their old ties in North Carolina and to promote greater fidelity to Virginia. Each tribe was to receive a tract of land equivalent to six square miles where the Indians could build a fort and make improvements on the land. The assigned land was to be held in common and could not be sold to members of the colony. Two provisos were included in the treaty: one permitted the governor of Virginia to set aside an area not exceeding 2000 acres for the support of a minister, schoolmaster, and the colonial detachment assigned as guards at the Indian town; the other stipulated that in case of considerable decrease in the number of Indians, the tract of land would be reduced to an area approximately 100 acres per native with the same privilege of hunting as before.[28]

The Saponi and Nottoway renewed their tributary status, and the Tuscarora agreed to become tributaries of the crown, submitting to "such forms of Government" and obeying "such rules as the Governor of Virginia shall appoint." Conspiracies against Virginia or other tributaries were to be suppressed; Indians guilty of murder or of theft causing injury to the colony were to be delivered for punishment according to Virginia law; and negotiations with foreign Indians without permission of the governor were forbidden. For the purpose of trade a "publick Mart and Fair" were to be held at least six times annually, and each was to be supervised by magistrates to prevent abuses to the natives. One other provision of the treaties included education and conversion of the Indians. As soon as possible a schoolmaster and minister were to be sent to each Indian reservation, and the three tribes promised to have all Indians children taught the English language and instructed in the principles of the Christian religion. Meanwhile, twelve boys were to be sent by each settlement to Saponi Town where the educational program was first to begin.[29]

The response to the three Indian treaties of 1713/4 was short of Spotswood's expectations. The Saponi readily fulfilled the provisions of the peace; the Nottoway only partially complied; and most of the Tuscarora effected a reconciliation with the colony of North Carolina and returned to their old home. The noncompliance of the Tuscarora modified the governor's plan for frontier defense. As altered, the defense provided for the Saponi to be on the Roanoke River, and the Nottoway—then joined by the Meherrin and the remnants of the Tuscarora tribe—to be located between the Roanoke and James rivers. The gap in the defense caused by the noncompliance of the Tuscarora was filled by the Germans located at Germanna. Two forts were added by Spotswood, one at Christanna on the south side of the Meherrin River where twelve men and an officer were stationed to act as rangers along with tributary Indians; the other fort was at Germanna which would ward off northern Indians. The original plan to decrease the cost of rangers was then possible. Spotswood informed the council, in August 1714, that he had disbanded the rangers of Prince George County and had decreased the remaining four detachments of rangers to six in each troop. While the expense for defending the frontier was reduced by one-third through the location of tributary Indians and the Germans, the security of the colony, Spotswood asserted, was strengthened.[30]

The dynamic Spotswood went beyond these arrangements to attempt a comprehensive revision of Indian relations. Considerable confusion still existed because small traders violated legal restrictions with apparent approval of public opinion, and arms and ammunition frequently reached tribes that were potential enemies of the colony. Another complication was that the fur and skin trade to the southwest declined, and the College of William and Mary suffered from the decrease of its income received from the export duties of the Indian trade. Attention also had to be given to frontier defense, which though greatly improved through the use of tributary Indians and the settlement of Germanna, was still essential. Moreover, the challenge to educate and to convert the natives to Christianity continued to prick the conscience of the colonial officials. All of these problems were addressed by Spotswood through the "Act for the Better Regulation of the Indian Trade," passed by the Assembly in 1714 with provisions for a single company to have a monopoly of most of the Indian trade.[31]

The act provided for the creation of the Virginia Indian Company, whose monopoly was to extend to all trade with the tributary Indians living south of the James and with all foreign Indians. The monopoly, with the king's approval, was to last for twenty years, and the trade with the tributaries was to be conducted at Fort Christanna, located on the Meherrin River near present Gholsonville, Brunswick County, Virginia. The company in return was to give £100 toward the construction of a magazine at Williamsburg. Powder used in the Indian trade was to be taken from the magazine and replaced by a new quantity, thereby guaranteeing at all times a supply of fresh, dry powder for the colony's defense. At their own expense the members of the company were to build a schoolhouse at Christanna, and after two years they were to assume the full expense of maintaining the fort and its detachment of twelve men and an officer. Even before organization of the new trading group, Spotswood had inaugurated work to be continued under sponsorship of the Indian company. Fort Christanna had been constructed and some 300 Saponi settled there. The governor engaged Charles Griffin as schoolmaster, paying him fifty pounds annually from his own pocket.[32]

Organization of the company began the very day the governor approved the act. The appeal for subscribers, though, generated mixed reactions; many colonists objected to trade under a monopoly as opposed to the free trade of private individuals. The Indian traffic involved in these plans was apparently controlled by as few as five or six entrepreneurs who employed, as Spotswood contended, "all of the lose fellows they can pick up."[33] These leading private traders were invited to subscribe to the company under the provision of a minimum of £50 or maximum of £100 investment per person. With an initial capitalization of £4000 that could be extended to £10,000, the company would involve forty or more investors. But there were few early subscribers because of opposition, including that of private traders, to the extensive obligations of the company and to the efforts to impose tighter regulations of the trade. Consequently, Spotswood appealed to leading citizens and pushed the investment to £10,000, including at least twenty prominent members of the colony. Spotswood, himself, "ventured" £100 and was elected head of the company.[34] Possibly larger amounts were invested by him and other members, but the governor's main concern seems clearly to have been to achieve the integrated frontier program of the company rather than efforts to engross the trade for himself.

Part of the plans of this program were soon implemented. The company erected the schoolhouse at Christanna and the number of Indian students increased. By October 1715, Spotswood could write that there were seventy native children under Griffin's care, most of whom "can already say the Lord's Prayer and the Creed"; by February 1715/6, the number had grown to 100.[35] The company also contributed to the construction of the powder magazine, and the cost of the operation of Fort Christanna came from the treasury of the Indian company after December 1716.

Steps for the development and recovery of Virginia Indian trade were a significant part of the objectives of the company. Experienced traders, when available, were employed, roads were improved, and bridges were built. Trading goods were obtained in the colony and from England, and the company established rates and supervised the exchange of commodities to prevent exorbitant prices. Plans were made in 1717 to dispatch one of the largest expeditions ever sent forth by a colony, consisting of "no less than 200 horse-loads of goods under a guard of 40 men." Apparently this caravan was never dispatched. But in the next year company traders did journey to the Cherokee country, returning in the fall "with about 70 horse load of skins" along with several Cherokee leaders who wished to arrange for continued trade.[36] The Catawba Indians also came to Virginia and left eleven of their children at Fort Christanna in April 1716 as hostages to guarantee peace with all of the English colonies.

Spotswood also encouraged a "company of Adventurers" to explore the western mountains one hundred miles above the settlements; they reported that the descent on the western side appeared to be as easy as the one from the east. Continuing these efforts, the Indian company in 1716 was responsible for an expedition which discovered a "Passage over the great mountains."[37] The members of the party are not known, but it is probable that they were Germans from Germanna who served as rangers along the frontier. Spurred on by the discovery, Governor Spotswood, with the approval of the council, led the well-known expedition of the "Knights of the

Golden Horseshoe" in 1716. Having gathered at Germanna, where the horses were shod, the expedition of Virginia gentlemen went along the falls of the Rappahannock and continued west to the Blue Ridge Mountains at Swift Run Gap. The group then continued west along an Indian trail to the Shenandoah River where the governor buried a bottle containing a paper signifying that he "took possession of this place in the name and for King George 1st of England." They then drank "the King's health in Champagne, and fired a volley, the Prince's health in Burgundy, and fired a volley, and all the rest of the Royal Family in Claret, and a volley."[38] Still another toast to the governor's health and another volley followed before their return to Germanna. No new Indian tribes were located for trade, but the exciting potential of the western area was glimpsed and several members of the expedition were later to form the vanguard of settlers who entered the piedmont section along the route they had traversed. The Golden Horseshoe expedition thus became a symbol for the advance from tidewater to piedmont.

The future of the trading company, however, became uncertain as complaints against it as a monopoly were lodged by London merchants and some Virginia colonists, including William Byrd II and Philip Ludwell, Jr. Memorial after memorial were submitted about the company, and the Board of Trade received complaints and petitions on both sides of the question. Finally, the Board of Trade passed over the many subsidiary arguments presented, and the crux of the issue was its monopolistic features. Governor Spotswood was asked why the act of 1714 did not violate royal instructions for free trade. Spotswood in his answer to the Board of Trade denied that the law engrossed the trade and stated that additional persons could still be admitted to membership in the company.[39] But the solicitor general reported that the act created a monopoly and thereby violated both the governors' instructions and acts of Parliament. The Board of Trade concurred with the report of the solicitor general and recommended to King George I and the Privy Council the disallowance of the "Act for the Better Regulation of the Indian Trade." The king and council endorsed the recommendation, and a proclamation for repeal was issued in November 1717.[40]

Most of the major features of the act for defense and Indian education were continued temporarily until the Assembly could consider these measures in the spring of 1718. The Assembly made some compensation for individuals who had spent money in the public interest, but it was in no mood to continue the activity of the organization at public expense. The company did continue as a private agency but was abandoned after four years as an unprofitable venture.

During its existence as a legal monopoly the company made definite contributions. Frontier security was improved; Spotswood claimed that during its time "there was not so much as one Alarm from any foreign

Indians, nor occasion for ordering out the militia for defending the Frontiers, as had been the practice for many years before."[41] Trade to the southwest was stimulated and abuses by traders reduced, but statistics are not available to make specific comparisons of the volume of the Indian traffic that resulted from the efforts of the company. Some progress in education was made through the work of Griffin at Christanna. In this combined program is found the real significance of the Virginia Indian Company—an effort to establish the relationship between "red man and white upon a basis of order and justice."[42]

Governor Spotswood was also much concerned with Virginia land policy and its relationship to western expansion. It is in this area that the pressures of the frontier and the availability of land made their greatest impact upon Spotswood and eventually overcame his efforts to administer effectively imperial and colonial requirements. Aware of the land acquisitions that some colonials were amassing despite regulations to the contrary, he in the end joined in the rush and acquired for himself large landholdings before the end of his term as governor.

Land policy had received increasing attention since the closing years of the seventeenth century. Edward Randolph, serving as surveyor general of customs in America, had submitted a report on the land system in Virginia to the Board of Trade during the first years of its organization in 1696. Pondering the question as to why Virginia was not more densely populated with the migration that had occurred, he placed greatest stress in his answer upon the planting of tobacco and to the condition that:

> servants are not so willing to go there as formerly because the members of Council and others who make an interest in the Government have from time to time procured grants of very large tracts of land, so that for many years there has been no waste land to be taken up by those who bring with them servants, or by servants who have served their time. But the land has been taken up and engrossed beforehand, whereby such people are forced to hire and pay rent for lands or to go to the utmost bounds of the Colony for land exposed to danger. . . .[43]

Randolph also criticized other aspects of the land system: the failure to collect quitrents; the failure or distortion of the requirement for "seating and planting"; and the failure of the requirement for keeping "four able men well armed" on land on the frontier of the colony. The annual quitrent was one shilling per fifty acres with omission of payment requiring forfeiture of the grant, but one report in 1697 indicated that no more than £800 had been collected from quitrents and there was no evidence of forfeiture for noncompliance. "Seating and planting," required to retain possession, had been defined by the Assembly in 1666 with the declaration that "Building an house and keeping a stock one whole yeare upon the land shall be accounted seating; and that cleering, tending and planting an acre of ground shall be accounted planting."[44] Either one fulfilled the condition for the patent, and throughout the seventeenth century there had been no relationship between the size of the tract and the amount of improvement required. The minimum performance satisfied the law; therefore, either the building of a small cabin, putting a few cattle or a few hogs on the tract for a year, or planting as little as an acre of ground—any one of the three protected the grant. As for the keeping of "four able men well armed" on lands on the frontier, Randolph reported that "this law is never observed. These grants are procured upon such easy terms and very often upon false certificates of rights."[45] Randolph was inclined to be hypercritical of administration in the American colonies, but his contentions about Virginia land policy had some validity.

Randolph's charge of "false certificates of rights" referred to irregularities in the administration of the grants by headrights that had been in effect in Virginia since the time of the London Company. The headright, instituted to ensure a balance between population and acquisition of private title in the soil, had not been achieved because of increasing abuses and evasions. Claims for headrights sometimes were based upon persons being listed as imported into the colony several times. Some shipmasters claimed lands on the basis of the full list of both passengers and crew, other sailors falsified the records for themselves, and eventually lists of fictitious names were recorded. The final stage in irregular procedure was reached at least by the 1690s when the clerks in the office of the secretary of the colony sold the headright claim to persons who would simply pay from one to five shillings. The abuses nullified attempts to rationalize settlement and land holding. Through perversion of the system and speculation in land, title was granted for large areas of wholly uncultivated and uninhabited lands. The headright was also originally intended to apply to inhabitants of the British Isles, but by the middle of the seventeenth century the names of persons imported from Africa appeared occasionally as the basis for headright, and by the last decade of the century they were frequently found.

Responding to the abuses set forth by Randolph, the Board of Trade issued instructions for a "new method of granting land in Virginia" to Francis Nicholson as he returned to Virginia in 1698 as governor. Stricter requirements were laid out for "seating and planting" and for the collection of quitrents. Neither the councillors nor the burgesses, however, were willing to grapple directly with land reform and no legislative action was taken by them to implement the recommendations of the Board of Trade. Governor Nicholson in 1699 was responsible for an order of the General Court that no more headrights be issued for the importation of Negroes. Nicholson also found the sale of headrights by the secretary's office to be still prevalent, but the practice was not eliminated completely. As a substitute measure that arose over the problem of land taken up in Pamunkey Neck and on the south side of Blackwater Swamp, the governor and council in 1699 authorized the acquisition of land by treasury right, stating that title to fifty acres of land would be granted for the payment of five shillings sterling to the auditor.[46] Thus the sale of land by treasury right reappeared, a practice that increased in importance as the eighteenth century progressed. This action seemed to be a revival of the system under the Virginia Company whereby individuals were awarded certain amounts of land in return for their investments of money or services to the colonizing efforts of the company. Actually, however, it was a new type of treasury right for it required only payment of a specific sum such as five shillings for fifty acres; and it, in effect, provided for transfer of land by sale. Grant by headright in most of Virginia continued for a few years to account for the great majority of land patents issued, but after the first quarter of the eighteenth century it gradually fell into disuse. For the Northern Neck which had been granted to proprietors faithful to the king during civil war in England, the headright never served as the basis of the land system. Rather the distribution of land by treasury right was employed in the seventeenth as well as the eighteenth century.

Nicholson's most significant reform in land policy was the collection of quitrents and the sale of quitrent tobacco. The new rent-roll of 1704 for all of Virginia except the Northern Neck proved to be the most complete up to that time. Analysis of this roll has also provided new insights into the social and economic structure of the colony. While a few large grants were evident, the implications of Randolph's criticisms that extensive lands were held by only a few persons must be modified to give proper perspective to the role of the small farmer. Examination of the rent-roll by one scholar has revealed that it was "the sturdy, independent class of small farmers who made up a full 90 per cent of the freeholders at the time." Furthermore, "Here and there, especially in the frontier counties, is listed a tract of four or five or even ten thousand acres, but such cases are very rare."[47] The figure of 19,500 acres for "Byrd Esqr" in Henrico County is the exception rather than the rule for 1704.[48]

The impetus for land reform by official direction from England continued under Spotswood. During his first few years in office, he attempted to implement changes in land policy either by influencing the action of the Virginia Assembly or by issuing proclamations to carry out instructions forwarded from London. The conditions for planting and clearing required under patents were stiffened by the Assembly and called for three acres for every fifty, an increase from the previous requirement of only one acre for a tract of any size.[49] By proclamation Spotswood added other stipulations, including (1) the right of the executive to review grants of more than 400 acres to determine the likelihood of their being tilled, and (2) the requirement that the width of the grant be at least one-third of its length.[50] The second provision was necessary to prevent unscrupulous individuals from preempting lands that bordered along rivers in small strips, thereby denying access to other landholders. After 1713, an evaluation of the quality of the land in relation to the requirements for seating and planting of new grants was instituted, and surveyors determined the amount that was "plantable" and the amount that was "barren." The plantable portion required the cultivation within three years of three acres out of every fifty, or the draining of at least three acres of swamp or marsh land. The barren area required for every fifty acres within three years the stocking of at least three cattle or six sheep or goats. For a tract in which all was barren, both a dwelling "after the manner of *Virginia* building" was to be completed and cattle were required in the same proportion as above. Significant for the interest of Spotswood, there was the alternative of having for every 100 acres "one good able hand" working for three years "in digging of any stone quarry, coal, or other mines."[51] The requirement of the Assembly in 1713 that land be forfeited on which quitrents had not been paid for three years met stiff opposition. It was either opposed directly by the council who had been leaders in obtaining large grants of land, or it was ignored by local officials.

Spotswood's initial zeal in land reform was one cause of the impasse that was eventually reached between the governor and Assembly. William Byrd II recorded that efforts had been made "to soften" Spotswood on pressing the land act of 1713, but to no avail.[52] There were other factors that were even more critical. The governor was at odds with the burgesses on the disposition of the quitrents by retaining some control for king and governor; he clashed sharply with the council over the question of the right of the governor or the council to designate members of the courts of oyer and terminer, which were established to meet at times other than the General Court to hear special and urgent cases; he generated opposition from leading colonials by criticism that led to the dismissal of Philip Ludwell, Jr. as deputy auditor and the decision of William Byrd II to abandon the office of receiver general; he skirmished long and bitterly over the governor's right of induction of Anglican ministers and the extent of influence of the local vestries and the Anglican commissary with James Blair, who as commissary represented the Bishop of London as the highest ecclesiastical officer in the colony.

The hostility that had been most intense beginning in 1714 began to subside by 1718 with the council, and by 1720 Spotswood made peace with the Assembly, if not with Blair and Ludwell. He won the right to appoint judges to the courts of oyer and terminer, but agreed to restrict the positions to members of the council. While still endorsing the integral and vital relationship between empire and colony, he became more sympathetic to the colonists and appeared to some to have joined hands with the colonials. This was particularly evident in matters of land policy, where he reversed his position from the early reforms of his administration and along with other leading Virginians laid claim to thousands of acres on the frontier in the new county of Spotsylvania.

Spotswood's vast accumulation of land came rapidly, and the acquisition violated some of the legal steps he had previously attempted to enforce. He had taken up land on which he settled the German servants in 1717; two years later with associates he took title to an additional tract of 15,000 acres for iron mines. With the authorization of Spotsylvania County, he was instrumental in the granting of several tracts, one of 20,000 acres, another of 40,000 acres, that were made in the name of other colonists and the title later transferred to Spotswood. Bonds for the grants were not always provided. In all, Spotswood obtained in his own name or that of associates some 85,027 acres in Spotsylvania.[53] Others inspired by his interest in the area had taken out thousands of acres for themselves. These irregular procedures contributed to the decision to remove him as govenor in 1722. Spotswood as private citizen then spent part of his time at Germanna and engaged in the production of iron and naval stores. He extended the line of settlement in Spotsylvania County by bringing in new families who were placed on small farms with leases that carried forward two generations. Spotswood's presence and his enthusiasm for western development inspired other leading citizens to invest in Virginia's new settlements, including many of his "Knights of the Golden Horseshoe." Both as colonial official and as private citizen, Spotswood's greatest interest was in the potential of frontier development.

7

New Blood in Piedmont and Valley of
Virginia and Maryland:
Imperial Plans and Land Speculation, 1720–50

The impact of territorial ambitions of rulers in Europe extended to colonies in America and often affected directly their status in both war and peace. At other times the alliance of powers in Europe changed so rapidly that there was a lag in reactions to the European scene. The treaty of Utrecht of 1713 at the end of Queen Anne's War soon fell apart with the realignment of powers in the Quadruple Alliance of 1718. Spain, which had been an ally of France in the War of Spanish Succession, then found herself an opponent as France joined with England, Holland, and Austria in resisting the territorial ambitions of Philip V of Spain and his wife, Elizabeth Farnese. The Franco-Spanish conflict that ensued in America from 1719 to 1721 culminated in the French capture of Pensacola, but it was restored to Spain with the return of peace.[1] Despite these rapid changes, the British still viewed both Spain and France as challengers in the New World, with particular concern for the French with their greater potential as a threat.

A study of colonial frontier history can too easily be limited to an examination of a restricted locale without adequate attention to plans that are formulated at higher levels of the imperial hierarchy. Both topics are worthy of note, and both should be considered in order to provide the proper perspective for the history of an area. With the continuation of the Anglo-Spanish and Anglo-French struggles during the eighteenth century, British officials were increasingly concerned with maintaining and expanding American colonies in relationship to these threats. In response to this challenge, the Board of Trade addressed itself to the problem of British policy for western America and prepared its report on the "State of the British Plantations in America" in 1721.[2]

Following the creation of the Board of Trade in 1696, it had received several important communications from the colonies that helped shape frontier policy. Francis Nicholson as governor of Virginia had urged Indian trading companies during the 1690s to maintain influence over Indians to the west and to counter French activities. Thomas Nairne in 1708, having observed in person the burgeoning influence of the French as far west as the

Mississippi River, submitted a memorial that has been described as "one of the most remarkable documents in the history of Anglo-American frontier 'imperialism'."[3] Accompanied by a map, which is no longer extant, the memorial stressed the strategic role of South Carolina in countering French activity, the value of trading posts on the Tennessee River, and the possibility of settling the old locale of the Apalache Indians in Florida. Alexander Spotswood as early as 1710 advocated a westward push by permitting settlement along one bank of the James River to counter the French. The challenge posed by French presence was spelled out by Richard Berresford, agent for the South Carolina Assembly, in the "Designs of the French to Extend their Settlements from Canada to Mississippi behind the British Plantations" in 1717.[4] Spotswood and other colonial governors promptly endorsed that report on the seriousness of the threat. The Virginia governor in 1718 urged the settlement of the Great Lakes and the securing of the mountain passes to the west. Spotswood even offered to brave the "uninhabited Wilderness" as the leader of an expedition to the Great Lakes and not to "grudge any fatigue" if authorized to be financed from the quitrents of the colony.[5] After the French seizure of Pensacola from the Spanish, he advocated that the English take over St. Augustine to foil a possible encirclement to the southeast. Sir William Keith, deputy governor of Pennsylvania, submitted his "report on the Progress of the French Nation" to the board in 1719.[6] He urged the elimination of bickering among the colonies over the Indian trade and advocated an intercolonial union that would promote their mutual interests in trade and western settlements. The following year the Board of Trade listened as John Barnwell and Joseph Boone of South Carolina outlined in person a plan to counter the French by a fort-building scheme that resembled closely the earlier proposals of Nairne. In a letter to the board in the same year, Governor William Burnet of New York reviewed the state of French forts in the Indian country and indicated his plans to build forts at Niagara and Onondaga.[7] With these and other suggestions from the colonies, the Board of Trade completed its report of 1721.

The board made three major recommendations of particular significance for the American colonies. First, it recommended the discovery and the fortification of the passes over the Appalachians, the erection of forts on the Great Lakes advocated by both Spotswood and Burnet, and the securing of the Carolina frontier by additional garrisons. The second step was "cultivating the good understanding of the native Indians." Some emphasis was given to the possibility of encouraging intermarriage between Indian and white, to a more zealous propagation of the Christian faith, and to imitation of the French example of sending certain Indian chiefs to the home country. Greatest stress was placed upon improving the regulation of Indian trade as an effective diplomatic tool in western expansion rather than a mere source of profit. In the third step for putting "the Government of the plantations upon a better foot," the report was critical of the proprietary governments for some of their laws "contrary to those of Great Britain" and for their failure in intercolonial cooperation, recommending that all be made royal colonies. The board also pointed out the failure of an efficient quitrent collection and the critical need for the preservation of the forests. As a means of implementing all of these needed reforms, the report put forth the suggestion that all of the colonies from Nova Scotia to South Carolina be placed under the control of "one Lord Lieutenant, or Captain General" with at least two councillors from each province, similar to the arrangement that then existed for the Leeward Islands.[8]

These proposals of the Board of Trade for western expansion were the essence of a general British western policy designed to counter both French and Spanish encirclement, but it did not immediately receive whole-hearted endorsement from the Privy Council. Except for approval of the Altamaha Fort as an advanced prong into the area of the future colony of Georgia still claimed by Spain, the Privy Council did not consent to the expenditures nor the aggressive measures necessary to implement the policy. During subsequent years the Board of Trade played a less vigorous role in colonial administration with the evolution of the position of prime minister, but the first two recommendations continued as the goals of British western policy. Action was taken, as recommended in the third step, to complete the transition of the Carolinas to royal colonies, but others, such as Pennsylvania and Maryland, remained under proprietary control. The proposal for a centralized direction of the colonies under one official represented an extension of the unsuccessful experiment of the Dominion of New England in 1688–89, and it foreshadowed similar ideas—again from the Board of Trade— in 1754 and the Albany Plan of Union of the same year.

The major impulse for western expansion on the southern frontier in the half-century following the Board of Trade's report in 1721 came from either land speculators, local settlers, or immigrants seeking land; occasional encouragement also came from colonial governors, assemblies, and crown officials in England. Spotswood's leadership had moved the Virginia Assembly in 1720 to authorize the counties of Spotsylvania and Brunswick in recognition that "the frontiers towards the high mountains are exposed to danger from the Indians, and the late settlement of the French to the westward." The Assembly also provided the expenditure of 1500 pounds Virginia currency: 500 to be used for the construction of "a church, court house, prison, pillory and stocks," and the remaining 1000 pounds to provide arms and ammunition for the new settlers. All "publick levies" were waived for the new inhabitants for ten years beginning in 1721.[9] Efforts were also made to get the crown to remit quitrents for ten years, but in 1723 the Privy

Council agreed to only a seven-year exemption with a maximum of 1000 acres of land to be taken up by each person. Spotswood's vast holdings of over 85,000 acres posed a special problem with 1000 acres as a limit, and his case was referred to the crown. The dilemma was resolved by the order in council of 1729 permitting him to retain his holdings because of his long service, but requiring full payments for headrights and yet permitting an exemption for the quitrents for seven years. Recognizing the potential of settlers of varied ethnic backgrounds, the Assembly also exempted "foreign Protestants" with their own minister from the tithe for ten years.[10]

The expansion across the piedmont section was primarily an east-west advance spearheaded by settlement along the river valleys of the Potomac, Rappahannock, James, and Roanoke, although some additions in population were also made by the southern movement of immigrants from Pennsylvania.[11] Spotswood's western interest had encompassed both the northern area along the Rappahannock and the southern area along the Roanoke and Meherrin rivers. Fort Christanna had been constructed along the Meherrin; the interests of William Byrd II and others in both land and mining deposits along the James as well as Spotswood's greater familiarity with the Rappahannock country from his trek with the "Knights of the Golden Horseshoe" prompted him to turn his major efforts to the northern area. Spotsylvania County, organized in 1721 under Spotswood's leadership, stood as the first Virginia county west of the piedmont and the first to run over the Blue Ridge into the Shenandoah Valley. Along the Rappahannock, Spotswood and some of his "Knights" led the way in taking up land grants and in colonizing the area, thereby providing a pattern of settlement that brought a group of well educated and well-to-do leaders seeking new land for cultivation of tobacco or land for speculation that was sold to small farmers or rented to tenants. By 1728 settlers moving across Spotsylvania County crossed the Blue Ridge, and the first grants made in the valley went to Larkin Chew, Thomas Chew, and their associates.

In the Northern Neck of Virginia, where Lord Fairfax then held proprietary rights, settlements moved along the Rappahannock River and its tributary the Rapidan, and up the Potomac beyond the present location of Washington, D.C., near the falls. They continued along the Potomac tributary, the Occoquon, which parallels the Potomac above the falls and feeds into the main stream about twenty miles south of the nation's capital. A grant of 1920 acres of land was made by the royal governor of Virginia as early as 1705 above the falls of the Rappahannock in an area that was later in dispute between the royal government and the Northern Neck proprietor until settled in 1746. The controversy did not deter settlers; they continued to move into the Northern Neck after purchasing land from the proprietor or into the disputed area between the Rapidan and Rappahannock after negotiating with either the proprietor or the royal officials in the colony. Prince William County was organized there in 1731.[12]

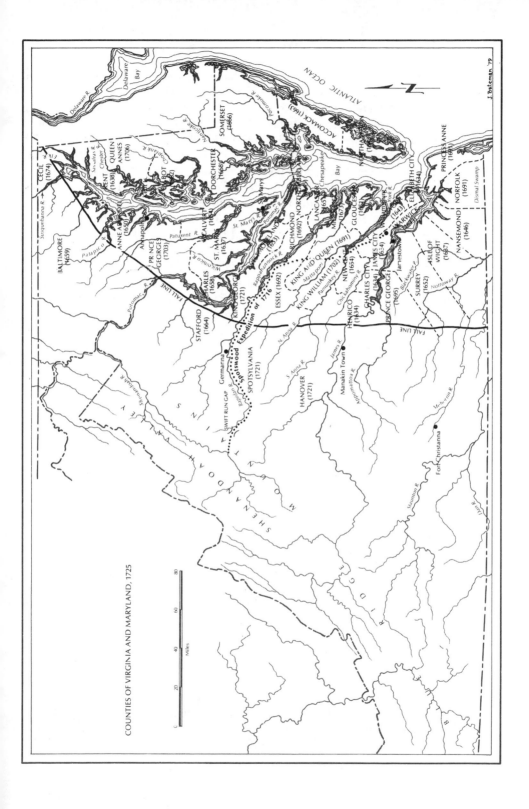

COUNTIES OF VIRGINIA AND MARYLAND, 1725

J. Bateman '79

ATLANTIC OCEAN

N

Miles
0   20   40   60   80

SHENANDOAH MOUNTAIN

BLUE RIDGE

Delaware Bay

Delaware R.

Susquehanna R.

BALTIMORE (1659)

CECIL (1674)

KENT (1638)

Chester R.

Sassafras R.

QUEEN ANNES (1706)

TALBOT (1662)

Choptank R.

DORCHESTER (1668)

SOMERSET (1666)

Nanticoke R.

Pocomoke R.

ACCOMACK (1663)

NORTHAMPTON

Chesapeake Bay

PRINCE ANNE (1691)

FALL LINE

Patapsco R.

ANNE ARUNDEL (1650)

Annapolis

PRINCE GEORGE (1703)

Patuxent R.

CALVERT (1654)

ST. MARY'S (1637)

St. Mary's

Potomac R.

St. Mary's

CHARLES (1658)

Wicomico R.

Potomac R.

STAFFORD (1664)

KING GEORGE (1721)

WESTMORELAND (1653)

Rappahannock R.

ESSEX (1692)

RICHMOND (1692)

NORTHUMBERLAND

LANCASTER (1651)

MIDDLESEX (1673)

GLOUCESTER

York R.

ELIZABETH CITY (1634)

NORFOLK (1691)

NANSEMOND (1646)

PRINCESS ANNE (1691)

Dismal Swamp

Germanna

Spotswood Expedition of 1716

SWIFT RUN GAP

Rapidan R.

Rappahannock R.

SPOTSYLVANIA (1721)

HANOVER (1721)

N. Anna R.

S. Anna R.

Pamunkey R.

Mattaponi R.

KING AND QUEEN (1691)

KING WILLIAM (1702)

NEW KENT (1654)

James R.

Manakin Town

HENRICO (1634)

Chickahominy R.

CHARLES CITY (1634)

JAMES CITY

Jamestown

PRINCE GEORGE (1695)

Appomattox R.

Blackwater R.

SURREY (1652)

ISLE OF WIGHT (1637)

Nottoway R.

Meherrin R.

WARWICK (1643)

YORK (1634)

Staunton R.

Fort Christanna

Dan R.

FALL LINE

Besides the route along the Rappahannock, the other major corridor of westward expansion was along the James River. The Byrd family, William I and II, dominated trade along the falls and owned substantial land to the west. The French Huguenots had also established the frontier settlement at Manakin Town twenty miles above the falls. The move up the James was led by the William Randolph family, who during the seventeenth century had resided at Turkey Island with one son, Richard, at Curles Neck. Another son, Thomas, went above the falls and started a plantation in 1710 at Tuckahoe to which he later moved. Still other sons or in-laws formed a part of the western tide, including Peter Jefferson, father of Thomas Jefferson and son-in-law of Isham Randolph. Peter moved beyond the falls in 1731 and later acquired land along the Rivanna River. Goochland County was organized from Henrico in 1728 and became the second county in the piedmont.

The neighbors and in-laws of the Randolphs extended their interests to the Rivanna and took up land as early as 1727 in the area of present Fluvanna and Albemarle counties. Grants went to families including the Carters, Cockes, and Pages in one group of friends and relatives. Another closely related family faction included Colonel Nicholas Meriwether, Dr. Thomas Walker, and Charles Lewis. Colonel Meriwether, coming to present Albemarle County by way of the South Anna River rather than up the James, obtained a land grant of 13,000 acres in 1727 that was later increased to 17,000. Charles Lewis obtained 12,000 acres in the same area in 1732. A few small land grants were also made in the Albemarle area during this time, but they do not appear in significant numbers until 1735. Albemarle County was organized in 1744 as population increased. This record of land grants delineates a pattern of settlement in which the substantial planter or speculator, such as Dr. Thomas Walker, came first into the area, providing a notable exception to the Turnerian procession of migration in which the pioneer farmer came in advance of the planter. These planters and speculators provided significant leadership for the local level of government as well as contributing to a social and cultural pattern not always associated with pioneer movements.

The penetration along the Appomattox River, a tributary of the James, under the leadership of many of the families prominent in political, social, and economic affairs led by Randolph, provided a link between the James and the settlements to the south and southwest along the Roanoke River. Although navigable waters did not run over the divide between the Appomattox and the Roanoke, settlers made their way along this route to the leading tributaries of the Roanoke under the guidance of the Randolphs and Colonel Clement Read. Colonel Read moved into the area along the Little Roanoke River during the 1730s and soon had neighboring families arriving from tidewater, and this settlement provided similar patterns of migration to those noted for the piedmont section to the north. The area was a part of Brunswick County established in 1732.

The social and economic development of the Roanoke Valley was, however, to proceed along somewhat different lines than had occurred along the James River mainly for three reasons: the geography of the area, the nature of the land grants, and the greater variety in the ethnic backgrounds of the settlers. First, there was missing the same superb waterways that traversed the piedmont and tidewater and flowed into the Chesapeake Bay where private wharves for commerce dotted the river banks, and from which the important staple of tobacco could be loaded directly on ships for Europe. From the piedmont section, tobacco was often floated downstream to accessible wharves or hauled overland for short distances;[13] the Roanoke River, however, emptied into Albemarle Sound, which provided no adequate port along the North Carolina coast and did not give the same opportunities to the tobacco trade. Consequently, an area of small farms primarily with subsistence agriculture and industry developed, and the trade in tobacco and other products had to be taken mainly to Norfolk by a difficult overland route.

While the area was one mainly of small farms, land speculators had preceded the small farmer and laid claim to the best lands. Some 60,000 acres were obtained by the Randolphs in 1740 along the Staunton River aproaching the Blue Ridge Mountains in present Bedford County. William Byrd II was even more active in the area. Serving as one of the Virginia commissioners to run the long-disputed boundary line with North Carolina in 1728, Byrd was so inspired by the appearance of the land that he bought 20,000 acres at the confluence of the Dan and Irvine rivers from the North Carolina commissioners who had received land in compensation for their work. To explore his new acquisition and prevent the encroachment of future grants, Byrd with ten white men, three Indians, three Negroes, twenty horses, and four dogs proceeded to survey the area during September and October, 1733. Their experience was recorded by Byrd in *A Journey to the Land of Eden* in which the Dan River Valley was described as a beautiful dwelling "where the Air is wholesome, and the Soil equal in Fertility in any in the World." "Happy will be the People," Byrd continued, "destin'd for so wholesome a Situation, where they may live to fulness of day, and which is much better Still, with much Content and Gaiety of Heart."[14] This was the "Land of Eden," an elaborate description designed to attract newcomers. Byrd later obtained a much larger tract of over 100,000 acres along the Dan River.

The "Happy . . . People" who Byrd hoped were destined to settle this area were Swiss emigrants. In July 1736 he offered to give 10,000 acres of land if 100 families were transported by the following May, and about the same time he sold some 33,400 acres on the Roanoke River to Samuel Jenner of Bern, Switzerland, an agent for a group called the Helvetian Society. In 1737, "at the command" of this Society, a glowing account of the area and a detailed description of the natural history of Virginia were printed in Switzerland in the German language, written by Byrd and translated with modifications by Jenner. Entitled *Neu-gefundenes Eden*,[15] which has been translated as the "New Found Eden" or the "Newly Discovered Eden," the publication helped stimulate the migration of some 250 Swiss and German settlers, who unfortunately were shipwrecked in January 1738/9 as they approached the Atlantic coast near Norfolk. Many of them perished at sea. Perhaps as many as seventy survived to reach the Roanoke River. Byrd then made attempts to get additional settlers from Pennsylvania but was able to attract only a few more newcomers.

Even though Byrd was not successful in settling the desired number of families, the Virginia council completed his patent. Byrd had not even fulfilled the more lenient stipulations available after 1730 of having to settle only one family per thousand acres with quitrents not required until the patent was issued. These favorable terms for the speculator replaced the previous provision for the sale of land at 10 shillings per 100 acres with requirements for cultivation of at least 3 acres out of every 50 with annual quitrents of 2 shillings for every 100 acres.[16] Even though William Byrd II did not survive to see substantial settlement of his lands, the way was prepared for the significant increase that came later.

Much of the subsequent increase came from the "New Blood" of the Scots-Irish and Germans who came into the western valleys of both Virginia and Maryland from Pennsylvania. The Scots-Irish were immigrants from Northern Ireland where either they or their ancestors had moved from Scotland, primarily from the Lowlands from which there was a large migration in the seventeenth century with the urging of King James I. Presbyterian in religion, they encouraged education and trained ministers, yet they were noted as fierce frontier fighters and sometimes evoked sharp criticism from other ethnic groups. William Byrd II, for example, had declared against these "mixed people" and warned that they "flock over thither in such numbers, that there is not elbow room for them. They swarm like the Goths and Vandals of old and will over-spread our Continent soon."[17] The German immigrants during the first half of the eighteenth century were mainly Lutherans of the German Reformed Church from the Palatinate and other provinces in Germany. Skilled in agriculture, thrifty, and trained in crafts including the making of wagons and guns, they made important economic contributions but were slow to interact with other colonists because of language differences and attachment to their Old-World culture. Philadelphia was the major port of arrival for both of these groups. For example, over twelve shiploads of Scots-Irish arrived in Philadelphia during the summer of 1717, and about 15,000 German immigrants reached Philadelphia in sixty-seven ships during the decade following 1737.[18]

These immigrants had been attracted to Pennsylvania by the colony's promotional campaign, its toleration of diverse religious views, the availability of fertile land during early settlement, and the convenience of the port of Philadelphia. The continued stream of immigration, however, began to fill the unclaimed areas and forced rents and prices for remaining tracts to levels that exceeded costs in Virginia and Maryland by one-half or more. Blocked by the mountains to the west, the immigrants made their way to the southwest to the valleys of Virginia and Maryland.

The most frequent route of migration was the Great Wagon Road (see map p. 103). Starting from the Schuylkill River at Philadelphia, the road moved across southern Pennsylvania through York, then along the Monocay River in Maryland, and westward over the Catoctin Mountains passing near Frederick and crossing the Potomac at Williams Ferry or Williamsport. Continuing through the Shenandoah Valley, it moved southwest through present Winchester, Staunton, and on to Roanoke where it then turned east through the Staunton River Gap. From there it led to the piedmont of the Carolinas, and was well traveled in subsequent years.[19]

The valley of Virginia lay between the Blue Ridge Mountains on the east and the Alleghenies to the west and was known in the northern part as the Shenandoah Valley for the stream of the same name, which flows in a northeasterly direction into the Potomac. The first known settler in the valley was Adam Miller or Müller, a German from Pennsylvania whose interest supposedly was stimulated by knowledge of Spotswood and the "Knights of the Horseshoe." Miller did not come by way of the Great Wagon Road but entered the valley from the piedmont over Swift Run Gap and had settled without title near present Elkton by 1727.[20] The first official grant was made of 10,000 acres in 1728 to Larkin Chew, sheriff of Spotsylvania County, on Happy Creek, a tributary of the Shenandoah. This grant, along with others to Chew and his associates, was later to be a part of the title controversy between Lord Fairfax of the Northern Neck and colonial officials.

Land speculators played a prominent role in the settlement of the new areas as large grants were obtained and sold directly to the German and Scots-Irish immigrants from Pennsylvania. Grants of 1000 acres per family had already been authorized for Spotsylvania County. Beginning with a grant in June 1730 to John Van Meter, a neighbor of Adam Miller, a new provision was included for 20,000 acres contingent upon his settling one family for each 1000 acres. The modification was significant. Previously the land went to the settler; now it went to the speculator. Land was obtained under the colonial grant at 10 schillings per 100 acres, but it was usually sold by the speculators to immigrants from Pennsylvania at 3 pounds for the same number of acres, a sixfold increase. The new settlers were willing to pay the higher price by period payments rather than having to go to Williamsburg to secure a grant direct from colonial officials. The land speculator became a self-interested immigration agent who stimulated migration from Pennsylvania and contributed to a larger number of Germans and Scots-Irish; their activities however, did not fully determine "the patterns of land subdivision or rural settlement."[21] These patterns were also influenced by other kinds of land speculation such as small landholders who often sold off small tracts at handsome profits. Immigrants from Pennsylvania mingled with older Virginia settlers who had moved west from piedmont or tidewater.

Beyond the line of main settlement, documentary evidence on frontier life is scarce, although a diary of Moravian missionaries in 1749 gives a glimpse of a few families of hunters in western Virginia. They encountered settlers of various nationalities in the primitive conditions of these fringe areas where usually no title to land had been obtained. Proceeding along the South Fork of the South Branch of the Potomac River and seeking the New River, the missionaries received assistance on November 12 from an Englishman who provided information on routes and accompanied one of the missionaries to his lodging place with two dogs to guard against attacks from wild beasts such as the large wolf they met along the way. Traveling early the next day, they received "a piece of bread and cheese" from a German woman. Upon reaching the source of the South Fork in present Pendleton County, West Virginia, they spent the night in what was called an English cabin. This was most likely a flimsy or temporary shelter made from bark or saplings rather than the well-known log cabin that had been introduced to the colonies by the Swedes in the seventeenth century but was not found in many frontier areas until after the middle of the eighteenth century. The missionaries slept on bear skins and noted that the people with whom they stayed gave them "some of their bear meat, which can be found in every house in this district." For the next two days they were in contact with Welshmen along the Cow Pasture River and by November 16 crossed the James River to the mountain area of the present Virginia counties of Bath and Allegheny. In the evening, the missionaries continued, "we came to a house, where we had to lie on bear skins around the fire like the rest. The manner of living is rather poor in this district. The clothes of the people consist of deer skins. Their food of Johnny cakes, deer and bear meat. A kind of white people are found here, who live like savages. Hunting is their chief occupation."[22]

While there were small numbers of Swiss, Dutch, and Swedes also in the Shenandoah Valley, the three major groups were the English, Scots-Irish, and Germans. These three groups were present in about equal numbers on the eve of the American Revolution in the northern portion of the valley, or the "Lower Shenandoah."[23] A recent analysis of population distribution for Berkeley and Frederick counties in 1775 found a preponderance of English with 38 percent, followed by Germans with 29.5 percent, and Scots-Irish with 28 percent. For the entire Shenandoah Valley in 1775, however, the population by nationality was 37.8 percent for Scots-Irish, 31.5 percent for Germans, and 26.6 percent for English.[24]

The leading land speculators were not confined to one ethnic group, and enterprising individuals were quick to grasp the economic potential of the valley frontier. Jacob Stover received 10,000 acres from the Virginia governor and council on June 17, 1730, the same day and in the same area as 40,000 acres were ceded to John and Isaac Van Meter. Adam Miller, having settled without patent, obtained title from Stover. Joist Hite, German, combined with Robert McKay, Scots-Irish, to gain control of the Van Meter claims in 1731 and secured the same year 100,000 acres more in the area of present Winchester. From tidewater, William Beverley of Essex County was aggressive in taking up land, obtaining with associates 20,000 acres in 1731 and 60,000 in 1734. The latter grant was extended to over 118,000 acres in 1736 to Beverley and other tidewater associates, Sir John Randolph and John Robinson. Beverley quickly gained control of the full tract and established Beverley's Manor in present Augusta County; by 1736 he had settled in the present area of Staunton some sixty-seven families, most of whom were Scots-Irish. His price of about 50 shillings for 100 acres was slightly under the speculator's usual figure of 3 pounds. Beverley offered one of the best bargains in the valley, selling eighty-four tracts with a total of 42,119 acres from 1738 to 1744 for the average price of £2 18s 4d per 100 acres. From 1745 to 1750, his sale price increased for 108 grants with a total of 37,762 acres to an average of £3 6s 6d for 100 acres. This was, nonetheless, a modest increase in comparison with the price hikes of many other speculators. Joist Hite, for example, made 44 grants of 19,182 acres from 1734 to 1744 at the average price of £6 13s 4d per 100 acres.[25]

To the south, Benjamin Borden and James Patton were the most important speculators during this period of settlement. Borden and William Robertson, seeking land for themselves and several families from East Jersey, were granted 100,000 acres in 1735 by the governor and council in the area of present Lexington. The grant included the stipulation that one family be brought in for each 1000 acres within two years and that it not interfere with the earlier concession to Beverley.[26] Additional time for settling was permitted two years later, and during the next few years predominantly Scots-Irish families settled on the Borden land with tracts ranging up to about 400 acres. James Patton from Northern Ireland had been active in bringing in Scots-Irish families for Beverley and became a leader in opening new areas. Patton, associated with twenty other men including John Preston, first asked for 200,000 acres in 1743 and in 1745 received authorization for half this amount along the New River and two other streams to the west. Four years were permitted for surveying and paying rights, and the land was to lie in the new county of Augusta.

Augusta County was created in 1745, the same year that the controversy over the boundaries of the lands of Lord Fairfax in the Northern Neck was resolved. The first grants in the valley in 1728 to Thomas Chew and associates had aroused a protest from Robert Carter as agent for Lord Fairfax.

Considerable confusion existed over the limits of the proprietary area claimed by Fairfax. His boundaries were based upon the new charter issued to Lord Culpeper by King James II in 1688, with the extension inserted by Culpeper to include "All that entire tract, territory or parcel of land" extending from the Chesapeake between the Rappahannock and Potomac rivers to "their said first heads or springs."[27] This last statement was interpreted as extending the proprietary claim beyond the Blue Ridge Mountains to the foot of the Alleghenies, and it brought into question land grants along the Rapidan River.

Several appeals were made to crown officials to settle the controversial boundary, and Lord Fairfax had come in person to the colony with the order in council for commissioners to be appointed to resolve the issue in 1735. Commissioners representing both sides arranged for surveys and maps, and the case of *Virginia v. Fairfax* was finally decided favorably for Fairfax.[28] The bounds as laid down by the court decree involved some six million acres with western boundaries extending from the Rapidan as the south fork of the Rappahannock to the north branch of the Potomac known as the Cohongorooten River. Survey lines and a map were completed for the boundaries. Grants made previously by the governor and council in the disputed area were recognized by Lord Fairfax.

The migration into the valley of Virginia was closely related to, or indeed was a part of, the simultaneous expansion of Maryland. After restoration of the Maryland colony to the rule of the proprietor in 1715 following years of royal control, settlement continued to be confined mainly to the tidewater for over a decade. By 1730 a few pioneers had occupied the area beyond the fall line and had staked their claims in the piedmont section. They settled mainly along the major streams, extending along the Potomac beyond the falls, up the Patuxent River beyond present Laurel, and along the Susquehanna to Octararo Creek. Most of tidewater Maryland had been occupied except for limited areas away from Chesapeake Bay, swamps on the Eastern Shore in southern Dorchester County, and along the controversial boundary line of Delaware.

As settlements moved farther west, Daniel Dulany the Elder played a significant role both as agent of the proprietor and as the leading land speculator. An Irish immigrant arriving in 1703, he began an illustrious career as lawyer, planter, land speculator, and colonial official, including the varied positions of receiver general, attorney general, commissary general or judge of the probate court, chief judge of the vice admiralty court, and ultimately a position on the proprietor's Council of State in 1742. As plantation owner, he acquired tracts both in tidewater and western Maryland, but he was so occupied with duties either as an official or as land speculator that he left the supervision of plantations to overseers or leased the land to tenants, a procedure prevalent among large landholders at the time. As land speculator,

Imperial Plans and Land Speculation 151

he acquired during his career over 55,000 acres of land warrants, representing an investment that he recovered as the land was surveyed and sold either in large or small amounts.[29]

The Maryland land system had evolved along somewhat the same lines as that of Virginia where the headright system by the eighteenth century had given way to acquisition by purchase. Maryland had used the headright from 1632 to 1683 when there was no provision for direct purchase. After 1683 the headright provision was eliminated and land was obtained by the payment of the purchase price, which in Maryland was also referred to as caution money. Originally designated only in terms of tobacco, the price in 1717 provided the money equivalent of 40 shillings sterling for each 100 acres. The quitrent rate of 4 shillings for 100 acres that had been in effect since 1671 was advanced to 10 shillings in 1733 except for special provisions for frontier or surplus land. Officials were authorized to "Determine and Direct a less Rent for any Distant Lands on the Borders and Frontiers" or to make exemptions as a reward for discovery of "Surplus Land." The above increase, however, brought a downward spiral of the issuing of land warrants to a scant 10 percent of previous years, contributing to the return to the former 4 shillings for 100 acres in 1738 but imposing at the same time an increase in the caution money from 40 to 100 shillings.[30] Special exceptions were again made for the frontier that encouraged both western settlement and land speculation.

Three individuals stand out as leading landholders and speculators in the second quarter of the eighteenth century in Maryland: Charles Carroll of Annapolis, Dr. Charles Carroll, and Daniel Dulany the Elder. Charles Carroll of Annapolis was for a time the proprietor's attorney general and represented the Catholic branch of the family. Dr. Charles Carroll, a physician and a relative from the Protestant side of the family, also had a significant interest in land speculation and joined Daniel Dulany the Elder and Charles Carroll of Annapolis as partners in the Baltimore Iron Company. From Charles Carroll of Annapolis in 1718, Dr. Charles received his first tract of 2400 acres in Anne Arundel County. He later turned his major interest to "western Maryland," which by definition was all a part of Prince George's County until the creation of Frederick in 1748.[31] The land transactions of Dr. Charles have been succinctly summarized from the rent-rolls as follows: "Altogether he warranted there [western Maryland] 91 tracts totalling 31,529 acres for an average of 352 acres per holding. Of that total he patented 83 tracts containing 28,480 acres. In addition he bought 13 tracts totalling 3049 acres. Of the 96 tracts he sold 57 containing 22,781 acres."[32]

The key role in the development of western Maryland during this period belongs to Daniel Dulany the Elder. As early as 1733 Lord Baltimore offered to remit quitrents for a number of years and to provide relief from duties for the church to stimulate western migration, but these offers had less of an impact upon populating the Monocay Valley than the migration from

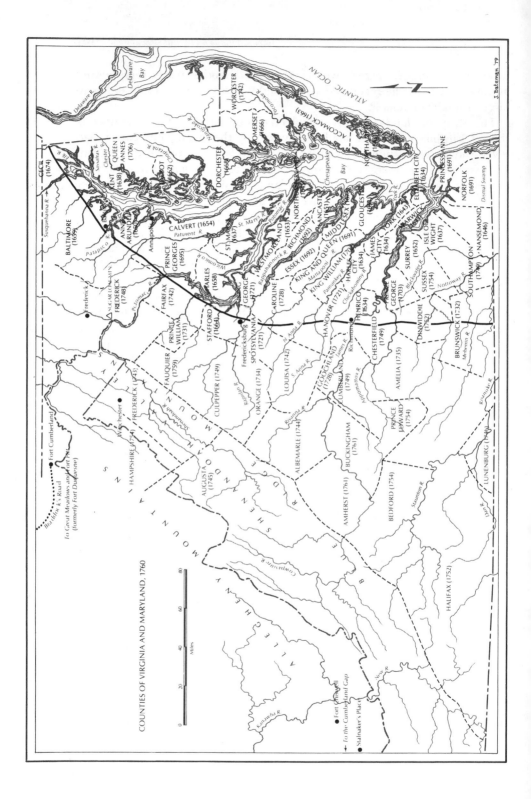

COUNTIES OF VIRGINIA AND MARYLAND, 1760

J. Bateman '79

ATLANTIC OCEAN

CECIL (1674)
BALTIMORE (1659)
KENT (1638)
QUEEN ANNES (1706)
TALBOT (1662)
DORCHESTER (1668)
WORCESTER (1742)
SOMERSET (1666)
ANNE ARUNDEL (1650)
CALVERT (1654)
PRINCE GEORGES (1695)
CHARLES (1658)
ACCOMACK (1663)
NORTHAMPTON (1634)

Chesapeake Bay
Delaware Bay
Delaware R.

Susquehanna R.
Patapsco R.
Frederick
Annapolis
Patuxent R.
Potomac R.
St. Mary's R.
Wicomico R.

FREDERICK (1748)
FAIRFAX (1742)
PRINCE WILLIAM (1731)
STAFFORD (1664)
KING GEORGE (1721)
SPOTSYLVANIA (1721)
Fredericksburg
CAROLINE (1728)
WESTMORELAND
RICHMOND (1692)
NORTHUMBERLAND
LANCASTER (1651)
ESSEX (1692)
KING AND QUEEN (1691)
MIDDLESEX (1669)
GLOUCESTER
KING WILLIAM (1701)
NEW KENT
JAMES CITY
YORK (1643)
WARWICK (1634)
ELIZABETH CITY (1634)
PRINCESS ANNE (1691)
NORFOLK (1691)
NANSEMOND (1646)
ISLE OF WIGHT (1637)
SURREY (1652)
SUSSEX (1754)
SOUTHAMPTON (1749)

Rappahannock R.
Mattapony R.
Pamunkey R.
York R.
Chickahominy R.
James R.
Nottoway R.
Blackwater R.
Dismal Swamp

FAUQUIER (1759)
CULPEPPER (1749)
ORANGE (1734)
LOUISA (1742)
HANOVER (1721)
GOOCHLAND (1728)
HENRICO (1634)
CHESTERFIELD (1749)
PRINCE GEORGE (1703)
DINWIDDIE (1752)
BRUNSWICK (1732)

Rapidan R.
Rivanna R.
S. Anna R.
N. Anna R.
Appomattox R.
Meherrin R.

ALBEMARLE (1744)
CUMBERLAND (1749)
AMELIA (1735)
PRINCE EDWARD (1754)
BUCKINGHAM (1761)
AMHERST (1761)
BEDFORD (1754)
LUNENBURG (1746)
HALIFAX (1752)

HAMPSHIRE (1753)
Winchester
FREDERICK (1743)
AUGUSTA (1745)

Shenandoah R.
SHENANDOAH VALLEY
BLUE RIDGE MOUNTAINS
ALLEGHENY MOUNTAINS
SUGAR LOAF MOUNTAIN
Cowpasture R.
Staunton R.
Roanoke R.
Dan R.

Fort Cumberland
Braddock's Road
To Great Meadows and Fort (formerly Fort Duquesne)

Fort Chiswell
To the Cumberland Gap
Stalnaker's Place
New R.
Kanawha R.

0 20 40 60 80
Miles

N

Pennsylvania, particularly of Germans. One group of Palatines founded the town of Frederick in 1745. Entering along the Monocay trail, the Germans branched off from the southward-moving stream of immigrants and readily took up the offers of land made available through speculators such as Dulany. Administratively a part of Prince George's County, the population of the area increased so rapidly that efforts to create a new county were sustained during the 1740s. Dulany the Elder made his first trip in person to the western area in 1744 and was excited by its potential. After failing to get a new county in both 1745 and 1747, Dulany pressed successfully for the creation in 1748 of Frederick County,[33] the last to be authorized in Maryland until 1773. Dulany also succeeded in getting Frederick established as the county seat, where he and his heirs reaped extensive profits from land sales. When the town of Frederick was first laid out, Dulany the Elder sold lots for two pounds, ten shillings, current money, with the additional return to Dulany and his heirs of British ground rent, annual payment by the purchaser for a perpetual lease of building land. This rent, found in colonial America primarily in Maryland and Pennsylvania, was imposed at the rate of one shilling each year for the first twenty-one years and double this figure after that. Later there was an increase in the price of the land and the amount of the ground rent; in some instances the increase came with the sale price, in others the amount of the perpetual ground rent.[34]

Income from farming in the western area derived mainly from growing wheat as a commercial crop. Tobacco, often a more lucrative cash crop, was not cultivated because the soil was ill-suited for it and because the German settlers had more experience with grains. The artisan skills of the inhabitants were applied to such industrial enterprises as mining. The Assembly encouraged economic diversification during this period with legislation that had provided bounties for hemp growing in 1727, for linen cloth made from flax or hemp in 1731 with renewals in 1740 and 1744, and for encouragement to mining such as the exemption of iron workers from both militia musters and road construction in 1732. The social and economic traditions of the Germans[35] and the transition to wheat growing in western Maryland shaped a society in Frederick County of predominantly small freeholders with few slaves except those of large landholders or speculators. Out of a total population of approximately 14,000 in 1755, only 12.5 percent of Frederick were slaves, a figure that is only half of the average for the colony as a whole; about 5 percent were indentured servants, and an undetermined number, including German settlers, were tenants.[36]

A statistical analysis of the land records for Frederick County of 1753 reveals a society of widespread landholding, but at the same time shows the existence of a small group of speculators and large landholders.[37] Out of 990 landholders, 10 percent held 56.8 percent of the total acreage with an approximate mean holding of 2155 acres. The next lower 10 percent in a decile breakdown dropped to 13.1 percent of the total acreage with a mean of 495. The lowest decile of owners held title to 1.1 percent of the acreage with an average holding of 40 acres. (See Table 4.) Of the total of 990 landholders, approximately 60 held 1000 acres or more. It is, however, impossible to determine how many of these were speculators, but it seems clear that the Carrolls and Dulanys were still active. Charles Carroll of Annapolis, for example, heads the list with 10 parcels and a total acreage of 23,306. Daniel Dulany the Younger was second with 13 parcels for 10,028 acres, while Daniel Dulany the Elder by 1753 held only 13 parcels and a total of 3075 acres. Dr. Charles Carroll was also listed with 43 parcels and a total of 6563 acres. The presence of these landholders and speculators from the beginning of Frederick gave a greater variety of social and economic standing in society than often existed in pioneer communities.

The shift to grain production in Frederick County, which also occurred in Maryland along the head of Chesapeake Bay in counties such as Baltimore and Cecil, posed special problems related to the use of tobacco as currency. From the early days of Maryland, tobacco, as in Virginia, had been used as the most important medium of exchange. Levies, court fines and expenses, and other official fees were usually designated in tobacco. In view of this problem, a paper money act of 1733 gave some relief in Maryland by permitting the use of paper money or coin for "dues" once requiring tobacco. Gold and silver coins were valued at the rate of 10 shillings for 100 pounds of tobacco. The act, however, excepted certain fees as payments for construction of churches. Two years later the substitution was extended to "provincial and county taxes" for a three-year period. In 1737 a bill passed the lower house for relief of the frontier areas with no tobacco, but it was rejected in the upper house. Again in 1739 a measure for special relief of the frontier failed, and it was not until the Tobacco Inspection Act of 1747 that special provisions were again made. Assessment for fees and levies were still made in tobacco, but for individuals not growing the crop during the previous year, payment could be made in money by the equivalent of 12 shillings 6 pence current money for each 100 pounds of tobacco. This relief for frontier and other areas not growing tobacco was continued in later acts of 1754 and 1763.[38]

The production of grain in western Maryland also had its impact upon the commerce of port cities and upon transportation routes over which the goods were sent for shipment. Road transportation in Maryland evolved along three courses, two of which are most relevant to the growth of western Maryland. One route developed on a north-south axis connecting Philadelphia with eastern Virginia and projecting prongs through Maryland that traversed both shores of Chesapeake Bay. This route affected the back country only indirectly. The other two transit lines were more relevant. One was the well-known Great Wagon Road that connected the back country of Maryland

TABLE 4
Decile Breakdown of Landholding, Frederick County,
Maryland (1753)[37]

Decile	%Total Acreage	Total	Acreage Held	Approx. Mean Holding
1	56.8%	99	213,423	2155 acres
2	13.1	99	49,182	495
3	8.4	99	31,559	320
4	6.1	99	22,963	230
5	4.7	99	17,828	180
6	3.5	99	13,097	130
7	2.6	99	9,900	100
8	2.3	99	8,609	85
9	1.4	99	5,098	50
10	1.1	99	4,092	40
Totals	100.0%	990	375,751	3785

and the valley of Virginia with Philadelphia and had served as the major line of migration of the Scots-Irish and Germans. Products such as grain were for a time sent to this market, although the 150 miles of transit was an arduous overland journey. The second route of importance for the back country was extended as English settlers moved up the Potomac and reached the Monocay by 1728, keeping their terminal trade connections with Georgetown and Alexandria. This route to the Potomac ports was more satisfactory for tobacco marketing where irregular ship connection in the upper reaches of the river would suffice, but it was less adequate for grain shipments where ports needed to be more accessible and where merchants as middlemen were desired. During the 1740s, settlers from western Maryland apparently developed trade connections with both Annapolis and Baltimore. The act uniting Baltimore with Jones Town in 1745 proclaimed the location was "very conveniently situated in regard to the back Inhabitants."[39] While thriving Baltimore did not capture the grain market of tidewater Maryland from the keen competition of ports such as Chestertown, it did benefit greatly by its connection with the back country. As one scholar has concluded: "Clearly it was from the frontier that came the impetus that differentiated the city of Baltimore from other towns of the province, and built up the large foreign trade of the metropolis."[40]

The multiplication of trade routes linking the seaboard with the back country eased, but by no means eliminated, the tensions that had long been mounting between those two areas. These "sectional" divisions, as they have been labeled by scholars, were, however, not as pronounced in the first half of the eighteenth century as they would later become. A brief examination of the question of sectionalism and politics in Virginia, though, reveals the origins of tensions stemming from the special needs and interests of frontier communities.

The addition of new counties or states often intensified sectionalism, as in such well-known examples in post-Revolutionary history as New England's opposition to new states in the Hartford Convention of 1814. The Virginia "Act for encouragement of the Land Frontiers" in 1705 seemingly appeared to discourage new counties by requiring that after division on "the land frontiers," there remain a minimum of 800 tithable persons and that the county before division provide for the new area "a decent church, court-house, and prison . . . after the form and manner now generally used within this colony."[41] The rationale for such provision, however, stressed the dangers of Indian attack and the heavy demand of both money and men in the militia for adequate protection. This reasoning, along with the procedure that was available and the frequent action that was taken to create new counties, militates against interpreting the legislation as sectionalism. Sectional conflicts were also minimized prior to the Revolution because new counties did not try to wrest political control from the tidewater.[42] Greater problems arose over the shifting of population westward because this required some of the older counties with loss of number to consolidate parishes. Governor Spotswood complained about another aspect of the problem of shifting county lines in the settled areas when his early efforts were defeated partly "through the dilligence of one leading man, who by the alteration proposed, would have lost many of his old friends that had voted for him in former elections, and got others into his county of whose friendship he was no ways confident."[43] Opposition to new counties in some instances came from the area itself and reflected no east-west cleavage at all, but during the American Revolution there was a more definite sectional stand in Virginia of eastern oppposition to new western counties.

Relocation of the colony's capital was another question that could produce then, as in later years, sectional reactions based on such parochial interests as the benefits or convenience for the particular area involved. The capital of colonial Virginia had been transferred in 1699 from Jamestown to Williamsburg, but by 1738 there was a campaign for another change. Some of the western counties favored a location upstream on the James, while some of the northern counties preferred a shift to the head of the York River. Votes were actually taken in the House of Burgesses on both Bermuda Hundred on the James and West Point on the York, but there was insufficient support for a move. In 1747 a mysterious fire consumed the capitol at Williamsburg, and once again its relocation was discussed that year. More potential sites were advocated, and the House of Burgesses went so far as to vote 43–33 to begin the construction of a new capital on the Pamunkey River.[44] The council promptly defeated this bill, and the controversy dragged out for the next two years with the council's continued opposition;[45] most council members were satisfied with Williamsburg because a number of large planters who held council seats resided nearby and were available for emergency sessions. The transfer of the capital was thereby delayed until the time of the Revolution.

Tobacco inspection provided another issue that eventually reflected a cleavage between the newer tobacco areas with small farms and the larger tobacco planter of tidewater; but in part this was simply the large planter versus the small planter, whatever his location. Under Governor Spotswood a tobacco law was passed in 1713 that was designed to improve the quality of the tobacco trade and of tobacco used as money by providing for inspection and for destruction of trash tobacco. Opposition came from all except four of Virginia's twenty-five counties, and bills for repeal were introduced in the Assembly. In 1717 the Privy Council terminated the law after receiving the recommendation of the Board of Trade advocating repeal upon insistence from several merchants.[46]

Governor William Gooch revived tobacco inspection in 1731, but a major effort on his part was required to revive regulation. While opposition to the measure came mainly from small farmers, a careful reading of Gooch's discussions on the controversial topic indicates opposition was stronger in the newer counties with a greater number of small farmers and from the Northern Neck, which remained in its ambivalent position between proprietor and colonial governor, resisting control from Williamsburg at every turn. The opposition was so acute in the Northern Neck that riots erupted in 1731–32 and destroyed tobacco warehouses.[47] This opposition notwithstanding, several factors were at work in behalf of continuing inspection. The persistence of Governor Gooch, the improvement of inspection provisions, the rise of tobacco prices, and the siege of bad weather increasing the amount of trash tobacco on the market all combined to provide sufficient support for the renewal of inspection for four years in 1735. The large planters, at least, were convinced that such regulatory steps were desirable, and with their backing inspection became an accepted tenet of the tobacco trade.

These regulations aided tobacco growers, but similar improvements were not forthcoming for those whose economic interests turned to the production of cattle and the growing of grain, particularly the new settlers in the northern portion of the piedmont and the valley. The Assembly under Governor Gooch did in 1742 recognize the problem by providing for inspection of pork and beef and for its shipment in barrels; and in the same act it included the continuation of the inspection of tar and pitch to eliminate trash.

Another critical problem faced by the Assembly was the required payment in tobacco of "levies and officers fees," a similar problem that confronted the Maryland areas engaged in tobacco culture. Temporary relief was provided by permitting the payment of both taxes and fees in current money.

Designation of the rates and prices in money were to be made by the county court, which was also to approve the individuals eligible for such substitution.[48] Unfortunately for those who obtained relief by this measure, it was enacted for only one year, and efforts to continue the provisions were defeated by the council in 1744.[49] Efforts to solve the problem in Virginia were less successful than the action noted for Maryland.

While these examples reflect some differences that emerged between tidewater and back country, they do not demonstrate the sharp political split that was more evident in later years. The economic ties in trade and the movement to piedmont and valley of a substantial number of large landholders and speculators tended to minimize sharp differences between the two areas.

The experiences of these landholders and speculators in the Shenandoah Valley whetted their interest in additional western expansion and in land acquisition and profits beyond the Allegheny Mountains. Both colonial and crown officials, while responding primarily to economic interests of the speculator, were aware of the French in the Ohio Valley as they deliberated over requests for land from both Virginia and Maryland during the 1740s and 1750s. The most significant results, initially, were the creation of an amazing number of new land companies. The pattern of large grants influenced the competition among the companies that emerged and spawned internal struggles in both colonies. Virginia was most directly involved, but the cleavage that occurred was not the traditional east-west split but a north-south division in which the alignment of families was important. The geographic dividing line between those involved in the competition was the Rappahannock River, which set off the Northern Neck along with the northern piedmont from the remainder of Virginia. The family alignments pitted the powerful Robinson-Randolph clique of tidewater Tuckahoes against the Lees, Washingtons, Fairfaxes, and others from the Northern Neck.[50]

The climax of the bidding for land came in 1749, but several extensive grants had been made prior to that time. The interest of Colonel James Patton has already been noted. As early as 1743, he and his partners sought a grant from the governor and council of Virginia across the Allegheny range on the New River, a stream that provides the natural phenomenon of rising east of the mountains and flowing west into the Kanawha and Ohio rivers. This request was delayed while local officials pondered the possible effects of such grants upon the French as well as the possible reaction of crown officials. The outbreak of King George's War in 1744 in the colonies as the counterpart of the War of Austrian Succession in Europe removed the concern for the French as a block to grants, for again Anglo-French hostility was resumed. Consequently, Patton and his associates received on April 26, 1745, 100,000 acres in what was then Augusta County on the Mississippi and New rivers and other streams to the west. The grant stipulated that the survey and payment of rights should be made in four years, although subject to extension of time by the council. On the same day John Robinson, president of the council, and his associates of the Greenbrier Company received 100,000 acres on the Greenbrier River under terms similar to those for Patton. Grants continued to be made by the governor and council until a request was submitted by the Ohio Company in 1747 for 200,000 acres for its members organized by Thomas Lee and consisting primarily of Virginians north of the Rappahannock. Governor William Gooch decided to refer this request for advice from crown officials, influenced either by the increasing demand for trans-Allegheny grants, or perhaps by the desire to delay action because of his closer association with the rival Robinson-Randolph faction. The response from Whitehall was favorable for the Ohio Company, and confirmation of the grant was authorized for the governor and council. There resulted on July 12, 1749, the granting of over one million acres for the trans-Allegheny area to the Ohio Company and rival groups and over 17,000 acres for the counties of Lunenberg and Albemarle east of the mountains.[51] Western lands were, indeed, the order of the day for that meeting of the governor and council.

The membership of the Ohio Company included initially such Virginia gentlemen from the Northern Neck as Thomas Lee, Lawrence and Augustine Washington, and George Fairfax; George Washington, Governor Robert Dinwiddie, and George Mason were added later. The company also included from outside Virginia a small group of London merchants led by John Hanbury, five members from Maryland including Thomas Cresap, and Governor Arthur Dobbs of North Carolina. Both John Hanbury, a Quaker with a strong imperialist view, and Dobbs played a more prominent role in exerting their influence among British officials than frequently recognized. Thomas Nelson, originally a member of the Ohio Company although not from the Northern Neck, later withdrew and was more active with rival groups.

The grant to the Ohio Company provided 200,000 acres along both sides of the Ohio River between the Monongahela and Great Kanawha. The company was to construct a fort near the Forks of the Ohio and to settle 100 families within seven years. When this was accomplished, the company would be eligible for an additional 300,000 acres in adjacent areas. The crown authorized the exemption of quitrents and land rights for ten years, and after ten years the quitrents would be imposed only upon cultivated lands. One of the distinguishing characteristics of the Ohio Company grant was its concern for the settlement of families. Christopher Gist, a well educated surveyor, made several explorations from 1750 to 1752 in behalf of the company, and its activities were directly involved in the challenge to the French that later brought the opening shots of the French and Indian War.[52]

The Loyal Land Company, representing a rival group of Virginians, received, on the same day of the grant to the Ohio Company, 800,000 acres

Dr. Thomas Walker's log cabin northwest of Cumberland Gap, 1750. Reconstruction of Dr. Thomas Walker's log cabin at the site where he and his companions constructed this pioneer building in 1750 after entering present-day Kentucky through Cumberland Gap. The site is now a part of the Dr. Thomas Walker State Park six miles from Barbourville. (Photograph courtesy of the Kentucky Department of Public Information, Frankfort, Kentucky.)

that were approved by the governor and council without a petition having been submitted to the crown. Designed more for speculation than for the family settlement policy of the Ohio Company, the grant did not include the special exemption from the payment of land rights and quitrents. Its lands were to be laid out in one or more surveys along the boundary between Virginia and North Carolina, extending to the west and north.

Membership in the Loyal Land Company was largely restricted to Virginians. Much of its membership was in Albemarle County, although other sections of Virginia were represented. Dr. Thomas Walker, Peter Jefferson, and Joshua Fry provided leadership from Albemarle County, while John Lewis came from the Shenandoah Valley and Edmund Pendleton from tidewater. Joshua Fry, who had vacated his professorship of mathematics at the College of William and Mary for the fortunes of the frontier, joined with Peter Jefferson of Shadwell to produce the valuable Fry and Jefferson Map of

1751. Dr. Thomas Walker's explorations and land interests have been more vividly impressed upon the pages of history than his efforts in medicine, although one recent scholar has described him as "one of the foremost physicians in the country."[53] Coming by marriage into possession of Castle Hill in present Albemarle County, Walker maintained his residence there. As agent for the Loyal Land Company, he was its most active member and trekked through Cumberland Gap into present Kentucky with four other explorers in 1750. This party constructed the first cabin by whites in the area of Kentucky, and it was listed by John Mitchell on his famous map of 1755 as "the extent of the English settlements 1750." The advance of the Loyal Land Company proved to be a less direct challenge to the French than that of the Ohio Company, but both companies were thwarted in their efforts by the renewal of the Anglo-French clash in the 1750s.

8

Foreign Protestants in the Carolinas and Georgia: South Carolina Townships in Middle and Back Country, 1720s–1760s

The 1720s were a decade of transition for the Carolinas. South Carolina had at musket's point pushed aside the proprietary governor in transition to royal control in 1719, but not until 1729 did the negotiations of the crown end proprietary rule for both Carolinas. South Carolinians resolutely pushed settlement beyond the tidewater or low country, while North Carolina's extension was more sporadic as its western settlers groped their way to and beyond the fall line along river valleys to form an irregular patchwork of protruding fingers of settlement.

South Carolina was confronted during the period with two major challenges. Spanish and French settlements to the south and southwest instigated unrest among Indians closer to Carolina settlements. Within the colony a balance between white settler and black slave was necessary as a precaution against possible devastation from servile insurrection.

Both challenges served as a background for the plan for frontier townships advanced by the new governor Robert Johnson, appointed in 1729. Governor Johnson came to grips immediately with the problems in increasing white immigrants and providing strategic defense posts that would encircle the colony. There were several possible influences on the details of the plan. It bore some similarity to the proposal in Virginia for "societyes of men" to cohabit the frontier, an idea that was set forth in 1701 while Francis Nicholson was governor in the Old Dominion before serving in South Carolina from 1721 to 1724. The instructions of the Board of Trade recognized the effectiveness of the township system in New England for an orderly expansion. Johnson's plan probably reflects more directly the thinking of Colonel John Barnwell and his recommendation for forts. There was also some similarity to the action of the South Carolina Assembly in 1716 in providing new colonists for the abandoned Yamassee lands.[1]

Johnson's "Scheem . . . for Settling Townships" was one of the most elaborate expounded for the southern colonial frontier and one of the most important because of the efforts made to implement it. Johnson proposed to the Board of Trade establishment of ten frontier townships; the board, in turn,

162

authorized eleven. They incorporated Johnson's major suggestions, but they altered them by projecting two settlements along the Altamaha River in the zone of Anglo-Spanish jurisdiction. The other townships advocated by the board were two on the Savannah River; two on the Santee; one each on the Wateree, Black, Peedee, Waccamaw, and the head of the Pon Pon. Twenty thousand acres were to be laid out along the river with land being distributed to each grantee at the rate of fifty acres for each individual in the family. An area of six miles around the township was reserved for expansion. The grantees would also be entitled to use of the 300 acres to be set aside as a "Common in perpetuity" as well as the "right of Common and Herbage" for other land not taken up. For administrative organization each township, when having 100 householders, was to constitute a parish and have two representatives in the Assembly. The board instructed Johnson to urge the Assembly to provide both a land grant of fifty acres and the exemption from quitrents for ten years for white servants at the end of their tenure of servitude, a measure prompted by concern over racial balance.[2]

Establishing new settlements and bringing in additional immigrants were, indeed, worthy goals; they were also expensive. The offer of free land attracted both the sponsors of settlement as well as the immigrants themselves, but it was not enough to assure success in these schemes. After discussion by both imperial and colonial officials of several alternatives for providing financial assistance, the South Carolina Assembly authorized expenditures for laying out townships, purchasing tools for immigrants, and assisting in the payment of passage for new colonists.[3] The way was thus cleared for aid to new settlements, but the extent to which this was forthcoming varied with the nature of the protection that the new areas would provide for the colony.

Nine townships under Johnson's plan were actually started on the South Carolina frontier. The two that were to go as far south as the Altamaha came within the area that would later be a part of Georgia and were never established as a part of Carolina. All of the nine formed a part of South Carolina that can be identified as middle country, a section covering the interior of the tidewater or low country and extending over the fall line and dotted with sand hills. Eastward along the Atlantic coast in the low country was an area of pine and oak tress interspersed among the swamps festooned with Spanish moss and known as the lower pine belt. More inviting to the early settlers was the upper pine belt in the middle country. Featuring also pine and oak trees but with fewer swamps and a rich sandy soil, the inland area could be easily cultivated. Beyond the sand hills and fall line to the west and northwest was the back country or piedmont, which has also been called up country. The townships in the middle country may be divided into eastern and western. Reaching from north to south and forming an arc that extended beyond the established areas near Charles Town, the eastern townships

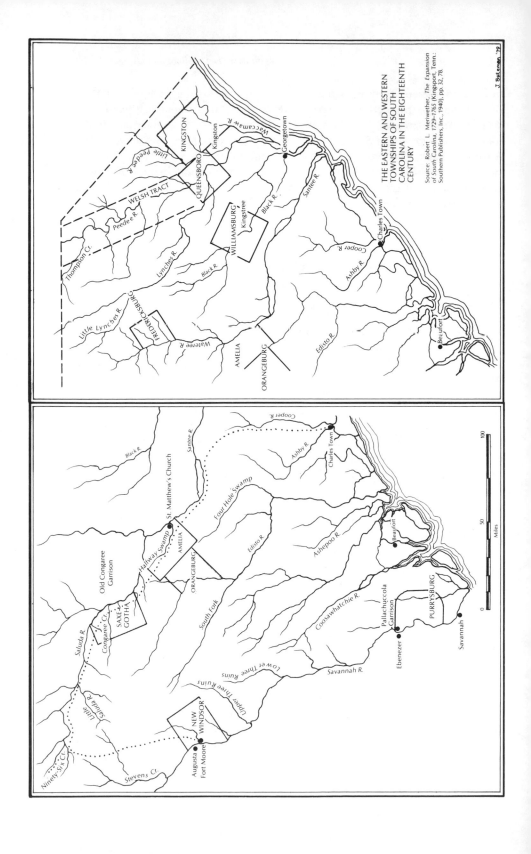

THE EASTERN AND WESTERN
TOWNSHIPS OF SOUTH
CAROLINA IN THE EIGHTEENTH
CENTURY

Source: Robert L. Meriwether, *The Expansion
of South Carolina, 1729–1765* (Kingsport, Tenn.:
Southern Publishers, Inc., 1940), pp. 32, 78.

J. Bateman '79

included Williamsburg, Kingston, Queensboro, and Fredericksburg; the western settlements were Amelia, Orangeburg, Saxe Gotha, New Windsor, and Purrysburg, the last one curving sharply toward the coast in the south.[4]

Williamsburg with its dominant Scots-Irish settlers has been appraised as the most successful of all the townships. Attracted by the bounty provided by the colony, the Scots-Irish came to Charles Town and were directed into the eastern sector of the middle country along the Black River, where their land was surveyed in 1732. Their experience of adjustment was probably typical of many of the newcomers of the time, for they "put up temporary huts of poles covered with earth, while they made a beginning of clearing and planting the land."[5] There, as in other areas, the new immigrants were unable to block out an entire section for themselves, even though many desired this, for the demands of other interested settlers and particularly land speculators foiled the fulfillment of the precise ratio of *bona fide* settlers to land granted. Williamsburg had a total white population of about 500 by the end of 1737; over half of the land granted from 1734 to 1737, however, went to nonresidents of the township in grants averaging about 550 acres. The grants of some 315 residents that can be clearly identified were only about 300 acres in size. But during subsequent years the area did not become one of frantic speculation, for many of the nonresident holders were interested in the area "for planting or investment."

Cattle raising had existed prior to the founding of the township, but it was curtailed in the interest of growing crops such as corn, rice, hemp, flax, and eventually indigo, which led Henry Laurens to claim in 1755 that Williamsburg produced "the best Indigo."[6] Certainly indigo was responsible for the healthy increase in the settlers' profits.

The cultural pattern of the township was shaped by the strong Scots-Irish heritage and the influence of the Presbyterian Church. The church as the social and cultural center inculcated a strict moral code and displayed the interest of the Scots-Irish for education. Their application in 1739 for the organization of a parish that would have brought an Anglican Church to the area is somewhat surprising, unless one considers that this could have been done mainly at the expense of the colony and would have cleared the way for representation in the lower house of the Assembly as provided in the plans for townships. Although approved in the lower house, the provision for a parish never cleared the Assembly, and the Williamsburg residents affiliated either with Prince Frederick's Parish, or after 1757 with St. Mark's.

Fredericksburg, authorized in 1733, pushed inland beyond Williamsburg to serve as a midpoint between the back country and the coastal area as well as to stabilize the country along the Wateree River claimed by the Catawba Indians. The Wateree Indians had lived with the Catawba following the Yamassee War.[7] The center of the township was selected by the surveyor at the confluence of Pinetree Creek and the Wateree, and about 1758 the settlement of the present area of Camden was started as a trading store. Support by the Assembly with bounty provisions was irregular, although some settlers apparently had the ten-year exemption from quitrents, probably from Scots-Irish immigrants who were a part of the migration that founded Williamsburg. Quakers and other Protestants from Ireland came in the early 1750s, receiving land with bounties for their settlement. The pattern of settlement reflected the distinction between the small farmer of the piedmont and the planter with slaves from the low country, with the small farmer concentrating in the northern or upper portion. The large planters were in tracts along the river bottoms, including more fertile soil as well as more swampy ground. By 1759 there was a population of about 900 in both Fredericksburg and the west side of the Wateree.[8] The area clearly revealed the ambivalent nature of settlement between low country and piedmont.

Kingston was a northwestern township near the North Carolina boundary that had little success and is not well recorded in the records of the colony. Originally designated to include both sides of the Waccamaw River, it was in 1773, at the instigation of the lower house, restricted to the north bank of the Waccamaw. The identity of the early inhabitants is difficult to establish, although it is evident that there were some Scots-Irish, perhaps an overflow from Williamsburg; it does seem clear, however, that land grabbing of tracts of over 500 acres of nonresidents was very prevalent. By 1757 there was a population of about 400, including a white milita of eighty-six men and fifty-seven male slaves between the ages of sixteen and sixty. As a frontier township it failed to get vigorous support from the Assembly because its location and proximity to North Carolina contributed little to the security of exposed areas of South Carolina[9]

Queensboro was adjacent to Kingston to the southwest and lay astride the Peedee River with an area reserved for the focal point of the township on the west bank near the confluence of the Lynches River. Like Kingston, the early settlement did not follow the pattern laid down in the program for townships. A request from James Gordon for aid to bring in 100 families was not honored by the Assembly because the need for stimulating the northern townships did not appear urgent. The Assembly did provide a partial bounty of eight bushels of corn and a peck of salt for each newcomer. Fragmentary records make the lines of development difficult to follow, but it is apparent that in the absence of a major importation of settlers directly from Europe the planters seeking substantial land grants entered the picture as in other townships.[10]

An area carved from Queensboro and known as the Welsh Tract, although not officially a township, did receive support from the Assembly and proved to be more successful in stimulating settlement than some of the official townships. The Welsh Baptists, from the area of the present state of Delaware, originally requested land in the Peedee Valley, including 10,000 acres in the northeastern part of Queensboro township with the addition of land upstream along the Peedee. Responding more generously than for townships such as Queensboro, the Assembly authorized £859 "as a bounty for the first two hundred settlers over twelve years of age who should come from Wales,"[11] and provided for each family six bushels of corn and a bushel of salt in 1737. Although few settlers apparently came directly from Wales, the population was about 500 in the Welsh Tract by 1745, about half of them being Welsh and occupying the area already known as the Welsh Neck.[12] The preference given Welshmen ended by 1745, and settlement continued with the arrival of a number of planters owning large estates; by 1757 there were about 3000 whites and 300 Negroes in the Welsh Tract proper.[13]

Originally the prospective Welsh settlers emphasized their interest in producing hemp, flax, and grain, and they had notable success in their economic endeavors. They responded promptly to a bounty offer from the governor and council of South Carolina in 1743 and received the special remuneration of fourteen shillings per barrel for the first twenty "of good and merchantable white flower." Like Williamsburg, the Welsh Tract settlers also had success with the production of indigo.

The five western townships were in more exposed positions and provided more frequent contact with Indian tribes in proximity to South Carolina than did the eastern townships. There was also a greater concentration of settlers primarily from Germany and Switzerland, while in contrast the eastern townships contained more immigrants from the British Isles, particularly the Scots-Irish. This ethnic difference was in part designed by the Assembly to encourage the success of the settlements, and in part resulted from new settlers with similar backgrounds being attracted to areas where others had preceded them.

Jean Pierre Purry, Swiss promoter of colonization and a native of Neuchâtel, was the mastermind as well as the namesake of the western township of Purrysburg. His so-called scientific calculations convinced him that the area along the thirty-third parallel provided the most desirable climate for living and therefore was the location in which colonization should be encouraged around the world. Pamphlets presenting this theory were published in the Netherlands in 1718, but Purry met with little encouragement from either the Dutch or the French. He then turned to the English with a *Memorial presented to his Grace the Duke of Newcastle*,[14] printed in 1724, in which he proposed to colonize some 600 Swiss in Carolina. Urging again the desirability of the area of the thirty-third parallel, Purry enumerated the blessings of the general area from Carolina to Florida. His agreement with the Carolina proprietors in 1724 to bring 600 Swiss to Carolina in return for 24,000 acres of land was not carried out. The proprietors modified the original terms thereby causing abandonment of the plan even though over 100 Swiss had already assembled for migration in Neuchâtel.

Purry persevered, though, and made a subsequent agreement with the crown in 1730 by which he was to receive 48,000 acres of land free of quitrents for ten years. The site of the settlement was selected along Yamassee Bluffs in the township of Purrysburg, providing protection for the lower Savannah River area and receiving the endorsement of Governor Robert Johnson for his township pattern of defense. Purry fulfilled his part of the bargain to bring 600 Swiss, and by 1736 he had received about 20,000 acres of the 48,000 promised. After his death, his son Charles petitioned in 1738 for the remainder of the land; although the grant was approved in the colony, apparently possession of the personal tract was never completed.[15]

Switzers arrived in such numbers that there were nearly 300 in Purrysburg by the beginning of 1734; an equally large group came in November of the same year. Arms including a cannon were provided to fortify the area and permitted the Assembly to abandon in 1735 the Palachacola garrison, which had previously provided protection. The early economic enterprises of the Switzers included experiments with silk culture, the growing of olives, and the production of wine; but most of the settlers soon turned primarily to agriculture and the raising of cattle. The first decade witnessed small land grants averaging about 150 acres worked mainly by free or indentured white labor. As the number of slaves increased, there was a clear change "from a frontier town of white laborers, free and indented, to a South Carolina parish dominated by slave labor."[16] The township and the area north of it formerly in St. Helen's Parish was organized into the parish of St. Peter in 1747 and authorized one member in the lower house of the Assembly. The church or chapel became the parish church.[17] Purrysburg proved to be one of the most valuable of the townships, providing a stronghold in the defense pattern of the colony. Its importance, however, was greatest in the middle of the eighteenth century, and it later declined when support was given to the development of Savannah in Georgia.

Along the Cherokee Path was the township of Amelia, which was located on the Congaree-Santee River and south of the mouth of the Wateree in the upper pine belt. Before its authorization, individual settlers such as Charles Russell entered the area as early as 1725 following his term as military commander of the Congarees. There was little active direction on the part of the Assembly in settling the area, probably since the problem of protection seemed less critical with settlers such as Russell already there. By 1757 population had reached approximately 750, including in this total some 100 slaves.[18] In general, the pattern of settlement reflected the infiltration of planters whose society resembled more the coastal plain than the piedmont.

Orangeburg was located just south of Amelia along the North Fork of the Edisto River and followed closely the spirit of the township plan by consisting mainly of foreign Protestants as bounty immigrants. To the township in 1735 came over 200 German-Swiss. By 1759 the continued migration and natural increase had pushed the population of Orangeburg to approximately 800. The terrain of the township contained mainly good soil with a "sandy loam," which was characteristic of the upper pine belt adjacent to the piedmont; only the southern part of the township extended to the swamps that spread over the lower pine belt and contributed for many years to the lack of roads, bridges, and convenient communication with Charles Town. Much emphasis was placed upon the production of cattle and grain, particularly wheat. Two other important characteristics of the township may be noted. First, landholding was mainly by residents in small tracts as contrasted to some of the townships where land speculators and large planters entered. The socioeconomic pattern was, therefore, one primarily of the small farmer with almost no black slaves. Second, the make-up of the population was predominantly German-Swiss, but the cultural chauvinism often associated with German immigrants gave way to some social and cultural intermingling.[19] With religious affiliation mainly as Presbyterians or Anglicans, the church records that are extant reveal there were at least twenty mixed marriages of German and English during a period of two decades and many examples of a family of one ethnic group serving as sponsor for a family of the other group in the sacrament of baptism.[20]

Reaching farther to the west and located on the Cherokee Path near the home of the Catawba Indians, the township designated in 1733 for the Congarees or Saxe Gotha was to serve for a time as a strategic point in the colony's defense as well as a crucible for the blending of German and English settlers. From 1716 to 1722 there had been a garrison at the Congarees, located on the western bank of the Congaree River about five miles downstream from the mouth of the Saluda River. The town later called Saxe Gotha was planted just above the garrison and extended along the river front. To this area came German-Swiss supported by the colony's bounty system in 1735. Land plats reveal grants also to a number of English in the settlement, and by 1748 the total population had reached slightly over 200.[21]

Saxe Gotha and the Congarees served as an important center of Indian trade with the Catawba and Cherokee, and the colony established both a palisaded fort and a patrol of rangers during a period of Indian troubles during the late 1740s. The area also produced wheat, some hemp and flax, hogs, cattle, and there are references to sheep by 1760. Like New Windsor, Saxe Gotha was in the most extreme western position of townships and was, therefore, subject to greater intermingling of the white and Indian civilization of the time.

New Windsor was placed along the eastern bank of the Savannah River opposite present Augusta, Georgia, and served as a post on the trading path to the Creeks, Choctaw, and Chickasaw. The township contained Fort Moore and extended from the confluence of Town Creek and the Savannah River upstream to some seven miles beyond the fort. In response to South Carolina's offer to supply "the settlers with food, tools and cattle, and furnishing lands free of all surveying charges and other fees," the Reverend Batholomew Zouberbuhler brought over in 1736–37 the first group of 192 Swiss, including fifty families, for New Windsor.[22]

To the vicinity of Fort Moore had come, probably during the 1720s, a band of Chickasaw, split from the main tribe farther west. They remained in the area for fifty years. Coming at the invitation of the colony of South Carolina and given a reserved tract of 21,774 acres after the Yamassee War, the Chickasaw under the Squirrel King at times proved an irritant with minor thievery, but more often as English allies they added to the protection of the southwestern frontier. Their presence no doubt enlivened the fort from time to time. Captain Daniel Pepper reported in 1742 that the

> Squirrel King and Mingo Stoby and the rest of the Cheekesaws with their wives came in with the War hoop from Frederica, and brought several Sculps to this garrison which they saluted by the discharge of their Guns and three huraas which I returned with my Cannon.
>
> On this particular occasion I knew they expected it, therefore provided a sufficient quantity of Victuals and Drink for them which has always been customary and with which they seemed well satisfied.[23]

From this survey of the townships planted by South Carolina, several observations or conclusions for frontier development may be noted. The encouragement that was given to the immigration of foreign Protestants definitely stimulated settlement and growth of some of the areas selected. There was not, however, always sufficient money available; yet despite the variations in amount and use from year to year, the overall total in the settlement fund was impressive. From its inception in the 1730s to 1765, there was a total of £60,000 available to stimulate settlement, and an indirect bonus was the exemption of immigrants from quitrents and taxes.

The success of the selections of locations for townships for the purpose of defense and economic growth varied. Settlements such as Purrysburg, Saxe Gotha, and New Windsor met a critical need for the time they were established, although the future growth of the colony of Georgia made both Purrysburg and New Windsor less vital by the 1760s. The location of Kingston near the North Carolina boundary proved to be less valuable for the colony, and the pragmatic Assembly, therefore, did not give the financial support to this township that was originally anticipated. There was also the problem of the development of areas not well equipped by nature for easy growth. Again the Assembly was practical and provided support for settlers in the Welsh Tract who were willing to develop the fertile land, although it was not one of the official townships. The Welsh Tract flourished. Natural advantages, then, were as important for the growth of the settlement as was the artificial stimulus provided by the Assembly.

The township planning did, on balance, give a substantial boost to populating the middle country and provided opportunities that were not readily available for the migration of foreign Protestants. This migration increased the ethnic variety of Carolina population and contributed to successful settlements such as Williamsburg with the influence of the Scots-Irish and Orangesburg with the German-Swiss. In general, foreign Protestants such as the Germans and German-Swiss were welcomed, although there were unsuccessful efforts of the Commons House to restrict the use of the settlement funds to immigrants from the British Isles during the early 1750s.

The balance of whites and blacks sought in the original plans for settlement was only partially achieved. In 1729 before the township plan was started, South Carolina had a total population of approximately 30,000, one-third white and two-thirds black.[24] By 1740 the population had nearly doubled to 59,000, including 20,000 whites and 39,000 blacks;[25] and by 1759 there was a further increase to 91,000 with a division of 36,000 whites and 55,000 Negroes.[26] While the discrepancy between the total of white and Negro settlers was still of great concern to Carolinians, there was some reduction in the overall ratio of one to two that existed before the township plan was implemented. For the tidewater area, however, the ratio had worsened. The encouragement to immigrants was one of the contributing factors to the ratio of more whites than Negroes in the middle and back country. The breakdown of population statistics reveals approximately 19,000 whites and 53,500 Negroes for tidewater; 10,400 whites and 2200 Negroes for the townships and the middle country; and 7000 whites and 300 slaves for the back country.

The back country or piedmont beyond the fall line developed mainly along the three main rivers of the Saluda, the Catawba-Wateree, and the Broad. The first two of these deserve special mention. In the area along the Saluda, settlement began during the late 1740s and the early 1750s around Saluda Old Town and Ninety-Six in the region sometimes identified as the "Northwest Frontier." This "Northwest Frontier" also encompassed the land reaching down to the Savannah River along both Long Cane and Stevens creeks, which empty into the Savannah. There was some interest in land speculation on this frontier, and by 1763 South Carolina was continuing in a limited way the establishment of townships and the encouragement of settlement by bounty.

The expansion of South Carolina involved the land speculator less than for Virginia and Maryland. The Board of Trade initially declined to support the petition of John Hamilton of London in 1737 for 200,000 acres planned for 1000 families. Four years later it did influence the crown to authorize the same amount of land for 1000 individuals, which stipulated only one white settler for 200 acres, to be settled in ten years by William Livingston and others. But there was inadequate support for the project, and Livingston's

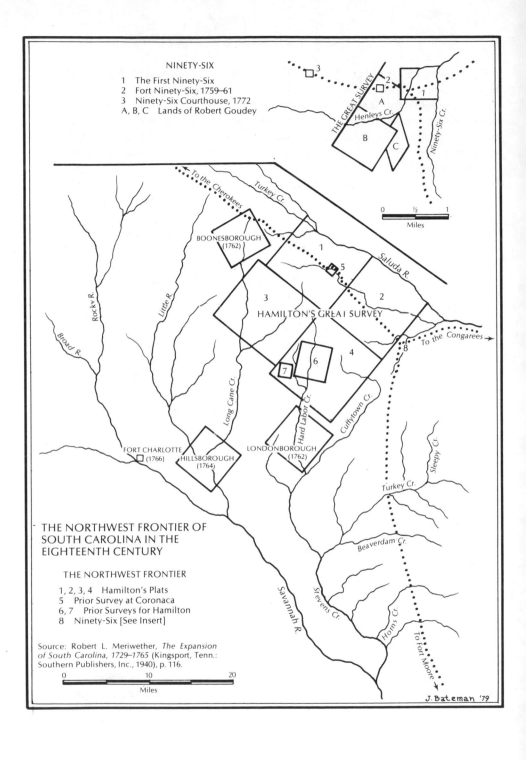

NINETY-SIX

1   The First Ninety-Six
2   Fort Ninety-Six, 1759–61
3   Ninety-Six Courthouse, 1772
A, B, C   Lands of Robert Goudey

THE GREAT SURVEY

Henleys Cr.

Ninety-Six Cr.

A

B

C

3

2

1

0   ½   1
Miles

To the Cherokees

Turkey Cr.

BOONESBOROUGH
(1762)

Saluda R.

1

5

Rocky R.

Little R.

3

2

HAMILTON'S GREAT SURVEY

Broad R.

8

To the Congarees

6

4

7

Long Cane Cr.

Hard Labor Cr.

Cuffytown Cr.

Sleepy Cr.

FORT CHARLOTTE
(1766)

HILLSBOROUGH
(1764)

LONDONBOROUGH
(1762)

Turkey Cr.

Beaverdam Cr.

Savannah R.

Stevens Cr.

Horn's Cr.

To Fort Moore

THE NORTHWEST FRONTIER OF
SOUTH CAROLINA IN THE
EIGHTEENTH CENTURY

THE NORTHWEST FRONTIER

1, 2, 3, 4   Hamilton's Plats
5   Prior Survey at Coronaca
6, 7   Prior Surveys for Hamilton
8   Ninety-Six [See Insert]

Source: Robert L. Meriwether, *The Expansion
of South Carolina, 1729–1765* (Kingsport, Tenn.:
Southern Publishers, Inc., 1940), p. 116.

0   10   20
Miles

J. Bateman '79

grant was turned over to John Hamilton in 1749.[27] Transporting over fifty people to South Carolina in 1751, he acquired "Hamilton's Great Survey" of 200,000 acres, lying along the south side of the Saluda River and reaching toward the Savannah.[28] Part of the tract was purchased by other speculators, but none of them seemed to have parcelled out their land in sales comparable to that in the valley of Virginia.

Continuing its interest in promoting white settlement and finding less use of the settlement fund because of Indian troubles, the Assembly in 1761 authorized more liberal support to immigrants, including increased amounts for transportation and renewing the exemption for ten years of quitrents and taxes. Two additional townships were established near "Hamilton's Great Survey": Boonesborough, consisting of 20,500 acres on Long Cane Creek, and Londonborough or Belfast of 22,000 acres along Hard Labor Creek. A third township, Hillsborough, was provided in 1764 with 28,000 acres near Londonborough for French Huguenots coming to the colony.[29] South Carolina thus continued during the 1760s to assist the migration of immigrants, including foreign Protestants, but the use of townships was much less extensive than Governor Robert Johnson's schemes of the 1730s.

For the second major area of the back country, settlement in the Upper Watcree un such tributaries as Waxhaw Creek and Cane Creek brought in a number of Scots-Irish. They had to confront, in addition to the usual rigors of frontier settlement, the long controversey over the boundary between North and South Carolina. Going back as far as the official separation of the two colonies in 1729, there was an ongoing debate involving the Board of Trade and both colonies over the question of whether or not the division of the two colonies should follow the course of the Cape Fear River or the Waccamaw River. The issue was not resolved until the 1770s, and complications of the disputes persist today with both North and South Carolina having conflicting markers for the exact birthplace of Andrew Jackson. Despite the uncertainties of land title created by this dispute, the area of the Upper Wateree had an estimated total population of 800 by 1760 and was stable enough for its religious organization "to make the Waxhaws the Presbyterian center of the South Carolina back country."[30]

Attention to immigration of foreign Protestants directly from Europe should not obscure the fact that the greater number of settlers in South Carolina expansion to the middle and back countries came either from the established areas in tidewater or from other colonies to the north. For the middle country the best analysis that has been made estimates from one-fourth to one-third of the white population migrating from tidewater South Carolina, while perhaps an equal number moved south from Virginia. In the back country, Virginia provided the largest group of settlers; other colonies such as Pennsylvania, Maryland, New Jersey, and North Carolina were next in number; and South Carolinians supplied the smallest group. Part of the local South Carolina migration included the movement of first or second generations of foreign Protestants who had originially settled townships such as Purrysburg but later preferred the higher ground of the piedmont over the swampy areas of the townships that bordered on tidewater.[31]

The push of settlement into the back country did not alter the sound economic base of the coast. Tidewater South Carolina had by that time pinned its prosperity on the production of rice and indigo. The cultivation of rice was centered primarily in the swampy areas of the low country, and by the middle of the eighteenth century it was South Carolina's most valuable crop, having recovered from the disruption of trade during the wars of the 1740s. Indigo, which had been tried as early as the seventeenth century, experienced a significant revival through the experiments of Eliza Lucas in the 1740s and through the stimulation of bounties, first by the province of South Carolina from 1744 to 1746 and then by the British Parliament beginning in 1748. For the year extending from March 25, 1749–50, exports from Charles Town increased to 138,299 pounds, but declined sharply for the next few years partly through the emphasis upon high-priced rice. The beginning of the French and Indian War in the 1750s revived the indigo exports and caused them to soar as high as 876,393 pounds for 1757–58, enhanced by the decline of West Indian competition.[32] While indigo was most extensively grown in the low country, it was planted in the middle country in the 1740s in such areas as Williamsburg, Queensboro, and the Welsh Tract, and it was also suitable for the back country but did not develop there until the 1760s.

In the middle and back country, corn was the most important food product followed closely by wheat, both of which were marketed mainly on a local scale. Rye, barley, and oats were also raised on a limited basis as were flax and hemp, and again primarily for local consumption. Indian trade, particularly in deerskins, engaged a number of settlers; at some of the trading centers or along the trading routes such as the Cherokee Path, food and other essentials were available to both whites and Indians who passed. A few cattle and hogs were also found in most frontier areas, but for South Carolina cattle raising with its cowpens deserves a brief analysis to determine its role in the agricultural economy and to identify its place in the historiography of the frontier.

The cattle raiser is included in that familiar suggestion of the "successive waves" of migration:

> Stand at Cumberland Gap and watch the procession of civilization, marching single file—the buffalo following the trail to the salt springs, the Indian, the fur-trader and hunter, the cattleraiser, the pioneer farmer—and the frontier has passed by.[33]

For the Carolina back country after the Tuscarora and Yamassee wars, the statement has also been made that the Carolina cattle raisers had the same opportunities as Virginians who "followed the fur-traders and erected scattered 'cow-pens' or ranches beyond the line of plantations in the Piedmont."[34] There are enough examples gleaned from the *South Carolina Gazette* to show that a few cattle raisers did precede the small farmer in the northern and eastern section of the colony of South Carolina, extending from the Santee River to the north and from the coast westward to the piedmont.[35] They were, for example, ordered by colonial officials to vacate the area of the township set aside for Williamsburg.[36]

Few contemporary descriptions of the cowpens have survived, but there are enough references to suggest a variety of arrangements. First, there might be a stationary location with crude housing for the cowpen keeper and an enclosed area clearly outlined by constructed fences or natural features; second, it might be a transient boundary with temporary enclosures for marking that could be easily shifted by cowkeepers on horseback. The isolation of the frontier deprived some of the cowkeepers of social and cultural contacts and contributed to the unfavorable descriptions that exist. Some were declared in the eighteenth century as guilty of "prophanation of the Lord's Day," and one was termed "a very mean and inconsiderable man."[37] But William Bartram provided a more favorable view by noting that they were "civil and courteous, and though educated as it were in the woods, no strangers to sensibility and those moral virtues which grace and ornament the most approved and admired characters in civil society."[38]

The South Carolina back country or piedmont had grasslands and rolling country with sufficient streams for watering, but apparently the problem of marketing seriously impeded the growth of cattle raising beyond the level of local subsistence. Only in the Saluda River Valley did cattle raising become a commercial venture prior to 1763, and its growth was made possible by the lines of communication along the Cherokee trail to and from Ninety-Six, providing a limited outlet to Charles Town. The distance, however, was so great that driving cattle on foot was discouraged, and barreling was impeded by the need for salt and for water transportation. Hides were tanned and sold, and butter was preserved with limited amounts of salt and saltpetre. Cattle holding, as revealed in some fifty property inventories of the back and middle country, was limited to six registrants with herds as large as one hundred. The back country had only one of these six.[39]

Cattle raising on a large scale and the existence of a significant number of cowpens were more characteristic of the low country than the frontier. A number of cattle growers remained close to Charles Town and benefited by the proximity to its markets. In 1741, for example, the *Gazette* noted the sale of 400 cattle by Thomas Drayton near Pon Pon, and a total of 500 to 1000 from the estate of Robert Beath near Dorchester.[40] A second concentration of cattle raising along the Edisto River included Orangeburg and other areas of cane swamps and dense foliage. The Edisto River between the north and south forks had limited grazing areas and transportation to market was often troublesome; cattle raising, nonetheless, continued. In 1742, for example, some 600 cattle were offered for sale by William Fuller at the Forks of the Edisto.[41] The third area of cattle raising had more grazing land south of the Edisto River to the Savannah River along the Salkehatchie and Coosawhatchie rivers, running occasionally up to 1000 acres. In 1736, just west of the Combahee River, some 300 cattle were noted, and Purrysburg had sales of 500 cattle in 1741.[42] Commercial cattle raising, then, was an adjunct to the staple producing plantations in the low country rather than on the edge of frontier settlements.

While South Carolinians were extending their settlements far into the interior, North Carolina experienced a similar era of growth after its transformation to a royal colony in 1729. This expansion, however, occurred in a more erratic pattern and with less prior planning than the township plan of South Carolina. As in both Virginia and South Carolina, the migration of the Scots-Irish and Germans accounted for much of the population increase. Their advance into the interior tended to transcend colonial boundaries both in cultural contacts and in economic activities where trade followed geographic lines rather than political boundaries.

By 1729 the 30,000 to 35,000 residents of North Carolina were found in two major areas of settlements.[43] The first extended from the Virginia border along both Albemarle and Pamlico sounds and clustered along the streams that flowed in a southeasterly direction. Settlements along Pamlico River had resulted in the creation of Bath in 1704 as the first town in the colony. The peopling of the Neuse and Trent river valleys included the German Palatines and Swiss settlers along with a few English and had resulted in the founding of the town of New Bern in 1710. The second major cluster of settlements had pushed northwestward from the coast along the Cape Fear River and had established the town of Brunswick about 1725 in the Lower Cape Fear with the addition of Wilmington a few miles upstream about 1733. Both Brunswick and Wilmington were a part of the Port of Brunswick that became the only major focal point of shipment that the colony could offer for frontier trade.

The significant increase in North Carolina population to 80,000 by 1755 constituted filling in the tidewater region as well as the gradual extension to the piedmont. By 1740, a few families settled in the piedmont along the Eno and Haw rivers and before the end of the decade other families moved west of the Yadkin River. Granville County was organized as the first county in the piedmont in 1746.[44] Some encouragement to immigrants was given by the efforts of Arthur Dobbs (later governor), Henry McCulloh, and others who obtained a grant of over a million acres in 1737 on the Yadkin, Catawba, and

Eno rivers for the purposes of bringing in Protestant families from Europe with the stipulation that over 3000 be settled. While their efforts fell short of the goal, they did assist over 800 immigrants by the early 1750s. Even more important as a source of population influx was the steady stream of newcomers present by the 1750s. These immigrants found their way to new homes mainly over the Great Wagon Road from the valley of Virginia, although some came by way of inland treks from Carolina ports such as Charles Town to uninhabited frontier areas. From present Roanoke, Virginia, the Great Wagon Road came through the water gap of the Blue Ridge and southward to the present area of Winston-Salem. German Moravians began their settlements there in 1753. Other settlers, particularly Scots-Irish, continued southward to present Salisbury which led to the organization of the county of Rowan in 1753 and the official establishment of the town two years later.[45] Salisbury was described by Governor Dobbs in 1755 as having "the Court House built and 7 or 8 log Houses erected,"[46] and by 1762 it had expanded to "at least thirty-five homes, inns, or shops," and with "74 of the 256 original lots in the township . . . purchased."[47] By 1762 continued southward movement led to the creation of Mecklenburg County, an important center for Scots-Irish settlers in which the town of Charlotte was later established in 1768.

Contemporaneous with the beginning of Rowan County and its seat of government at Salisbury was the creation of Orange County in 1752 with its county seat of Hillsboro founded two years later.[48] Both Scots-Irish and Germans moved into the area with the Scots-Irish locating mainly in the eastern part of the county, while the Germans, mostly Lutherans, concentrated west of the Haw River. The development of Hillsboro was recorded in the "Autobiography of Col. William Few." Having moved to the frontier on the banks of the Eno River in 1758 with his father, he noted that

> In that country, at that time, there were no schools, no churches or parsons, or doctors, or lawyers; no stores, groceries or taverns, nor do I recollect to have seen during the first two years any officer, ecclesiastical, civil or military, except a justice of the peace, a constable, and two or three itinerant preachers. The justice took cognizance of the controversies to a small amount, and performed the sacerdotal functions of uniting by matrimony. There were no poor laws or paupers.[49]

By 1764 when moving near Hillsoboro, he found it

> the metropolis of the county, where the courts were held and all the public business was done. It was a small village, which contained thirty or forty inhabitants, with two or three small stores and two or three ordinary taverns, but it was an improving village. . . . A church, court-house and jail were built, but there was no parson or physician. Two or three attorneys opened their offices and found employment.

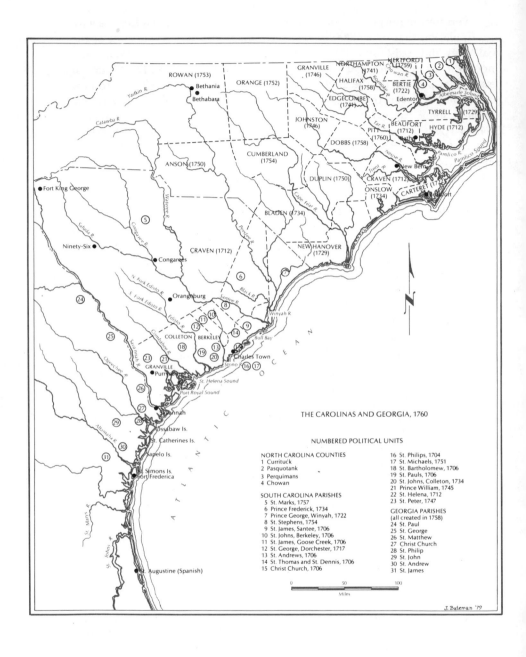

THE CAROLINAS AND GEORGIA, 1760

NUMBERED POLITICAL UNITS

NORTH CAROLINA COUNTIES
1 Currituck
2 Pasquotank
3 Perquimans
4 Chowan

SOUTH CAROLINA PARISHES
5 St. Marks, 1757
6 Prince Frederick, 1734
7 Prince George, Winyah, 1722
8 St. Stephens, 1754
9 St. James, Santee, 1706
10 St. Johns, Berkeley, 1706
11 St. James, Goose Creek, 1706
12 St. George, Dorchester, 1717
13 St. Andrews, 1706
14 St. Thomas and St. Dennis, 1706
15 Christ Church, 1706

16 St. Philips, 1704
17 St. Michaels, 1751
18 St. Bartholomew, 1706
19 St. Pauls, 1706
20 St. Johns, Colleton, 1734
21 Prince William, 1745
22 St. Helena, 1712
23 St. Peter, 1747

GEORGIA PARISHES
(all created in 1758)
24 St. Paul
25 St. George
26 St. Matthew
27 Christ Church
28 St. Philip
29 St. John
30 St. Andrew
31 St. James

0   50   100
Miles

J. Bateman '79

Superior and inferior courts of justice were established, and a fair field was opened for the lawyers.[50]

For the back country the addition and growth of small towns for trade maintained some of the connections with colonies to the north or south, and at the same time they also improved connections with the limited seaports in eastern North Carolina. For the period before 1763 there were two groups of inland towns that have been described as "midland towns," including Campbelltown, Cross Creek, Halifax, and Tarboro; and "western towns," including Hillsboro and Salisbury with the founding of Salem not coming until 1766.

Of the "midland towns," lying in the general area of the fall line, Halifax and Cross Creek were most important. Founded in 1757 on the Roanoke River some fifteen miles from the Virginia border, Halifax served as an entrepôt of trade in its location at "the limit of navigability for small craft." With connecting trade links either eastward to Edenton or northeastward to Virginia, Halifax funnelled through its trade marts the main products of the back country: wheat, Indian corn, pork, and lumber. In the area later named Fayetteville, both Cross Creek and Campbelltown were started as trading centers. Strategically located for grist mills, Cross Creek like Halifax to the north became an overland channel for products from the back country, particularly wheat, and developed vigorous trade links with Wilmington both by land and water.[51]

Salisbury and Hillsboro provided trade centers along the "Western Great Road," connecting Virginia to western Carolina over the trail that had been used for trade with the Cherokee and Catawba.[52] Although expanding slowly during their first few years, they maintained contacts in several directions. Salisbury sustained frequent transactions with South Carolina and Hillsboro with Virginia. Scottish merchants were also very active in stimulating trade connections with the back country, particularly with agents in Hillsboro. To promote trade within the colony and its seaports, the North Carolina legislature in 1755 authorized construction of a road from Hillsboro (then Orange Court House) to ports along the Cape Fear River. While North Carolina merchants were eager to reap the benefits from these additions, the implementation of the provision moved too slowly for major improvements within the period of this study.

North Carolina during the eighteenth century did not develop a staple economy in either the coastal area or the back country comparable to the Chesapeake area or the low country of South Carolina. Tobacco did continue as a money crop primarily in the northern and eastern part of the colony. More important for the back country after mid-century was the increase in the production of wheat. The piedmont also turned to wheat as a money crop, exporting through Virginia from the northern area or through South Carolina near the southern border. The intermediate region directed its products through Cross Creek at the fall line of the Cape Fear. Corn was a subsistence crop used mainly for bread, except by the Moravians who preferred wheat.

Livestock was important in both the local market as well as for export. The number of cattle or hogs was exaggerated in some of the contemporary accounts of the mid-eighteenth century, particularly those suggesting numerous herds of 1000 to 2000. Hogs and small herds of less than 100 cattle were widespread as a part of self-sufficient economy, and they were one of the most important products in trade as both cattle and hogs were driven during this period to market in South Carolina and Virginia with cattle continuing as far north as Philadelphia and New Jersey.

Many of the crops and livestock of the Carolinas were eventually introduced in the frontier colony of Georgia founded in 1732 and settled by foreign Protestants seeking new opportunities. Their social and economic experiences, however, differed from other colonies because of the unique experiment in planning in Georgia. The blueprint was conceived under the dual influence in England of humanitarian and Utopian impulses of the period and of imperialistic and mercantilistic schemes of the British ministry.

Many of the promoters of Georgia were on the Board of Trade or the Parliamentary Committee to examine jails under the chairmanship of James Edward Oglethorpe in 1729, or were the followers of Thomas Bray, who organized during the 1720s and were known after his death in 1730 as the Associates of the Late Dr. Bray.[53] Bray, commissary of the Anglican Church in Maryland, sponsored social reform through educational programs: he was an ardent proponent of parochial libraries in the colonies; in 1699 in England he launched the Society for the Propagation of Christian Knowledge (S.P.C.K.) to distribute religious books; and in 1701 he organized the Society for the Propagation of the Gospel in Foreign Parts (S.P.G.) as the mission arm of the Anglican Church to foster Negro and Indian education.[54] Bray's followers carried on his zeal for humanitarian causes, but this missionary spirit was just one influence in the founding of Georgia. The idea for a colony stemmed from a complicated series of discussions that began with Martin Bladen and Edward Ashe of the Board of Trade working with Oglethorpe's committee to investigate prisons. Oglethorpe confided his plans for a debtor colony to his friend and fellow Bray Associate, John the Viscount Percival, later the first Earl of Egmont. In 1730 the recently expanded Bray Associates applied to the king for a colony "on the south-west of Carolina for settling poor persons of London."[55] Through the contact of Bladen and Ashe the site petitioned for was coordinated with the frontier communities of South Carolina, particularly the two that were to extend to the Altamaha. The interest and influence of the Bray Associates in securing the grant was striking, for all trustees appointed in the king's charter were members.

A blend of motivations was behind the founding of the only frontier colony started in the eighteenth century. Release of imprisoned debtors and relief to the impoverished unemployed, some formerly debtors, highlighted the humanitarian ideal. The potential of the Indian trade in furs and skins and the possible economic development of the colony and its trade enlisted the mercantilists. The challenge to secure the frontier to the south and southwest against the Spanish, French, and their Indian allies appealed to the imperialists. These provisions pertained mainly to Englishmen, but the opportunities for "poor Protestants" seeking a haven from Europe extended the invitation beyond England.

The initial settlement of Georgia began with the arrival in February 1733 of the ship *Anne* with at least 114 colonists under the direction of Oglethorpe, a trustee who came to the colony and was responsible for its direct supervision during its early years. Most of the initial settlers were English, but soon to follow were other national groups who were assisted financially by the trustees. Within a year after settlement the colony contained 437 Caucasians. Out of this number, 259 were located in Savannah which was laid out according to a detailed plan for public squares, and lots for houses, gardens, and farms. The other 178 colonists started nearby settlements and were a part of the increasing number of immigrant groups in the early history of Georgia. Included in the eight or nine settlements modelled on the Savannah town plan were the French at High-Gate, Germans at Hamstead, and Scots at Joseph's Town.[56]

The social and economic ideals of the trustees were evident in their efforts to administer the colony. The twenty-one trustees were to serve without profit for twenty-one years. To discourage the growth of large plantations and provide for compact settlements for defense, land grants were limited to 500 acres per person and slavery was prohibited. As a further safeguard for this experiment, land inheritance was entailed by which property under "tail-male" could pass only to sons, not to daughters who might marry persons not in sympathy with the colony's objectives. Rum was also prohibited in hopes a sober and industrious society would emerge. Finally, representative government was not provided because colonists had little experience in politics; rather the rules set down by the trustees were the primary means of control and only three laws were passed in the two decades of the trusteeship.

The aid to immigrants in the early years of the colony came mainly in contributions to charity colonists, financed by private donations and support from Parliament to the trustees. Only a very small number of prison debtors have been identified, but charity colonists numbered 1700 to 1850 with over 1000 of these coming from Great Britain.[57] After 1738 the trustees brought over indentured servants whose service for the average of four to seven years was sold in the colony. Over 1100 of these servants were sent by the trustees during their two decades of rule with a preponderance of them being non-English. Consequently, in the first two or three decades of Georgia history a diverse number of Europeans arrived: Scots, Irish, Scots-Irish, French, Salzburgers, Moravians, other Germans, Swiss, Welsh, and a small number of Jews. Examination in greater detail of two of these, the Salzburgers and Scots, will exemplify some of the experiences and adjustments that occurred in the frontier colony of Georgia.

Thousands of Salzburgers—mostly Lutherans, suffering from religious persecution by Catholic rulers of the archbishopric-principality of Salzburg —fled in search of a better life to other parts of Europe, mainly to Prussia, Holland, and England. Two pastors in London in important court or royal chapels, Frederick Michael Ziegenhagen and Dr. Samuel Urlsberger, stimulated interest in the S.P.C.K. for aiding the oppressed Salzburgers, and the latter along with Chretien von Munch, both of the Georgia Board of Trustees, promoted interest in them as colonists to Georgia. Through the collections made by the S.P.C.K. and the initiative taken by the trustees, transportation was provided to port, particularly from Frankfurt to Rotterdam, then on to Georgia.

Seeking isolation to perpetuate their way of life, the Salzburgers were first located by Oglethorpe at a point named Ebenezer, or "the Stone of Help" in 1734. Although pleased at first with the prospects of their location, they soon discovered its shortcomings of unfertile soil and difficulty in transportation because a low creek bed was often jammed with broken logs. In 1736 they prevailed upon Oglethorpe to move them to higher ground along the Savannah River at Red Bluff, where they continued the name of their original site with New Ebenezer.[58]

In both Old and New Ebenezer the Salzburgers experienced many problems of adjustment in an exposed frontier community. There was a power struggle at Old Ebenezer in which the Reverend John Martin Bolzius sustained his influence over that of John Vatt, storekeeper and secretary of the Salzburg community, and assured the continuation of practically a theocratic domination. The settlement was subject to orders from Oglethorpe and the trustees, but their local civil administration was essentially ecclesiastical and their conduct guided to a great extent by the code or "Regulations" subscribed to as the "fundamental constitution, articles and rules" for a German Evangelical Lutheran congregation in 1733.[59]

Their housing developed along natural lines for such a community. In 1736 Old Ebenezer included "four good framed timber houses built at the expense of the trustees for the two ministers and the schoolmaster, and for a public store. A chapel and guardhouse as well as a great number of split board houses had been built by the people." The move to New Ebenezer brought new building assignments. In 1738 the population was reported to be 146, including 60 families, and the houses were described as huts constructed of clapboards and laid out in long straight rows. Two years later another report stated that Ebenezer "thrives very much; there are very good Houses built for each of the Ministers, and an Orphan House; and they have partly framed Houses, and partly Huts, neatly built, and formed into regular Streets."[60]

In economic and cultural development, the Salzburgers typify the reluctance of many immigrants to take on new ways dictated by a new environment and by association, slight though it may be, with the tenets of other cultural traditions. Initially land was held communally, but the Salzburgers obtained individual allotments in 1738. They were encouraged with their yields of corn, Indian peas, potatoes, and rough rice. Other grains were included, such as wheat and oats, and they were able to sell some of their products in Savannah. Innovation came slowly. The German settlers were reluctant to adapt to new land in the pine section, even though an experimental farm by Bolzius demonstrated its possibility. Furthermore, having used oxen and hoe in Germany, the Salzburgers were hesitant to adapt to use of the oxen with the plow, to say nothing of horses that were even more difficult to obtain. Some farmers were "just plain obstinate," lamented Bolzius, and "I cannot persuade them to break Oxen for that purpose, to which they were not used in their native Country."[61]

Two areas of economic activity—silk culture and lumber production—required the Salzburgers to adapt in order to succeed. Efforts to create in the American colonies a silk culture that would provide an adequate supply of silk for England persisted in the seventeenth and eighteenth centuries. Mulberry trees were sent to Georgia, and a bounty was provided for the production of silk. Oglethorpe passed on the trees to the Salzburgers, who for the remainder of the colonial period profited from the venture. In 1747 they sold 366 pounds of silk in Savannah, and in 1750 their efforts netted 1000 pounds of cocoons, which led Savannah to set up a filature for unwinding the silk.[62]

Lumber production became an important item with the first sawmill erected by Bolzius in 1745. After overcoming the problem of a fraudulent agent in the sale of lumber, the Salzburgers produced boards from the red pine wood that "Captains and Merchants" assured Bolzius "fetch a better Price than others."[63] While successful in use of lumber products, the Salzburgers did not develop beyond a limited experiment the production of naval stores.

Another distinct group of immigrants brought to Georgia were the Scottish Highlanders, who were placed in a highly exposed area of the frontier at New Inverness or Darien. Recruited from Scots seeking better economic opportunities and from some still suffering from participation in the Jacobite uprising of 1715, these immigrants were needed to counter the Spanish threat and were aided financially by the trustees. The trustees paid the passage of most of the 180 Scots (130 men and 50 women and children) and promised fifty acres of land to each settler. First reports from Darien were favorable, indicating that within the first two months the settlers had built a small fort to contain a battery of four cannon and some fourteen huts thatched with palmetto fronds.[64] Crops of corn, peas, and vegetables were promising until hit by rats and mice, but the industrious Scots filled in partly with the erection of a sawmill, the cutting of lumber, and cattle grazing. Servants were hard to obtain because of scarcity and high prices, yet the Scots at Darien did not sign the proslavery petition opposing the trustee policy of excluding slaves. Clan influence was still important among the Scots, but more than one was represented among the forty families. Political and military control was exercised under Oglethorpe mainly by John Mohr Mackintosh, who was commissioned a lieutenant. Even in the exercise of military authority Lt. Mackintosh had to rely upon the influence of clan leaders who were subordinate military officials.

The lofty ideals the trustees hoped to implant in Georgia were no match for the urge to benefit from the vast area of land available and the demands of the settlers to have the same opportunities as other American colonists. The restrictions upon landholding were changed in the early 1740s as the limit of individual holdings of 500 acres was raised to 2000, and "tail-male" was eliminated so daughters could then inherit land. Recognizing the commercial value of rum in the Indian trade and in sales to the colonists, the trustees relaxed enforcement of the alcohol prohibition in 1742. Slaves were brought into the colony in violation of the original restriction, and the trustees were finally pressured into repealing their antislavery law in 1750. The following year they added their final major change by calling a representative assembly of the colonists before yielding their control of Georgia to the crown as a royal colony in 1752.

The frontier conditions of Georgia throughout the period were evident from the limited growth of population both before and after the rule of the trustees. Over 2800 white colonists came to Georgia from its beginning to 1741, but by 1751 the total population was only 2300, including 1900 whites and 400 Negroes. During the next decade under royal control, population increase greatly accelerated, particularly during the years immediately preceding the American Revolution. The rapid increase in blacks resulted from lifting the slavery restriction and from expansion of plantations along the coast and on sea islands.

TABLE 5
Population Increase[6][5]

Date	Whites	Blacks	Total
1751	1900	400	2300
1753	2381	1066	3447
1760	6000	3578	9578
1773	18,000	15,000	33,000

Prior to these increases, though, the colony's attractiveness to new settlers was diminished by the continued Spanish threat, particularly during the 1740s, and by the international conflicts associated with its exposed position on the southern colonial frontier.

9

International Intrigue:
The Spanish Thrust, 1720s–1740s

In the international contest on the southern colonial frontier during the first half of the eighteenth century, the Anglo-Spanish conflict at times assumed more critical proportions than the Anglo-French, although eventually for the whole of North America the latter was more important. By the 1720s Spain was still in possession of Florida and maintained its claim northward toward Carolina in the disputed territory with the English that has been called the "Debatable Land."[1] The Treaty of Utrecht of 1713 ending the War of Spanish Succession had not altered this territorial dispute, but the victory of the English had extracted from the Spanish the *asiento*—the agreement for the British South Sea Company to take black slaves into Spanish colonies. After the treaty, France continued building its outposts on the Mississippi River and Mobile Bay. The hostility that developed in Europe between France and Spain between 1719 and 1721 over the territorial ambitions of Spanish rulers gave the French the opportunity to seize Pensacola, but the restoration of peace in 1721 returned the city to the Spanish. The British, therefore, continued to view seriously the challenge from both nations.

South Carolina pressed the British claim by the construction of more forts in strategic locations. Following the Yamassee debacle, Carolinians had completed Fort Moore at Savannah Town in 1716, a fort at Port Royal in the same year, and one at the Congarees in 1718. Included in the various recommendations submitted by John Barnwell and Joseph Boone to the Board of Trade in 1720 to counter Spanish and French claims was a suggestion for more frontier posts. They advised locations such as Palachacola Town, one in the Creek country on the Chattahoochee, and another at the mouth of the Altamaha River. They envisioned the fortifications as nuclei of frontier settlements.

The Board of Trade endorsed the whole scheme, but the Privy Council's enthusiasm was mainly for the Altamaha Fort. John Barnwell was picked to erect the fort, and he returned to South Carolina with the new royal governor, Francis Nicholson, in May 1721. With Barnwell and Nicholson came an independent company of British troops to aid in frontier fortification, the first regular troops dispatched to South Carolina. This contingent, while significant in beginning the use of such troops, fell far short of expectations and needs, for the company did not have the artisans and skilled workmen that were necessary. Barnwell, meanwhile, recruited "province scouts," and Nicholson influenced the Assembly to provide £1000 sterling for the new Altamaha Fort. Built as a temporary structure under great hardship because of the difficulty in getting material from the swampy area, Fort King George stood as a planked blockhouse on the north side of the north branch of the Altamaha. Twenty-six foot square and rising three levels high, it served as the stronghold for smaller huts encompassed in an area of some 60,000 square feet.[2] Although hardly a formidable outpost, the fort's existence raised the ire of the Spanish, who demanded its destruction; fire, however, overcame the fort rather than the Spanish. Having burned in January 1725/6, the fort was rebuilt with quarters that were even more temporary; in the fall of 1727 it was abandoned when its occupants were shifted to the stronger Port Royal.[3] Although Governor Robert Johnson urged its reoccupation with his township plan, it remained for the colony of Georgia to secure the area between the Savannah and the Altamaha.

The humanitarian impulses of the Georgia experiment were soon overshadowed by the imperialistic challenges from the Spanish. Fort King George was no longer a problem, and Anglo-Spanish trade irritants were in part alleviated by the Treaty of Seville in 1729, an agreement between Spain, England, France, and Holland relative to Spanish claims to Italian duchies. For England the treaty provided continuation of the *asiento* and a submission to a joint Anglo-Spanish commission of the English complaints of harassments by the Spanish coast guard (*guarda costas*).[4] But the boundary dispute continued, and the thrust of Georgia southward in the 1730s rekindled the hostile fires.

James Edward Oglethorpe concerned himself with the defense of his exposed colony from the beginning, and perhaps his most distinctive contributions while in America were his providing both security for Georgia, including skillful negotiations with the Indians, and the simultaneous challenge to Spain. Protecting the initial location at Yamacraw Bluffs soon after its settlement with five cannons, he continued to cultivate good relations with Tomo-Chi-Chi of the Yamacraw, a separate town of Creek Indians.[5] His reconnaissance southward in early 1734 uncovered several strategic locations for defense that were later established. Augusta, founded in 1735 at the fall line of the Savannah River, was primarily a trading post although it also was an area of defense. The Scottish Highlanders were located at New Inverness or Darien along the south bank of the Altamaha near its mouth where the settlement could contribute to Oglethorpe's most vital fortifications—Fort Frederica. Located on St. Simons Island, Frederica challenged Spanish claims and was established as a "military town" where Oglethorpe preferred to dwell—a decision emphasizing his commitment to confront the Spanish. On the southern extremity of the island he located Fort St. Simons to guard the

Fort Frederica, Georgia. Part of the remains of the fortifications at Fort Frederica, established during the 1730s by James Edward Oglethorpe on St. Simons Island at the mouth of the Altamaha River. (Photograph by the author.)

approach to Frederica, and he strung a series of other fortifications that reached toward the Spanish: Cumberland Island included St. Andrew's Fort to the north and Fort William to the south, and San Juan Island was the site of Fort St. George in the most extreme southerly position across from the mouth of St. Johns River.

The location of these fortifications as well as the nature and extent of their strength became a matter of much concern for the Spanish in negotiations that took place both in England and on the southern frontier. The Spaniards' strong suspicion of the aggressive actions of Oglethorpe was even faintly echoed by Robert Walpole as prime minister, and the Duke of Newcastle as Secretary of State sent from England Charles Dempsey to conduct negotiations in the interest of peaceful relations between Oglethorpe and the Spanish governor of Florida, Francisco del Moral Sánchez.

Spanish administration of colonies was centered in the king, who ruled them as his "personal and private possessions" without participation by the parliamentary body known as the *Cortes*. The prime agency for the king's administration was the Royal and Supreme Council of the Indies. It nominated officials for the king's approval, was responsible for legislation relating to the colonies, and served as the highest court to which colonial cases were appealed. Assisting the Council of the Indies was the *Casa de Contratación*, which has frequently been referred to as a board of trade concerned with the commercial development of the colonies in the empire. In the colonies, viceroys represented the king and presided over the Spanish possessions in America. The region of the present southeastern United States was a part of the viceroyship of New Spain with headquarters in Mexico. Below the viceroy were other officials including the captain general or governor, responsibile for areas such as Florida or Cuba.[6] Because of distance from the viceroy and difficulty in communication, the governors often exercised considerable independence in their actions.

Sánchez followed this course in the negotiations that took place with Oglethorpe. English commissioners visited St. Augustine under tense and trying conditions in 1736. A return visit from the Spanish commissioners to Frederica gave Oglethorpe an opportunity to provide a false impression of the extent of the strength of his fortifications, and he was able by the ruse of staging Indian protests against the Spanish to disguise his true plans for use of Indian allies.

The result of the exchange of visits was the Treaty of Frederica of October 11, 1736, agreed to by Oglethorpe and Sánchez. Both sides were to use their influence in curbing Indian raids. Further boundary disputes were to be referred to the home governments, and Oglethorpe agreed to withdraw from Fort St. George on San Juan Island with the stipulation that the Spaniards also stay free of the area and that the English claim not be jeopardized by his move. The provisions were most favorable to the English, for in effect it gave some recognition of their title as far south as the St. Johns River, a claim based mainly upon their *de facto* position in contrast to the superior *de jure* claims of the Spanish. Concerned about these negotiations, the Spanish repudiated the agreement and recalled Sánchez, who was prosecuted before the Council of the Indies.[7]

Oglethorpe's return to England following this agreement and Spanish memorials protesting English encroachments in Georgia resulted in a stiffening of British defense with the consent of King George II, even though the move was not favored by Prime Minister Robert Walpole for fear of war. The protection of Georgia was not left locally to the militia it could muster nor to troops that might be inveigled from neighboring colonies. Parliament agreed to shoulder the burden of defense when appealed to by the trustees. Oglethorpe emphasized to Walpole in February 1736/7 the need for regular troops rather than militia in the defense of Georgia, and he suggested that regulars should be used in other colonies at their own expense. As he estimated the situation of men and money, he concluded that "he could form about 300 men capable of bearing arms in Georgia, that South Carolina had money but no men, that North Carolina had men but no money, that Pennsylvania had both, and Virginia only money. That New England had men but no money, and New York had money and few men."[8] For immediate aid, troops from Gibraltar were released to proceed to Georgia, and Oglethorpe was placed in command of a regiment that was later brought to Georgia in 1738. Furthermore, Oglethorpe had in January 1736/7 been given the dual command of all royal forces in both Georgia and South Carolina.

The Treaty of Frederica failed to ease tension. Consequently, charges and countercharges along with numerous memorials went back and forth between the English and Spanish. The disputes revolved around numerous problems, both old and new. Boundary disputes originated in seventeenth century claims, and the English were guilty in the eighteenth century of subtly adding Georgia within the extensive Carolina boundaries. The Spanish resented English trade rights from the Treaty of Utrecht of 1713, particularly the provision for one five-hundred ton English ship to trade each year with Spanish colonies and the *asiento* for the English importation of 4800 slaves each year. To make matters more difficult, the British South Sea Company in this trade had accumulated a debt of £68,000 to Spain. Other trade competition in the West Indies led to controversy over the Spanish rights of search and the severe actions of the Spanish coast guard in surveillance of English ships. The most sensational of the protests to the searches was by Captain Robert Jenkins, who maintained that the Spanish boarded his ship *Rebecca* near Havana and the Spanish captain "took hold of his left ear and slit it down with his cutlask."[9] In 1738 Jenkins appeared before the House of Commons and aroused its members to fever pitch by exhibiting the carefully preserved ear which he claimed resulted from the Spanish assault some seven years before. The sensation of the moment was enough to provide the name for the renewal of war that was soon to come.

The welter of conflicting issues forced Spain and England to make another attempt at a settlement. With the encouragement of Prime Minister Walpole, representatives met at the palace of El Pardo near Madrid and signed the Convention of El Pardo on January 14, 1738/9.[10] The agreements were subject to ratification by each country. Two major issues were provided for in the convention: (1) settlement of the debts for depredations, which through bargaining resulted in the Spanish owing the English £95,000; and (2) resolution by commissaries of the boundary conflict with the stipulation that during the deliberations of the settlement "things shall remain . . . in the situation they are in at present without increasing the fortifications there or taking any new posts."[11] In effect, this looked upon the Altamaha as the boundary with the restriction that no additions be made between there and St. Johns River. The Walpole ministry, after considerable debate, won approval of its action relative to the Convention of El Pardo on two different votes in the Commons. But the criticism of truckling to Spain was so sharp and bitter that the continuation of peaceful negotiations was jeopardized. The convention itself had failed to end certain recurring grievances by not eliminating the Spanish right of search, by not providing for a payment by the South Sea Company to Spain, and by postponing settlement of the boundary dispute in its referral to commissaries. Worse still, even the agreement made by Spain to pay £95,000 for depredations was not honored because of the South Sea Company's obligation, and Spain revoked the *asiento* in May 1739.[12] The British refused to accede to Spanish demands for the withdrawal of certain naval squadrons from Gibraltar, and the Spanish were not satisfied that adequate steps had been taken to restrict further fortifications on the southern frontier. In Georgia and South Carolina there were protests against Spanish efforts to unleash attacks by Indians and by Carolina slaves, who had "found kind Reception" at St. Augustine.[13] A proclamation from St. Augustine that escaping Negro slaves would be given their freedom contributed to the Stono slave revolt of September 9, 1739, an uprising of blacks on the Stono River near Charles Town who seized arms from a warehouse and attempted unsuccessfully to fight their way to St. Augustine.[14] At least twenty whites and forty Negroes died in the insurrection. In its wake, fear and consternation greatly increased in both South Carolina and Georgia.

The alignment of Indian tribes was also critical to the Anglo-Spanish conflict. To understand the intricacies of the Indian allegiance, it is essential to examine the state of native affairs during the years preceding the outbreak of war. The major English burden of Indian negotiations and formulation of Indian policy with the tribes of the Southeast at that time fell more upon South Carolina and Georgia than upon North Carolina. This was true largely because of North Carolina's relatively protected position and small number of natives, plus the absence of officials with a strong commitment to dealing with the Indians. None of the small North Carolina tribes numbered more than twenty families except the Tuscarora, who could muster as many as 200 warriors. Following their defeat in the Tuscarora War, the survivors of the tribe remaining in Carolina acceded to English pressure in the approval of their leaders. Bishop Augustus Spangenberg later commented that they had no king but simply a captain selected from among them by the English.[15] As in Virginia and South Carolina, these tribes had assumed the status of tributaries and rendered in return for protection a donation of deerskins once or twice each year when they came to dine with the governor.

South Carolina, as previously noted, had modified the experiment of a public monopoly of the Indian trade started in 1716. The Assembly first continued it in March 1718/9 as a public corporation without the monopoly, since private traders could then participate. In 1721 the government withdrew and then provided three commissioners, nominated by the Commons House, as regulators of the trade. They continued until crown officials nullified the act. Control then went to the governor and council, probably through Francis Nicholson's bid for power, but the arduous duties were such that the governor was willing to return the supervision of trade to the Commons. This body then provided for control by a single commissioner, which was to remain in effect until 1761 except for a brief period in 1751 when legislative jurisdiction was challenged by the executive, Governor James Glen.[16]

The Indian trade, an important part of the colonial economy and Indian diplomacy, aroused antagonism in intercolonial relations as South Carolina and Georgia clashed over its control. By 1724 South Carolina had recovered its trade lost during the Yamassee War and through the challenge from Virginia. These gains declined slightly during the remainder of the decade due to Spanish agitation of the Lower Creeks, but the colonizing of Georgia enhanced the deerskin trade through Charles Town. Rivalry with Georgia, though, soon emerged; interestingly enough, the regulations imposed in Georgia in 1735 that created a crisis with South Carolina were actually taken from the South Carolina statute of 1711.[17] The situation was doubly ironical. Not only were the regulations copied from South Carolina, but the Georgia restrictions placed Carolina in a similar position to Virginia's experience earlier in the century. For South Carolina the shoe was on the other foot, and the pinch was similar to the squeeze she had exerted on the Old Dominion. Traders engaging in the traffic with Georgia Indians had first to take out a license from the Georgia commission; failure to do so was subject to a penalty of £100 sterling and confiscation by the Georgia Indian commissioner. Oglethorpe was appointed the first commissioner in 1735 and served diligently until his duties in prosecuting the war against the Spanish necessitated the appointment of William Stephens as co-commissioner in 1741.[18]

Enforcement of the Georgia act in 1736 intensified the intercolonial conflict. Ill feelings were further exacerbated by Georgia's stopping trade on the Savannah River by Carolina traders for violating the colony's prohibition of rum. South Carolina counterd the Indian trade restrictions by an act promising to reimburse from the public treasury losses sutained in the trade by South Carolinians. Even though crown approval had been given to the Georgia Indian Act, South Carolina filed a strong protest to the Privy Council with the urgency of the matter being emphasized more by Charles Town traders than by the planters. The matter was referred in December 1736 to the Board of Trade, which started hearings on the matter in May 1737. The crux of the issue, as in the earlier South Carolina-Virginia dispute, proved to be the monopolistic violation of free trade. The Board of Trade sought legal opinions and was advised that the Georgia monopoly was unwarranted but that requirement of a Georgia license was justified for trade regulation. This opinion favorable to the Georgia trustees was not followed, however, for the Board of Trade recommended to the Privy Council that the trade remain open to traders licensed either in Charles Town or in Georgia. Despite appeals by the trustees, the decision of the King in Council in 1738 recommended that acts be passed by both Georgia and South Carolina for regulating the trade "for the mutual benefit and satisfaction of both the said provinces," and, meanwhile, Georgia was to issue licenses without charge to any traders approved by the governor of South Carolina.[19]

The controversy continued because of Georgia's concern for abuse by a flood of traders. It was not until the 1740s that an acceptable formula was devised by the trustees and the newly appointed governor of South Carolina, James Glen. In view of the difficulty of identifying Georgia Indians and determining the boundaries of Georgia, the agreement provided that South Carolina could license half of the Indian traders in Georgia, and in return Georgia traders would have the right to trade in Carolina. While it was intended that acts be passed in both colonies to this effect, they were never completed, and considerable confusion existed because traders of one colony did not heed the commission of the other. Yet this resolution of the problem reduced the earlier tension between the two colonies and permitted the focusing of attention on the external threats from hostile Indians, Spanish, and French.

Both South Carolina and Georgia were involved during the second quarter of the eighteenth century with the major tribes of the Southeast: the Cherokee, Creeks, Chickasaw, and Choctaw. The Catawba were then a friendly, small group and would continue to be of special interest to South Carolina, as well as to North Carolina and Virginia. The Yamassee, who had fled to the protecting arm of the Spanish near St. Augustine, were also a small tribe and hostile to the English. Generally speaking, the Cherokee with over 4000 warriors in 1740 were pro-English and English influence upon their political organization increased steadily. The Chickasaw, numbering only about 500 fighters in 1740, continued as English allies and upheld their reputation as the bravest of warriors. The Choctaw, still a large group with over 5000 warriors in 1739, remained pro-French, although the English attempted to woo them away. The Creek Confederacy, through its geographical location and the inclination of its leaders, was most vulnerable to the international intrigues of the English, Spanish, and French. Consisting in 1740 of both the Lower Creeks with about 1500 warriors along the Chattahoochee and the Upper Creeks with about 2000 fighters along the Coosa and

Tallapoosa rivers, the Confederacy tried to be neutral in the international struggle. At times, though, the Lower and Upper Creeks were at odds on their attitude toward colonists of different nations.

South Carolina had concluded peace with the Creeks in 1717 in a treaty at Charles Town, which was later acknowledged in Coweta, the headquarters of the Lower Creeks. This was done at a time when Old Brims, Creek "emperor," was conscientiously pursuing the neutralist's role, even though his son, Seepeycoffee, and other leaders vacillated. They leaned first toward the Spanish as some enjoyed a visit to St. Augustine while others were taken to Mexico City, and then they bowed to the French as Seepeycoffee accepted an invitation to visit and receive gifts from the French in Mobile. The neutralist policy of Old Brims, however, prevailed, while the Creek feud with the Cherokee continued. South Carolina was also on friendly terms with the Cherokee although relations were strained by Virginia competition for trade. With this setting, South Carolina entered upon the devious and precarious course of peace with both nations, but encouraging the continuation of their war. Efforts to achieve the goal were abandoned in view of the problems of maintaining security for trade in both nations and of maintaining respect for the English when more open assistance, including white warriors, had to be withheld from both groups.[20]

Peace between the Creeks and Cherokee was then worked out by Carolina agents, and confirmed by representatives of both nations before the South Carolina legislature with President Arthur Middleton as the presiding official. While relations were thus improved and the English emphasized the value of their trade over that of the competing Spanish and French, problems continued. The situation was still critical with the Lower Creeks who were susceptible to the blandishments of the Spanish and French, and with the Overhill Cherokee who continued to be exposed to attacks from Indians from the Ohio Valley encouraged by the French. The Overhill Cherokee were of particular concern because of the possibility of peace with the French Indians and because both the French and English wanted forts in their territory. Their eventual alliance with the British resulted from an unexpected and fortuitous development in behalf of the English through the incredible feats of Sir Alexander Cuming.

A Scottish baronet and member of the Royal Society, Cuming came to Charles Town in 1729 with an interest in collecting scientific information. Full of schemes that bordered on the bizarre and impossible, he experimented with alchemy, proposed the colonization of 300,000 Jewish families in the Cherokee territory to pay off the national debt of England, and again concerned himself with the national debt in proposing a currency and national bank. The national bank, he asserted, would benefit the British colonies, retain them in "a natural state of dependency," civilize the Indians in America, and pay off the national debt and provide money for lending to foreign nations by bringing in 200 million pounds sterling of gold and silver specie within forty years.[21] These schemes made little impact.

Cuming journeyed to the Cherokee country in March and April of 1730. His interest in science soon turned to Indian politics as he learned more about the state of affairs among the natives and the threat of the French. With extraordinary boldness and persuasive oratory, he appeared in many of the villages, armed with "Pistols, a Gun, and a Sword," and prevailed upon the Cherokee to accept the pro-English Moytoy of the Overhill villages as their "emperor," and to designate Cuming as "Governor and Lawgiver of the Cherokee Nation."[22] Designation of the warrior Moytoy as the emperor contributed to the transition of the Cherokee nation from an aggregate of independent villages with no explicit structure for tribal decisions to the establishment of an explicit structure for tribal government.[23] While this was an important step in the internal organization of the Cherokee nation, Cuming's next move in taking seven Indians to London in 1730 paved the way for an Anglo-Cherokee agreement. The Board of Trade seized the opportunity, without recognizing or satisfying Cuming's bid for power, to conclude a treaty with the group. Consisting of only two chiefs and five warriors, the delegation had one warrior who did not sign the agreement since he had been added to the group along the route to Charles Town for embarkation; another one was later to play a prominent role in Cherokee affairs under the name of Attakullakulla, or the Little Carpenter.

The treaty to "brighten the chain of friendship" was designed to promote closer relations between the English and the Cherokee, and to obtain Cherokee recognition of their subjection to the king of England. The Cherokee agreed to assist against the enemies of the English, "to keep the trading path clean," and to deliver to the justice of English law both Indians and whites guilty of murder. As an encouragement to trade, the king ordered "the English in Carolina to trade with the Indians" and "to plant corn from Charles Town towards the Town of the Cherokees."[24] While not resolving all Anglo-Cherokee problems such as subsequent trade crises, the treaty did help bind the Cherokee to the English for three decades.

A somewhat different impact upon Anglo-Cherokee relations was made by another European schemer, Christian Gottlieb Priber. More of a dreamer than Cuming, Priber was an enigma to his eighteenth-century contemporaries as he journeyed to the Indian country in the 1730s. To many of the English he appeared to be an agent of the French with designs to tear the Cherokee away from the English friendship. James Adair, noted Indian trader and writer of Indian history, described him as "a gentleman of a curious and speculative temper" and a "philosophic" person.[25] The Indian trader Ludovick Grant termed him "a most Notorious Rogue and inniquitous fellow" who "was certainly an Agent for the French" among the Cherokee. Since he was "a great Scholar he soon made himself master of their Tongue, and by his insinuating manner Indeavoured to gain their hearts, he trimm'd his hair in the indian manner and painted as they did going generally almost naked except a shirt and a Flap."[26] A contemporary in Georgia designated him "a very extraordinary Kind of a Creature; he is a little ugly Man, but speaks almost all Languages fluently, particularly English, Dutch, French, Latin and Indian; he talks very prophanely against all Religions, but chiefly against the Protestant."[27] The Frenchman Antoine Bonnefoy, who was held captive by the Cherokee, correctly recorded that Priber, whom he called Pierre Albert, had no direct connection with the French but had been forced to leave his native Saxony because of opposition to his efforts to establish his perfect society.[28]

Priber proposed to bring his utopia to the Cherokee and establish a society to be known as the "Kingdom of Paradise," which he had been planning for twenty years. While the Cherokee already had collective ownership common to most tribes, Priber's scheme went beyond this in proposing a communistic society, where all would be equal, where all "goods should be held in common," and "lodging, furniture and clothing should be equal." There would be equality of women and the abandonment of traditional family ties. There would be "no marriage contract" and the women would "be free to change husbands every day." Children would be the responsibility of the republic for care, maintenance, and adequate instruction; "the law of nature" was to be the "sole law."[29]

Priber's influence over the Indians in urging an independent or neutral role in dealing with Europeans disturbed the English, who usually held sway over the Cherokee. Several efforts to seize him were at first foiled by the Indians who had adopted him in their tribe. Finally, however, the Creeks, spurred on by English traders, laid hold of Priber when he was on a mission to their nation. He was delivered prisoner to the colony of Georgia after living with the Indians for about seven years; he died while held at Fort Frederica. When turned over to Georgia, one contemporary recorded that "There was a Book found upon him of his own Writing ready for the Press, which he owns and glories in, and believes it is by this Time privately printed, but will not tell where."[30] Unfortunately the book referred to has been lost to posterity, and no evidence has been found that it was ever privately printed.

A more realistic approach in Indian-white relations was followed by Oglethorpe as he held a firm hand over Indian negotiations in Georgia. He exerted a positive influence for the English in Creek affairs even though creating uncertainty and confusion in the Georgia-South Carolina battle for Indian trade. From the very beginning Oglethorpe in Georgia as well as other trustees in England recognized at least the title of occupation, if not the sovereign rights, of the natives, and they were solicitous in getting the Indians to relinquish the use title. Faced by an earlier treaty in 1715 that South Carolina had made with the Yamassee restricting English settlement south of the Savannah River, Oglethorpe arranged for a new treaty in 1733. Arranging this treaty brought to the fore two of the most important persons in Indian affairs in early Georgia history: Tomo-Chi-Chi and Mary Musgrove. Tomo-Chi-Chi was the chief of the local Yamacraw, formerly a part of the Creek Confederacy. He became a fast friend of Oglethorpe and the recipient of his favors and support, including the colorful visit to England in 1734. Upon his death in 1739, there was an English funeral with Oglethorpe serving as one of the pall bearers; at the grave in one of Savannah's squares "At the Depositing of the Corpse, seven Minute Guns were fired, and about forty Men in Arms (as many as could instantly be found) gave three Vollies over the Grave."[31] The ceremony was another way of rewarding faithful friendship to the English.

Mary Musgrove was the half-breed daughter of an English trader and an Indian "princess" who was the sister of Old Brims of the Creeks. Having lived in South Carolina part of the time and being fluent in both English and the language of the Creeks, she rendered valuable service to Georgia from the beginning of its settlement, serving not only as an interpreter but as an effective advocate of friendly relations with Georgia. Calling herself "Queen of the Creeks," she was very much under the influence of Oglethorpe, who treated her "very kindly on all Ocassions,"[32] although apparently promising at times more payments than she ever received for her services to the colony. Mary's later controversy with the colony over these payments need not minimize her earlier contributions.

A Creek delegation to Georgia arranged by Mary in 1738 informed Oglethorpe of a large conference scheduled the following year at Coweta and invited him to attend. Aware of the imminence of war with Spain, Oglethorpe engaged in bold and effective diplomacy by taking the long and hazardous journey into the heart of the Lower Creek country on the Chattahoochee River near present Columbus, Georgia. The many risks of the journey were offset by the valuable contacts, for in addition to Creeks there were representatives of the Cherokee, Chickasaw, and several small groups. The Cherokee at the time were secure in English interest, and so were the Chickasaw, although they were hard pressed by combined French and Choctaw assaults.

The major goal of the negotiations was to hold the Creeks secure for the English. Oglethorpe was concerned at the time with the Spanish and even found himself encouraging peace between the Creeks and the French to leave him free to concentrate on the expected Spanish assaults. In so doing, he gave aid indirectly to the French, who were left free to continue war against the already harassed Chickasaw. For Georgia and the English, the Coweta negotiations promoted better trade relations and confirmed Creek cession of lands between the Savannah and St. Johns rivers.[33] Stronger allegiance to the English was thus established by Oglethorpe for the Creeks. As he was returning to the colony from Coweta in November 1739, he received news of the beginning of hostilities in the War of Jenkins' Ear pitting Spain against England. Primarily a naval war in America, it was affected by the beginning of the War of Austrian Succession in 1740 in Europe in which Spain and France aligned against Austria, which had England as an ally.

The English effort in prosecuting the War of Jenkins' Ear focused upon two areas: naval expeditions to the Caribbean and the attacks and counterattacks along the Georgia-Florida frontier. Personnel participating in these campaigns included regular naval and military troops from Britain, militia from the colonies including soldiers recruited by the local assemblies for specific missions, and Indian allies. Admiral Edward Vernon commanded the naval expedition to the Caribbean and with six ships captured Porto Bello in November 1739.[34] For other expeditions to the West Indies, Major General Alexander Spotswood was designated quartermaster general and was to coordinate the raising of troops from the "Northern" colonies, a designation that included the southern colonies of Maryland, Virginia, and North Carolina but excluded South Carolina and Georgia which were to support General Oglethorpe. From a total British force of 12,000 some 3600 were recruited from the "Northern" colonies in the proportions given in Table 6.

TABLE 6
Northern Recruitment[35]

Colony	Companies	Men
Pennsylvania	8	800
New England	5	500
New York	5	500
Virginia	4	400
North Carolina	4	400
New Jersey	3	300
Maryland	3	300
Rhode Island	2	200
Connecticut	2	200
Total	36	3600

The successful recruiting was greatly aided by the lure of Spanish booty and mineral riches and by the opportunity to remove Spanish challenges to English trade. Individual colonies added a stimulus. Maryland, for example, offered a bounty of five pounds for enlisted men and special privileges upon their return, including freedom from military duty for a time, immunity from arrest as debtor, and exemption from taxes and fees for ferries.[36]

Meanwhile, General Oglethorpe was authorized to seize St. Augustine when practicable. Except for limited naval aid and some assistance from

England in the form of additional guns, he had to rely upon resources in the colonies. His successful trip to Coweta and the continued cooperation of Mary Musgrove paved the way for valuable Indian allies, and he solicited troops from both Georgia and South Carolina. Early skirmishes found Oglethorpe probing the defenses of St. Augustine; in January 1739/40 he burned the Spanish wooden fort of Picolata along the St. Johns River and seized Fort St. Francis de Pupa across the river.

Oglethorpe went in person to Charles Town in March to make an appeal for additional assistance against the Spanish, buttressed by his official status of commander of crown forces in South Carolina as well as Georgia. His reception was not without suspicion and moments of pique in view of Georgia's challenge in the Indian trade and navigation of the Savannah River; nevertheless, he secured authorization of 400 troops with the promise of an additional 100, enrolled for four months under the command of Colonel Alexander Vanderdussen. While awaiting both military and naval forces at the mouth of the St. Johns, Oglethorpe with assistance from both Creek and Cherokee fighters moved south of the St. Johns and captured Fort Diego and secured it with a force of about sixty men in anticipation of his major effort on St. Augustine. Returning to the mouth of the St. Johns River, he met the assembled forces and coordinated their movement toward St. Augustine, taking part of his troops by water and sending the Highlanders and the South Carolinians under Vanderdussen by land. With a force of some 900 white troops—both regulars and provincials—and 1100 Indians, Oglethorpe was ready to challenge by direct assault the forces of Manuel Montiano, Spanish governor of Florida. Montiano's support totalled some 462 regulars, 61 militia, 43 Negroes, and 50 Indians in March of 1739/40. By the middle of May, initial forays took the English forces into Fort Moosa, about two miles from St. Augustine, and raids were made up to the gates of the city.[37]

Oglethorpe's major assault on the city and fort was set for June 5, 1740. The master plan called for a naval bombardment to neutralize the fort and to silence the six Spanish half galleys that had recently slipped in with supplies from Havana. Oglethorpe's call for the naval attack, however, met with a terrifying silence. The shallow waters of the harbor and the threat of the half galleys had checked the naval units, and Oglethorpe was reluctantly forced to turn to a siege of the city. But the lackadaisical attitude of the sieging troops, the alertness of the Spanish in recapturing Fort Moosa and opening a small wedge in communication, and the upcoming hurricane season forcing withdrawal of British naval forces all produced such a discouraging situation that Oglethorpe had to call off the siege.[38] By July 10 he was back at Frederica with dejected spirits but embroiled in controversy over the conduct of South Carolina troops. To what extent, if any, had the Carolinians been guilty of improper conduct in the campaign? Lost battles seem to demand a scapegoat, and the blame in this case was both widespread and contradictory.

There was criticism of English naval officers, criticism of Oglethorpe for inadequate and inefficient coordination, and criticism of Vanderdussen and the South Carolina troops for being dilatory and either deserting or withdrawing too soon from the siege. The conflicting views of the period have been carried forth in the partisan views of historical writers. South Carolina historians have not failed to criticize Oglethorpe and to come to the defense of Vanderdussen to show, as one writer contended, "how groundless are the charges . . . carelessly made against the South Carolina contingent."[39]

The most critical part of the controversy was its impact upon South Carolina relations at the time when cooperation was needed to thwart the likely Spanish attack. Oglethorpe turned both to England and to South Carolina to improve Georgia's defenses. The British Admiralty alerted officers in the American theater to the potential threat to Georgia and South Carolina from St. Augustine; but in response to appeals from Oglethorpe for additional assistance, the ministry because of its involvement with war in Europe could provide little more than an additional company of grenadiers. Oglethorpe's appeal to South Carolina for additional troops was regarded suspiciously and rebuffed, and the general found himself left to his own resources in Georgia and to the assistance he could obtain from Indian allies.

The delay of assaults from St. Augustine was caused in part by the activity of British forces in the Caribbean. After Vernon's earlier capture of Porto Bello, twenty-five additional ships under Sir Chaloner Ogle joined him along with Brigadier General Thomas Wentworth's force of some 12,000, including the 3600 troops from the "Northern" colonies under Colonel William Gooch, successor to General Spotswood. The combined forces of Vernon and Wentworth failed disastrously in their assault on Cartagena on April 9, 1741; they likewise faltered at Santiago in Cuba in the following July, a failure influenced in part by the ineptness of Wentworth. Open feuding ensued between Vernon and Wentworth, and both were recalled in September 1742.[40]

With failure of these efforts the Spanish stepped up their plans for an expedition from St. Augustine against both Georgia and South Carolina, including Port Royal as one of their targets. Juan Francisco de Horcasitas, governor of Havana, was ordered to prepare the expedition; he in turn designated Montiano at St. Augustine to command the attack. Ships and troops from Cuba reached St. Augustine in early summer; the force then proceeded toward Georgia with a superiority of both ships and men. The exact count, however, has not been determined for estimates have ranged from thirty-three to fifty-six ships and from 2000 to 7000 soldiers. Despite Oglethorpe's efforts to improve the defense of his string of forts, the Spanish force moved past the outposts, had a stiff fight overwhelming Fort St. Simon, and then landed troops in preparation for an advance on Fort Frederica, the major target of the attack. A series of skirmishes and ambushes involving the

Spanish and Georgia forces reached a climax in the Battle of Bloody Marsh in July 1742 when Oglethorpe's troops successfully ambushed the enemy and killed or took prisoner some 200 Spaniards.[41] Montiano still had a force superior in number, but the hazardous terrain and the partial deception by a contrived note of the true strength of the Georgia force contributed to the Spanish decision to withdraw. Oglethorpe's aggressiveness was an important factor in the battle, and much credit should also go to the determined Highlanders and to the assistance of Indian allies. One Spanish sergeant exclaimed that "the woods around Frederica were so full of Indians that the devil himself could not get through."[42] A final compelling factor was the threat that British naval units would trap the Spanish ships in Frederica River. Some British ships were already on the horizon.

A brief surge of intercolonial concern prompted South Carolina to dispatch a few troops on the British ships that arrived too late to catch the retreating Spaniards. The Georgians had only jibes for the South Carolinians who had refused troops earlier and then arrived too late to fight. There was a more cordial air toward other colonies for notes of congratulation and gratitude came to Oglethorpe from New York, Pennsylvania, New Jersey, Maryland, Virginia, and North Carolina. Virginia also dispatched 200 troops to assist Oglethorpe, who in March of 1743 knocked at the gates of St. Augustine again but provoked no decisive battle. Although unknown to the participants, the major fighting was over on the southern frontier. The War of Austrian Succession did continue in Europe and brought the American colonies into conflict with France with King George's War beginning in 1744.

France renewed with Spain the Second Bourbon Family Compact in 1743, part of a series of agreements linking the interests of their blood-related rulers, and became an active participant in the international struggle. France long had wanted to curtail England's commercial advantages and her privileges in the Spanish *asiento;* she also stood on common ground in opposing the extension of English jurisdiction on the southern frontier because of its threat to French possessions. France, however, was concerned about the freedom of the seas and possible infringement by Spain upon her trade in the Caribbean and the Gulf of Mexico and hoped to force commercial concessions upon Spain in negotiations for the renewal of the family compact. The course of diplomatic events in Europe, which united Sardinia and Austria in a defensive pact in September 1743 for fear of Spanish desires in Italy, spurred France to proceed with the renewal without the treaty of commerce she sought. The significance of the second family compact for the southern frontier was to renew the Franco-Spanish challenge to British territorial claims and particularly English encroachment upon both Florida and Louisiana with the founding of Georgia. For the trade in slaves under the *asiento*, the Spanish heeded French beckoning by "promising" not to renew British privileges.[43]

The official declaration of the Anglo-French hostilities in 1744 in King George's War did not bring vigorous activity on the southern frontier. The most intense efforts were made to the north in expeditions such as the English conquest of Louisbourg. On the southern frontier, limited attacks and counterattacks occurred, but the most active efforts exerted were to align the Indians on one side or the other. Oglethorpe went back to England in 1743, never to return to Georgia. The duties of president of Georgia were assumed by William Stephens.

The peace at Aix-la-Chapelle ending the war in 1748 returned boundaries to the *status quo ante bellum*. The Indian furor on the southern frontier escaped the final provisions of the treaty. Despite earlier promises by Spain to France, the *asiento* for England was renewed for four years, but it would soon be the subject of further negotiations. The threat of Spanish raids diminished and the Georgia regiment was discharged. The status of French expansion was less certain and Anglo-French hostility soon erupted in the French and Indian War that dominates the remaining period of this study.

10

War for Empire:
The French Thrust, 1750s–1760s

The three major European powers—England, France, and Spain—had a temporary interlude of peace in the mid-eighteenth century. Rivalries persisted, however, and on the southern colonial frontier France replaced Spain as the active colonial threat. England's relations with Spain eased after the old irritants of trade in the Spanish colonies were removed by the English agreeing in negotiations at Madrid in 1750 to relinquish the *asiento* for a money payment of £100,000 by Spain and to a cancellation of mutual debts between the British South Sea Company and the king of Spain.[1] Tension was also eased between Spain and England by the Spanish falling back into a defense posture in the areas of St. Augustine, St. Marks, and Pensacola as she faltered upon the threshold of the surge of expansion upon which both the English and French were gaining momentum. Florida was primarily a military outpost with little to recommend it economically.[2] Governor James Glen of South Carolina reported in 1749 that there was a total population of all colors in St. Augustine of only about 2300;[3] and while recent estimates for the number of troops in the area ranged up to 600, the number of effective soldiers appeared closer to 100. The Spanish did, however, remain a threat in Indian relations and maintained friendly overtures to the Lower Creeks, who sought English trade but continued resentment for the Anglophile Cherokee and for the Georgia settlers encroaching on their vacated lands on the Savannah River.

France, on the other hand, was gathering momentum at mid-century in her bid to extend her control over more of America. Francis Parkman has likened the French empire in North America to a large animal with its head in the snows of Canada and its tail in the canebrakes of Louisiana. The head displayed the greater vigor, although there was increased activity all the way from New France to Louisiana. Administration of these colonial efforts came under a political organization that contrasted sharply with that of the English.

In the administration of colonies, France employed a system that was structured to provide checks and balances for the home government headed by the king. The tradition of absolute government placed less responsibility upon the individual colonists then the English representative system. In North

America the French created two areas of administration and modeled their government for the most part after that of a French province. New France or Canada had a governor and intendant, while Louisiana had a governor and ordonnateur. The governor was considered higher in rank and was responsible for military, foreign, and Indian relations. The intendant or ordonnateur, on the other hand, served as a check on the governor and had responsibility for the administration of "finance, justice, and police." In effect, their authority overlapped and was frequently confused, which in part served the purpose of having one official check on the other; however, this led to extended controversies argued in long and tedious reports to the home country. Differences of opinion between these officials were also aired in the Supreme or Superior Council on which both were members. Exercising "original and appellate jurisdiction," the council along with the governor and the intendant or the ordonnateur had full responsibility for executive, legislative, and judicial matters subject only to the approval of the king.[4]

The officials of New France outranked the officials of Louisiana in the hierarchy of authority, but confusion existed over the status of the Illinois country relative to these two centers of administration. Lying between the mountains to the east and west that contained the Mississippi Valley, the Illinois country encompassed a vast area along the Ohio, Missouri, and Illinois rivers. While many views were expressed over its disposition and over the Forks of the Ohio, the French placed control during war under the governor of New France.[5]

Religious leaders played a prominent role in the French Catholic settlements, but there did not exist the same confusion over authority as for civil leaders. Only one diocese was established and the Bishop of Quebec had authority extending from New France over both Illinois and Louisiana. The bishop served on the Supreme Council along with the governor and the intendant or the ordonnateur, and he had supervision of missionaries, priests, and the establishment of parishes, which were first provided in New France in 1722.[6]

In Louisiana in 1748, the lower Mississippi basin had 12 companies of French troops and one Swiss regiment. On paper there were 750 soldiers, but actually the companies, authorized 50 men, had only about 15 and the strength of 9 companies was only 141 fusiliers. An order of 1750 raised the miltiary strength to 37 companies with a table of organization for 50 men plus commissioned officers. The number of troops then surged upward to about 2000 men in 1751 dispersed over both Louisiana and the Illinois country in the following locations: 875 at New Orleans, 475 at Mobile, 100 at the German village, 100 at Point Coupée, 50 at Natchitoches, 50 at Natchez, 50 on the Kansas River, and 300 in the Illinois country.[7]

At mid-century the conflict between the French and English centered in the Ohio Valley. While there had been little miltiary activity in the Ohio and

Mississippi valleys during King George's War from 1744 to 1748 as a part of the War of Austrian Succession, portents of future clashes were at hand. New France or Canada had earlier established fortified points south of the Great Lakes to guard the portages of their trade routes, to provide connecting links with other French settlements in Illinois and Louisiana, and to maintain French influence over important Indian tribes in the area such as the Miami (Twightee) and the Huron. The Fox Indians of the Wisconsin River country had harassed and blocked French trade routes to the Sioux and other western tribes during the first three decades of the eighteenth century and were not successfully challenged until 1734. To protect more easterly trade routes connecting Canada with Illinois and Louisiana, the French had established military strongholds, including Fort Miami on the Maumee River and Fort Vincennes on the Wabash. Although suffering at times from high prices of trade goods, from inadequate supplies of essential articles of commerce, and from limited markets for furs and skins on the continent of Europe, the French continued to dominate trade along the lower Ohio River Valley as the English became more active in its upper reaches.

Explorers and traders from Pennsylvania were most zealous in pushing English influence into the Ohio Valley along with a few Virginians. During the 1730s and 1740s they took advantage of the invitations to trade with migrating natives such as the Shawnee and Delaware who were forced westward along the junction of the Allegheny and Monangahela rivers in western Pennsylvania. One of the most influential Pennsylvania leaders was George Croghan,[8] an immigrant from Ireland in 1741 who quickly adapted to the frontier as Indian trader and diplomat by learning Indian languages and developing rapport with the tribes. As early as May 1747 he reported the shifting allegiances of a group of the Six Nations or Iroquois living along Lake Erie but still under the jurisdiction of their confederacy in New York. "Those Ingans," he wrote, "ware always in the French Interest till now, Butt This Spring, allmost all the Ingans in the Woods, have Declared against the French, and I Think this will be a fair Opertunity, if purshued by some Small Presents, to have all the French Cut off in them parts."[9] By the following year Croghan's influence was also at work because the leader of the Miami, known as "Old Briton" to the English and "La Demoiselle" to the French, changed the Indians' allegiance to the English and established on the upper Great Miami River the fortified town of Pickawillany. In a real sense, this fortification for a few years was the weathervane of dominant influences in the Ohio River Valley; for the moment, the winds favored the English.

Aroused by this increasing Anglo-American threat, the Marquis de la Galissonière, governor general of New France from 1747 to 1749, envisaged a string of French forts south of the Great Lakes. In 1749 he dispatched Céloron de Blainville on an expedition down the Ohio, or "Beautiful River," to boast a show of military force, to recover the allegiance of Indian tribes, and most important of all to assert French claim to the area while collecting information about the intruding challengers. Planting lead plates at strategic points to claim the land for the king of France, Blainville also made several speeches to Indians as he solicited their friendship for France. Galissonière felt the English threat so strongly that he produced a long proposal for French officials upon his return to France in 1749, a proposal that was soon to encourage other French fortifications.

Before the Marquis de Duquesne, appointed governor general of New France in 1752, proceeded with construction of additional forts, a vigorous attack by the Chippewa and Ottawa Indians from the Michilimackinac area under the leadership of Charles-Michel Langlade, a French trader, destroyed English influence at Pickawillany. In a surprise dawn raid on June 21, 1752, the attacking forces of about 240 warriors overpowered the post; defenses had been temporarily weakened by the absence of warriors out on the hunt. The victors feasted upon the boiled body of "Old Briton" and the roasted heart of an English trader killed in the raid. Taking five other English traders as prisoners for the French, the raiders burned the cabins and hoisted the French flag over the remaining fortification. Even though a passing Virginia expedition restored an English flag to the deserted post, French influences resurged with the downfall of Pickawillany. Duquesne stepped up the Gallic challenge with the addition of a string of forts to control the area south from Lake Erie along the upper waters of the Ohio: Fort Presqu'Isle on Lake Erie and Fort Le Boeuf on a tributary of the Allegheny River in 1753, and Fort Duquesne in 1754 at the Forks of the Ohio at the important junction of the Allegheny and Monongahela rivers, present-day Pittsburgh.[10] The Forks of the Ohio as the "gateway to the West" became the object of both trade and military rivalry as well as sparking competition between Anglo-American land companies that added yet another dimension to international tensions.

In Virginia both the Ohio Company and the Loyal Land Company, organized in 1749, soon pursued their interests in western lands. Dr. Thomas Walker of Virginia penetrated Kentucky as a member of the Loyal organization in 1750. The Ohio Company dispatched the able and experienced explorer, Christopher Gist,[11] on missions in 1750 and 1751 to the Ohio Valley to reconnoiter the land, to discern the most expedient transportation routes, and to invite Indian representatives to the proposed treaty of Logstown, located about eighteen miles below present Pittsburgh. Part of the purpose of the Logstown meeting was to get confirmation of an earlier conference at Lancaster, Pennsylvania, in 1744. By that treaty the colonies of Virginia, Maryland, and Pennsylvania had prevailed upon the Six Nations or Iroquois to give up their claim to lands south of the Ohio River. But the Indians soon complained of the agreement, stating that they did not understand "Pen and Ink work, and that their Interpreter did not do them Justice."[12] At Logstown in June 1752 the Six Nations again confirmed the land cession of Lancaster, provided approval was later given by the Onondaga Council.[13] They also consented to the construction of a fort at the Forks of the Ohio by the Ohio Company and promised not to harass the English settlers on company land. But the pictographic signatures of the Indian negotiators were never ratified by the Onondaga Council which had no representative at the meeting, so the provisions of the treaty were of dubious standing. The status of the Forks of the Ohio remained uncertain.[14]

In the years preceding the outbreak of wars in the 1750s, five alternatives had been opened to British leaders in providing for the protection and defense of the colonies. First of all, the problem had been left to local initiative with only occasional supplies of weapons from England; neighboring colonies were to come to the aid of those in danger with military commands authorized by the respective colonies and involving duplication of commissions from colonies with troops. While there were several examples of intercolonial aid, such as the Tuscarora and Yamassee wars, cooperation was not easily achieved. The particularism of the respective colonies often hampered joint assistance, and to overcome it a second approach was tried in the northern but not in the southern colonies. This was the imposition of government over the colonies by the Dominion of New England (1686–89) with full control over military and civil affairs. While the Board of Trade again proposed a similar union in their report of 1721, it was never realized. The search for an answer to the problem of colonial defense then shifted to schemes that would place the greater part of the financial burden for protection upon revenue from Britain rather than from America. This was attempted in a third approach by bringing to the colony regular British regiments that might serve for a limited mission and then depart, or they might be given a permanent or extended assignment to a specific fort or area such as the regiment of Oglethorpe stationed in Georgia and South Carolina.

The heavy demands upon manpower that this plan entailed, particularly if troops were needed elsewhere in the empire, ushered in a fourth approach that would still be a financial burden on the British taxpayer but would minimize the personnel demands from England. Troops were to be recruited from the colonies, trained by a small cadre of British regulars, and merged when ready for regular duty with a British unit. Local legislatures were encouraged to aid in the expenditures of equipping and training, but England provided what the colonies did not. Both colonial officers and troops were integrated into a regular British unit and benefited from the superior status a regular regiment assumed. The American response to this plan was favorable and transcended the pesky bickering that frequently marred the efforts of intercolonial cooperation. There was no undertaking that drew entirely upon the southern colonies, but in the 1740s Maryland, Virginia, and North Carolina supplied troops for the West Indian expedition led by Vernon and

Wentworth. The fifth and final approach was tried in the mid-eighteenth century and provided both a stated number of troops and specific expenditure by having colonials enlist in regular British regiments for regular terms, not just for one campaign. Tried in New England, the scheme failed to work as well as the previous arrangement for a more limited mission. British regulars and colonials never developed the essential rapport for an effective unit.[15]

As the French threat intensified at mid-century, the British ministry sought a course of action consistent with past experiments in colonial defense and that also reconciled conflicting mercantile and political goals. When Robert Dinwiddie, the new lieutenant governor of Virginia in 1751, forwarded to England two years later the information about construction of Fort Le Boeuf, members of the Cabinet Council were stirred to action. They brushed aside opposition to sending guns for forts; they issued anew the direction for intercolonial aid if fighting erupted; they endorsed the recommendation of the Board of Trade to convene an intercolonial conference to maintain the loyalty of the Iroquois. By January of 1754 independent companies, including the one in South Carolina, were ordered to garrison the forts being built on the Ohio. By the summer of 1754 special funds, including £8500 from tobacco duty and £5000 in specie, were authorized for use by Dinwiddie in negotiations with the Indians and in completing the anticipated forts. The amount was increased to £20,000 when news arrived that the French had taken the English fort started at Logstown.[16] The intercolonial congress for negotiations with the Iroquois met in Albany, New York, in 1754 and is best known for the Albany Plan of Union that was proposed, but never endorsed either by the colonists or crown officials.

Additional reports of the advance of the French into the Ohio Valley had led Governor Dinwiddie to dispatch young George Washington with a warning message to the French in October 1753. The French commander at Fort Le Boeuf received the communication and promised to forward it to Canada, but he stated vigorously that he intended to remain in his location by authorization of his military orders. The firm answer brought back by Washington in January 1754 resulted in the dispatch of a Virginia regiment under Joshua Fry and Washington. Dinwiddie had by this time received the "Instructions" to "repell force by force" from crown officials transmitted by Lord Robert Holdernesse, Secretary of State for the Southern Department.[17] The campaign began with Washington's surprise attack upon the French at Great Meadows of the Youghiogheny in western Pennsylvania and the resulting French counterattack and ended with Washington's hasty construction and later forced evacuation of Fort Necessity on July 5, 1754.

News of this defeat forced the ministry to pursue more actively other alternatives for protecting the American frontier. Consideration was given to two possibilities: either providing British pay for soldiers recruited in

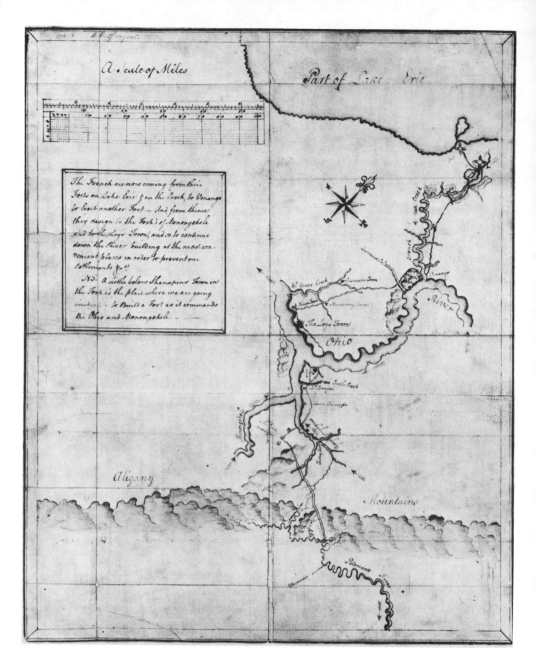

George Washington's map of the Ohio, 1753–54. Sketch map of the Ohio River made by George Washington in 1753–54 and forwarded to England by Governor Robert Dinwiddie of Virginia along with a copy of Washington's report on his mission to warn the French. Washington describes the French advance south of Lake Erie and their plans to build more forts. He states that Virginians plan to build a fort at the Forks of the Ohio which "commands the Ohio and Monongahela." (Reproduced by permission of the Public Record Office, London. Document MPG 118.)

America or dispatching British troops from the British Isles. After extended discussion that involved George II and his son, the Duke of Cumberland—then Captain General of the British Army—a combination of the above alternatives was followed. The decision provided for the appointment of Edward Braddock, a favorite of the Duke of Cumberland, as the general in command of all British forces in North America. Two Irish regiments with a full contingent of officers were also dispatched, and authorization was given for bringing to full strength the colonial forces and the revival of two other regiments previously disbanded—the 50th and 51st. Plans were then formulated for the proposed attack in 1755 at Niagara, Crown Point, and Fort Duquesne, with General Braddock to lead the march on Fort Duquesne. A fourth group was sent to conquer the Acadians, which it did by the attack upon Fort Beauséjour in Nova Scotia.[18] For these campaigns the colonies were requested through their governors to provide wagons, housing for troops, and contributions to a general fund to be used by Braddock. In case of failure of colonial contributions, he was assured of British payment. Braddock was also authorized to implement the recommendation of the Board of Trade for greater imperial supervision of Indian relations by the appointment of Sir William Johnson as Superintendent of Indian Affairs.

The response of the colonies to these requests was not impressive, and some of the colonies used their contributions to assert themselves against royal dictates. Several of the northern colonies contributed to a provincial command, and a grant authorized by the Virginia Assembly for £16,000 was to be administered by a legislative committee rather than being turned over to a collective fund for Braddock. Establishing control of funds through the legislative committee reflects the means by which the lower house of the assemblies in its "Quest for Power" encroached upon the executive prerogatives of royal governors in military policy.[19]

Worse still, the colonies were not always willing to cooperate in efforts that did not necessarily involve money but required only a concert of action to provide support from Indian allies. The most flagrant case in point during this period was the conflict between Governor Dinwiddie of Virginia and Governor Glen of South Carolina over Indian allies for Braddock. While on a number of occasions serious threats to one or more colonies had resulted in intercolonial assistance, the Glen-Dinwiddie struggle was complicated by a history of competition for influence over certain Indian tribes and for profits from the Indian trade, and by differences of opinion about securing the frontier.

Dinwiddie was aware of the need for Indian allies for Braddock's campaign. So critical was the problem that one historian later concluded that "success for the one side or the other depended largely on holding the Indians fast in allegiance."[20] George Washington's frontier experience led him to state that "Indians are only match for Indians; and without these, we shall ever fight upon unequal Terms."[21] But Dinwiddie had little knowledge or experience in handling Indian negotiations; nonetheless, he actively sought native allies. The Virginia tributary Indians could provide little support, for Dinwiddie reported they had not over sixty warriors in 1755.

As early as May 1753, Dinwiddie had appraised Governor Glen of the French threat in the Ohio Valley and sought both military aid from South Carolina as well as assistance from Glen in persuading the Catawba, Cherokee, and also the Creeks to send warriors to oppose the French. Glen refused to provide aid until instructions from the crown could be obtained; furthermore, his council had advised him not "to promise any great assistance."[22] Dinwiddie persisted and appealed again to Glen for assistance with the Catawba and Cherokee, also with the Creeks and Chickasaw in early 1754. Continuing a vigorous course, Dinwiddie invited several tribes to send delegations to Winchester in May 1754 to receive presents from the king. He included the Iroquois and some Indian leaders from the Ohio Valley, and he sent invitations through Abraham Smith direct to the Catawba and Cherokee. This dispatch of an emissary angered Glen, and in response to the contention from South Carolina that Glen was the "proper Channell of . . . Correspondence" to the two tribes, Dinwiddie pleaded the urgency of the situation and explained that the Winchester meeting was not a "New Treaty" but a friendly meeting "to concert the common Welfare."[23]

Glen tended to minimize the French threat in the Ohio Valley. Yet he recognized French encroachment upon territory claimed by the English and advocated some form of union or "confederacy" for common protection. He wrote the following to Dinwiddie on March 14, 1754:

> Massachusets New York, Pensilvania Maryland Virginia North Carolina and South Carolina, they will keep all the power of France in this part of the world at a distance, at least from their own territories, but they must be determined to stand and fall together, to feel when any one of them is hurt, and in general to act upon every occasion like members of the same body.[24]

Glen proposed that Dinwiddie organize a meeting in Virginia to create the desired union in June of 1754. While Dinwiddie favored some form of joint effort, he opposed this specific step because of the delay that it would entail in resisting the French advances he was certain were imminent.

Upon receipt of instructions from Lord Holdernesse, Glen was forced to dispatch one of the independent companies of regulars for service in Virginia during 1754 and 1755.[25] After considerable delay, caused partly by controversy with the Assembly, Glen approved the appropriation for aid to Braddock's expedition of £4000 to be paid in bills of exchange.[26]

But Glen gave no assistance in providing Indian warriors for Braddock. Dinwiddie stated in 1754 that the Catawba and Cherokee had promised 800 to 1000 warriors for action against the French. When they were sorely needed for Braddock's campaign, they failed to arrive, caused in part by a conflicting meeting called by Glen. Braddock marched off into the wilderness without enough Indians to serve even as scouts. The defeat of his forces on July 9, 1755, is a well-known story. The French with a force of around 850, over 600 of whom were Indians, inflicted a total of 977 casualties on an English force of 1459, which at the time of the Monongahela crossing included only 8 Indians.[27]

Evaluations of the outcome of this battle have varied greatly. Contemporary reactions to the rout placed great emphasis upon the ineffectiveness and possible cowardice of British regular enlisted troops. These opinions, however, were based upon reports from British officers who may have been eager to protect their own military reputation and future assignments. Yet these criticisms still have support among recent scholars. Other twentieth-century critics, described by one writer as modernists, have pointed an accusing finger at Braddock, emphasizing that he and his staff did not on that fatal day adequately adhere to approved eighteenth-century tactics in such decisions as formations and flank protection to give Old World methods a chance for victory.[28] Still other twentieth-century analysts have returned to the traditional, persuasive arguments that the nature of the terrain permitted a surprise attack by the French and that Braddock failed to respond to New World challenges by not taking advice from the Americans, by not having sufficient Indian allies, and by retaining an "unshakable faith in British tactics and in British troops."[29]

The blame for the lack of Indian allies cannot be attributed wholly to any one person. Braddock's inexperience in commanding the natives discouraged some of the few that were available, for one Pennsylvania chief complained that "he never appeared pleased with us; and that was the reason that a great many of our warriors left him and would not be under his command."[30] Dinwiddie blamed Glen for the failure to use his influence in obtaining the cooperation of the Catawba and Cherokee and chided him to search his conscience about how well he had done his duty for the crown.[31] Glen had scheduled a conference with the Cherokee at Saluda Old Town in South Carolina in June of 1755, which conflicted with the time for sending allies for Virginia. Apparently French intrigue had increased among the Cherokee, and the Indians themselves had requested a meeting. Glen had the approval of the South Carolina council for the conference and was very eager to complete the purchase of Cherokee lands that extended almost to the edge of expanding English settlements. He negotiated with Old Hop, so-called by the English because of a limp, who had emerged as the most influential Cherokee leader during the 1750s. He was one of the beloved men, not a warrior, and brought the elders into political affairs at the tribal level. This created an explicit structure for general councils and a means of formulating and expressing Cherokee tribal opinion. The purchase from Old Hop, however, was of dubious value since control over the area was not exercised.[32] Dinwiddie minimized its importance on the grounds that the same area had been previously purchased; furthermore, he asserted that Glen had been a victim of French "Cunning and Chicanery" through a plot designed to prevent the cooperation of the Cherokee with Braddock's expedition.[33] There is no evidence to substantiate the last charge by Dinwiddie.

Continuing his criticism, Dinwiddie pointed an accusing finger at Glen in his letter of September 25, 1755, about the Cherokee:

> five of th[a]t Nat'n were lately in here and declar'd their Intent'n of com'g with a great No. to our Assistance, but . . . the G'r of So. Carolina had so frequently and earnestly desir'd a Meet'g with their Great Men th[a]t on their determining to meet him put a Stop to their intended March to our Aid.[34]

Governor Arthur Dobbs of North Carolina sided with Dinwiddie and was also critical of Glen. The South Carolina governor chose the very time the Cherokee were wanted "to appoint a meeting" for a treaty, Dobbs stated, and thus he has "regarded himself and not the Public Service."[35] The opinion of Dobbs, however, is not entirely unbiased. He was a fellow member of the Ohio Land Company with Dinwiddie and also had sharply disagreed with Glen over the boundary line between North and South Carolina.

Glen, in turn, was critical of Dinwiddie for meddling in Indian affairs that he thought should be handled by South Carolina. In a letter to Dinwiddie on August 15, 1754, he complained:

> The Government of Virginia knows little of our Indians, and can have no great knowledge in any Indian affairs; they have nevertheless busied themselves extreamly for these three or four years past, with all the Indians contiguous to and in alliance with this Province which has been a matter of great Concern to every Member of this Community, as they are sensible how dangerous it may be when matters of so great delicacy are handled by Gentlemen that can have no great experience in them.[36]

Again claiming control over the Cherokee, Glen reiterated that South Carolina was "extremely Jealous of any other Colonies intermingling with our Indians, by long experience we have become acquainted with their nature and Inclinations and have managed them so as to keep them steadily in the British interest."[37]

Braddock was also critical of Dinwiddie's failure to provide the Indian allies that he had promised. Although commending Dinwiddie most highly in March of 1755 for "the zeal which he has shown, and the pains which he has taken, for the good of the service," he referred two months later to "the folly of Mr. Dinwiddie and the roguery of the assembly." When the Catawba and

Cherokee failed to arrive, Braddock naively inquired why arrangements had not been made with the Carolinas since these Indians were their "natural allies."[38]

After Braddock's defeat and the criticism that followed, Glen modified his earlier position and encouraged the Catawba to send warriors to Virginia but still maintained until the end of his administration in 1756 that he should be the intermediary for the Cherokee. Virginia, nevertheless, negotiated directly with the tribe. Both Catawba and Cherokee warriors came to Virginia and accompanied Major Andrew Lewis in the Sandy Creek expedition against the Shawnee during the winter of 1755–56.[39]

What appraisal, then, can be made of the role of the two governors in this controversy over Indian affairs and intercolonial cooperation? Glen was undoubtedly more skillful in Indian negotiations and had the opportunity to gain much wider influence and experience with the southern Indians, particularly the Catawba and Cherokee. In fact, Glen ranks well among colonial officials who attempted to guard the rights and welfare of the Indian and to satisfy the persistent demand for more land for western expansion of colonial settlers.

Both governors were expansionist or imperialist and were of the same mind as members of the English ministry such as Lord Halifax, who favored extension of the colonies beyond the Appalachian Mountains rather than restrictions of the colonials east of the mountains. Some mercantilists, though, preferred restriction and argued that the colonies would most safely remain as producers of staples and raw materials rather than develop as competing manufacturers. Both Glen and Dinwiddie provided for forts to the west that would protect friendly natives as well as colonial settlers and that also would serve as a wedge for territorial expansion. Dinwiddie displayed a more universal view of British interests and was more zealous in his efforts to solicit intercolonial cooperation in challenging the French threat to British expansion. On the other hand, Dinwiddie had one of the major French threats appearing in the Ohio Valley, which was more contiguous to Virginia than to South Carolina, and he was a member of the Ohio Company with land claims in the contested area. Glen's warnings about serious threats to the Tennessee Valley did not materialize, and his estimation of the enemy situation was less sound than that of Dinwiddie. The extent of his involvement in land and Indian trading companies has never been determined. Glen's particularistic emphasis upon South Carolina's prerogatives with the Indians and his interest only in South Carolina expansion modified his imperialism to the point that in a sense it became provincialism.

Both governors must share the responsibility for lack of closer cooperation between the colonies. Glen was guilty of frustrating the various proposals suggested for better cooperation of Indian affairs, and Dinwiddie suffered from lack of experience in Indian negotiations. The results for the overall English effort were that the Indians could not only play the English off against the French, but they could also frequently play one English colony against another. The chaos that resulted prompted the decision to establish Indian superintendents as imperial officials. They addressed not only the matter of Indian allies but the related problems of regulation of Indian trade for both diplomatic and economic purposes and the negotiations that were attempted to obtain title to Indian lands. Sir William Johnson had already been appointed superintendent for the North in 1755. By 1756 Edmund Atkin, who had submitted an elaborate report on Indians in the Southeast,[40] received the appointment as superintendent for Indians in the South.

This administrative action was a bright spot in a bad year for colonial affairs. The military campaigns planned for 1755 were not the successes anticipated. Braddock's expedition was a debacle, and William Shirley, governor of Massachusetts, was unable to get his troops organized in time to attack Fort Niagara, which guarded the portage between Lake Ontario and Lake Erie. Sir William Johnson's campaign to take Crown Point on Lake Champlain was foiled by the French, and the English were able only to build Fort Edward and Fort William Henry on Lake George to protect the water route to the Hudson River. The only successful attack was upon Fort Beauséjour on the Bay of Fundy that led to the expulsion of the Acadians to secure the Nova Scotian frontier for the English.

Braddock's defeat left the southern frontier exposed and impelled the colonies to provide protection for their own area. Virginia's position was most seriously jeopardized and led to a variety of preparations. George Washington was appointed by Governor Dinwiddie as "Colonel of the Virginia Regiment" and other forces organized for defense in August 1755. The Virginia Assembly authorized a poll tax for support for a Virginia force not to exceed 1200 men; it also stiffened the militia law but still restricted the use of the militia beyond colonial boundaries. The Assembly took decisive action against its Indian foes by providing bounties for scalps. In August 1755 a two year authorization was made for payment of £10 to any member of the colony killing or taking prisoner any hostile male Indian over twelve years of age; it was a felony, however, to kill any native in alliance with the English. Upon recommendation from Dinwiddie, the Assembly two months later authorized paying the bounty to any friendly Indians who killed or captured hostile ones.[42] Renewed in 1757 with an increase in the amount of the bounty, the provision was, however, repealed in 1758, the Assembly stating that it did not "answer the purposes thereby intended."[43] Use of the bounty along with increased expeditions of friendly Indians was noted by Dinwiddie in correspondence to William Pitt in May 1757:

> We've now near 400 Indians from the Catawbas, Cherokees, Tuscaro-
> ros, Saponies and Notowas, w'ch are order'd to our frontiers to proceed

in Parties w'th some of our People a scalping. . . . This is a barbarous Method of conducting warr, introduc'd by the French, w'ch we ware oblig'd to follow in our own Defence.[44]

Immediately after Braddock's defeat, several western Virginia counties volunteered both men and money for defense, with Hanover County being the first to provide a company. It was recruited under the inspired leadership of the Reverend Samuel Davies, an eloquent Presbyterian minister. Yet turmoil continued to plague the patient Washington, whose troops were exhausted as much from missions prompted by false as from true reports of hostile raiders. Seeking further action by Virginia officials, Washington wrote Governor Dinwiddie emphasizing the "people's distresses" and his own frustration from being unable to relieve them:

> If bleeding, dying! would glut their insatiate revenge, I would be a willing offering to savage fury, and die by inches to save a people! I *see* their situation, know their danger, and participate their sufferings, without having it in my power to give them further relief, than uncertain promises.[45]

The appeal moved Dinwiddie to order to Washington's assistance half of the militia, or some 4000 additional troops, from the western counties of Fairfax, Frederick, Prince William, Culpeper, Orange, Stafford, Spotsylvania, Caroline, Albemarle, and Louisa. The Assembly also responded by providing funds from an additional tax on tithables and on land. Most important, it authorized a "chain of forts" extending from Hampshire County to Halifax County, the number and location to be determined by Dinwiddie.[46] He in turn left the selections largely to Washington, who was more familiar with the peculiar needs of each section of Virginia's exposed frontier. Consisting of fortified cabins, blockhouses, stockades, and forts, these fortifications were strongholds for military personnel as well as a haven for frontier settlers when Indians were on the warpath. Eighty-one of these fortifications were built under Washington's direction in 1756.[47]

In Maryland, Governor Horatio Sharpe took the initiative in providing frontier protection through his own action and delayed calling the Assembly into session unless steps taken by Pennsylvania set an example that Maryland could emulate. Colonel Thomas Dunbar, military subordinate to Braddock and responsible for the command of the expedition after his death, decided to vacate Fort Cumberland constructed at Wills Creek on the upper Potomac River before Braddock's campaign. The decision to abandon this fort and to take to Philadelphia what was left from Braddock's two regiments and three independent companies had created consternation among Maryland settlers. Some concluded "twas better for them to fly naked & leave their habitations then remain an easy Prey to an enraged & cruel Enemy, who may now have free & uninterrupted Access to these two infatuated & defenceless Colonies."

Governor Sharpe encouraged many of the settlers to stay by assuring them of the continuation of troops at Fort Cumberland and the addition of four small forts where he was to "place a small Garrison with Orders to them to patroll from one to the other and to Fort Cumberland and in case of Alarms to receive the neighbouring Families into their Protection."[48] Support for Sharpe's action came from subscription "among the Gentn & People," and even though the procedure was opposed by the Assembly for fear of being bypassed on subsequent measures, Sharpe continued the scheme and helped stabilize the Maryland frontier.[49]

The very day Braddock died in battle, Governor Dobbs of North Carolina was on tour of the frontier of his own province, "to view my Lands, and at the same time the Western Frontier and fix a place to station our Frontier Company," as well as to observe the South Carolina boundary line and the condition of the Catawba Indians.[50] Dobbs selected a fort site for the frontier company of Captain Hugh Waddell on the South Yadkin River and "fixed upon that as most central to assist the back settlers and be a retreat to them as it was beyond the well settled Country, only straggling settlements behind them."[51] News reached Dobbs of Braddock's defeat while still on his survey of the back country, and he immediately summoned the militia of Anson and Rowan counties to help secure the area by cooperating with Waddell's frontier company. Returning to New Bern by the middle of August, Dobbs exhorted the Assembly to action in a fervid and moral tone:

> The flame has already reached our Border and God Almighty has extended his correcting arm and made a Breach upon us, upon account of our wantoness, luxury and neglect of the practice of our religious duties and moral virtue, and we are now to fight *pro aris et facis,* and it requires the united forces of all the Colonies notwithstanding our great superiority to withstand their arms supported by the whole power of France.[52]

The Assembly responded to the crisis by recruiting three additional companies. The new troops were sent north for the Oswego campaign, and Dobbs saw to the improvement of coastal forts as well as to the construction by Waddell of Fort Dobbs near present Statesville, or about twenty-seven miles west of Salisbury. In December 1756 the governor's inspecting commissioner described the fort as manned by about fifty competent men and officers under the command of Waddell; it was

> a good and Substantial Building . . . Oblong Square fifty three feet by forty, the opposite Angles Twenty four feet and Twenty-Two In height Twenty four and a half feet, . . . The Thickness of the Walls which are made of Oak Logs regularly Diminished from sixteen Inches to Six, it contains three floors and there may be discharged from each floor at one and the same time about one hundred Musketts.[53]

The remainder of North Carolina back country settlements away from Fort Dobbs was, however, reported in "a Defenceless Condition."

The year 1756 ushered in the official declaration of hostilities known as the Seven Years' War, the European designation of the conflict that had started two years before as the French and Indian War in the American colonies. A "diplomatic revolution" resulted in a different alignment of European powers from the War of Austrian Succession in the 1740s with England now on the side of Frederick II of Prussia while France joined with both Austria and Russia to challenge the territorial ambitions of Frederick in Poland. The fortunes of the English in America, however, did not immediately improve for their campaign to take Louisbourg on the St. Lawrence River failed. The new French commander, the Marquis de Montcalm, captured Fort Oswego on Lake Ontario in 1756 and Fort William Henry on Lake George the following year.

The persistent military reverses of the English aroused such a popular clamor in the home country that King George II reluctantly agreed to bring William Pitt, the "Great Commoner," into the ministry in the fall of 1757 with primary responsibility for conduct of the war. Pitt immediately instituted major changes. He recalled ineffective senior officers, appointed younger ones on the basis of ability rather than seniority, ordered military moves by direct communications from his office, appealed for greater support of the war effort at home, dispatched more regular troops to America, and encouraged greater cooperation among the English colonies for a united war effort. By 1758 the fruits of his efforts began to turn the tide of victory as Louisbourg fell to the English in July, Fort Frontenac on Lake Ontario surrendered in August, and by November Brigadier General John Forbes, marching directly across Pennsylvania, occupied Fort Duquesne which was partially destroyed by the French as they withdrew without a fight when their Indian allies deserted. The reconstructed fort was then appropriately named Fort Pitt. The momentum of the English effort continued with the most significant victory of the war coming at Quebec in 1759 as the young general, James Wolfe, defeated Montcalm on the Plains of Abraham in the heroic struggle in which both men lost their lives. General Jeffrey Amherst followed this victory with the concluding major engagement of the war in the colonies as Montreal was forced to yield to the English in 1760. Frontier style fighting did not play a prominent role in these concluding battles as continental military tactics of formal battle lines were most often employed, even by the Canadian provincial troops who constituted a substantial part of French forces.

Elsewhere, in the southern colonies, the continuing conflict with Indians made conventional military campaigns difficult and resulted in protracted hostilities. South Carolina continued to be heavily involved in the fighting as the colony most directly concerned with the Cherokee War on the southern frontier that erupted in 1760. Before the end of Governor James Glen's administration in 1756, he had been very active in the efforts to build a fort among the Cherokee; his disagreements with Dinwiddie included this project as well. Dinwiddie had been authorized by crown officials to expend £10,000 for colonial defense and to cooperate with Glen in the construction of a fort among the Overhill Cherokee.[54] Glen requested £7000 of the total but Dinwiddie allotted him only £1000, since he considered Glen's figure much too high and recommended that the South Carolina Assembly provide additional funds needed.[55] The Assembly demurred, stating that the fort would benefit all southern colonies and should be financed either by their cooperative contribution or by the royal treasury. Again both governors were partly in error: Dinwiddie had made inadequate funds available, and Glen had made an excessive request. Glen persuaded the South Carolina Assembly to provide funds by loan for the construction of a fort and had proceeded in person with Captain Raymond Demeré and a task force as far as Ninety-Six when he was notified of the arrival of his gubernatorial successor, William Henry Lyttelton. He was forced to abandon the task, but the new governor later completed it.

Lyttelton reorganized the expedition and persuaded the Assembly in behalf of the crown not only to change the loan of £2000 to a direct appropriation, but to increase the figure to £4000. The new force of over 200 provincial troops and regulars from independent companies was again placed under the command of Captain Demeré and again included the temperamental engineer, William Gerard De Brahm. Meanwhile, Dinwiddie had dispatched Major Andrew Lewis with a smaller Virginia detachment of about sixty workers with the intention that the two groups cooperate in building one fort.[56]

The project that started out to be a cooperative venture ended with the construction of two fortifications. The clever Cherokee seized the opportunity to request two forts along the Little Tennessee River, one on the south side to guard the western approaches and the other on the north side for security against possible attacks from the Francophiles in the Ohio Valley. Major Lewis from Virginia completed a flimsy fort on the north side about one mile from Chota during July of 1756, motivated largely by the desire to get Cherokee warriors for Virginia campaigns. Demeré completed by the spring of 1757 a more substantial fort on the south side despite the erratic performance of De Brahm and his eventual abandonment of the project on Christmas night of 1756. The fort was named Fort Loudoun in honor of the new commander of British forces in America, John Campbell, fourth Earl of Loudoun.[57]

Deep in the heart of Cherokee territory, these forts had the positive potential of strengthening Anglo-Cherokee diplomatic relations and trade. But for each side, they also had their perils. For the Indians, they could provide excessive English control over Cherokee internal affairs; for the English, a small detachment might well become hostages to the Indians in case of hostility. Fort Loudoun, the stronger of the two forts, was of greater concern, for the Virginia-built fort was never properly manned.

Anglo-Cherokee relations had deteriorated by 1760. Why this disruption of the long-standing good relations that had in general prevailed? The French continued their influence through Fort Toulouse and through Creek Indian leaders such as the Mortar. The control of Cherokee leaders that had emerged with the evolution of tribal government under the elders or beloved men began to lapse as individual villages proceeded on an independent course or as mixed reactions to the English emerged in Indian towns. Ill will toward the whites stemmed in part from continued abuses of Indians by unscrupulous traders who took advantage of the southern colonies' failure to work out an effective intercolonial policy for trade. There was also increasing apprehension on the part of the Cherokee with the white settlements that moved closer and closer to their own villages, such as the Long Cane settlements. The Cherokee, recruited for the expedition of General John Forbes against Fort Duquesne in 1758, lost interest when it was delayed from May until the fall, and a number of them were murdered by Virginia frontiersmen in clashes resulting from the Indians' horse stealing in the Bedford area.[58] The long tradition of blood revenge was very much at work. Perhaps this influence plus the lack of wisdom on the part of Governor Lyttelton of South Carolina in handling the Cherokee were the two most important factors in provoking the bloody conflict in 1760.

The major events of the war with the Cherokee as a part of the larger conflict with the French and Indians required the participation of both imperial and provincial troops, with only limited assistance from Indians friendly to the English. Moreover, the conflict challenged anew intercolonial cooperation particularly for Virginia and the two Carolinas. Governor Lyttelton of South Carolina was concerned about local affairs, not international or intercolonial issues, as he pushed the colony toward war. When a Cherokee delegation led by Oconostota appeared in Charles Town seeking ammunition and other trade, Lyttelton upon mixed advice from the council declined to negotiate with these unauthorized representatives and decided upon two dubious steps: to hold part of the delegation as hostages for the exchange of Cherokee guilty of recent murders, and to march in force into the Indian country to Fort Prince George among the Lower Cherokee, and perhaps on to the harassed garrison at Fort Loudoun among the Overhills.[59]

Lyttelton did not correctly anticipate the demands of his mission and sought aid primarily from neighboring North Carolina and not from the imperial force then commanded by Sir Jeffrey Amherst. Both Governor Dobbs and the North Carolina Assembly responded favorably to Lyttelton's call, but Colonel Hugh Waddell, designated by Dobbs to lead the contingent, was delayed too long when most of his 500 militiamen refused to participate until legal provisions were specifically stipulated about the militia serving beyond the bounds of the colony. Lyttelton, therefore, started in October 1759 to Fort Prince George with 150 independent regulars and additional militia to total 1500 troops with small supporting groups from the Catawba and Savannah River Chickasaw. Holding Oconostota and twenty-seven other Cherokee leaders as hostages, he hoped to force the delivery of Indians guilty of recent white murders in accord with the treaty of 1730, and he was also concerned about contact with Fort Loudoun. Confronted by sickness from measles and smallpox, by the absence of further reinforcements, and by the time limit of the first of the year on the recruitment of most of his troops, Lyttelton decided to conclude before departure on December 31 another treaty with the Little Carpenter and other Cherokee leaders. It was to encourage trade and Cherokee support to the English, but it also provided for the continued detention of twenty-two Cherokee as hostages to be exchanged for those guilty of murder. Fort Loudoun was not reached, and Fort Prince George was left with twenty additional whites to its garrison as well as twenty-two hostages, a situation that proved to be a corrosive ferment among the Cherokee.[60]

Concern over the hostages was one of the major factors in escalating the Anglo-Cherokee conflict. Oconostota, who had been released, tricked Lieutenant Richard Coytmore, then in command of Fort Prince George, into a fatal ambush on February 16, 1760, under pretense of a friendly discussion. The resulting confusion brought death to all the Cherokee hostages still in the fort and threatened the colony to the point that Governor Lyttelton called for assistance from General Amherst and from neighboring colonies, including a special appeal to Virginia to dispatch an expedition to relieve Fort Loudoun by way of the more accessible route from the Old Dominion.[61]

General Amherst responded by assigning Colonel Archibald Montgomery of the Seventy-seventh Regiment to the mission against the Cherokee. Montgomery arrived in Charles Town on the first of April 1760, just before Lyttelton departed to be governor of Jamaica and at a time that Lieutenant Governor William Bull was interim governor. With a regimental force of a little over 1300 Scottish Highlanders, Montgomery sought even more support in men, material, and transportation. Although more troops were authorized by the South Carolina Assembly, only 335 rangers from the colony and some 80 Catawba and Savannah River Chickasaw accompanied the expedition.[62] North Carolina failed to provide aid to Montgomery because an impasse developed between Governor Dobbs and the Assembly over the problem of paper currency and financing the troops. In Virginia in response from requests by both Lyttelton and Bull, the governor and Assembly provided 700 additional troops beyond the 300 stationed on the southwestern frontier the previous year. William Byrd III was appointed commander of the expedition that was to be coordinated with Montgomery's moves and was to take advantage of the superior route into Cherokee lands from Virginia.[63]

Montgomery's forces were needed by Amherst in the planned expeditions for Canada. After inflicting considerable damage upon the Lower Towns, Montgomery arrived at Fort Prince George on June 4. He abandoned the hope of continuing to Fort Loudoun because of the difficulty of the terrain and the problem of logistics. After his peace bids failed, he made other raids upon the Middle Settlements before returning to Charles Town in early July. Byrd was slow in completing the organization of his expedition and had little optimism for the possibility of relieving Fort Loudoun and apparently little heart to press on with the campaign. Montgomery's withdrawal with his force of seasoned troops from the Indian country made Byrd's chances for success even less and caused Governor Francis Fauquier of Virginia to take the position that then "it was not thought advisable to let Colonel Byrd with 1000 men mostly new levies, march into the enemy's country."[64]

The starving garrison at Fort Loudoun, which had held out by limited trade with the Indians, particularly Indian women, was finally forced to agree to terms of capitulation on August 8. Promised safe conduct from the Indian country, the garrison started out the next morning but soon a mass of Indians attacked them, killing or taking captive all of the garrison save John Stuart. He was taken from the slaughter by an Indian who seized him and was conducted to safety by his friend, the Little Carpenter. He was later appointed to succeed Atkin as Superintendent of Indian Affairs in the South. One of the striking lessons from the demise of Fort Loudoun was the vulnerability of a fort so isolated in the Indian country that in time of trouble it could not be resupplied or relieved.

The fall of Fort Loudoun moved Amherst to dispatch another expedition of regulars, stronger than Montgomery's force, to wage war on the Cherokee. Governor Bull was to conduct peace negotiations, and assistance from South Carolina was prerequisite for the campaign. Lieutenant Colonel James Grant, who had been an effective officer with Montgomery's Cherokee march, arrived in Charles Town on January 6, 1761. Waiting for better weather and for spring to provide essential grass for his march, Grant did not proceed to Fort Prince George until May 27. Having stationed some of his force of about 2800 along the route to maintain supply and communication lines, he then struck out in early June with a force of about 2250 for a month's raid that successfully chastised the Cherokee.[65] Peace feelers were then extended, but it was not until September 21 that a preliminary treaty was concluded with Indian negotiators led by the Little Carpenter. Terms were worked out along the guidelines that Bull had provided to Grant. Both sides were to restore prisoners, and the English were to resume trade with the Indians at Keowee.

The Cherokee were to relinquish property seized during the fighting, to permit English forts in their nation, and to put to death Cherokee guilty of murdering Englishmen. The omissions from the first draft of the treaty provide important insights into Indian-white relations. The severe demand by the English that four to eight Cherokee, drawn from all sections of the nation, be turned over to the English to be put to death to avenge the death of Englishmen was deleted; and the original provision to force the Cherokee to make Little Carpenter emperor was also dropped.[66] This was done perhaps either at his own suggestion or through realization that an effective leader would have to gain acceptance with the tribal council, which played a more prominent role in Cherokee affairs than was the case when Sir Alexander Cuming seated Moytoy as emperor in 1730.

The Cherokee were thus brought to terms largely through the efforts of regular troops assisted by rangers and other provincial troops from South Carolina, along with a limited number of Indian allies. In the concluding phase of the war with Grant's expedition, North Carolina had again provided little assistance, although the Assembly did authorize 500 provincials in April who were not ready for action until August. Assigned to the command of William Byrd III, they played the same inactive role as his 600 Virginia troops. Without the support of regular troops, and again with little enthusiasm for the campaign itself, Byrd failed to move from Stalnaker's Place to the Cherokee country to coordinate with Grant's attack. Byrd later resigned. Lieutenant Colonel Adam Stephen, successor to Byrd, advanced with Hugh Waddell and his North Carolina contingent to the Great Island of the Holston, only about 100 miles from the Overhill towns. Their major contribution to the end of the conflict was the potential of their attack that made the Cherokee more willing to accept the end of fighting.[67] Implementation of the terms worked out under the direction of Bull, including return of white prisoners, came slowly as the Great Warrior emerged as the new leader of the Cherokee to wield the influence formerly exercised by Old Hop.

The Cherokee War had involved primarily the expeditions of organized troops, but the settlers in advanced frontier positions were sometimes caught in the conflict and had to adjust to the hazards that confronted them. One of the best known encounters was the killing or capture of from forty to fifty Scots-Irish settlers on Long Cane Creek in the back country on February 1, 1760, after an unsuccessful Cherokee assault on Fort Prince George the previous month. En route to refuge in Augusta when the attack occurred, Patrick Calhoun's mother, the grandmother of John C. Calhoun, died in the attack. Patrick reported in the *South Carolina Gazette* that he believed "all fighting men would return and fortify settlement if aided by Rangers for assistance and protection."[68] Without relying fully on rangers, many of the settlers in areas such as the Congarees, Saxe Gotha, and Augusta turned to

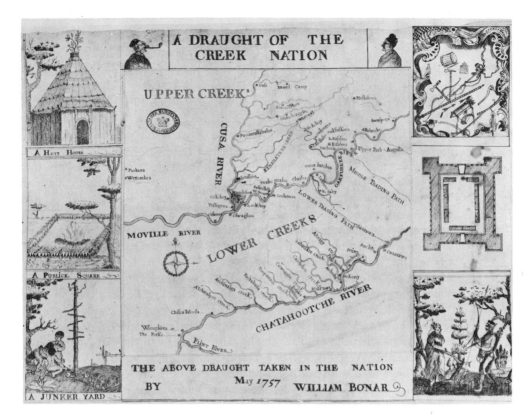

Map of the Creek Nation, 1757. "A Draught of the Creek Nation" by William Bonar drawn while serving among the Creeks as aide to Samuel Pepper. Governor William H. Lyttelton of South Carolina had sent Pepper to confer with the Indians. (Reproduced by permission of the Public Record Office, London. Document C O 700 / Carolina 21.)

their own resources and converted private homes into "settler's forts." In cramped and often unsanitary conditions approximately 1500 settlers spent the miserable winter of 1760–61 in some thirty "settlers' forts" of the upper piedmont.[69] The end of the Cherokee conflict brought relief and opened the routes for both old and new settlers to press farther into the back country.

The young and exposed colony of Georgia played a minor role in the French and Indian War. While France was an antagonist throughout the conflict, the Spanish, who were closer to Georgia, did not enter the fray until 1762 after the Third Bourbon Family Compact of 1761, too late to be an active belligerent before the war ended. In answer to requests by the crown for contributions of men and money in 1755 under John Reynolds as governor and in 1757 under Henry Ellis as his successor, the colony pleaded lack of resources to do more than look to the defense of its own borders. Reynolds stressed building up the militia and projected a series of forts to encircle the colony, both coastal and interior, but they proved to be too expensive to construct. Ellis, however, did complete a series of log forts, and he also worked to place Indian relations on a better footing. Ellis cooperated with Edmund Atkin, Superintendent of Indian Affairs in the South, for his trek into the Creek country where he displayed considerable personal courage in negotiating with both Creeks and Choctaw. A temporary peace between the Chickasaw and the Francophile Choctaw provided for trade with the Choctaw when the French supplies had grown scarce because Louisiana had been unable to get Indian goods from France from the beginning of the conflict until 1758.[70]

James Wright succeeded Ellis as governor of Georgia and joined other southern governors and John Stuart, the new Superintendent of Indian Affairs whose life had been spared at Fort Loudoun, in a conference with representatives of southern Indians at Augusta, Georgia, in November 1763. Authorized by Lord Egremont, Secretary of State for the Southern Department, the conference was designed to explain the significant changes relative to the French and Spanish resulting from the Treaty of Paris and to deal with any other problems the Indians might raise. The end of the war had brought both East and West Florida into British hands, and the Spanish had been pushed beyond the Mississippi while the French had been forced off the continent. Assisting Stuart were Governors Fauquier of Virginia, Dobbs of North Carolina, Thomas Boone of South Carolina, and Wright of Georgia. Indians representing the Cherokee, Catawba, Chickasaw, Choctaw, and Creeks attended. Several Choctaw chiefs, however, did not attend because of fear of passing through Creek country, and some of the Francophile leaders of the Upper Creeks were not present.[71]

At the Augusta Conference more extensive trade was assured the Indians as well as better control and selection of traders, but the Cherokee's complaint of the South Carolina public monopoly of trade was forwarded for crown consideration. The Catawba obtained satisfactory arrangements for their reservation boundaries. The Cherokee were critical of Virginia settlements west of the Kanawha River and of South Carolinians who had advanced beyond Long Cane Creek; but in neither case was a clear resolution of these complaints worked out at the conference. A boundary proposed by the Creeks was agreed to for Georgia that included all of the colony's settlements to that date. The line ran from the Savannah River southward by Little River, Briar Creek, along the Lower Creek path, then along the Ogeechee River, south to the Altamaha River and on beyond as Georgia would extend in the future.[72] The Congress of Augusta successfully maintained stability on most of the southern frontier in Indian-white relations in the period of transition of territorial control, but no such accord was reached on the northern frontier.

Even before the Augusta Conference convened, Indian assaults on the northern colonial frontier extended turmoil to the advanced areas of Maryland and Virginia settlements. The disturbance that swept the northern sector in 1763 stemmed from the fear that the explusion of the French left the Indian at the mercy of the English and under the arbitrary oppression of their traders. No longer would the natives be able to play one European power against the other. When British agents decreased the annual gifts to the Indians that spring, they went on the warpath in an uprising since known as Pontiac's Rebellion.

A brief look at the southwestern Virginia frontier will exemplify the impact of this uprising. By 1762, as noted by one writer, "the people from the sources of James were crossing the dividing ridges and descending upon the Greenbrier, New River and other tributaries of Kenhawa. Others from Roanoke and North Carolina were advancing westward upon the sources of the Stanton, Dan, Yadkin, Catawba and Broad, along the eastern base of the Blue Mountains, with wistful eyes upon the beautiful country of the Cherokees."[73] The Greenbrier settlements of approximately one hundred settlers, however, were either killed or driven out in 1763 in the attacks of Pontiac's Rebellion. The area remained unoccupied until near the end of the decade. Some advanced settlements precariously held on as evidenced by the report of the Reverend John Brown from Greenfield on July 27, 1763:

> All the valleys of Roanoke River and along the waters of the Mississippi are depopulated, except Captain English with a few families on New River, who have built a fort, among whom are Mr Thompson and his family alone remaining. They intend to make a stand until some assistance be sent them. . . .
>
> I have built a little fort in which are eighty-seven persons, twenty of whom bear arms. We are in a pretty good posture of defence, and with the aid of God are determined to make a stand. In five or six other places in this part of the country they have fallen into the same method and with the same resolution.[74]

In the midst of this confusion in Indian-white relations, British imperial officials were moved to establish the Proclamation Line of 1763, setting up a temporary restraining barrier for further white migration west of the watershed of the Appalachian Mountains. This was designed to prevent further encroachment upon Indian lands until formal negotiations could be conducted under imperial supervision for the peaceful acquisition of Indian land titles. The result was an element of instability for advanced white settlers who often did not understand the restriction. There was also a pause in these years of transition before a more vigorous advance into new areas resulted —some in defiance of the delimiting line, others advancing as Indian titles were cleared largely through the efforts of John Stuart as Superintendent of Indian Affairs.

11

Religion and Education on the
Southern Colonial Frontier, 1700–1763

Immigrants to the New World brought with them ideas and institutions, "culture in knapsacks," which was based upon their heritage and experience. These ideas and institutions were shaped and reshaped by the environment of the new country and by the interaction of one group with another in the process of Americanization. While development of cultural institutions was often slow, particularly in isolated frontier areas, there was evidence by the eighteenth century in religion and education of the contribution of many ethnic groups, the interaction of Afro-Americans and Indians with migrating Europeans, and the transforming experience of New World environment upon Old World ideas. For religion and education, the most significant aspect of the process was the preservation and modification of European civilization under the conditions of a new country.

The seventeenth century has often been referred to as a period when immigrants were predominantly and distinctly English, while the eighteenth century witnessed immigration that was primarily non-English. The English cultural foundation of the seventeenth century was so prominent that it continued to pervade the patchwork of culture. The normal pattern of migration from east to west helped to spread English influence from established eastern areas to new western ones, but the extensive north-south movement of new immigrants, such as the Germans and Scots-Irish, created cultural ties that transcended colonial boundaries and at times were more influential than the traditional east-west relationships. Some of the inter-colonial ties were in trade and were enhanced by personal contacts of those engaged in economic pursuits. But the strongest forces at work in the cultural pattern that developed were the common European heritage and the sharing of similar experiences in the American environment.

In contrast to New England, the Anglican Church—the state church of England—became officially the prime religious organization for the southern colonies since it was by law established at some time in all of them. Having been set up in Virginia in the seventeenth century, it received official establishment in Maryland in 1702, in South Carolina in 1706, in North Carolina in 1715, and in Georgia in 1758. Some modifications developed from practice in England. Provision for more local control over the selection of ministers emerged with the vestry wielding more influence than the governor in Virginia and with the choice in South Carolina being made by the parishioners. The shortage of Anglican ministers, which was aggravated by the absence of a bishop in America with the power of ordination, resulted in laymen sometimes filling the pulpit and presiding over exclusive functions of the church such as funerals. The needs of the Anglican Church and the opportunity to serve both Indians and Negroes resulted in the creation in 1701 of the Society for the Propagation of the Gospel in Foreign Parts, the mission arm of the church generally known as the S.P.G.

From reports sent to the Secretary of the S.P.G., the following summary reflects the religious needs in the southern colonies at the beginning of the eighteenth century.

> In *South Carolina* there were computed seven thousand souls, besides negroes and Indians, living without any minister of the Church of England, and but few dissenting teachers of any kind, above half the people living regardless of any religion. In *North Carolina,* above five thousand souls without any minister, or any religious administration used; no public worship celebrated, neither the children baptized, nor the dead buried in any Christian form. *Virginia* contained about forty thousand souls, divided into forty parishes, but wanting near half the number of clergymen requisite. *Maryland* contained about twenty-five thousand, divided into forty parishes, but wanting also half the number of ministers requisite.[1]

By 1750, according to a recent compilation, Virginia had a total of ninety-six Anglican churches that were heavily concentrated in the eastern area of the tidewater, and Maryland had some fifty Anglican groups that were clustered along each side of Chesapeake Bay or in the lower reaches of the Potomac. Only seven in Maryland stretched westward along the upper waters of the Potomac. Besides the ninety-six Anglican churches in 1750, Virginia had seventeen Presbyterian, five Lutheran, five German Reformed, and three Baptist congregations. The majority of these dissenting churches were in frontier counties in the piedmont and valley[2] where immigrant communities predominated.

During the eighteenth century dissenters succeeded in clearly achieving the right to worship with their own group. Although a Virginia statute of 1699 stated that persons over twenty-one should be fined if they "doe neglect or refuse to resort to their parrish church or chapell once in two months to heare devine service upon the sabbath day," it also exempted dissenters who qualified under the English Toleration Act of 1689 and who attended their own religious meetings with the same regularity designated above.[3] Some confusion remained over the exemption of dissenters from church attendance until the law was changed in 1744, but their right to preach was recognized by the governor and council in the same year, 1699, when the Reverend Francis Makemie obtained by his petition the ruling that "all Dissenters under His Governmt Shall have such Liberty allowed them as the Law directs Provided they use it Civily and Quietly."⁴ By act of 1720 authorizing the frontier counties of Spotsylvania and Brunswick, the Virginia Assembly further stipulated that "Because foreign Protestants may not understand English readily, if any such shall entertain a minister of their own, they and their titheables shall be free for ten years."⁵ When adding the new counties of Frederick and Augusta, an additional provision was made to delay organization of the parish until county government had been organized and to permit foreign Protestants to set up their own religious organization without immediate support to the Anglican Church. Frederick County, for example, was organized in 1743, but Frederick Parish was not established until June of 1744 with the selection of vestrymen, even though Quakers had had congregations there for ten years. Augusta Parish, organized in 1747 in Augusta County, had a similar delay even though Presbyterians had been meeting there for almost a decade.

The recognition of the right of dissenters was reiterated by Lieutenant Governor William Gooch in his inaugural address of February 1, 1728/9, when he stated that an indulgence to dissenters was "so consistent with the Genius of the Christian Religion, that it can never be inconsistent with the Interest of the Church of *England.*"⁶ Dissenting ministers were, however, required to file with the county court and to signify where they expected to preach and establish churches, a requirement that proved difficult for some of the Quakers without an established meeting place. As dissenters increased in number—particularly in the piedmont and valley—they did not always adhere to these requirements. For example, the Reverend James Maury protested against Presbyterians preaching in his parish in Louisa County without either license or an officially designated place.

One other unusual arrangement that resulted from the preponderance of dissenters in the early settlements of the valley of Virginia and in North Carolina was the composition of the vestries of some Anglican churches. Many members, sometimes a majority, were either German or Scots-Irish. The first vestry in Augusta Parish in Virginia, for example, had a majority of Presbyterians. Vestries were needed in frontier settlements to provide essential functions, particularly civil ones such as processioning of land to verify boundaries and to care for orphaned children, especially those who had lost their parents in Indian attacks. Augusta Parish had to arrange for the care of forty-seven orphans between 1748 and 1752. While these essential duties apparently justified this composition of some of the early Anglican vestries in the valley, steps were taken by the Assembly to change the situation as soon as the number of Anglicans increased. By act of 1759 dissenters were no longer permitted to continue on a vestry where at least seven, which constituted the quorum for business, belonged to the Church of England. They were to have successors named by other members of the vestry; but if there was not a majority of Anglicans on the vestry, the matter was to be referred to the Assembly.[7] The change in composition of the vestry was delayed in some areas, for Augusta Parish did not replace its Presbyterian members until 1767.

The Anglicans had some success in adapting themselves to foreign groups with limited knowledge of English. In Purrysburg, South Carolina, in the middle country, for example, the French predominated in 1739, but there were also Germans and some English who had taken up claims either ahead of or along with the Switzers brought by Jean Pierre Purry. By 1763 the German speakers were reported to be the most numerous. Although having some members preferring either the Lutheran or German Reformed preaching, there was limited ministration by men of their faith except upon visits from Ebenezer in Georgia. The French were better served by ministers of French extraction, but they rather quickly turned to the services of official Anglicanism. The Reverend Henry Francis Chisselle, serving Purrysburg from 1734 until his death twenty-four years later, conducted Anglican services as an ordained minister but also made special language provision for the French and Germans, providing sermons in French but only giving to the Germans a translation of the English prayer book. Chisselle received financial support from both the S.P.G. and the South Carolina Assembly. One of his successors, the Reverend Abraham Immer, took up duties in Purrysburg in 1760 and continued services in both French and German, providing sermons in German which Chisselle had not done.[8]

The settlement during the 1730s of the township of Orangeburg in the middle country of South Carolina provides another example of the modification of language usage as well as of social interaction of the Germans and English. The Orangeburg settlers were served at first by the ministry of John Ulrick Giessendanner, a Swiss immigrant without formal religious training who kept the church registry in German but died in 1738 after little more than a year in the colony. He was succeeded by his nephew, John Giessendanner, who at first was ordained by the Presbyterians but by 1750 had received ordination in the Church of England. Continuing the Orangeburg registry in English after Anglican ordination until near his death in 1761, the nephew recorded baptisms and marriages for the Germans and the English. The two groups tended to stand apart, and yet a German or English family occasionally assisted each other in baptisms and the registry recorded nineteen intermarriages for the twenty-three years it covered.[9]

The Anglican Church was less influential in North Carolina and in back country or piedmont South Carolina. It never achieved a strong foothold in the unsettled conditions of North Carolina even with the efforts of S.P.G. missionaries, and Governor Arthur Dobbs reported for all of North Carolina in 1764 that "there is not at present more than Six established Clergymen in the province, to officiate in near Parishes; and that there are not above three or four Churches finished in the Province fit for divine Service."[10] In back country South Carolina in 1759, there were no organized Anglican churches, only the efforts of an occasional Anglican missionary.

The difficulties that the Anglican Church had in extending an effective ministry to the southern colonial frontier can be attributed in part to the problems inherent in transmitting the institutions of an older established area to new settlements as well as reflecting to some extent a cleavage between tidewater and piedmont. But the most significant differences arose from the innovations of the variety of immigrant groups who brought their religious heritage to the new settlements. A few examples will illustrate the diversity of these groups and will demonstrate north-south cultural ties that were at times more vital than east-west relationships.

Presbyterians in the valley of Virginia began with the organization of Christian societies and reading houses that evolved into churches. Apparently the first service held by them in the valley was in Frederick County along the Potomac River in 1736. Other ministers came into Augusta County under the encouragement of the Philadelphia Synod, including the Reverend John Craig, who has been called the "first settled minister in western Virginia."[11] Having come in 1740 to the triple forks of the Shenandoah River, he served both Tinkling Spring Church and Augusta Stone Church. Still other Presbyterians turned back across the Blue Ridge along the Staunton and Roanoke rivers to form such churches as those at Cub Creek and Hat Creek. They were a part of the Donegal Presbytery in Pennsylvania, which was under the Synod of Philadelphia. Other congregations in Hanover County looked north in the cultural link that brought them assistance and leadership from the New Castle and New Brunswick presbyteries that became a part of the Synod of New York. Many of the Hanover County Presbyterians turned to the emotional and evangelical appeal of the Great Awakening, a religious movement of international significance with its emphasis upon personal piety and evangelism which were most evident in the southern colonies in the 1730s and 1740s. The Hanover Presbyterians were fortunate in obtaining the services of the Reverend Samuel Davies whose influence also extended to new settlements in other colonies.[12]

Links with northern synods also prevailed among Presbyterians in new settlements in North Carolina. Stimulated by the evangelical nature of the Great Awakening, the Synod of Philadelphia sent ministers during the 1740s to North Carolina. Reverend Davies noted that one minister on a tour during the early 1740s "underwent great Hardships in *Carolina,* without much Success, by Reason of the Fewness of the Inhabitants at that Time; who were generally such uncultivated Savages, that there was little Prospect of doing them much Service without continuing a long Time among them to teach them the first Rudiments of Christianity; and so scattered, that but very few of them could convene in one Place to hear."[13] By the middle of the century, Davies noted a definite improvement in number, attitude, and educational background of ministers as he referred to a request from a congregation on the Peedee River for a minister that the New Castle Presbytery was unable to fill.

North Carolina was particularly affected by migration from the north, and apparently a greater number of Presbyterians than other religious groups were new arrivals. On the "Northwest Carolina Frontier," embracing the Yadkin and Catawba rivers and including Salisbury, a majority of the newcomers migrated from older settlements in the colonies and many had been in America for thirty years or more. Furthermore, a greater number of Anglicans, Baptists, and Quakers came directly from established families in the colonies than was true for the Presbyterians.[14] That many Presbyterians were recent arrivals is not surprising in view of the heavy migration from northern Ireland. But the preponderance of migrants coming from established northern settlements contributed to the religious ties that turned northward and likewise helps to explain the degree to which adaptations were made in the Americanization of religious organizations as well as the emergence of psychological outlooks that eventually came to be distinctly American.

Considerable diversity of religious beliefs characterized German settlers, and their delay in promoting formal religious organizations complicates the problem of identification. Most extensive among them were the Lutherans and German Reformed, and during their early years of settlement they often resorted to meeting only in homes or schoolhouses with religious services conducted by the schoolmaster or other laymen without the sacraments that required an ordained minister. When church buildings were first completed, the two groups sometimes shared the same one. The Germans had fewer organizational ties with churches to the north, but in Virginia, for example, new congregations were visited by German missionaries from both Maryland and Pennsylvania which helped to fill the empty pulpits that often existed. In Georgia, one of the most distinctive religious groups were the Salzburgers, who carved out of the wilderness only a few miles from Savannah both Old and New Ebenezer. Living under the strong arm of John Martin Bolzius, they developed a Lutheran community with excellent religious conditions, and with law and order maintained without resort to the usual court system.[15]

One small group of Germans, Sabbatarians from Johann Beisel's Ephrata settlement in Pennsylvania, apparently penetrated the far reaches of the western area of Virginia and were visited by Dr. Thomas Walker in the spring of 1750 on his land hunting venture in behalf of the Loyal Land Company. Walker encountered this German group while visiting William English (Ingles), a Scots-Irishman from Pennsylvania who had settled with a Draper family in the area called "Draper's Meadows" near present Blacksburg, Virginia. About English and the Sabbatarians, Walker wrote:

> He has a mill, which is the furthest back except one lately built by the Sect of People, who call themselves the Brotherhood of Euphrates, and

are commonly called the Duncards; who are the upper inhabitants of the New River, which is about 400 yards wide at this place. They live on the west side, and we were obliged to swim our Horses over. The Duncards are an odd set of people, who make it a matter of Religion not to Shave their Beards, ly on Beds, or eat Flesh, though at present, in the last, they transgress, being constrained to it, as they say, by the want of a sufficiency of Grain and Roots, they having not long been seated here. I doubt the plenty and deliciousness of the Venison and Turkeys has contributed not a little to this. The unmarried have no private Property, but live on a common Stock. They dont baptize either Young or Old, they keep their Sabbath on Saturday, and hold that all men shall be happy hereafter, but first must pass through punishments according to their Sins. They are very hospitable.[16]

More numerous and important were the Moravians who were one of the most interesting and successful groups on the entire southern colonial frontier. Well known for their great zeal in missionary work among the Indians and for the assistance they gave to other frontier settlers during times of turmoil, they also provide a study in social and economic experiments with a communal organization based upon their religious beliefs and later modified as frontier conditions changed. Descending originally from followers of John Hus, they revived the "Renewed Church" or United Brethren (*Unitas Fratrum*) in 1722 with the migration of "Brethren of the Ancient Church" from Bohemia and Moravia because of religious persecution to the lands of Count Nicholas Ludwig von Zinzendorf in Saxony. On his lands was established the community of Herrnhut, which became the major fountainhead for migration of Moravians to America. To implement the vigorous missionary policy advocated by the group, the Herrnhut community arranged for the acquisition of land for new communities, or "settlements," which have been described as "societies or communities of missionaries." The United Brethren usually held title to the land in the name of an individual, and there were varying experiments in the social and economic organizations of the "settlements," some adopting community living more than others.[17]

Count Zinzendorf's plans to settle a group of Schwenkfelders in the new colony of Georgia were altered when they unexpectedly accepted arrangements to go to Pennsylvania. August G. Spangenberg, Moravian clergyman and later bishop, was then authorized to negotiate with the Georgia trustees in behalf of Zinzendorf in 1734, and fifty acres were also granted to Spangenberg and David Nitschmann. As it turned out, the Moravians who came to Georgia in 1735 and 1736 occupied only the two fifty-acre tracts in Savannah which were used in common for the group. In 1739 and 1740 they abandoned Georgia for Pennsylvania, primarily because of opposition to military service in the buffer frontier colony.[18]

The Moravians in Georgia introduced the community of labor that was later developed more elaborately in the General Economy at Bethlehem, Pennsylvania. While retaining the general religious organization of Herrnhut, their economic activities were influenced by the challenges of frontier life. Encouraged by Spangenberg, they adopted a modified community of labor and based their inspiration for this *Gemeinschaft* on the second chapter of Acts, particularly verses 44 and 45 (King James version): "(44) And all that believed were together, and had all things common; (45) and sold their possessions and goods, and parted them to all men, as every man had need." The manuscript diary of the Savannah congregation for 1736 describes their decisions to adopt the *Gemeinschaft*:

> There has been no "society" like that at Jerusalem, but at this present time it becomes necessary, for material reasons. Were we only individuals all would fear to give one of us credit, for they would think, 'he might die,' but nothing will be denied the 'Society,' for each stands for the other. Each member must work diligently, since he does not labor for himself alone but for his brethren, and this will prevent much laziness. No one must rely on the fact that he understands a handicraft, and so on, for there is a curse on him who relies on human skill and forgets the Divine power. No one will be pressed to give to the 'Society' any property which has hitherto belonged to him—Each person present was asked if he had any remarks to make, but there were no objections raised.[19]

In Bethlehem, Pennsylvania, the General Economy, which has been termed "a typical American experiment in religious communism," was more fully developed and was effective from 1744 to 1762. Evidence of the communal organization was present in the "Sea Congregations" of immigrants to Pennsylvania as early as 1742 with a division of labor according to the Choir system. The Choir division, also evident in Europe, was more highly developed in America with separate housing provided for many of the groups. In Bethlehem the Choirs included the "married people, the widowers, the widows, the unmarried men, the unmarried women, the older boys, the older girls, the little boys, and the little girls." Settlers in the General Economy were also divided according to specific trades and occupations with special abilities influencing the designation.[20] There was, then, a community of labor, but there was not an absolute community of property because individuals were permitted to retain title to private property when joining the group.

Essentially the same organization was followed in the new Moravian settlements in North Carolina during the 1750s, although their social and economic organizations were never as complex as the General Economy in Pennsylvania. Lord Granville, retaining land in North Carolina as his share of the original Carolina proprietary grant, offered to sell a large area to the

Moravians after Parliament in 1749 encouraged them to settle in America.[21] Spangenberg and a party came from Pennsylvania in 1752 and selected the Wachovia tract in present Forsyth County of 98,985 acres, which was purchased by the *Unitas Fratrum* for £500 sterling and an annual quitrent of £149 9s. 2½ d. The initial heavy expenses for land purchase, surveying, and colonizing led to the selling of shares in return for which the shareholder could claim 2000 acres of land as one of the members of the Wachovia Society. The Wachovia tract contained, therefore, during the early years lands designated as belonging to the Unity and lots that were set aside for the shareholders in the Society.[22]

In the settlement of the North Carolina land, Count Zinzendorf had proposed a "Patriarchal Plan" whereby "each family would live alone, and work for its own support." Spangenberg, more familiar with frontier hazards and the limitations of the experience of the settlers, advocated in the beginning some common effort with six to ten families working together under one overseer.[23]

At the first Moravian settlement at Bethabara ("Old Town") in 1753, the communal organization prevailed with the establishment of the Bethabara "Oeconomie." As in other Moravian settlements, pure communism was not followed, for private property did not have to be surrendered when joining the group. But under the community of living in early Bethabara, "the farm was tilled for the common good, income from farm products and the industries went into the general purse, housing, food, and clothing was supplied to each member."[24] The Choir divisions were also used and were most important for the social and religious life of the settlement.

In 1759, Bethania ("New Town") was founded about three miles from "Old Town" under somewhat different organization. Designed in part to accommodate some of the refugee families that made their way to the Moravian settlements during the French and Indian War, the new settlement differed from the original one in providing less communal living. Some thirty lots were provided in Bethania for lease or rent, half for the refugees and half for the Bethabara settlers who preferred "to begin husbandry and housekeeping for themselves."[25] Frontier conditions had, thus, contributed to the decision for community living, but gradually this was abandoned as the settlement matured and the area was afforded protection. It was not until the middle of the nineteenth century, however, that the lease system of land use was discontinued, and the supervision by the religious group of economic activities was completely abandoned.

This unique experience of the Moravians was effective to an unusual degree for the time. With justification, it has been described as "the best integrated and most successful community in the Southern colonies." With deserved pride in their achievements, the Moravians in 1763 stated that "Bethabara has been so far the pantry for all the settlers in this neighborhood."[26]

The influence and growth of the Baptists were widespread and cut across ethnic lines more than most other groups. With the Great Awakening, two separate groups emerged during the 1750s. The Regular or General Baptists were more inclined toward Calvinism and predestination, and were members of the Philadelphia Association. The Separate Baptists were more receptive to Arminianism and the belief that salvation was open to all through repentance. The Regular Baptists were the first to come to Virginia and made their appearance in the western settlements in the early 1740s, having come to the Shenandoah Valley from Maryland. During the 1750s Shubal Stearns, the founder of the Separate Baptists, came first to western Virginia but met opposition by the General Baptists. He then moved in 1755 to North Carolina, where Sandy Creek Church became a leader of the Separate Baptists. The Anglican preacher, Charles Woodmason, noted in 1765 for North Carolina "that the Baptists are now the most numerous and formidable Body of People which the Church has to encounter with, in the Interior and Back Parts of the Province. . . . these Baptists . . . have taken such deep Root there that it will require long Time and Pains to grub up their Layers."[27]

It is not to be assumed that most, or even a majority, of the frontiersmen always subscribed to the beliefs of the various religious groups, nor that they succeeded in living a godly life that matched the high moral standards for which the churches stood—standards that not even some of its ministers were always able to achieve. This problem is not peculiar to the frontier, but conditions there made it difficult to achieve these ideals. Chaos of the moral order was, however, less evident where strong religious organizations, such as that provided by the Moravians and Salzburgers, extended their influence and control over every facet of life.

One prime example of religious extremes on the frontier was the fanaticism of a strange religious sect of Weberites, whose short-lived orgies on the South Carolina frontier has been referred to as the Weber heresy. In the absence of a "Dutch Minister" in Saxe Gotha and the Dutch Fork, "these ignorant Germans," as noted by Lieutenant Governor William Bull, "from a pious desire of having some religion had unhappily formed a Sect of Enthusiasts."[28] Led by Jacob Weber with the assistance of John George Smithpeter, the sect gathered strength during the late 1750s and burst into an uncontrolled frenzy amid the tension created by the Cherokee War. Jacob Weber, a man who vacillated from emotional extremes of depression to exhilaration and who was stimulated by popular support, referred to himself as "the most High" and the head of the Trinity. The triune was completed with John George Smithpeter as the Son, and Dauber, "a godless, colored preacher," as the Spirit. The harmony of the triune, however, was soon disrupted by internal quarreling. Weber and Smithpeter concluded that Dauber, the Spirit, was too "lukewarm," and incited the sect to smother him by trampling upon him in a pit filled with mattresses. Weber later turned upon Smithpeter and again the sect responded by "trampling upon his throat" until he was dead.[29] For these deeds, seven Weberites were tried in Charles Town for murder and four were convicted, but only Jacob Weber was put to death by hanging on the gallows after three of his compatriots were pardoned by Bull. While the so-called heresy was reported to have infiltrated to North Carolina, Virginia, and Maryland among both German and English settlers, it apparently was of little, if any, consequence following the death of Weber. The episode is significant in reflecting the extremes to which religion could go in a frontier area without the controls usually imposed by organized churches, regular ministers, and a better educated laity.

Religion and education were twin facets of American colonial culture. In the colonial South the official Anglican Church established a few free schools such as in Maryland. Some schools were private with restricted enrollments or simply instruction by private tutors; others were public schools admitting all able to pay tuition; still others were charity schools often sponsored by counties; and finally there were various educational provisions by immigrant groups who usually emphasized religious training to further their sectarian point of view. There were not, however, the numerous tax-supported schools that had developed in New England. Legislation did provide in most of the southern colonies for training in reading and writing for orphans, the poor, illegitimate and mulatto children, and apprentices. Education in frontier areas of the eighteenth century, to the extent that it existed, was in part the extension of the agencies from the more stable eastern settlements; there were also the sectarian innovations of various immigrant groups; and in many instances the educational efforts were left to the individual families.

A variety of reports emphasized the poor state of education in frontier settlements such as those for South Carolina. Governor James Glen noted in 1753 about many of the children in the back country that their parents failed to "bestow the least Education on them, they take so much Care in raising a Litter of Piggs, their Children are equally naked and full as Nasty, The Parents in the back Woods come together without any previous Ceremony, and it is not much to be wondered at that the Offspring of such loose Embraces should be little looked after."[30] *The South Carolina Gazette* in June 1765 proclaimed: "We present as a grievance the want of public schools in the back parts of this province, for the education and instruction of the children of the poor people who are settled there."[31]

Yet much learning took place even in the remote districts of the colonies, particularly within the family. Mothers instructed their daughters in the art of cooking at the hearth, in the use of the spinning wheel and loom, and in the sewing of homespun cloth. Daughters also learned the duties of a wife and mother in preparation for their own marriage. Among German immigrants particularly, both mother and daughter learned to assist in the cultivating and harvesting of crops. Sons, unless apprenticed to a master to learn a special trade, were taught by their fathers the elementary requirements of agriculture, the use of the ax in its many functions, the skill of tools and perhaps the anvil, and sometimes the workbench for crafts. Joseph Doddridge, for example, described the useful art he had mastered in the valley of Virginia:

> It was that of weaving shot-pouch straps, belts and garters. I could make my loom and weave a belt in less than one day. Having a piece of board about four feet long, an inch auger, spike gimlet, and a drawing knife, I needed no other tools or materials for making my loom. It frequently happened that my weaving proved serviceable to the family, as I often sold a belt for a day's work, or making an hundred rails. So that, although a boy, I could exchange my labor for that of a full grown person for an equal length of time.[32]

The use of the rifle and other firearms was most certainly also included in the instruction of young men, and often even for women who needed this skill for emergencies where they might confront danger alone. In areas without formal schooling, either the mother or father, though most often the mother, provided some form of basic instruction in reading and writing; and when favorably disposed to religion, they added the use of the Bible.

The role of the family is not always documented, but there is enough evidence to demonstrate that relatives also assisted in the instruction of adults. Daniel Boone, for example, although never developing a high degree of literacy, did learn to read and write with the assistance of his brother's wife, and this ability in an area with limited education aided Boone in his election as a representative to the state legislature of Virginia during the Revolution. James Read, a Baptist preacher who moved from the valley of Virginia to North Carolina at the time of the French and Indian War, started his ministry without being able to read or write, but with the aid of his wife he studied sufficiently to be able to understand the Bible on his own. In South Carolina, it was noted about John Pearson living at the Congarees in the 1750s that "Under the instruction of his father, and with a little school education, he became a very good English scholar."[33]

Maryland had established in its older settlements more formal education with the beginning of King William's School in Annapolis in 1701 under authorization of an earlier act of 1696. Subsequent legislation of 1723 provided for at least one school in each county with 100 acres of land and compensation for Anglican schoolmasters. Although this joint church-state enterprise was not realized in every county, several institutions were set up and support was authorized for schools from a variety of tax sources such as tobacco, furs and skins, pork, and naval stores. A Maryland report in 1754 on schoolmasters in each county, which was designed to thresh out the papists, is valuable for the additional insight it gives about schools and teachers.

Frederick, the frontier county established six years before, reported four teachers of private schools subscribing to the oath of abjuration. The report on Prince George, although no longer primarily a frontier county, revealed the range of schoolmasters from the better trained ministers to at least two indentured servants and four convict servants.[34]

Practical studies were favored in both old and new settlements, particularly near the end of the colonial period. Hugh Jones in the 1720s noted the inclination of many Virginians to become involved in trade and to educate themselves through the daily experience in business rather than through a liberal education with books. The great majority of books emphasized classical education, but a number devoted primarily to practical problems did appear. For example, the inventory of Mathew Hopkins in Frederick County, Maryland, in 1751 included *The Mariners Compass Rectified* and *Every Man His Own Doctor*.[35] One Georgia family was also prepared for self-medication with a handwritten book identified as the "Doctrine of Inflim Diseases." Books in Virginia in the 1750s included instructions for self-education in business in *The American Instructor: or Young Man's Best Companion*. For back country South Carolina, Anglican Woodmason in 1757 urged schools for children, for if their "Heads and Hands, be employ'd in Exercises of the Manual and Useful Arts: Tradesmen would increase—Manufactures be follow'd up—Agriculture be improv'd."[36]

The most extensive discussion of this call for a more utilitarian education came from the Reverend James Maury, Anglican minister and director of a small boarding school in piedmont Virginia where young Thomas Jefferson was a student. Rector of Fredericksville Parish in Louisa County, Maury exerted himself in serving three churches and a chapel. He complained that his charge was "the most extensive and inconvenient Parish in the colony" and that he lived "just a post-boy's life in which one galloped away one's constitution." Despite these duties he still managed to run his boarding school, to invest in the Loyal Land Company, and to stand later as the plaintiff in the celebrated Parson's Cause.

Upon receipt of the discourse of Jonathan Boucher, a fellow Anglican minister, in defense of classical education, Maury responded in 1762 on 100 half sheets of paper. While he acknowledged the value of classical education, he emphasized the need for instruction in "Branches of useful, practical Knowledge" and urged that a young man "while under his Tutor, be chiefly employed in Studies, that will be useful to him in the approaching active Scenes of Life." He reiterated in conclusion:

> For *our Youth*, I repeat it again; because the Genius of our People, their Way of Life, their Circumstances in Point of Fortune, the Customs and Manners and Humors of the Country, difference us in so many important Respects from Europeans, that a Plan of Education, however

judiciously adapted to these last, would no more fit us, than an Almanac, calculated for the Latitude of London, would that of Williamsburg.[37]

While Maury was primarily concerned with the future of Virginia gentlemen as estate owners, his views were put forth in an area near the frontier line and they voiced the same emphasis upon utilitarian education that applied to other members of society.

Several colonies passed a series of impressive laws during the seventeenth and eighteenth centuries for the care and education of children who were orphans, poor, illegitimate, or mulatto. Motivated by economic and humanitarian reasons, the colonies provided education for many of these children mainly through the apprentice system in which many of the indentures for service of the apprentice included the requirement of teaching the basic skills of reading and writing. The responsibility for administering the compulsory education requirement usually rested with the county court and the churchwardens of the parishes, who served as the representative of the vestry of the Anglican Church. For example, the county courts in Virginia, made up of justices of the peace appointed by the governor, assumed much of the responsibility for enforcing the provisions for orphans, while it shared with the churchwardens the authority over the poor and illegitimate.

To what extent did western expansion influence these provisions for the less privileged members of society? The existence of fewer schools in frontier areas suggests the possibility of greater resort to the apprentice system for education, but the increased number of counties and parishes without adequate officials made administration difficult. Yet the need for schools persisted because war conditions in frontier areas in periods such as the French and Indian War increased the number of orphans and compelled action by local officials. In the valley of Virginia the Augusta County Court bound out at least 150 orphans in a ten-year period, while Frederick County arranged for some 220 during the same time. In Frederick County, Maryland, in 1750 an indenture exemplified both the provision for education as well as the freedom dues when the November Court stipulated that during the six-year indenture of Edward Bullen the master shall provide one year of schooling and give Bullen at the expiration of his contract a horse, saddle, and a decent suit of clothes.[38] Implementing the provision for education often depended to a great extent upon the attitude of the master in charge, and it is likely that many county justices and churchwardens were more concerned with the economic burden upon the county and the need for more skilled tradesmen than in assuring the education of youth with books.

Beyond these legal provisions for education, many immigrant groups made their own contribution to the educational pattern. The Presbyterians were noted for their insistence upon a well educated ministry, and the training of their leaders was done either in Scotland or England, at Gilbert Tennent's

"Log College" once it had been set up at Neshaminy in Pennsylvania in 1727, or at the College of New Jersey (Princeton) after 1746. As early as 1749 the Reverend John Brown established the important Augusta Academy in the valley of Virginia, and in North Carolina the Presbyterians added several schools by the time of the Revolution.

German immigrants, particularly the Lutherans and German Reformed, were slow to establish formal churches but did attempt to satisfy both their religious and educational needs with a school and schoolmaster. By the late 1740s Germans in Maryland benefited by the school of Thomas Schley at Frederick. In Virginia, the Lutherans, who built Hebron Church in 1740 in present Madison County, were reported in 1748 as having "a beautiful large church and school"; and the German Reformed were listed as having a "church and school" at Germantown,[39] their location in present Fauquier County just south of Warrenton. In Georgia the Germans sustained three or four schools, again closely related to the church under Lutheran control. They were committed to teaching in both English and German and emphasized traditional moral values as well as the necessities of a vocation. The school at Zion on an outlying plantation, for example, met in the church where space was provided by a partition in the sanctuary.

Moravians in North Carolina were likewise concerned about education, and the challenge of frontier conditions did not eliminate the opportunities for both adults and children. In 1756, for example, the *Records of the Moravians* reveal for adults that "After supper an English class was begun for the Single Brethren"; and for children, "Br. Petersen has begun a day school for our boys and his wife assists Sr. Kalberlahn with the girls. Br. and Sr. Bachoff have taken charge of the children in Bethania."[40]

The extent of literacy is one index to the effectiveness of educational efforts, but there is some difficulty in getting precise evidence for frontier areas. One reliable estimate for the South Carolina back country in the 1740s and 1750s places illiteracy between ten and twenty percent.[41] The ability of settlers to provide their own signature indicates more widespread literacy than one might anticipate, although in some cases this might be the limit of their writing skill. A petition of 1756 from the Saluda country in South Carolina had sixteen out of fifty-six signing with their mark, one of the higher rates of illiteracy for the colony at that time. Most or all of these petitioners were likely Caucasian, and these figures do not reflect the educational level of other racial groups.

The presence of the Indian and the Negro challenged Anglicans and other immigrant groups to provide for education and conversion to Christianity. Charters for colonization had included exhortations for missionary programs and several Christian organizations in Great Britain, including the S. P. G., initiated efforts to fulfill these goals for both the Indian and Negro. More efforts were initiated than has often been recognized, although the success during the colonial period was limited.

Virginia, for example, inaugurated during the seventeenth century the plans of educating Indian boys, bringing in whole families among the English, and training young Indians in the grammar school of the College of William and Mary.[42] Governor Alexander Spotswood also had a keen interest in these efforts in behalf of Virginia, and arranged for education by Charles Griffin of as many as 100 Indian students in 1716 as a part of his integrated plan for the Virginia Indian Company, an effort that came to an end with the termination the following year of the company because of its monopolistic features in trade. Commissary James Blair was instrumental in arranging for part of the proceeds from the estate in England of Robert Boyle, author of Boyle's law in science, to support Indian boys at William and Mary. The income annually received in Virginia in the eighteenth century was used to clothe, feed, and educate from eight to twelve Indian boys at a cost of about fourteen pounds per year for each student. By 1723 sufficient funds had accumulated to construct Brafferton Hall on the campus of William and Mary for Indian education, and classes, usually segregated, were conducted for them in the grammar school. For the year 1754, for example, the Bursar's Report identifies eight of the seventy-five students at William and Mary as Indians supported under the Boyle fund.[43] The prime goal of these efforts was to send the boys back to their tribes as agents of both Christianity and education.

South Carolina's most notable missionary was Dr. Francis Le Jau, a Huguenot refugee who became a firm Anglican in England before coming to America. From 1706 until his death in 1717, he served in South Carolina among the Huguenots in Goose Creek as a missionary of the S. P. G. Master of six languages, he strove with all the energy of his physically ailing frame to realize the objectives of the society: to educate and Christianize both the Indian and the Negro, and to establish Anglicanism firmly among white settlers. Although meeting with many difficulties and disappointments, he had moments of success such as the response of about fifty Negroes and Indians to his invitation to remain beyond the regular Sunday service for about thirty minutes: "I teach 'em the Creed, the Lords Prayer, and the Commandments; I explain some portion of the Catechism, I give them an entire Liberty to ask questions, I endeavour to proportion my answers and all my Instructions to their want and Capacity: I must acknowledge that the hand of God does visibly appear on this particular occasion."[44] The Indians to which Le Jau referred were most likely either Indian slaves or small groups of free natives often referred to as "settlement" Indians, living in proximity to whites and participating in a tribute system which was more extensively used in Virginia. Le Jau was also interested in Indians in other areas and set out to learn their language in order to overcome this barrier to communication. In 1708 he forwarded a copy of the Lord's Prayer in the Savannah Indian language to the secretary of the S. P. G. Later in 1714 he expressed his continued interest in this problem but lamented the poor cooperation of the Indian traders: "I will take pains to get those several Dialects of which I have sent to You a small Specimen. . . . I only complain of the dulness and laziness of those Traders that cou'd inform me; There is no Scholar and hardly a Man of sense among them all."[45] For some traders, it was not a question of laziness; it was opposition to missionaries who would scorn their unscrupulous dealings with the natives and their conspiring to foment intertribal wars from which they expected monetary gain.

Another missionary, Samuel Thomas, complained of the difficulty of overcoming the problem of language and used this as one of his excuses for never working among natives. He complained that the Indian language was "utterly void of such Terms as we express the most necessary Truths of Christian Religion in, they have no word for God, or heaven, or Kingdom for a mediator or for his death and satisfaction."[46]

Several other efforts by individuals were made in various southern colonies, but the most concerted one was the project for the school at Irene initiated by the Moravians in Georgia in 1737 under the leadership of Benjamin Ingham with the assistance of Peter Rose and his wife. Serving the Creek Indians on an island in the Savannah River about a mile upstream from Savannah, the school thrived as a combined project of the Moravians and the trustees of Georgia until its progress was ended in 1739 and 1740 by hostility with the Spanish, the departure of the Moravians from Georgia, the death of the Indian leader Tomo-Chi-Chi, and the decision of Ingham to return to England.[47]

Various views were expressed about the progress of missionary and educational efforts among the Indians. In Virginia, for example, Governor Spotswood was optimistic for his program and stated that the Indian boys were "as much desirous of a liberal education as can be expressed."[48] Hugh Jones and William Byrd II were more pessimistic, Byrd stating that after the Indian boys returned to their tribe, "instead of civilizeing and converting the rest, they have immediately Relapt into Infidelity and Barbarism themselves."[49] Governor Dinwiddie, writing to the Cherokee leader, Old Hop, noted another aspect of the problem:

> The Young Men that came here for Education at our College did not like Confinement, and, in Course, no Inclination to Learning. They were too old. If you sh'd think proper to send any, they sh'd not exceed the Age of 8 Years. Those that came here were well cloath'd and properly taken Care of, but they co'd not be reconcil'd to their Books: they went away of their own accord with't leave.[50]

A variety of difficulties on the part of the colonists prevented full realization of the educational and missionary goals for work among the

Indians. Most colonists did not persevere in the projects that were started, influenced in part by either an anti-Indian bias or by hostilities that disrupted peaceful relations. Even a minister like Samuel Davies complained, particularly during the French and Indian War, of the Indians as "blood-thirsty savages" and "infernal furies in human form."[51] Traders, as previously noted, offered little assistance either because of lethargy or deliberate opposition for selfish reasons. More basic was the failure of the English to devise plans of education that gave adequate recognition to the cultural heritage and traditions of the Indians, and the unyielding attempts to make Englishmen of them. This has been a perennial problem in race relations that has not yet been fully resolved.

Work among Negroes also received some attention in frontier areas where in general there were fewer blacks than in eastern established settlements. In the valley of Virginia embracing the area from the Potomac River to the headwaters of the James, the population for 1763 has been estimated as 20,000 whites and 1000 blacks. Piedmont Virginia, however, had a substantial increase in Negroes during the eighteenth century, particularly in Louisa and Spotsylvania counties which by 1755 had a population of over 52 percent slave.[52] South Carolina had by 1759 a total population of 36,000 whites and 55,000 blacks with the great portion of the slaves in the tidewater. In the middle country of the upper belt there were approximately 9000 whites and only 1300 slaves, while the back country was about 10 percent slave.[53]

Several projects for Negroes were actually initiated in eastern settlements and had potential influence for frontier areas. In Maryland the commendable work of the Reverend Thomas Bacon, Anglican minister in Talbot County on the Eastern Shore, included the preaching of several sermons in behalf of Negroes and the solicitation of funds that made possible the establishement in 1750 of a Charity Working School, open to all without "distinction of sex, race, or condition of servitude." Bacon moved west to Frederick County in 1758 and continued his interest in the poor, proposing a charity school for Negro girls and the possible use of "Circulating Schoolmasters." But Bacon's declining health and his heavy involvement with the compilation of his Laws of Maryland, which were published in 1765, prevented his pressing these goals in Frederick as effectively as in Talbot.[54]

In 1743 the Reverend Alexander Garden, Anglican minister who also served as commissary in assisting the Bishop of London, succeeded in the establishment of the Charles Town Negro School which featured several perceptive innovations. Referring to the Negro as a "Nation within a Nation," Garden advocated the training of "Home Born Male Slaves," between the ages of twelve and sixteen by "Negro Schoolmasters, Home-born," and recommended that, once the slaves were trained, they should be assigned to work under appropriate persons in designated places.[55] Garden had excellent success with the Negro Harry as teacher, and the school continued beyond his death in 1756 but declined after 1764 with the death of Harry and the lessening of support by the S. P. G. in South Carolina. Increasing to seventy boys and girls and also reaching adult slaves interested in studying, the school had the unrealized potential of providing black teachers for much of the colony.

While these efforts for special schools had significant possibilities for the colonies, the more enduring work came from individual ministers. Once plantation owners received assurances that baptism did not provide freedom for the slave, ministers worked more freely with both whites and blacks. Samuel Davies in Virginia reported about 300 Negroes in his ministry, and his neighboring Presbyterian parson, John Todd, referred to having about 200 or more attend his services.[56] In South Carolina the Reverend Thomas Thompson reported for his frontier parish of St. Bartholomew in 1736 that there were "120 Families of White People, and 1200 Negroes." While several blacks attended his services and were baptized by him, he did not reach as many as the Reverend John Fordyce in the parish of Prince Frederick along the northernmost edge of settlement in South Carolina. Fordyce, for example, reported for 1742 the baptism of "39 white Children, 5 Black, 2 Mullato's and 3 adults"; for 1743, "42 white and 2 negro children"; and for 1744, "35 children, 4 Negro Children, and Two Adult Negro Women."[57]

To reiterate, both religion and education on the southern colonial frontier were promoted by colonial governments, by religious groups, and by families. Only partial success, however, was achieved in these efforts. The extension of official Anglicanism to new settlements was more effective in Maryland and Virginia than in the Carolinas and Georgia, particularly in areas such as the piedmont section and the county of Frederick in Virginia where migration of leading families from the east gave support to its continuation. Modified by adjustment to the new country, the Established Church was further challenged by the religious preferences of various immigrant groups whose migration from northeast to southwest created north-south ties that had greater cultural significance than the traditional east-west relationship. Attempts to convert and educate both Indians and Negroes continued on the frontier primarily as individual efforts and were less formal than such projects in established coastal areas as the Negro School of Alexander Garden in Charles Town.

The influence of the environment upon the pioneer settler and the social interaction of the various immigrant groups contributed to the process of Americanization. Yet in cultural affairs where religion played the dominant role, diversity of culture rather than uniformity was a major characteristic throughout the eighteenth-century colonial era.

Retrospect

Past studies of the American frontier have not examined in detail the full span of the southern colonial frontier to 1763. While there have been intensive investigations for limited times and areas, there have been only general interpretations in such essays as "The Old West" by Frederick Jackson Turner. Concerned primarily with later periods of American history, Turner was most interested in the expansion to piedmont and back country beyond the fall line and dismissed too hastily the tidewater, stating that "the Atlantic coast was in such close touch with Europe that its frontier experience was soon counteracted, and it developed along other lines."[1] But European institutions on the first Atlantic frontier were subjected to some of the same reforging that was evident on later frontiers, and one might well argue that some of the institutional changes that occurred during the early years along the Atlantic coast were more drastic than the changes that resulted in successive stages of westward advance.

Old World institutions were quickly modified in the tidewater colonies. Maryland, for example, established manors, some of which conducted feudal courts leet and baron; all were finally abandoned. In Virginia and Maryland eventually such local officials as the sheriff assumed positions in the evolution of county government similar to, but not identical with, the position in England. In the Chesapeake the sheriff had greater financial responsibility and had the advantage of the more democratic nature of his office and of its association with local rather than royal or provincial government. On the other hand, his authority and influence in judicial matters were less with the absence of some of the courts that existed in England. In the Carolinas, while the Fundamental Constitutions exerted more influence in their early settlements than often is recognized, many of their provisions such as the proposed feudalistic social organizations were rejected from the beginning as impractical for the new country with the availability of land and a relatively fluid social order.

The lure of land for the European immigrant was a powerful factor in attracting newcomers to America, and the proponents of southern colonies all used this to people their desired settlements. The proprietors of Carolina increased the land allotments for individuals in their campaign for immigrants, but the trustees of Georgia attempted without success to restrict sharply the total landholding of each individual. The headright system was intended to control the settlement patterns by restricting the number of acres granted, such as fifty acres per person, to avoid the disposition of vast tracts without population for their settlement. While Virginia and Maryland, for example, used the headright system for most of the seventeenth century, the pressures for more land forced both colonies to abandon it and permit sale of larger amounts by purchase. This facilitated the acquisition of thousands of acres by land speculators. Yet the results of these accumulations were not always detrimental to the growth of the colonies as exemplified in the valley of Virginia and in western Maryland. These speculators proved to be self-interested immigration agents who stimulated settlements by offering land at a profit to Scots-Irish and German immigrants who preferred dealing with speculators rather than with colonial officials in the provincial seats of government.

The position of land speculators in the vanguard of settlement represents a procession of civilization contrary to the familiar line of "the buffalo following the trail to the salt springs, the Indian, the fur-trader and hunter, the cattle-raiser, the pioneer farmer. . . ."[2] Outstanding examples of the important role of the land speculator occurred in the eighteenth century in both the piedmont and valley of Virginia and in Frederick County, Maryland. South Carolina provided a different approach to this procession by setting up townships in the middle country where the colony stimulated directly the importation of foreign Protestants for predetermined areas in the plan of frontier protection.

The availability of land also contributed to social mobility and to the opportunities for less fortunate members of society such as the indentured servants. For example, the demand for larger individual landholdings in Georgia forced the trustees to modify their regulations both on the total number of acres allowed each person as well as the entail prohibiting daughters from inheriting real estate. Recent demographic studies for colonial Maryland clearly show the social mobility and opportunities for leadership in society that existed for ex-indentured servants.

Relative to Indian affairs, the frontier experience of colonial days provided a background for formulation of national policy. The recognition of the Indian's right of occupation of the land, which through experience became widespread in the colonies, was later explicitly stated by the United States Supreme Court in 1823. The question of Indian titles to land and land values at the time of treaty negotiations still remain critical issues in the 1970s. The provision for Indian boundaries and reservations in the nineteenth century were foreshadowed in colonies such as Virginia and South Carolina. The contention that "Particularism was strongest in colonies with no Indian frontier"[3] is only partially true. South Carolina's competition with both Virginia and Georgia for Indian trade and for influence over the same Indian tribes resulted in an exaggeration of the interests of the individual colonies and strongly militated against intercolonial cooperation and union. This was especially evident in the Virginia-South Carolina competition that involved Governor Alexander Spotswood of Virginia at the time of the Yamassee War in South Carolina, and governors Robert Dinwiddie of Virginia and James Glen of South Carolina in preparation for General Edward Braddock's expedition in 1755. The Indian frontier promoted dissension rather than cooperation in the crises involving these two colonies.

Sectionalism with bitter antagonism between tidewater and interior as identified later in the eighteenth or nineteenth centuries did not clearly emerge before 1763. Factionalism existed along geographical lines, and this could be on a north-south basis as well as an east-west positioning. In the competition for land grants in Virginia during the 1740s and 1750s, the major alignment of competition placed the Robinson-Randolph tidewater group versus the Lees, Washingtons, and Fairfaxes of the Northern Neck. There were, nonetheless, seeds for later antagonisms in which the newly settled interior was usually discriminated against by the older, established coastal settlements. The South Carolina proprietors, however, attempted the opposite alignment during the 1680s in their struggle with the local merchants and planters when they experimented with distributing a larger number of Assembly delegates in proportion to population to the newer and more sparsely settled areas. The conflicts of the late 1760s and 1770s involving the Regulators in both North and South Carolina were still a few years away.

The influences of the frontier in the process of Americanization and the role of various immigrant groups were important parts of the development of American civilization. While this process was at work prior to 1763, it did not come to full fruition until the later years of the American Revolution and the national period of the late eighteenth and early nineteenth centuries. The influences of the rural and agricultural frontier were only a part of the process along with urban contributions in more established sections. For the immigrant groups, the French Huguenots in most areas of South Carolina rather quickly moved in religion to the Anglican Church and adopted the English language. Scots-Irish also adapted readily to American frontier conditions, but they were less accommodating to the Anglican Church which they as Presbyterians opposed vigorously on the eve of the American Revolution because of its preferred official position in the southern colonies. German immigrants were the most persistent in perpetuating their own language and culture through control of their churches and schools. There were, however, some social and cultural intermingling with other groups as noted by the intermarriage of Germans and English in the township of

Orangeburg in South Carolina. The cultural link among immigrants, particularly in the eighteenth century, transcended colonial boundaries and followed more a north-south line than the traditional east-west one. One writer noted for Presbyterians in piedmont North Carolina: "Indeed it is likely that the inhabitants of this region knew more about Philadelphia at that time than Newbern or Edenton."[4]

Many "intellectual traits" or "striking characteristics" have been identified that presumably were influenced by the frontier experience. Certainly there was frontier influence on individualism that for the most part had positive contributions in the adaptations necessary in the southern colonies. Some settlers did for a time turn to cooperative ventures such as the Moravians who for a few years had a communal organization. Moreover, individualism in its extreme form had the potential of negative results as evidenced by the Weber heresy in South Carolina. Certainly there was "that practical, inventive turn of mind" that was evident in the self-help books of the colonial period as well as in the changing ideals of education as stated by the Reverend James Maury. Additionally, attitudes of social democracy were encouraged by the availability of land, although democracy in the form of universal manhood suffrage was not widespread until later years.

Interpretations of history and the explanations of causation have been constant challenges over the years and often they have been reduced to dimensions that are too narrow, or that focus on one factor in monistic terms rather than in a pluralistic approach. In the philosophy of history, no "laws" of history have been successfully formulated and demonstrated. Interpretations of factors shaping the course of human events have sometimes been limited to economic determinism, geographical determinism, inertia of the past, class conflict and materialism, the role of the hero, or even to chance. While any one of these explanations may be emphasized for a particular situation without submitting to a deterministic position, no one of them will consistently provide adequate answers to all of the complexities of human history.

The influence of the frontier in the southern colonies was important in shaping the society of the time and in contributing to the emerging American civilization. But it was only one of the factors at work. The European heritage abounded and must be given a prominent position in the complex of influences. The persistence of this heritage at times outweighed the forces of change in the American environment. A monocausationist approach explaining the history of the southern colonies only in terms of frontier influences is not valid. Yet for the predominantly agricultural society that developed in a rural setting in the southern colonies, the frontier was one of the strongest factors shaping its growth.

Notes

Preface

1. Henry S. Commager, ed., *Documents of American History,* 5th ed. (New York, 1949), p. 5.
2. Ibid., p. 6.
3. For the best reproductions of the White drawings, see Paul H. Hulton and David B. Quinn, *The American Drawings of John White,* 2 vols. (London and Chapel Hill, 1964).

Chapter 1

1. Alexander Brown, ed., *The Genesis of the United States,* 2 vols. (Boston and New York, 1890), I, 52–63.
2. C. F. and F. M. Voeglin, compilers, *Map of North American Indian Languages* (n.p., 1966).
3. Wendell H. Oswalt, *This Land was Theirs: A Study of the North American Indian* (New York, 1973), pp. 24–30.
4. Henry C. Forman, *Virginia Architecture in the Seventeenth Century* (E. G. Swem, ed., *Jamestown 350th Anniversary Historical Booklets* Williamsburg, 1957), pp. 6–12.
5. Edward Arber and A. G. Bradley, eds., *Travels and Works of Captain John Smith,* 2 vols. (Edinburgh, 1910), I, 67.
6. Nancy O. Lurie, "Indian Cultural Adjustment to European Civilization," in James M. Smith, ed., *Seventeenth-Century America: Essays in Colonial History* (Chapel Hill, 1959), p. 40.
7. Charles M. Hudson, *The Catawba Nation* (Athens, 1970), pp. 7–8.
8. Brown, *Genesis of the United States,* I, 62.
9. Thomas Hariot, *A brief and true report of the new found land of Virginia* (1588; facsimile reprint New York, 1903). All three parts of this famous work deal in part with commodities: the first part with merchantable commodities, the second with food, and the third with building materials.
10. Edmund S. Morgan, *American Slavery, American Freedom: The Ordeal of Colonial Virginia* (New York, 1975), pp. 63–8. This volume incorporates Morgan's earlier article on "The Labor Problem at Jamestown, 1607–18," *American Historical Review,* 76 (June 1971), pp. 595–611.
11. Arber and Bradley, *Travels and Works of John Smith,* I, 126.
12. Sigmund Diamond, "From Organization to Society: Virginia in the Seventeenth Century," reprinted in Stanley N. Katz, ed., *Colonial America: Essays in Politics and Social Development* (Boston, 1976), p. 11. Morgan, *American Slavery, American Freedom,* p. 84, gives a higher figure of thirty-six gentlemen out of 105 settlers on the first expedition.
13. Lyon G. Tyler, ed., *Narratives of Early Virginia, 1606–1625* (J. Franklin Jameson, ed., *Original Narratives of Early American History* New York, 1907), pp. 21–2.
14. The charters of early Virginia have been reproduced in *The Three Charters of the Virginia Company of London, with Seven Related Documents: 1606–1621,* introduction by Samuel M. Bemiss (E. G. Swem, ed., *Jamestown 350th Anniversary Historical Booklets* Williamsburg, 1957).

15. Wesley Frank Craven, *The Southern Colonies in the Seventeenth Century, 1607–1689* (Wendell H. Stephenson and E. Merton Coulter, eds., *A History of the South* Baton Rouge, 1949), pp. 105–7.

16. Brown, *Genesis of the United States*, II, 776.

17. Ibid., II 778.

18. Philip A. Bruce, *Economic History of Virginia in the Seventeenth Century*, 2 vols. (New York, 1896). Vol. 1, chap. 8 has a good discussion of "Acquisition of Title to Land—The Patent."

19. Susan M. Kingsbury, ed., *The Records of the Virginia Company of London*, 4 vols. (Washington, 1903–35), III, 103–4.

20. Quoted in Charles E. Hatch, Jr., *The First Seventeen Years, Virginia, 1607–1624* (E. G. Swem, ed., *Jamestown 350th Anniversary Historical Booklets* Williamsburg, 1957), p. 39.

21. The most valuable extant records relate to Berkeley Hundred and are in the Smith of Nibley papers in the New York Public Library. Part of them have been published in vols. 3 and 4 of Kingsbury, *Records of the Virginia Company*.

22. Ibid., 3, 98–109. For details of identification of "the greate Charter," see Craven, *Southern Colonies in the Seventeenth Century*, pp. 126–7 and 127n.

23. The land policy of Colonial Virginia is examined in greater detail in W. Stitt Robinson, Jr., *Mother Earth: Land Grants in Virginia, 1607–1699* (E. G. Swem, ed., *Jamestown 350th Anniversary Historical Booklets* Williamsburg, 1957), and in Manning C. Voorhis, "The Land Grant Policy of Colonial Virginia, 1607–1774," Ph.D. diss., University of Virginia, 1940.

24. Brown, *Genesis of the United States*, II, 549n–550n.

25. Voorhis, "Land Grant Policy of Colonial Virginia," p. 27.

26. Kingsbury, *Records of the Virginia Company*, III, 155–8, 162–4.

27. Ibid., III, 164–74.

28. The English use of the term "corn" usually referred during the seventeenth century as in later periods to grain. Except in direct quotations where the English designation is retained, corn in this study refers to maize or Indian corn. There is, however, some confusion in the use of the term in the Maryland laws of this period.

29. Kingsbury, *Records of the Virginia Company*, III, 166.

30. Ibid., III, 166.

31. Quoted in Lyman Carrier, *Agriculture in Virginia, 1607–1699* (E. G. Swem, ed., *Jamestown 350th Anniversary Historical Booklets* Williamsburg, 1957), p. 25.

32. Kingsbury, *Records of the Virginia Company*, IV, 23–4, 565.

33. *King James: His Counterblast to Tobacco* (London, 1672). For the history of tobacco and a commentary on a 1791 study, *Traité Complet de la Culture, Fabrication et Vente du Tabac*, as well as an illustrated account of tobacco, see *Tobacco: Its History Illustrated by the Books, Manuscripts, and Engravings in the Library of George Arents, Jr., Together with an Introductory Essay, a Glossary, and Bibliographic Notes by Jerome E. Brooks*, 5 vols., (New York, 1937–52), IV, 145–7.

34. Lewis C. Gray, *History of Agriculture in the Southern United States to 1860*, 2 vols. (Washington, 1933), I, 217–8; Melvin Herndon, *Tobacco in Colonial Virginia: "The Sovereign Remedy,"* (E. G. Swem, ed., *Jamestown 350th Anniversary Historical Booklets* Williamsburg, 1957), pp. 19–22, 46.

35. Avery O. Craven, *Soil Exhaustion as a Factor in the Agricultural History of Virginia and Maryland, 1606–1860* (Urbana, 1926), pp. 30–2.

36. James Mooney, "The Powhatan Confederacy, Past and Present," *American Anthropologist*, new series, 9 (1907), pp. 129–30.

37. Monacan has frequently been spelled Manakin. James Mooney, *The Siouan Tribes of the East*, Bureau of American Ethnology, Bulletin 22 (Washington, 1894), pp. 18–27; David I. Bushnell, Jr., *Native Villages and Village Sites East of the Mississippi*, Bureau of American Ethnology, Bulletin 69 (Washington, 1919), p. 16.

38. Lewis Hanke, *The Spanish Struggle for Justice in the Conquest of America* (1949; reprint Boston, 1965), p. 19.

39. Kingsbury, *Records of the Virginia Company,* III, 18–9.

40. Ibid., III, 19.

41. Arber and Bradley, *Travels and Works of John Smith,* I, 163.

42. John Daly Burk, *History of Virginia from its First Settlement to the Present Day,* 4 vols. (Petersburg, 1804–16), I, 170–1.

43. Alexander Brown, *The First Republic in America* (Boston and New York, 1898), pp. 456–7; Brown, *Genesis of the United States,* I, 384–6.

44. Quoted in Robert H. Land, "Henrico and its College," *William and Mary College Quarterly,* 2d series, 18 (October 1938), pp. 470–1.   1.

45. Kingsbury, *Records of the Virginia Company,* III, 14.

46. Robert Johnson, *The New Life of Virginea* (London, 1612; reprinted in Peter Force, ed., *Tracts and Other Papers relating principally to the . . . Colonies in North America,* 4 vols. Washington, 1836–46), I, no. 7. Hereafter cited as Force, *Historical Tracts.*

47. Kingsbury, *Records of the Virginia Company,* III, 552.

48. Ibid., III, 551.

49. Land, "Henrico and its College," p. 493.

50. Kingsbury, *Records of the Virginia Company,* III, 612.

51. Ibid., III, 671–2.

52. "Minutes of the Council and General Court," *The Virginia Magazine of History and Biography,* 19 (April 1911), p. 117. Hereafter cited as *Va. Mag. of Hist. & Biog.*

53. Kingsbury, *Records of the Virginia Company,* IV, 74.

54. Published editions of the original of the "Musters of the Inhabitants in Virginia, 1624/5" include John C. Hotten, ed., *The Original List of Persons of Quality . . . and Others Who Went from Great Britain to the American Plantations, 1600–1700* (London, 1874; facsimile reprint New York, 1931), pp. 201–65; and Annie L. Jester and Martha W. Hiden, eds., *Adventures of Purse and Person: Virginia, 1607–1625* (Princeton, 1956).

55. The writer is indebted for this analysis to the excellent article of Irene W. D. Hecht, "The Virginia Muster of 1624/5 As a Source for Demographic History," *William and Mary Quarterly,* 3d series, 30 (January 1973), pp. 70–71. Morgan, *American Slavery, American Freedom,* p. 396n, has a different count for the Muster list. He gets a total of 1210 rather than 1218, notes only 53 men over age 39 rather than 63, and finds 8 rather than no women over 39.

56. Hecht, "The Virginia Muster of 1624/5," pp. 71–2.

57. Ibid., p. 80.

58. Ibid., p. 84.

59. Ibid., pp. 81–2.

60. Ibid., pp. 75–8.

Chapter 2

1. Clayton C. Hall, ed., *Narratives of Early Maryland, 1633–1684* (J. Franklin Jameson, ed., *Original Narratives of Early American History* New York, 1910), p. 102.

2. Ibid., pp. 41–2.

3. Ibid., pp. 43–4.

4. John R. Swanton, *The Indian Tribes of North America,* Bureau of American Ethnology, Bulletin 134 (Washington, 1952), pp.56–61.

5. Hall, *Narratives of Early Maryland,* pp. 41–2.

6. Charles M. Andrews, *The Colonial Period of American History*, 4 vols. (New Haven, 1934–38), II, 282–3.

7. Hall, *Narratives of Early Maryland*, pp. 67–8.

8. William H. Browne et al., eds., *The Archives of Maryland* (Baltimore, 1883–), III, 47–8, 99–100, 221–8, 231–7. Hereafter cited as *Archives of Maryland*.

9. Ibid., III, 48.

10. "Proceedings of the Manor Court of St. Clement's Manor, 1659–1672" are found in ibid., LIII, 627–37.

11. Ibid., LIII, lxi–lxv, 628–9.

12. W. W. Hening, ed., *Statutes at Large: being a Collection of All the Laws of Virginia from the First Session of the Legislature in the year 1619*[to 1792] 13 vols. (Richmond, 1809–23), I, 224.

13. Craven, *Southern Colonies in the Seventeenth Century*, pp. 166–7.

14. Cyrus H. Karraker, *The Seventeenth-Century Sheriff: A Comparative Study of the Sheriff in England and the Chesapeake Colonies, 1607–1689* (Chapel Hill, 1930), pp. 144–59.

15. The Maryland Toleration Act entitled "An Act concerning Religion" is found in *Archives of Maryland*, I, 244–7.

16. Hening, *Statutes of Virginia*, I, 277.

17. Andrews, *Colonial Period of American History*, II, 317–21; Craven, *Southern Colonies in the Seventeenth Century*, pp. 260–1; contemporary documents relating to the controversy with the proprietor and the resulting conflict are included in Hall, *Narratives of Early Maryland*, pp. 163–275.

18. The basic study for counties in Maryland is Edward B. Mathews, *The Counties of Maryland, their Origin, Boundaries, and Election Districts* (Baltimore, 1907).

19. Arthur E. Karinen, "Numerical and Distributional Aspects of Maryland Population, 1631–1840," Ph.D. diss., University of Maryland, 1958, p. 39; for two articles by the same author based upon this dissertation, see *Maryland Historical Magazine*, 54 (December 1959), pp. 365–407 and 60 (June 1965), pp. 139–59; Evarts B. Greene and Virginia D. Harrington, *American Population Before the Federal Census of 1790* (New York, 1932), p. 123.

20. Arthur P. Middleton, *Tobacco Coast: A Maritime History of Chesapeake Bay in the Colonial Era* (Newport News, 1953), p. 31.

21. Kingsbury, *Records of the Virginia Company*, III, 168–9.

22. *Archives of Maryland*, I, 97–8.

23. Hening, *Statutes of Virginia*, I, 164, 189–90, 399, 478; II, 119–20, 222–3.

24. Ibid., I, 487–8; Newton D. Mereness, *Maryland as a Proprietary Province* (New York, 1901), pp. 109–10.

25. Hening, *Statutes of Virginia*, I, 141–2, 152, 164, 204–6, 212–3, 488; II, 32.

26. Ibid., I, 310.

27. Ibid., I, 469–70.

28. Ibid.

29. Ibid., I, 425; Gray, *History of Agriculture*, 1, 184–5.

30. Reprinted in Force, *Historical Tracts*, III, no. 13.

31. Hening, *Statutes of Virginia*, I, 420, 425, 481.

32. Quoted in Wesley N. Laing, "Cattle in Seventeenth–Century Virginia," *Va. Mag. Hist. & Biog.*, 67 (April 1959), p. 146.

33. Hening, *Statutes of Virginia*, I, 153.

34. Ibid., I, 218–9.

35. Ibid., I, 199.

36. Ibid., I, 228, 244, 351.

37. Ibid., I, 176, 199.

38. Ibid., I, 244–5.

39. Ibid., 332, 458.

40. *Archives of Maryland*, I, 96, 344.

41. *William and Mary College Quarterly*, 2d series, 6 (April 1926), pp. 118–9.

42. Hening, *Statutes of Virginia*, I, 208–9.

43. *A Perfect Description of Virginia* (London, 1649); also reprinted in Force, *Historical Tracts*, II, no. 3.

44. Robert Beverley, *The History and Present State of Virginia*, ed. Louis B. Wright (Chapel Hill, 1947), p. 60, gives a figure of near 500.

45. Hening, *Statutes of Virginia*, I, 285, 287, 292–3.

46. Ibid., I, 293–4, 326.

47. Especially expensive were the salaries of the four commanders, each of whom received 6000 pounds annually. Clarence W. Alvord and Lee Bidgood, *The First Exploration of the Trans-Allegeheny Region by the Virginians* (Cleveland, 1912), p. 30.

48. Hening, *Statutes of Virginia*, I, 326–7.

49. Beverley, *History of Virginia*, pp. 61–2.

50. John D. Burk, *The History of Virginia from its First Settlement to the Present Day*, 4 vols. (Petersburg, 1804–16), II, 98–9.

51. Hening, *Statutes of Virginia*, I, 323–4.

52. Ibid., I, 323–6.

53. Ibid., I, 328–9, 349.

54. Ibid., I, 352–4.

55. In addition to the citations for new counties in Hening's *Statutes of Virginia*, the standard work on Virginia counties is Morgan P. Robinson, *Virginia Counties: Those Resulting From Virginia Legislation*, Bulletin of the Virginia State Library, 9, nos. 1–3 (Richmond, 1916).

56. William A. Reavis, "The Maryland Gentry and Social Mobility, 1637–1676," *William and Mary Quarterly*, 3d series, 14 (July 1957), pp. 418–22.

57. Russell R. Menard, "From Servant to Freeholder: Status Mobility and Property Accumulation in Seventeenth-Century Maryland," *William and Mary Quarterly*, 3d series, 30 (January 1973), pp. 40–1.

58. Ibid., pp. 42–4, 46.

59. In a study of "Servitude and Opportunity in Charles County, Maryland, 1658–1705," Lorena S. Walsh provides a detailed statistical analysis of 1387 servants brought to Charles County from its creation in 1658 to 1705, noting that "those who arrived earliest had the greatest success." Political, economic, and social opportunities declined after the first few years with distinct evidence of these limitations by the 1670s and 1680s. See Aubrey C. Land, Lois G. Carr, and Edward C. Papenfuse, eds., *Law, Society, and Politics in Early Maryland* (Baltimore, 1977), pp. 111–33.

Chapter 3

1. Alvord and Bidgood, *First Explorations*, p. 93.

2. F. N. Robinson, ed., *The Works of Geoffrey Chaucer*, 2 vols. (Boston, 1957), I, 19.

3. Quoted in Murray G. Lawson, *Fur: A Study in English Mercantilism, 1700–1725* (Toronto, 1943), p. 4.

4. Quoted in Paul C. Phillips, *The Fur Trade*, 2 vols. (Norman, 1961), I, 9.

5. Hening, *Statutes of Virginia*, I, 262.

6. The report of this expedition entitled "The Discovery of New Brittaine" is reprinted in Alvord and Bidgood, *First Explorations*, pp. 103–30.

7. William P. Cumming, ed., *The Discoveries of John Lederer* (Charlottesville, 1958), pp. 28–31, 34–7, 87–90.

8. William N. Sainsbury et al., eds., *Calendar of State Papers, Colonial Series, America and West Indies* (London, 1860–), 1669–1674, pp. 604–7; Alvord and Bidgood, *First Explorations*, pp. 70–5, 181–205.

9. Identity of this river is uncertain. "The likeliest conjecture," according to Alvord and Bidgood, is "the French Broad or the Little Tennessee." See Alvord and Bidgood, *First Explorations*, p. 82.

10. Ibid., pp. 34–45; Hotten, *Original List of Persons of Quality*, pp. 179, 233; Frank Monaghan, "Abraham Wood," *Dictionary of American Biography*, 20 (1946), p. 454.

11. For sketches of the career of William Byrd II, see John S. Bassett, ed., *The Writings of Colonel William Byrd of Westover, Esqr.* (New York, 1901); Louis B. Wright, ed., *The Prose Works of William Byrd of Westover: Narratives of a Colonial Virginian* (Cambridge, 1966); and Pierre Marambaud, *William Byrd of Westover, 1674–1744* (Charlottesville, 1971).

12. Alvord and Bidgood, *First Explorations*, pp. 192–3.

13. Wright, *Prose Works of William Byrd*, pp. 307–8.

14. Pierre Marambaud, "Colonel William Byrd I: A Fortune Founded on Smoke," *Va. Mag. Hist. & Biog.*, 82 (October 1974), p. 443.

15. "Letters of William Byrd, First," *Va. Mag. Hist. & Biog.*, 24 (June 1916), pp. 231–2.

16. Ibid., 24 (June and October 1916), pp. 233–4, 351, 354; 25 (January and April 1917), pp. 49, 51–2, 132, 135.

17. Hening, *Statutes of Virginia*, II, 336–8.

18. The events of Bacon's Rebellion are analyzed in Wilcomb E. Washburn, *The Governor and the Rebel: A History of Bacon's Rebellion in Virginia* (Chapel Hill, 1957); and Richard L. Morton, *Colonial Virginia*, 2 vols. (Chapel Hill, 1960), I, chaps. 13–16. See also Warren M. Billings, "The Causes of Bacon's Rebellion: Some Suggestions," *Va. Mag. Hist. & Biog.*, 78 (October 1970), pp. 409–35.

19. Warren M. Billings, ed., *The Old Dominion in the Seventeenth Century: A Documentary History of Virginia, 1606–1689* (Chapel Hill, 1975), p. 273.

20. *William and Mary College Quarterly*, 1st series, 4 (1895–96), p. 86.

21. British Museum, London. Egerton Manuscripts, vol. 2395, folio 550.

22. British Public Record Office, London. Colonial Office Papers 5:1310, no. 2; *Cal. State Papers, Col. Ser.*, 1699, p. 310.

23. *Va. Mag. Hist. & Biog.*, 1(July 1893), pp. 57–8.

24. T[homas] M[athews], "The Beginning, Progress, and Conclusion of Bacon's Rebellion in Virginia, 1675–1676," Force, *Historical Tracts*, 1:no. 8, p. 11. This account is also included in Charles M. Andrews, ed., *Narratives of the Insurrection, 1675–1690* (J. Franklin Jameson, ed., *Original Narratives of Early American History* New York, 1915).

25. *Cal. State Papers, Col. Ser.*, 1675–1676, p. 448.

26. Winder Abstracts (Abstracts in Virginia State Library, Richmond, made by F. A. Winder from originals in the British Public Record Office, London), II, 240.

27. Hening, *Statutes of Virginia*, II, 326–333.

28. Andrews, *Narratives of the Insurrection*, pp. 110–1.

29. Hening, *Statutes of Virginia*, II, 341–65.

30. Thomas J. Wertenbaker uses this designation in *The Torchbearer of the Revolution: The Story of Bacon's Rebellion and its Leader* (Princeton, 1940). His portrayal of Bacon as a leader for democratic reform is sharply challenged by Washburn in *Governor and the Rebel*, which is critical of Bacon and gives a more sympathetic view of Sir William Berkeley.

31. Bernard Bailyn, "Politics and Social Structure in Virginia," in James M. Smith, ed., *Seventeenth-Century America: Essays in Colonial History* (Chapel Hill, 1959), pp. 102–3.

32. Hening, *Statutes of Virginia*, II, 366–406, gives the acts of the Assembly of February 1676/7; Washburn, *Governor and the Rebel*, pp. 60–2, provides a convenient identification of the acts that were repassed.

33. Quoted in Wertenbaker, *Torchbearer of the Revolution*, pp. 135–7.

34. The most extensive treatment thus far on this subject is in Wilcomb E. Washburn, "Bacon's Rebellion, 1676–1677," Ph. D. diss., Harvard University, 1955, pp. 665–85.

35. An extensive Protestant protest was set forth in 1676 in "Complaint from Heaven with a Huy and crye and a petition out of Virginia and Maryland," *Archives of Maryland*, V, 134–49.

For the Charles County unrest, see Andrews, *Colonial Period of American History*, II, 343–4.

36. "Treaty between Virginia and the Indians, 1677," *Va. Mag. Hist. & Biog.*, 14 (January 1907), pp. 289–96.

37. *Archives of Maryland*, I, 228.

38. Ibid., III, 462.

39. Ibid., III, 522–5.

40. Ibid., XV, 56, 58.

41. Ibid., II, 557–60.

42. This theme is explored in David L. Davis, "The Colonial Rangers," M. A. thesis, University of Kansas, 1973, chaps. 1–2.

43. Hening, *Statutes of Virginia*, II, 433–40.

44. Ibid., II, 498–501.

45. Ibid., III, 17–22.

46. W. P. Palmer et al., *Calendar of Virginia State Papers, 1652–1869, Papers and Other Manuscripts, 1652–1869*, 11 vols. (Richmond, 1875–93), I, 67.

47. *Cal. State Papers, Col. Ser.*, 1714–1715, p. 234.

48. *Archives of Maryland*, VIII, 77–8, 83–4, 90–1.

49. Ibid., VIII, 82.

50. Many of the original records on this revolt were destroyed in the Stafford County courthouse fire during the Civil War. Examination of extant records has been completed by Frank W. Read in " 'Grevances Wiy The Have Taken Op Arms': Virginia and Maryland in the Glorious Revolution," M. A. thesis, University of Kansas, 1972.

51. For an excellent sketch of the career of William Fitzhugh, see Richard B. Davis, ed., *William Fitzhugh and his Chesapeake World, 1676–1701* (Chapel Hill, 1963), pp. 3–55.

52. *Archives of Maryland*, VIII, 94.

53. For a detailed analysis of the Associators' Convention, see Lois G. Carr and David W. Jordan, *Maryland's Revolution of Government, 1689–1692* (Ithaca, 1974).

54. Hening, *Statutes of Virginia*, III, 82–5, 98–101, 115–7, 119–21, 126–8.

55. *Cal. State Papers, Col. Ser.*, 1689–1692, pp. 308–9, 339–40, 674.

Chapter 4

1. William L. Saunders, ed., *The Colonial Records of North Carolina*, 10 vols. (Raleigh, 1886–90), I, 5.

2. Alexander S. Salley, Jr., ed., *Narratives of Early Carolina, 1650–1708* (J. Franklin Jameson, ed., *Original Narratives of Early American History* New York, 1911), p. 6.

3. John R. Swanton, *The Indians of the Southeastern United States*, Bureau of American Ethnology, Bulletin 137 (Washington, 1946), see names of tribes; Frederick W. Hodge, ed., *Handbook of American Indians North of Mexico*, Bureau of American Ethnology, Bulletin 30 (Washington, 1907–10), see names of tribes; Douglas L. Rights, *The American Indian in North Carolina* (Winston-Salem, 1957), p. 259, projects much higher Indian population figures for the time of first contact with Europeans: 1200 for the Chowanoc, 1000 for the Cape Fear, 1200 for the Machapunga.

4. Hudson, *Catawba Nation*, pp. 12, 26.

5. Chapman J. Milling, *Red Carolinians* (Chapel Hill, 1940), chap. 2; see also Swanton, *Indians of Southeastern United States*, sketches of individual tribes.

6. Hudson, *Catawba Nation*, p. 33n.

7. Hodge, *Handbook of American Indians*, II, 851–2.

8. Swanton, *Indians of Southeastern United States*, p. 105; for problems of correct identity of the Catawba, see Hudson, *Catawba Nation*, chap. 2.

9. Swanton, *Indians of Southeastern United States*, p. 114.

10. Salley, *Narratives of Early Carolina,* p. 53.

11. Ibid., p. 52.

12. The charters to the proprietors may be conventionally found in Saunders, ed., *Colonial Records of North Carolina,* I, 20–30, 102–14; and in Mattie E. E. Parker, ed., *North Carolina Charters and Constitutions, 1578–1698* (Raleigh, 1963), pp. 74–104.

13. Both the Spanish text and the above translation are given in David B. Quinn, *North America from Earliest Discovery to First Settlements: The Norse Voyages to 1612* (Henry S. Commager and Richard B. Morris, eds., *The New American Nation Series* New York, 1977), pp. 259, 259n.

14. Herbert E. Bolton and Mary Ross, *The Debatable Land: A Sketch of the Anglo-Spanish Contest for the Georgia Country* (1925; reprint New York, 1968), pp. 1–27; John Tate Lanning, *The Spanish Missions of Georgia* (Chapel Hill, 1935), pp. 212–3 and passim.; Ray A. Billington, *Westward Expansion: A History of the American Frontier* (New York, 1967), pp. 26–8.

15. Saunders, *Colonial Records of North Carolina,* I, 19.

16. Ibid., I, 48–50, 56.

17. Ibid., I, 57.

18. Ibid., I, 87–8. The "Concessions and Agreements" are also reproduced in Parker, *North Carolina Charters,* pp. 107–27.

19. Saunders, *Colonial Records of North Carolina,* I, 86–9.

20. Salley, *Narratives of Early Carolina,* pp. 77–108.

21. Saunders, *Colonial Records of North Carolina,* I, 159.

22. Louise F. Brown, *The First Earl of Shaftesbury* (New York, 1933), p. 156.

23. The portion of the Fundamental Constitutions relating to land distribution is found in Saunders, *Colonial Records of North Carolina,* I, 188–92.

24. Andrews, *Colonial Period of American History,* III, 217–8, 218n, provides a corrective figure to the one given in Edward McGrady, *The History of South Carolina under the Proprietary Government, 1670–1719* (New York, 1901), pp. 717–9.

25. The proprietors offered colonists entering before March 25, 1670, a headright of 150 acres for freemen, women over age sixteen, and menservants (including slaves); 100 acres for female servants and boys less than sixteen. Beyond 1670 the grants decreased until after 1682 the provision for 150 acres was reduced to 75 or 70, the 100 acres to 50. These varying amounts may be traced through the separate publication for *Commissions and Instructions from the Lords Proprietors of Carolina to Public Officials of South Carolina, 1685–1715,* ed. Alexander S. Salley (Columbia, 1916).

26. Quoted in McGrady, *South Carolina Under Proprietory Government,* p. 124.

27. Langdon Cheves, ed., *The Shaftsbury Papers and Other Records relating to Carolina* (*Collections of the South Carolina Historical Society,* V, Charleston, 1897), p. 379. Hereafter cited as *Shaftsbury Papers.*

28. David D. Wallace, *The History of South Carolina,* 4 vols. (New York, 1934), I, 90–1.

29. Saunders, *Colonial Records of North Carolina,* I, 202–3.

30. Ibid., I, 204.

31. These instructions from Colonial Office Papers 5:286 are reproduced in William J. Rivers, *A Sketch of the History of South Carolina to the Close of the Proprietary Government by the Revolution of 1719* (1856; reprint Spartanburg, 1972), pp. 347–51.

32. *Shaftesbury Papers,* p. 167.

33. Ibid., p. 187.

34. Ibid., p. 338.

35. Ibid., p. 334.

36. Milling, *Red Carolinians,* pp. 58–9. The date for the deed should be March 10, 1675/6.

37. Verner W. Crane, *The Southern Frontier, 1670–1732* (1928; reprint Ann Arbor, 1956), p. 17; *Shaftesbury Papers,* pp. 456–62.

38. Public Records of South Carolina (Transcripts and Microfilm of manuscript records in

the British Public Record Office, London, available in the South Carolina Archives, Columbia, South Carolina. Volume numbers refer to the bound volumes of the transcripts), I, 60–1.

39. Crane, *Southern Frontier*, p. 35.

40. Rivers, *Historical Sketch of South Carolina*, p. 389.

41. Salley, *Narratives of Early Carolina*, p. 329.

42. Hodge, *Handbook of American Indians*, II, 532.

43. "Letter of Thomas Newe from South Carolina, 1682," *American Historical Review*, 12 (January 1907), p. 323.

44. Wallace, *History of South Carolina*, I, 149.

45. Quoted in Oscar T. Barck, Jr. and Hugh T. Lefler, *Colonial America* (New York, 1958), p. 291.

46. Thomas Cooper and David J. McCord, eds., *The Statutes at Large of South Carolina*, 10 vols. (Columbia, 1836–41), II, 329.

47. Ibid., II, 268–9.

48. Saunders, *Colonial Records of North Carolina*, I, 192–7.

49. Public Records of South Carolina, II, 33–4.

50. Part of the opposition to the proprietors came from the group of early settlers, primarily from Barbados, who were known as Goose Creek men because of their location along this tributary of the Cooper River. As Anglicans they clashed with the proprietors over their policy of toleration of dissenters, and the proprietors opposed some of their activities such as their traffic in Indian slaves. M. Eugene Sirmans, *Colonial South Carolina: A Political History, 1663–1763* (Chapel Hill, 1966), pp. 17–8.

51. McGrady, *South Carolina under Proprietary Government*, p. 199.

52. Wallace, *History of South Carolina*, I, 123–5.

53. Salley, *Narratives of Early Carolina*, p. 143.

54. Ibid., p. 149.

55. Ibid., p. 171.

56. Crane, *Southern Frontier*, p. 111.

57. Greene and Harrington, *American Population Before 1790*, p. 173.

58. Converse D. Clowse, *Economic Beginnings in Colonial South Carolina, 1670–1730* (Columbia, 1971), p. 102.

59. Saunders, *Colonial Records of North Carolina*, I, 229.

60. Ibid., I, 260.

61. There are several other estimates of population for North Carolina of the late seventeenth century. Craven, *Southern Colonies in the Seventeenth Century*, p. 408, suggests 3000; Andrews, *Colonial Period of American History*, III, 258, indicates a little more than 4000; Greene and Harrington, *American Population before 1790*, p. 156, give George Bancroft's figure of 4000 and another estimate of 5000.

62. Saunders, *Colonial Records of North Carolina*, I, 467.

63. Ibid., I, 663.

64. Hening, *Statutes of Virginia*, II, 445–6.

Chapter 5

1. Quoted in Crane, *Southern Frontier*, p. 5.

2. Swanton, *Indians of Southeastern United States*, p. 91. Charles Hudson, *The Southeastern Indians* (Knoxville, 1976), p. 5, notes that recent general estimates for Indians of the Southeast at the time of European contact have been much higher than the total assigned by Swanton, perhaps ten times greater. No specific figure, however, is given for the Apalache.

3. Swanton, *Indians of Southeastern United States*, pp. 119, 123; John R. Swanton, *Early*

History of the Creek Indians and Their Neighbors, Bureau of American Ethnology, Bulletin 73 (Washington, 1922), p. 442.

4. Swanton, *Early History of Creek Indians,* p. 122; Crane, *Southern Frontier,* pp. 79–80; Charles H. Fairbanks, "Ethnohistorical Report on the Florida Indians," in *Florida Indians,* 3 vols. (New York, 1974), III, 92, gives higher figures for Indian captives.

5. Fairbanks, "Ethnohistorical Report," p. 98; see also Howard F. Cline, "Notes on Colonial Indians and Communities in Florida, 1700–1821," in *Florida Indians,* I, 57–60.

6. Quoted in Crane, *Southern Frontier,* p. 23.

7. W. L. McDowell, ed., *Journals of the Commissioners of the Indian Trade, 1710–1718,* Colonial Records of South Carolina (Columbia, 1955), p. 104.

8. Ibid., p. 269.

9. Ibid., p. 117.

10. Ibid., p. 186.

11. David I. Bushnell, Jr., describes the preparation of skins by the Choctaw in *The Choctaw of Bayou Lacomb, St. Tammany Parish, Louisiana,* Bureau of American Ethnology, Bulletin 48 (Washington, 1909), pp. 11–2.

12. McDowell, *Journals of Commissioners of Indian Trade,* p. 82.

13. Ibid., pp. 98–9.

14. Crane, *Southern Frontier,* p. 124.

15. Cooper and McCord, *Statutes of South Carolina,* II, 309–16.

16. Sirmans, *Colonial South Carolina,* pp. 93–4; Crane, *Southern Frontier,* pp. 89–95.

17. R. A. Brock, ed., *The Official Letters of Alexander Spotswood, Lieutenant-Governor of the Colony of Virginia, 1710–1722,* Collections of the Virginia Historical Society, new series, 2 vols. (Richmond, 1882–85), II, 331. Hereafter cited as *Spotswood's Letters.*

18. Pryce [Price] Hughes to the Duchess of Ormond, October 15, 1713, Price Hughes manuscripts, South Caroliniana Library , University of South Carolina, Columbia, S.C.

19. Crane, *Southern Frontier,* p. 99.

20. Hodge, *Handbook of American Indians,* II, 851–2.

21. Saunders, *Colonial Records of North Carolina,* I, 921–2.

22. Ibid., I, 933.

23. Ibid., I, 826–7.

24. Crane, *Southern Frontier,* 158–60.

25. A journal of John Barnwell's expedition against the Tuscarora was printed in the form of letters from Barnwell in the *Va. Mag. Hist. & Biog.,* 5 (April 1898), pp. 391–402 and 6 (July 1898), pp. 42–55; reprinted in *South Carolina Historical and Genealogical Magazine,* 9 (January 1908), pp. 30–54.

26. *Spotswood's Letters,* I, 170.

27. H. R. McIlwaine et al., eds., *Executive Journals of the Council of Colonial Virginia,* 6 vols. (Richmond, 1925–66), III, 293–5. Hereafter cited as *Virginia Executive Journals.*

28. Ibid., III, 313.

29. Saunders, *Colonial Records of North Carolina,* II, 26, 29.

30. Ibid., II, 15.

31. Crane, *Southern Frontier,* pp. 159–61.

32. Cooper and McCord, *Statutes of South Carolina,* II, 317.

33. McDowell, *Journals of Commissioners of Indian Trade,* p. 11.

34. Crane, *Southern Frontier,* p. 162.

35. McDowell, *Journals of Commissioners of Indian Trade,* p. 59.

36. Milling, *Red Carolinians,* pp. 137–9.

37. Details of the Yamassee War are covered in Crane, *Southern Frontier,* chap. 7; Milling, *Red Carolinians,* chap. 9; Wallace, *History of South Carolina,* I, chap. 21.

38. *Cal. State Papers, Col. Ser., 1716–1717,* pp. 223–4.

39. *Spotswood's Letters,* II, 136.

40. Frederick J. Turner, *The Frontier in American History* (New York, 1920), p. 15.

41. Crane, *Southern Frontier*, pp. 229–34.

42. Cooper and McCord, *Statutes of South Carolina*, III, 24. The full Act of 1717 is found in III, 23–30.

43. Ibid., II 677–80.

44. McDowell, *Journals of Commissioners of Indian Trade*, p. 123.

45. Cooper and McCord, *Statutes of South Carolina*, III, 86–96.

46. The various experiments for control of trade are examined in Jack P. Greene, *The Quest for Power: The Lower Houses of Assembly in the Southern Royal Colonies, 1689–1776* (Chapel Hill, 1963), pp. 310–3.

47. Swanton, *Early History of Creek Indians*, p. 226.

48. Quoted in Wallace, *History of South Carolina*, I, 213.

49. Max Savelle, *The Origins of American Diplomacy: The International History of Angloamerica, 1492–1763* (New York, 1967), pp. 309–313; Max Savelle, *Empires to Nations: Expansion in America, 1713–1824* (vol. 5 of *Europe and the World in the Age of Expansion* Minneapolis, 1974), pp. 123–4.

50. Analysis of these and other factors in the overthrow of the proprietors may be found in Sirmans, *Colonial South Carolina*, chap. 6.

Chapter 6

1. Hening, *Statutes of Virginia*, III, 84–5.

2. "Report of the Journey of Francis Louis Michel," *Va. Mag. Hist. & Biog.* 24 (April 1916), pp. 125–34.

3. *Archives of Maryland*, XIX, ix, 211.

4. *Cal. State Papers, Col. Ser.*, 1701, pp. 140–2, 630–4.

5. Ibid., p. 634.

6. *Virginia Executive Journals*, II, 172–7.

7. Hening, *Statutes of Virginia*, III, 204–9.

8. Turner, *Frontier in American History*, pp. 86–7.

9. *Archives of Maryland*, XIX, 227, 244; XX, 487, 523; XXIII, 111, 214.

10. Colonial Office Papers, V, 1313, no 25; *Cal. State Papers, Col. Ser.*, 1701, pp. 539–40, 548, 586; 1702–1703, pp. 339–40.

11. Herbert L. Osgood, *The American Colonies in the Eighteenth Century*, 4 vols. (New York, 1924), II, 175–6, 208–9.

12. The official authorization for the forts may be found in *Archives of Maryland*, VIII, 461.

13. *Archives of Maryland*, XX, 154.

14. James L. Bugg, Jr., "The French Huguenot Frontier Settlement of Manakin Town," *Va. Mag. Hist. & Biog.* 61 (October 1953), pp. 366–7.

15. "Journey of Michel," *Va. Mag. Hist. & Biog.* 24, pp. 122–3.

16. Hening, *Statutes of Virginia*, III, 228.

17. Bugg, "French Huguenot Frontier Settlement," pp. 382–5, 390–3.

18. *Spotswood's Letters*, II, 217.

19. Ibid., II, 78.

20. Edward P. Alexander, ed., *The Journal of John Fontaine: An Irish Huguenot Son in Spain and Virginia, 1710–1719* (Williamsburg, 1972), p. 88.

21. Wright, *Prose Works of William Byrd*, p. 356.

22. Cooper and McCord, *Statutes of South Carolina*, II, 309–16; *Virginia Executive Journals*, III, 177–8; William Grant et al, eds., *Acts of the Privy Council of England, Colonial Series, 1613–1783*, 6 vols. (London, 1908–12), II, 610–3; Depositions on actions of South Carolina in the Indian trade are found in Colonial Office Papers, 5:1316, no 47, in Robert Hix, pp. 189–90 and in David Crawley, pp. 190–1.

23. Colonial Office Papers, 5:1316, no. 46; *Cal. State Papers, Col. Ser.,* 1706–1708, pp. 765–6 and 1708–1709, p. 479.

24. Cooper and McCord, *Statutes of South Carolina,* II, 357–9.

25. *Acts of the Privy Council,* II, 613–4; Colonial Office Papers, 5:1316, no. 40.

26. Leonidas Dodson, *Alexander Spotswood: Governor of Colonial Virginia, 1710–1722* (Philadelphia, 1932), p. 74. The act for appointing rangers may be found in Hening, *Statutes of Virginia,* IV, 9–12.

27. *Spotswood's Letters,* II, 37, 41–2.

28. The three Indian treaties may be found in Colonial Office Papers, 5:1316, nos. 162, 163, 164.

29. Ibid., *Cal. State Papers, Col. Ser.,* 1712–1714, pp. 306–10; *Virginia Executive Journals,* III, 363–6.

30. *Spotswood's Letters,* II, 70–1; *Virginia Executive Journals,* III, 368.

31. The Indian trade Act was not in the original edition of Hening's *Statutes,* but it is now included in Waverly K. Winfree, comp., *The Laws of Virginia: Being a Supplement to Hening's The Statutes at Large, 1700–1750* (Richmond, 1971), pp. 104–13.

32. *Spotswood's Letters,* II, 209.

33. Ibid., II 149.

34. Ibid., II, 209.

35. Ibid., II, 138, 141.

36. W. Neil Franklin, "The Indian Trade of Colonial Virginia," Ph. D. diss., Princeton University, 1928, chap. 5, p. 20. See also by the same author, "Virginia and the Cherokee Indian Trade, 1673–1752," *East Tennessee Historical Society's Publications,* no. 4 (January 1932), pp. 3–21; and "Virginia and the Cherokee Indian Taade, 1753–1775," ibid., no. 5 (January 1933), pp. 22–38.

37. *Virginia Executive Journals,* III, 428.

38. Alexander, *Journal of John Fontaine,* p. 106.

39. *Spotswood's Letters,* II, 231–2.

40. *Cal. State Papers, Col. Ser.,* 1716–1717, pp. 328, 335; Colonial Office Papers, 5:1318, p. 457.

41. *Spotswood's Letters,* II, 302.

42. Leonidas Dodson, *Alexander Spotswood: Governor of Colonial Virginia, 1710–1722* (Philadelphia, 1932), p. 98.

43. *Cal. State Papers, Col. Ser.,* 1696–1697, pp. 88–9.

44. Hening, *Statutes of Virginia,* II, 244.

45. *Cal. State Papers, Col. Ser.,* 1696–1697, p. 89.

46. *Virginia Executive Journals,* I, 457.

47. Thomas J. Wertenbaker, *The Planters of Colonial Virginia* (Princeton, 1922), pp. 53–4. This volume has been reprinted in *The Shaping of Colonial Virginia* (New York, 1958).

48. The rent-roll of 1704–1705 has been reproduced in the Appendix of ibid., pp. 183–245.

49. Hening, *Statutes of Virginia,* III, 524–5.

50. Osgood, *American Colonies in the Eighteenth Century,* II, 221–2.

51. Hening, *Statutes of Virginia,* IV, 37–40.

52. Dodson, *Spotswood,* pp. 281–2.

Chapter 7

1. J. Leitch Wright, Jr., *Anglo-Spanish Rivalry in North America* (Athens, 1971), pp. 71–2.

2. E. B. O'Callaghan and B. Fernow, eds., *Documents Relative to the Colonial History of the State of New York,* 15 vols. (Albany, 1856–87), V, 591–630.

3. Crane, *Southern Frontier,* p. 93.

4. Ibid., p. 209.

5. *Spotswood's Letters*, II, 297–8.

6. Crane, *Southern Frontier*, p. 203.

7. O'Callaghan, *Documents of the Colonial History of New York*, IV, 577, 579–80.

8. Ibid., V, 623, 627–30.

9. Hening, *Statutes of Virginia*, IV, 77.

10. Ibid., IV, 78.

11. The details of western expansion during this period may be followed in Morton, *Colonial Virginia*, II, chaps. 13, 14; and in Thomas P. Abernethy, "The First Transmontane Advance," *Humanistic Studies in Honor of John Calvin Metcalf* (Charlottesville, 1941), pp. 120–38.

12. Robinson, *Virginia Counties*, p. 95.

13. Middleton, *Tobacco Coast*, pp. 39–40.

14. Bassett, *Writings of Colonel William Byrd*, pp. 306–8.

15. Richard C. Beatty and William J. Mulloy, eds., *William Byrd's Natural History of Virginia or The Newly Discovered Eden* (Richmond, 1940).

16. Thomas P. Abernethy, *Three Virginia Frontiers* (Baton Rouge, 1940), p. 54.

17. Byrd to Mr. Collenson, July 18, 1736, *Va. Mag. Hist. & Biog.*, 36 (October 1928), pp. 353–5.

18. Louis B. Wright, *The Cultural Life of the American Colonies, 1607–1763* (Henry S. Commager and Richard B. Morris, eds., *The New American Nation Series* New York, 1957), pp. 60, 66.

19. Parke Rouse, *The Great Wagon Road from Philadelphia to the South* (vol. 11 of America Trail Series New York, 1973); for a detailed, scholarly analysis of travel routes in all of Virginia, see Edward Graham Roberts, "The Roads of Virginia, 1607–1840," Ph.D. diss., University of Virginia, 1950.

20. For a brief sketch on Adam Miller by Charles E. Kemper, see *Va. Mag. Hist. & Biog.*, 10 (July 1902), pp. 84–6.

21. Robert D. Mitchell, *Commercialism and Frontier: Perspectives on the Early Shenandoah Valley* (Charlottesville, 1977), p. 79; see pp. 78–84 for the "Typology of Land Speculation."

22. William J. Hinke and Charles E. Kemper, eds., "Moravian Diaries of Travels through Virginia," *Va. Mag. Hist. & Biog.*, 11 (October 1903), 113–31. Quotations in this paragraph are on pp. 121–3. The two Moravian missionaries were Leonhard Schnell and John Brandmueller.

23. Miles S. Malone, "The Distribution of Population on the Virginia Frontier in 1775," Ph.D. diss., Princeton University, 1935, pp. 3, 64.

24. These tabulations are based upon the chart in Mitchell, *Commercialism and Frontier*, p. 43.

25. See chart on p. 76 of ibid. for land sale prices of speculators; see also Robert E. and B. Katherine Brown, *Virginia, 1705–1786: Democracy or Aristocracy?* (East Lansing, 1964), pp. 16–8.

26. *Virginia Executive Journals*, IV, 351, 408–9.

27. Robinson, *Mother Earth*, p. 69.

28. *Acts of the Privy Council*, III, 385–91.

29. Aubrey C. Land, "A Land Speculator in the Opening of Western Maryland," *Maryland Historical Magazine*, 48 (September 1953), pp. 191–203; Aubrey C. Land, *The Dulanys of Maryland* (Baltimore, 1955), passim.

30. *Archives of Maryland*, XXVIII, 45–6; Clarence P. Gould, *The Land System in Maryland, 1720–1765*, Johns Hopkins University Studies in Historical and Political Science, series 31, no. 1 (Baltimore, 1913), pp. 56–7.

31. Information on Maryland counties may be found in Mathews, *Counties of Maryland*.

32. R. Bruce Harley, "Dr. Charles Carroll—Land Speculator, 1730–1755," *Maryland Historical Magazine*, 46 (June 1951), p. 106.

33. *Archives of Maryland*, XLVI, 91, 142–4.

34. Aubrey C. Land, "Genesis of a Colonial Fortune: Daniel Dulany of Maryland," *William and Mary Quarterly*, 3rd series, 7 (April 1950), pp. 268–9.

35. Richard H. Shryock in "British versus German Traditions in Colonial Agriculture," *Mississippi Valley Historical Review*, 26 (June 1939), pp. 39–54, argues for a significant difference between German and English practices in agriculture because of cultural influences, concluding that the Germans were often more efficient. For a contrary view based upon a statistical analysis of Pennsylvania tax lists and estate inventories that minimizes agricultural differences among national groups, see James T. Lemon, "The Agricultural Practices of National Groups in Eighteenth-Century Southeastern Pennsylvania," *Geographical Review*, 56 (October 1966), pp. 467–96.

36. Charles A. Barker, *The Background of the Revolution in Maryland* (New Haven, 1940), p. 7.

37. For this statistical analysis, I would like to thank Professor David C. Skaggs of Bowling Green State University, Ohio, and Mr. Gary Bailey who included it in his student paper in 1974 entitled "Property Distribution and Social Status in Pre-Revolutionary Maryland."

38. Clarence P. Gould, *Money and Transportation in Maryland, 1720–1765*, Johns Hopkins University Studies in Historical and Political Science, series 33, no. 1 (Baltimore, 1915), pp. 125–7.

39. Clarence P. Gould, "The Economic Causes of the Rise of Baltimore," in *Essays in Colonial History Presented to Charles McLean Andrews by his Students* (New Haven, 1931), p. 240.

40. Ibid., p. 247.

41. Hening, *Statutes of Virginia*, III, 284.

42. Brown and Brown, *Virginia*, pp. 219–20.

43. Quoted in David Alan Williams, "Political Alignments in Colonial Virginia, 1698–1750," Ph.D. diss., Northwestern University, 1959, p. 112.

44. J. P. Kennedy and H. R. McIlwaine, eds., *Journals of the House of Burgesses of Virginia, 1619–1776*, 13 vols. (Richmond, 1905–15), 1742–47, 1748–49, pp. 242, 245.

45. H. R. McIlwaine, ed., *Legislative Journals of the Council of Colonial Virginia*, 3 vols. (Richmond, 1918–19), II, 999.

46. Morton, *Colonial Virginia*, II, 454, 456.

47. *Virginia Executive Journals*, IV, 469.

48. Hening, *Statutes of Virginia*, V, 168–70.

49. *Legislative Journals of the Council*, II, 944, 946.

50. Williams, "Political Alignments in Colonial Virginia," pp. 329–30.

51. Morton, *Colonial Virginia*, II, 571–3; there is a summary of many of these grants in "A List of Early Land Patents and Grants," *Va. Mag. Hist. & Biog.*, 5 (October 1897), pp. 173–80, and 5 (January 1898), pp. 241–4.

52. For more details about the Ohio Company, see Kenneth P. Bailey, *The Ohio Company of Virginia and the Westward Movement, 1748–1792* (Glendale, California, 1939), and Alfred P. James, *The Ohio Company: Its Inner History* (Pittsburgh, 1959).

53. Morton, *Colonial Virginia*, II, 575.

Chapter 8

1. Robert L. Meriwether, *The Expansion of South Carolina, 1729–1765* (Kingsport, Tenn., 1940), pp. 17–18; Crane, *Southern Frontier*, pp. 229–31, 282–3; Wallace, *History of South Carolina*, I, 334.

2. Public Records of South Carolina, XIV, 174–6; Meriwether, *Expansion of South Carolina*, pp. 19–21.

3. Cooper and McCord, *Statutes of South Carolina*, III, 340.

4. See map p. 164.

5. Meriwether, *Expansion of South Carolina,* p. 79; for full discussion of Williamsburg, see ibid., pp. 79–87.

6. Phillip M. Hamer et al., *The Papers of Henry Laurens* (Columbia, 1968–), I, 279.

7. For additional information on the Wateree Indians, see Milling, *Red Carolinians,* pp. 209–10, 215–6, 225.

8. For discussion of Fredericksburg, see Meriwether, *Expansion of South Carolina,* pp. 99–109.

9. Ibid., pp. 86–8.

10. Wallace, *History of South Carolina,* I, 353–4; Meriwether, *Expansion of South Carolina,* pp. 89–90, 94.

11. Meriwether, *Expansion of South Carolina,* p. 92.

12. An interesting addition to the limited material on Welsh migration is Arthur H. Dodd, *The Character of Early Welsh Emigration to the United States* (Cardiff, 1957).

13. Meriwether, *Expansion of South Carolina,* pp. 90–8.

14. The writer has used in the Rare Book Room, Library of Congress, an 1880 edition of this *Memorial* which was privately printed in Augusta, Georgia.

15. The writer has traced the activities of Purry and his son through the following volumes of the microfilm of original documents in the British Public Record Office, London: Colonial Office Papers, 5:359, 361, 362, 363, 366. See also Crane, *Southern Frontier,* pp. 283–7; Meriwether, *Expansion of South Carolina,* pp. 34–6.

16. Meriwether, *Expansion of South Carolina,* p. 38; for full discussion *of Purrysburg,* see ibid., pp. 34–41.

17. Cooper and McCord, *Statutes of South Carolina,* III, 668–9.

18. Meriwether, *Expansion of South Carolina,* pp. 42–4, 50–1.

19. Ibid., pp. 44–8.

20. The church register kept by John Ulrick Giessendanner and his nephew, John Giessendanner, has been printed in Alexander S. Salley, Jr., *The History of Orangeburg County, South Carolina, from its First Settlement to the Close of the Revolutionary War* (Orangeburg, 1898), pp. 91–216.

21. Wallace, *History of South Carolina,* I, 346–51.

22. Meriwether, *Expansion of South Carolina,* p. 66; for full discussion of New Windsor, see ibid., pp. 66–72.

23. Milling, *Red Carolinians,* p. 191.

24. Sirmans, *Colonial South Carolina,* p. 132, using figures of Governor James Moore for tax returns, gives a total population for 1721 of 19,600 with a breakdown of 7800 whites and 11,800 black slaves. For 1729, see Meriwether, *Expansion of South Carolina,* p. 6.

25. Sirmans, *Colonial South Carolina,* p. 207.

26. Meriwether, *Expansion of South Carolina,* p. 160.

27. *Acts of the Privy Council,* III, 572–3, 699–700.

28. Meriwether, *Expansion of South Carolina,* pp. 125–7.

29. Wallace examines the question of whether there were three or four townships resulting from the confusion over the identification of Belfast and Londonborough. See David D. Wallace, *South Carolina: A Short History 1520–1948* (Chapel Hill, 1951), pp. 220n and 221n.

30. Meriwether, *Expansion of South Carolina,* p. 144.

31. Ibid., pp. 161–2.

32. Gray, *History of Agriculture,* I, 290–2.

33. Turner, *Frontier in American History,* p. 12.

34. Ibid., p. 88.

35. James S. Maag, "Cattle Raising in Colonial South Carolina," M.A. thesis, University of Kansas, 1964, pp. 36–8.

36. *South Carolina Gazette,* February 15, 1734/5.

37. Maag, "Cattle Raising," pp. 21–2.

38. William Bartram, *Travels through North & South Carolina, Georgia, East and West Florida* (Philadelphia, 1791), p. 310.

39. Meriwether, *Expansion of South Carolina*, p. 168.

40. *South Carolina Gazette*, April 2 and April 9, 1741.

41. Ibid., April 10, 1742.

42. Ibid., May 1, 1736 and July 2, 1741.

43. Harry Roy Merrens, *Colonial North Carolina in the Eighteenth Century: A Study in Historical Geography* (Chapel Hill, 1964), p. 53.

44. Information on the beginning of counties may be found in D. L. Corbitt, *The Formation of North Carolina Counties, 1663–1943* (Raleigh, 1950), passim.

45. The beginning of Salisbury is examined in Robert W. Ramsey, *Carolina Cradle: Settlement of the Northwest Carolina Frontier, 1747–1762* (Chapel Hill, 1964), pp. 152–70.

46. Saunders, *Colonial Records of North Carolina*, V, 355.

47. Ramsey, *Carolina Cradle*, p. 169.

48. A valuable county history, although not documented, is Hugh T. Lefler and Paul Wager, eds., *Orange County, 1752–1952* (Chapel Hill, 1953).

49. "Autobiography of Col. William Few of Georgia," *Magazine of American History*, 7 (November 1881), p. 344.

50. Ibid.

51. The "midland towns" are discussed in Merrens, *Colonial North Carolina*, pp. 155–62.

52. The "western towns" are examined in ibid., pp. 162–6.

53. For a detailed examination of the Bray Associates, see Crane, *Southern Frontier*, pp. 303–25.

54. Edwin S. Gaustad, *A Religious History of America* (New York, 1966), pp. 76–7.

55. E. Merton Coulter, *A Short History of Georgia* (Chapel Hill, 1933), p. 15.

56. Ibid., p. 53.

57. Kenneth Coleman, *Colonial Georgia: A History* (New York, 1976), pp. 20–3, 52, 223–4.

58. P. A. Strobel, *The Salzburgers and their Descendants* (Baltimore, 1855), provides a useful account of the background and history of the Salzburgers in Georgia, even though very laudatory of their efforts.

59. Ibid., pp. 94–9.

60. Allen D. Candler and Lucian L. Knight, eds., *The Colonial Records of the State of Georgia*, 26 vols. (Atlanta, 1904–16), IV, 665, V, 59–60.

61. Ibid., XXV, 219.

62. M. T. McKinstry, "Silk Culture in the Colony of Georgia," *Georgia Historical Quarterly*, 14 (September 1930), pp. 225–35; J. M. Hofer, "The Georgia Salzburgers," ibid., 18 (June 1934), pp. 99–117.

63. *Colonial Records of Georgia*, XXVI, 74.

64. Ibid., XXI, 115–6, 120.

65. Harold E. Davis, *The Fledgling Province: Social and Cultural Life in Colonial Georgia, 1733–1776* (Chapel Hill, 1976), p. 32.

Chapter 9

1. See Bolton and Ross, *Debatable Land*.

2. For the problems in building this fort, see Joseph W. Barnwell, ed., "Journal of Col. John Barnwell (Tuscarora) in the Construction of the Fort on the Altamaha in 1721," *So. Car. Hist. & Gen. Mag.*, 27 (October 1926), pp. 189–203; Crane, *Southern Frontier*, pp. 236–7.

3. Trevor R. Reese, *Colonial Georgia: A Study in British Imperial Policy in the Eighteenth Century* (Athens, 1963), p. 13.

4. Savelle, *Origins of American Diplomacy*, pp. 323–5.

5. John P. Corry, *Indian Affairs in Georgia, 1732–1756* (Philadelphia, 1936), pp. 69–72.

6. Charles Gibson, *Spain in America* (Henry S. Commager and Richard B. Morris, eds., *The New American Nation Series* New York, 1966), pp. 91–5; C. H. Haring, *The Spanish Empire in America* (New York, 1947), pp. 76–8, 105–7.

7. For a commentary on the fate of Sánchez, see George T. Lanning, "The Legend that Governor Moral Sánchez was Hanged," *Ga. Hist. Quar.* 38 (December 1954), pp. 349–55.

8. Reese, *Colonial Georgia*, pp. 58, 75.

9. Quoted in Wright, *Anglo-Spanish Rivalry*, p. 87.

10. Savelle, *Origins of American Diplomacy*, pp. 348–50.

11. Quoted in Reese, *Colonial Georgia*, p. 66.

12. John T. Lanning, *The Diplomatic History of Georgia: A Study of the Epoch of Jenkins' Ear* (Chapel Hill, 1936), p. 178.

13. *Colonial Records of Georgia*, IV, 427.

14. For a perceptive examination of the background and events of this revolt, see Peter H. Wood, *Black Majority: Negroes in Colonial South Carolina from 1670 through the Stono Rebellion* (New York, 1974).

15. Rights, *Indian in North Carolina*, p. 58.

16. Greene, *Quest for Power*, pp. 311–5.

17. *Colonial Records of Georgia*, I, 31–42.

18. Corry, *Indian Affairs in Georgia*, p. 45.

19. Leonard W. Labaree, ed., *Royal Insturctions to British Colonial Governors, 1670–1776*, 2 vols. (New York, 1935), II, 475–6; Corry, *Indian Affairs in Georgia*, pp. 54–61; Reese, *Colonial Georgia* pp. 109–12.

20. International rivalries involving negotiations with Indians in the "Old Southwest" are ably developed in Crane, *Southern Frontier*, chap 11.

21. Sir Alexander Cuming, "Scrapbook," Edward E. Ayer Collection, Newberry Library, Chicago, 24 pages.

22. Sir Alexander Cuming, "Gerogia and the Cherokees," in ibid., pp. 22, 47–8.

23. William H. Gilbert, Jr., "The Eastern Cherokee," *Anthropological Papers*, Bureau of American Ethnology, Bulletin 133 (Washington, 1943), pp. 321, 363; Fred Gearing, *Priests and Warriors: Social Structures for Cherokee Politics in the 18th Century*, Memoir 93, *American Anthropologist*, 62, no. 5, part 2 (October 1962), pp. 5–6, 85–7. The theories of Indian government set forth by these writers are challenged in John P. Reid, *A Law of Blood: The Primitive Law of the Cherokee Nation* (New York, 1970), pp. 18–27.

24. Saunders, *Colonial Records of North Carolina*, III, 129–33.

25. James Adair, *The History of the American Indians* (London, 1775), pp. 240, 242.

26. "Historical Relation of Facts Delivered by Ludovick Grant, Indian Trader, to His Excellency the Governor of South Carolina," *So. Car. Hist. & Gen. Mag.*, 10 (January 1909), pp. 59, 61.

27. *South Carolina Gazette*, August 15, 1743.

28. Newton D. Mereness, ed., *Travels in the American Colonies* (New York, 1916), p. 248.

29. Mereness, ed., *Travels*, p. 249; see also the two articles by Knox Mellon, Jr., "Christian Priber's Cherokee 'Kingdom of Paradise,'" *Ga. Hist. Quar.*, 57 (Fall 1973), pp. 319–31 and "Christian Priber and the Jesuit Myth," *So. Car. Hist. Mag.*, 61 (April 1960), pp. 75–81.

30. *South Carolina Gazette*, August 15, 1743.

31. *Colonial Records of Georgia*, IV, 428.

32. E. Merton Coulter, "Mary Musgrove, 'Queen of the Creeks': A Chapter of Early Georgia Troubles," *Ga. Hist. Quar.*, 11 (March 1927), pp. 1–30.

33. The terms of the Coweta treaty may be found in ibid., 4 (March 1920), pp. 3–8.

34. Wright, *Anglo-Spanish Rivalry*, p. 89.

35. Lanning, *Diplomatic History of Georgia*, p. 206.

36. *Archives of Maryland,* XL, 581–4.

37. Lanning, *Diplomatic History of Georgia,* pp. 223–4; Wright, *Anglo-Spanish Rivalry,* pp. 90–2; Reese, *Colonial Georgia,* pp. 78–80.

38. For documentary sources on this campaign, see John T. Lanning, ed., *The St. Augustine Expedition of 1740: A Report to the South Carolina General Assembly* (Columbia, 1954); *Letters of Montiano, Siege of St. Augustine,* Collections of the Georgia Historical Society, vol. 7, part 1, (Savannah, 1909).

39. Wallace, *History of South Carolina,* I, 440.

40. Lanning, *Diplomatic History of Georgia,* pp. 199–219; Wright, *Anglo-Spanish Rivalry,* p. 94.

41. Wright, *Anglo-Spanish Rivalry,* pp. 95–7; Coulter, *Short History of Georgia,* p. 46; *The Spanish Official Account of the Attack on the Colony of Georgia, in America, and of its Defeat on St. Simons Island by General James Oglethorpe,* Collections of the Georgia Historical Society, vol. 7, part 3 (Savannah, 1913).

42. Corry, *Indian Affairs in Georgia,* p. 127n.

43. Savelle, *Origins of American Diplomacy,* pp. 376–7.

Chapter 10

1. Savelle, *Origins of American Diplomacy,* p. 422.

2. Lawrence H. Gipson, *Zones of International Friction: North America, South of the Great Lakes Region, 1748–1754* (vol. 4 of *The British Empire Before the American Revolution* New York, 1939), pp. 11–2.

3. Ibid., p. 16.

4. Clarence W. Alvord, *The Illinois Country, 1673–1818* (Springfield, 1920), pp. 190–4; W. J. Eccles, *France in America* (Henry S. Commager and Richard S. Morris, eds., *The New American Nation Series* New York, 1972), pp. 68–71.

5. Alvord, *Illinois Country,* pp. 191, 191n.

6. Ibid., pp. 197–8.

7. Gipson, *British Empire,* IV, 106–7, 107n.

8. For a more detailed examination of Croghan, see Nicholas B. Wainwright, *George Croghan: Wilderness Diplomat* (Chapel Hill, 1959).

9. Croghan to R. Peters, May 26, 1747, *Pennsylvania Archives,* First Series, 12 vols. (Philadelphia, 1852–60), I, 742.

10. Gipson, *British Empire,* IV, 221–4; Billington, *Westward Expansion,* pp. 124–5; W. J. Eccles, *The Canadian Frontier 1534–1760* (Ray A. Billington and Howard R. Lamar, eds., *Histories of the American Frontier* Albuquerque, 1974), pp. 160–2.

11. For a recent biography of Gist, see Kenneth P. Bailey, *Christopher Gist: Colonial Frontiersman, Explorer, and Indian Agent* (Hamden, Conn., 1976).

12. Colonial Office Papers, 5:1327, pp. 188–9.

13. "The Treaty of Logg's Town, 1752: Commission, Instructions, etc., Journal of Virginia Commission, and Text of Treaty," *Va. Mag. Hist. & Biog.,* 13 (October 1905), pp. 143–74.

14. Morton, *Colonial Virginia,* II, 615.

15. Stanley M. Pargellis, *Lord Loudoun in North America* (New Haven, 1933), pp. 4–16.

16. Ibid., pp. 22–4.

17. R. A. Brock, ed., *The Official Records of Robert Dinwiddie, Lieutenant-Governor of the Colony of Virginia, 1751–1758,* 2 vols., Collections of the Virginia Historical Society, vols. 3–4, New Series (Richmond, 1883–84), I, 89, hereafter cited as *Dinwiddie Records;* O'Callaghan, *Documents of the Colonial History of New York,* VI, 794–5.

18. Pargellis, *Lord Loudoun,* pp. 30–35.

19. Greene, *Quest for Power,* pp. 302–9.

20. Justin Winsor, *The Mississippi Basin* (Boston and New York, 1898), p. 324.

21. John C. Fitzpatrick, ed., *The Writings of George Washington from the Original Manuscript Sources, 1745–1799*, 39 vols. (Washington, 1931–44), I, 305.

22. Dinwiddie to Glen, May 23, 1753 and Glen to Dinwiddie, June 21, 1753, Colonial Office Papers 5:13.

23. *Dinwiddie Records*, I, 61–3, 131–3.

24. Glen to Dinwiddie, March 14, 1754, in *Robert Dinwiddie Correspondence Illustrative of his Career in American Colonial Government and Westward Expansion*, Louis K. Koontz, ed., Microfilm (Berkeley and Los Angeles, 1951), p. 481.

25. *Dinwiddie Records*, I, 97.

26. Captain Orme stated in his *Journal* that these bills were the only money contributed by the colonies that "passed through" Braddock's hands. Winthrop Sargents, ed., *The History of an Expedition Against Fort Du Quesne, in 1755* (Philadelphia, 1855), p. 325.

27. For a discussion of the conflicting reports on the total strength and casualties of each force, see Douglas Southall Freeman, *George Washington: A Biography*, 7 vols. (New York, 1948–57), II, 68n, 86; Sargent, ed., *Expedition*, p. 310.

28. Stanley Pargellis, "Braddock's Defeat," *American Historical Review*, 41 (January 1936), pp. 253–4, 269.

29. Freeman, *Washington*, II, 94–9; Paul E. Kopperman, *Braddock at the Monongahela* (Pittsburgh, 1977), gives a detailed review of both contemporary and twentieth-century criticisms of the expedition, concluding that British troops were responsible for the failure and that "the weight of evidence places the onus on them, rather than on Braddock or other officers" (p. 121). See chapters 5 and 6.

30. Sargent, ed., *Expedition*, p. 173.

31. *Dinwiddie Records*, II, 125.

32. Meriwether, *Expansion of South Carolina*, pp. 209–10.

33. *Dinwiddie Records*, II, 212–4.

34. Ibid., II, 213.

35. Saunders, *Colonial Records of North Carolina*, V, 359–60.

36. Quoted in Lawrence H. Gipson, *The Great War for the Empire: The Years of Defeat, 1754–1757* (vol. 6 of *The British Empire Before the American Revolution* New York, 1946), pp. 25–6.

37. Glen to Dinwiddie, June 1, 1754, Colonial Office Papers, 5:14.

38. Louis K. Koontz, *Robert Dinwiddie: His Career in American Colonial Government and Westward Expansion* (Glendale, California, 1941), pp. 322–3, 322n.

39. F. B. Kegley, *Kegley's Virginia Frontier: The Beginning of the Southwest, The Roanoke of Colonial Days, 1740–1783* (Roanoke, Virginia, 1938), pp. 224–8.

40. For further information on Atkin, see Wilbur R. Jacobs, ed., *Indians of the Southern Colonial Frontier: The Edmond Atkin Report and Plan of 1755* (Columbia, 1954).

41. Hening, *Statutes of Virginia*, VI, 530–50; Morton, *Colonial Virginia*, II, 676.

42. Hening, *Statutes of Virginia*, VI, 550–2, 565; *Dinwiddie Records*, II, 254; Williamsburg *Virginia Gazette* (Dixon and Hunter), Oct. 31, 1755.

43. Hening, *Statutes of Virginia*, VII, 241.

44. *Dinwiddie Records*, II, 620.

45. Fitzpatrick, ed., *Writings of Washington*, I, 324–5.

46. Hening, *Statutes of Virginia*, VII, 17–8; Hampshire County was formed in 1754 from Augusta, Frederick, and Hardy counties, and the area is now a part of West Virginia. Robinson, *Virginia Counties*, p. 144.

47. For an identification of these forts, see Louis K. Koontz, *The Virginia Frontier, 1754–1763*, Johns Hopkins University Studies in Historical and Political Science, series 43, no. 2 (Baltimore, 1925), pp. 111–48.

48. William H. Browne, ed., *Correspondence of Governor Horatio Sharpe, 1753–1761*, 2 vols., *Archives of Maryland* 6 (1888–90), I, 262.

49. Hays Baker-Crothers, *Virginia and the French and Indian War* (Chicago, 1928), pp. 87–8.

50. Saunders, *Colonial Records of North Carolina*, V, 353.

51. Ibid., V, 357.

52. Quoted in Desmond Clarke, *Arthur Dobbs, Esquire, 1689–1765: Surveyor-General of Ireland, Prospector and Governor of North Carolina* (Chapel Hill, 1957), p. 125.

53. Saunders, *Colonial Records of North Carolina*, V, 849.

54. Thomas Robinson to Dinwiddie, July 5, 1754, Colonial Office Papers, 5:211.

55. *Dinwiddie Records*, II, 281–2.

56. John R. Alden, *John Stuart and the Southern Colonial Frontier: A Study of Indian Relations, War, Trade, and Land Problems in the Southern Wilderness, 1754–1775* (Ann Arbor, 1944), pp. 57–8.

57. Ibid., pp. 58–9.

58. David H. Corkran, *The Cherokee Frontier: Conflict and Survival, 1740–62* (Norman, 1962), pp. 149–52.

59. Alden, *John Stuart*, pp. 83–4.

60. Ibid., pp. 85–8.

61. Corkran, *Cherokee Frontier*, p. 195.

62. Ibid., p. 207; Alden, *John Stuart*, p. 107.

63. Morton, *Colonial Virginia*, II, 733.

64. Quoted in ibid., p. 734.

65. Corkran, *Cherokee Frontier*, pp. 246–54.

66. Ibid., pp. 256–62.

67. Morton, *Colonial Virginia*, II, 735.

68. *South Carolina Gazette*, February 23, 1760.

69. Richard M. Brown, *The South Carolina Regulators: The Story of the First Vigilante Movement* (Cambridge, 1963), p. 5.

70. Alden, *John Stuart*, pp. 95–8.

71. Ibid., pp. 181–6.

72. A record of the conference was printed as the *Journal of the Congress of the Four Southern Governors, and the Superintendent of That District, with the Five Nations of Indians, at Augusta, 1763* (Charleston, S. C., 1764).

73. Lyman Chalkley, "Before the Gates of the Wilderness Road," *Va. Mag. Hist. & Biog.*, 30 (April 1922), p. 184.

74. Quoted in *Kegley's Virginia Frontier*, pp. 284–5.

Chapter 11

1. David Humphreys, *An Historical Account of the Incorporated Society for the Propagation of the Gospel in Foreign Parts,* cited in William W. Sweet, *Religion in Colonial America* (New York, 1949), pp. 54–5.

2. Edwin Gaustad, *Historical Atlas of Religion in America* (New York, 1962), p. 167.

3. Hening, *Statutes of Virginia*, III, 170.

4. *Virginia Executive Journals*, I, 427.

5. Hening, *Statutes of Virginia*, IV, 78.

6. *Journals of the House of Burgesses*, 1727–34, 1736–40, p. 4.

7. Hening, *Statutes of Virginia*, VII, 301–3.

8. Meriwether, *Expansion of South Carolina*, p. 40; Wallace, *History of South Carolina*, I, 339.

9. This registry is printed in Salley, *History of Orangesburg County*, pp. 91–216.

10. Saunders, *Colonial Records of North Carolina*, VI, 1091.

11. Morton, *Colonial Virginia*, II, 584.

12. For a biography of Davies, see George W. Pilcher, *Samuel Davies: Apostle of Dissent in Colonial Virginia* (Knoxville, 1971).

13. Samuel Davies, *The State of Religion among the Protestant Dissenters in Virginia: in a Letter to the Rev. Mr. Joseph Bellamy, of Bethlem, in New England: From the Reverend Mr. Samuel Davies, V. D. M. in Hanover County, Virginia* (Boston, 1751).

14. Ramsey, *Carolina Cradle,* pp. 201–2.

15. Additional material on Bolzius in journals include Klaus G. Loewald, Beverly Starika, and Paul S. Taylor, eds. and trans., "Johann Martin Bolzius Answers a Questionnaire on Carolina and Georgia," *William and Mary Quarterly,* 3d series, 14 (April 1957), pp. 218–61 and 15 (April 1958), pp. 228–52; Lothar L. Tresp, trans. and ann., "August, 1748 in Georgia, from the Diary of John Martin Bolzius," and "September, 1748 in Georgia, from the Diary of John Martin Bolzius," *Ga. Hist. Quar.,* 47 (June and September 1963), pp. 204–16, 320–32; George F. Jones, ed. and trans., "John Martin Bolzius Reports on Georgia in 1739," *Ga. Hist. Quar.,* 47 (June 1963), pp. 216–9; George F. Jones, "The Secret Diary of Pastor Johann Martin Bolzius," *Ga. Hist. Quar.,* 53 (March 1969), pp. 78–110.

16. J. Stoddard Johnston, ed., *First Exploration of Kentucky,* Filson Club Publication No. 13 (Louisville, 1898), 38–9.

17. Jacob J. Sessler, *Communal Pietism among Early American Moravians,* American Religion Series, VIII (New York, 1933), passim.

18. Adelaide L. Fries, *The Moravians in Georgia, 1735–1740* (Raleigh, 1905), pp. 51, 126.

19. Ibid., pp. 136–7.

20. Sessler, *Communal Pietism,* pp. 76, 90–1, 97.

21. A copy of the Act of Parliament of 1749 is included in Adelaide L. Fries et al., eds., *Records of the Moravians in North Carolina,* 7 vols. (Raleigh, 1922–), I, 23–5.

22. Ibid., I, 65–9.

23. Ibid., I, 48–9.

24. Ibid., I, 241n.

25. Saunders, *Colonial Records of North Carolina,* V, 1149; Fries, ed., *Moravians in North Carolina,* I, 293–4.

26. Quoted in Carl Bridenbaugh, *Myths and Realities: Societies of the Colonial South* (Baton Rouge, 1952), p. 151.

27. Richard J. Hooker, ed., *The Carolina Backcountry on the Eve of the Revolution: The Journal and Other Writings of Charles Woodmason, Anglican Itinerant* (Chapel Hill, 1953), pp. 45, 47.

28. Public Records of South Carolina, XXIX, 80–2; Brown, *South Carolina Regulators,* pp. 19–20.

29. Theodore G. Tappert and John W. Doberstein, trans., *The Journals of Henry Melchoir Muhlenberg,* 3 vols. (Philadelphia, 1942–58), II, 577–9.

30. Quoted in Hooker, *Journal of Woodmason,* p. xxv.

31. *South Carolina Gazette,* June 1, 1765.

32. Joseph Doddridge, *Notes on the Settlement and Indian Wars* (Martin Ridge and Ray A. Billington, eds., *America's Frontier Story: A Documentary History of Westward Expansion* New York, 1969), p. 106.

33. Quoted in Meriwether, *Expansion of South Carolina,* p. 157.

34. Bernard C. Steiner, *History of Education in Maryland,* United States Bureau of Education, Circular of Information No. 2, 1894 (Washington, 1894), p. 34.

35. Inventories, Frederick County, Maryland, 1750/51, Hall of Records, Annapolis, Maryland, p. 111.

36. Hooker, *Journal of Woodmason,* p. 226.

37. Comments of the Reverend James Maury on education have been edited by Helen D. Bullock in the *Papers* of the Albemarle County Historical Society, Virginia.

38. Judgments, Frederick County Court, Maryland, 1751, Hall of Records, Annapolis, Maryland, p. 170.

39. "Moravian Diaries," *Va. Mag. Hist. & Biog.*, 11 (October 1903), pp. 230, 233.

40. Edgar W. Knight, ed., *A Documentary History of Education in the South before 1860*, 5 vols. (Chapel Hill, 1949–53), I, 708.

41. Meriwether, *Expansion of South Carolina*, p. 177.

42. For an examination of these efforts, see W. Stitt Robinson, "Indian Education and Missions in Colonial Virginia," *Journal of Southern History*, 18 (May 1952), pp. 152–68.

43. Bursar's Book Ledger, William and Mary College, 1763–1770, William and Mary College Library, pp. 3, 19, 32, 43, 61, 65, 89.

44. Frank K. Klingberg, ed., *The Carolina Chronicle of Dr. Francis Le Jau, 1706–1717*, University of California Publications in History, vol. 53 (Berkeley and Los Angeles, 1956), p. 76.

45. Ibid., p. 95.

46. "Mr. Samuel Thomas's Remonstrance in Justification of himself," Records of the Society for the Propagation of the Gospel in Foreign Parts, Microfilm, The Journals, 1701–1850, Appendix A, document no. 79, pp. 469–70.

47. Fries, *Moravians in Georgia*, pp. 154–5, 214, 221.

48. *William and Mary College Quarterly*, 1st series, 1 (1892–3), p. 217.

49. Bassett, *Writings of William Byrd*, p. 99.

50. *Dinwiddie Records*, II, 446.

51. Samuel Davies, *Sermons on Important Subjects*, 3 vols. (New York, 1849), III, 42, 43.

52. See the map and tables in Brown and Brown, *Virginia*, pp. 73 ff.

53. Meriwether, *Expansion of South Carolina*, pp. 160, 260.

54. For additional information on Bacon, see Harris E. Starr, "Thomas Bacon," *Dictionary of American Biography*, 1 (1946), p. 484; Bernard C. Steiner, "A Pioneer in Negro Education," *Independent*, 51 (August 24, 1899), pp. 2287–90; Lawrence C. Worth, "A Maryland Merchant and His Friends, in 1750," *Maryland Historical Magazine*, 6 (September 1911), pp. 213–40.

55. Frank J. Klingberg, *An Appraisal of the Negro in Colonial South Carolina* (Washington, 1941), pp. 104–5.

56. H. Warren Gardner, "The Dissenting Sects on the Southern Colonial Frontier, 1720–1770," Ph.D. diss., University of Kansas, 1969, pp. 228, 238.

57. Klingberg, *Negro in Colonial South Carolina*, pp. 82, 85.

Retrospect

1. Turner, *Frontier in American History*, p. 68.

2. Ibid., p. 12.

3. Ibid., p. 15.

4. Statement by John Spencer Bassett, quoted in ibid., p. 106.

Bibliography

Limitations of space prohibit a comprehensive listing of all published and unpublished materials relevant to the study of the southern colonial frontier to 1763. A selection of the most significant and most useful is provided in this bibliography.

Manuscripts and Unpublished Records

Supplementing the basic published sources for each of the southern colonies are collections of both public and private records in depositories both in the United States and Great Britain. The basic guides to material available in Great Britain are Charles M. Andrews, *Guide to the Materials for American History, to 1783, in the Public Record Office of Great Britain,* 2 vols. (Washington, 1912–14), and Charles M. Andrews and Frances G. Davenport, *Guide to the Manuscript Materials for the History of the United States to 1783, in the British Museum, in Minor London Archives, and in the Libraries of Oxford and Cambridge* (Washington, 1908). Additional assistance is in B. R. Crick, Miriam Alman, and H. L. Beales, eds., *A Guide to Manuscripts Relating to America in Great Britain and Ireland* (London, 1961). Information about transcripts may be obtained in Grace G. Griffin, *A Guide to Manuscripts Relating to American History in British Depositories reproduced for the Division of Manuscripts of the Library of Congress* (Washington, 1946). Identification of microfilm is in Lester K. Born, *British Manuscripts Project: A Checklist of the Microfilm Prepared in England and Wales for the American Council of Learned Societies, 1941–1945* (Washington, 1953). Assistance with local records is in William S. Jenkins, *A Guide to the Microfilm Collection of Early State Records* (Washington, 1950). Among these many records, I have found most useful the correspondence of colonial governors and Indian treaties such as those from the Public Record Office in Colonial Office Papers, class 5, vols. 13, 14, 211, 1310, 1313, 1316, and from the British Museum, the Egerton Manuscripts and the Sir Alexander Cuming Papers. The Virginia Colonial Records Survey, sponsored as a part of the 350th anniversary of the settlement of Jamestown, includes reports on collections and about 1000 reels of microfilm of records in Great Britain and a few archives on the continent of Europe. Both reports and microfilm are available at the Virginia State Library in Richmond, Alderman Library of the University of Virginia in Charlottesville, and the Research Library of Colonial Williamsburg. A much-needed guide to this collection is being prepared by Dr. John D. Neville of the Virginia State Library, and he kindly permitted me in 1978 to use the parts thus far completed.

Other depositories abroad of particular value are two in London: Lambeth Palace with correspondence of the Archbishop of Canterbury and the Bishop of London relative to missionary work in the American colonies, and the Society for the Propagation of the Gospel in Foreign Parts whose records relating to the American colonies are also now available on microfilm. The Public Record Office of Northern Ireland in Belfast has the papers of Arthur Dobbs, governor of North Carolina from 1754 to 1765, and valuable letters of emigrants to America. In Edinburgh, the Scottish Record Office's "Source List of Manuscripts Relating to the U. S. A. and Canada" greatly expedited in 1967 the use of such collections as the John Forbes papers with correspondence to and from southern governors in the 1750s.

Several other archives and private libraries in the United States provide valuable assistance

271

with unpublished records. The Edward E. Ayer Collection of the Newberry Library, Chicago, has excellent Indian material, most useful of which related to the Cherokee. The papers of Governor William H. Lyttelton of South Carolina in the Clements Library, Ann Arbor, Michigan, contain material on the Cherokee War of 1760–61. The Hall of Records in Annapolis, Maryland, includes among its well organized collections the County Court Judgments of Frederick County and Inventories of Property. The South Carolina Department of Archives and History has many unpublished records of the colonial period, including the 38 volumes of the Journals of the Council and Upper House of the Assembly from 1721 to 1775. The Georgia Department of Archives and History has the typescript of the unpublished volumes of Colonial Records of the State of Georgia: volume 20 and volumes 27–39. Kenneth Coleman and Milton Ready are serving as editors for the publication of these remaining volumes with volume 27 published in 1977.

British Published Sources

Four major sets provide valuable British material for the colonial period: W. Noel Sainsbury et al., eds., *Calendar of State Papers, Colonial Series, America and the West Indies, 1574–*, over 40 vols. to date (London, 1860–); *Journals of the Commissioners for Trade and Plantations preserved in the Public Record Office, 1704–1775*, 14 vols. (London, 1920–38), generally known as the Board of Trade Journals; William Grant et al., eds., *Acts of the Privy Council of England, Colonial Series, 1613–1783*, 6 vols. (London, 1908–12); and Leonard W. Labaree, ed., *Royal Instructions to British Colonial Governors, 1670–1776*, 2 vols. (New York, 1935).

Geography, Maps, and Population

Physiographic divisions and descriptions of terrain may be found in Nevin M. Fenneman, *Physiography of Eastern United States* (New York, 1938), and Wallace W. Atwood, *The Physiographic Provinces of North America* (Boston, 1940).

Maps, both manuscript and published, have provided assistance in identifying essential geographical locations and delineating the advance of settlements. The most authoritative source for identification of maps relating to the southern colonial frontier is William P. Cumming, *The Southeast in Early Maps* (Princeton, 1958). John Smith's "Map of Virginia, 1612" is available in vol. 2 of Edward Arber and A. G. Bradley, eds., *Travels and Works of Captain John Smith*, 2 vols. (Edinburgh, 1910). The following maps of particular value are all identified in chronological order with details about available reproductions in Cumming, *Southeast in Early Maps:* Augustine Herrman, "Virginia and Maryland, 1673"; J. B. Homann, "Virginia Marylandia et Carolina, 1714"; John Barnwell, ["Southeastern North America"], ca. 1722, photographic reproduction kindly provided the author by the Library of Congress of this important manuscript map; Edward Moseley, "A New and Correct Map of the Province of North Carolina, 1733"; Joshua Fry and Peter Jefferson, "A Map of the Inhabited Part of Virginia Containing the Whole Province of Maryland with Part of Pensilvania, New Jersey and North Carolina, 1751 [1753]"; and John Mitchell, "A Map of the British and French Dominions in North America, 1755."

General population compilations include Evarts B. Greene and Virginia D. Harrington, *American Population Before the Federal Census of 1790* (New York, 1932), and the more interpretative work of Stella H. Sutherland, *Population Distribution in Colonial America* (New York, 1936). Herman R. Friis portrays the westward-moving frontier by dots (about 200 persons each) for ten different periods in "A Series of Population Maps of the Colonies and the United States, 1625–1790," *Geographical Review*, 30 (July 1940), pp. 463–70, mimeograph copy also available from the American Geographical Society (1940). Fulmer Mood uses the above maps to identify many frontiers of settlement in his "Studies in the History of American Settled Areas and Frontier Lines," *Agricultural History*, 26 (January 1952), pp. 16–34. More specialized approaches to population by colonies include Arthur E. Karinen, "Numerical and Distributional Aspects of Maryland Population, 1631–1840" (Ph.D. diss., University of Maryland, 1958), from which two articles are available in the *Maryland Historical Magazine*, 54 (December 1959), pp. 365–407 and 60 (June 1965), pp. 139–59; population maps for different periods in Morgan P. Robinson, *Virginia Counties: Those Resulting From Virginia Legislation*, Bulletin of the Virginia State Library, 9, nos. 1–3 (Richmond, 1916); Miles S. Malone, "The Distribution of Population on the Virginia Frontier in 1775" (Ph.D. diss., Princeton University, 1935) which now needs corrections; and Wilbur Zelinsky, "An Isochronic Map of Georgia Settlement, 1750–1850," *Georgia Historical Quarterly*, 35 (September 1951), pp. 191–5.

Indians of the Southern Colonial Frontier

For the period prior to 1763, descriptions of the American Indians come almost exclusively from European immigrants to America or their descendants and from the more recent scholarly work of anthropologists and historians. C. F. and F. M. Voegelin have compiled the *Map of North American Indian Languages* (1966). Indian languages and culture areas are effectively described in Wendell H. Oswalt's *This Land Was Theirs: A Study of the North American Indian* (New York, 1973), a volume which then examines selected Indian groups in detail. A more general cultural study is Harold E. Driver, *Indians of North America* (Chicago, 1969). Wilcomb E. Washburn has added a comprehensive view of the American Indian including social and psychological analyses and major attention to the first half of American history in *The Indian in America* (Henry S. Commager and Richard B. Morris, eds., *The New American Nation Series*, New York, 1975). For bibliographies, see the "Bibliography" by Lyman H. Butterfield, Wilcomb E. Washburn, and William N. Fenton in *American Indian and White Relations to 1830: Needs and Opportunities for Study* (Chapel Hill, 1957), and the more comprehensive one by Francis Paul Prucha, *A Bibliographical Guide to the History of Indian-White Relations in the United States* (Chicago, 1977).

The following descriptions give contemporary observations of southern Indians: Paul H. Hulton and David B. Quinn, *The American Drawings of John White*, 2 vols. (London and Chapel Hill, 1964); Arber and Bradley, eds., *Travels and Works of Captain John Smith;* James Adair, *The History of the American Indian: Particularly Those Adjoining to the Mississippi, East and West Florida, Georgia, South and North Carolina and Virginia* (London, 1775); and Wilbur R. Jacobs, ed., *Indians of the Southern Colonial Frontier: The Edmond Atkin Report and Plan of 1755* (Columbia, 1954).

Twentieth-century studies of Virginia Indians include James Mooney, "The Powhatan Confederacy, Past and Present," *American Anthropologist*, new series, 9 (1907), pp. 120–52; Maurice A. Mook, "Aboriginal Population of Tidewater Virginia," *American Anthropologist*, new series, 46 (April-June 1944), pp. 193–208. Special attention is called to the excellent article by Nancy O. Lurie, "Indian Cultural Adjustment to European Civilization," in James M. Smith, ed., *Seventeenth-Century America: Essays in Colonial History* (Chapel Hill, 1959), pp. 33–60, and to the best study of Pocahontas by Philip L. Barbour, *Pocahontas and her World: A Chronicle of America's First Settlement* (Boston, 1970). A recent critical look at the ethnocentric views of European immigrants is J. Frederick Fausz, "The Powhatan Uprising of 1622: A Historical Study of Ethnocentrism and Cultural Conflict" (Ph.D. diss., College of William and Mary, 1977).

Anthropologists have extended their identifications to larger areas of the frontier, including James Mooney, *The Siouan Tribes of the East*, Bureau of American Ethnology, Bulletin 22 (Washington, 1894); David I. Bushnell, Jr., *Native Villages and Village Sites East of the Mississippi*, Bureau of American Ethnology, Bulletin 69 (Washington, 1919). John R. Swanton deserves special notice for his studies of the Southeast as well as other areas, including the useful descriptions of *The Indians of the Southeastern United States,* Bureau of American Ethnology, Bulletin 137 (Washington, 1946); *The Indian Tribes of North America,* Bureau of American Ethnology, Bulletin 134 (Washington, 1952); *Early History of the Creek Indians and their Neighbors,* Bureau of American Ethnology, Bulletin 73 (Washington, 1922); and *Source Material for the Social and Ceremonial Life of the Choctaw Indians,* Bureau of American Ethnology, Bulletin 103 (Washington, 1931). Frederick W. Hodge, ed., *Handbook of American Indians North of Mexico,* 2 vols., Bureau of American Ethnology, Bulletin 30 (Washington, 1907–10) will be superseded by a new publication of the Smithsonian Institution.

Other useful studies of one or more tribes of the Southeast have been completed. William H. Gilbert, Jr., examines the social and political structure of "The Eastern Cherokee," *Anthropological Papers,* no. 23, Bureau of American Ethnology, Bulletin 133 (Washington, 1943). Fred Gearing goes further, sometimes with limited evidence, in describing Cherokee society and government in *Priests and Warriors: Social Structures for Cherokee Politics in the 18th Century,* Memoir 93, *American Anthropologist,* vol. 62, no. 5, part 2 (October 1962). Some of the conclusions of these writers are challenged by the two recent studies of the lawyer, John P. Reid, entitled *A Law of Blood: The Primitive Law of the Cherokee Nation* (New York, 1970), and *A Better Kind of Hatchet: Law, Trade, and Diplomacy in the Cherokee Nation during the Early Years of European Contact* (University Park, Pennsylvania, 1976). Douglas L. Rights adds information on *The American Indian in North Carolina* (Winston-Salem, 1957), and Chapman J. Milling gives a sympathetic treatment for South Carolina in *Red Carolinians* (Chapel Hill, 1940). In two recent scholarly studies, Charles M. Hudson, anthropologist, examines *The Catawba Nation* (Athens, 1970), and the culture of *The Southeastern Indians* (Knoxville, 1976), an extensive analysis of Indian society with particular attention to the Cherokee, Creeks, Chickasaw, Choctaw, and Seminoles. The research stimulated by the action of the Indian Claims Commission has resulted in several publications, including two ethnohistorical studies for Florida: Charles H. Fairbanks, "Ethnohistorical Report on the Florida Indians," *Florida Indians,* 3 vols. (New York, 1974), vol. 3; and Howard F. Cline, "Notes on Colonial Indians and Communities in Florida, 1700–1821," *Florida Indians,* vol. 1.

General and Regional Studies

General studies of the colonial period are still valuable in presenting an overall view of all of the colonies as well as detailed examinations of specific ones. Most reliable among these are Charles M. Andrews' *The Colonial Period of American History,* 4 vols. (New Haven, 1934–8), and Wesley F. Craven's two studies: *The Southern Colonies in the Seventeenth Century, 1607–1689* (vol. 1 of Wendell H. Stephenson and E. Merton Coulter, eds., *A History of the South,* Baton Rouge, 1949), indispensable for early Virginia and Maryland; and *The Colonies in Transition, 1660–1713* (Commager and Morris, eds., *The New American Nation Series,* New York, 1968). Lawrence H. Gipson provides a wealth of information, especially on international relations and western expansion, in *The British Empire Before the American Revolution,* 14 vols. (New York, 1936–69). Herbert L. Osgood gives useful details, although less valuable for interpretations, in *The American Colonies in the Seventeenth Century,* 3 vols. (New York, 1904–7), and *The American Colonies in the Eighteenth Century,* 4 vols. (New York, 1924–5). The best one-volume study of western settlements is Ray A. Billington's *Westward Expansion: A History of the American Frontier* (New York, 1967), containing up-to-date bibliographies for every revision including the most recent one in 1974. Frederick J. Turner devoted limited attention to the southern colonial frontier. Most germane are the essays in *The Frontier in American History* (New York, 1920). The economy of all the agrarian region is examined in the detailed study of Lewis C. Gray, *History of Agriculture in the Southern United States to 1860,* 2 vols. (Washington, 1933). Jack P. Greene effectively analyzes the gains of the legislature in *The*

Quest for Power: The Lower Houses of Assembly in the Southern Royal Colonies, 1689–1776 (Chapel Hill, 1963). Culture is described in the critical essays of Carl Bridenbaugh, *Myths and Realities: Societies of the Colonial South* (Baton Rouge, 1952). A more balanced view is found in Louis B. Wright, *The Cultural Life of the American Colonies, 1607–1763* (Commager and Morris, eds., *The New American Nation Series*, New York, 1957), and *Culture on the Moving Frontier* (Bloomington, Indiana, 1955).

Virginia

Virginia has published many of its public records for the colonial period, although not collecting them under one series title. For the early years, Susan M. Kingsbury, ed., *The Records of the Virginia Company of London*, 4 vols. (Washington, 1903–45) are most important. Laws are available in W. W. Hening, ed., *Statutes at large: being a Collection of All the Laws of Virginia from the First Session of the Legislature in the Year 1619* [to 1792], 13 vols. (Richmond, 1809–23), with additions in Waverly K. Winfree, comp., *The Laws of Virginia: being a Supplement to Hening's The Statutes at Large, 1700–1750* (Richmond, 1971). Other important sources include J. P. Kennedy and H. R. McIlwaine, eds., *Journals of the House of Burgesses of Virginia, 1619–1776*, 13 vols. (Richmond, 1905–15); H. R. McIlwaine, ed., *Legislative Journals of the Council of Colonial Virginia*, 3 vols. (Richmond, 1918–9); H. R. McIlwaine et al., eds., *Executive Journals of the Council of Colonial Virginia*, 6 vols. (Richmond, 1925–66), the most valuable in this group; and W. P. Palmer et al., *Calendar of Virginia State Papers, 1652–1869*, 11 vols. (Richmond, 1875–93).

Contemporary accounts and other documents may be effectively utilized in Alexander Brown, ed., *The Genesis of the United States*, 2 vols. (Boston and New York, 1890); Lyon G. Tyler, ed., *Narratives of Early Virginia, 1606–1625* (J. Franklin Jameson, ed., *Original Narratives of Early American History*, New York, 1907); and the more recent well-edited volume by Warren M. Billings, ed., *The Old Dominion in the Seventeenth Century: A Documentary History of Virginia, 1606–1689* (Chapel Hill, 1975). *The Virginia Gazette* (Williamsburg), beginning in 1736, is especially valuable with the assistance of the modern index by Lester J. Cappon and Stella M. Duff, eds., *Virginia Gazette Index, for the Years 1736–1780*, 2 vols. (Williamsburg, 1950).

Letters, journals, diaries, contemporary histories, and more recent studies are available for the colonial period. Many of these have been published for travelers or for individuals either living on the frontier or directly involved in official policies affecting the area. Among the most valuable are Richard B. Davis, ed., *William Fitzhugh and his Chesapeake World, 1676–1701* (Chapel Hill, 1963); Robert Beverley, *The History and Present State of Virginia*, ed. Louis B. Wright (Chapel Hill, 1947); Edward P. Alexander, ed., *The Journal of John Fontaine: an Irish Huguenot Son in Spain and Virginia, 1710–1719* (Williamsburg, 1972); Wm. J. Hinke, ed. and trans., "Report of the Journey of Francis Louis Michel from Berne, Switzerland, to Virginia, October 2, 1701–December 1, 1702," *Va. Mag. Hist. & Biog.*, 24 (January–June 1916), pp. 1–43, 113–41, 275–303; R. A. Brock, ed., *The Official Letters of Alexander Spotswood, Lieutentant-Governor of the Colony of Virginia, 1710–1722* (Collections of the Virginia Historical Society, new series, 2 vols., Richmond, 1882–5); and the study of *Alexander Spotswood: Governor of Colonial Virginia, 1710–1722* (Philadelphia, 1932) by Leonidas Dodson. Both William Byrd I and II had land, Indian trade, and other frontier interests. Letters of William Byrd I are scattered through several volumes of the *Va. Mag. Hist. & Biog.*, vols. 24–28 (1916–20). See also Pierre Marambaud's article on "Colonel William Byrd I: A Fortune Founded on Smoke," *Va. Mag. Hist. & Biog.*, 82 (October 1974), pp. 430–57. Several volumes provide essential information about William Byrd II: John S. Bassett, ed., *The Writings of Colonel William Byrd of Westover, Esqr.* (New York, 1901); Louis B. Wright, ed., *The Prose Works of William Byrd of Westover: Narratives of a Colonial Virginian* (Cambridge, Mass., 1966); Richard C. Beatty and William J.

Mulloy, eds., *William Byrd's Natural History of Virginia or The Newly Discovered Eden* (Richmond, 1940); and the biography by Pierre Marambaud, *William Byrd of Westover, 1674–1744* (Charlottesville, 1971). Rare views of isolated areas are found in William J. Hinke and Charles E. Kemper, eds., "Moravian Diaries of Travels through Virginia," *Va. Mag. Hist. & Biog.*, 11 (October 1903), pp. 113–31. The interest of Virginians in western expansion during Anglo-French conflicts is evident in R. A. Brock, ed., *The Official Records of Robert Dinwiddie, Lieutenant-Governor of the Colony of Virginia, 1751–1758*, 2 vols. (Collections of the Virginia Historical Society, vols. 3–4, new series, Richmond, 1883–4); Louis K. Koontz, ed., *Robert Dinwiddie: Correspondence Illustrative of his Career in American Colonial Government and Westward Expansion*, Microfilm (Berkeley and Los Angeles, 1951); and the biography by Louis K. Koontz, *Robert Dinwiddie: His Career in American Colonial Government and Westward Expansion* (Glendale, Ca., 1941). The frontier role of young George Washington may be traced through vols. 1–2 of John C. Fitzpatrick, ed., *The Writings of George Washington from the Original Manuscript Sources, 1745–1799*, 39 vols. (Washington, 1931–44), and the new on-going edition of Washington Papers in vol. 1 of Donald Jackson and Dorothy Twohig, eds., *The Diaries of George Washington, 1748–1765* (Charlottesville, 1976). Douglas Southall Freeman provides an evaluation of this role in *George Washington: A Biography*, 7 vols. (New York, 1948–57), vols. 1–3.

Other secondary works have provided excellent assistance for the study of Virginia's frontier experience prior to 1763. Information on population and social change may be found in Thomas J. Wertenbaker, *The Planters of Colonial Virginia* (Princeton, 1922); Sigmund Diamond, "From Organization to Society: Virginia in the Seventeenth Century," reprinted in Stanley N. Katz, ed., *Colonial America: Essays in Politics and Social Development* (Boston, 1971), pp. 3–31; and the statistical analysis by Irene W. D. Hecht, "The Virginia Muster of 1624/5 As a Source for Demographic History," *Wilaim and Mary Quarterly*, 3d series, 30 (January 1973), pp. 65–92. Edmund S. Morgan's innovative study of *American Slavery, American Freedom: The Ordeal of Colonial Virginia* (New York, 1975) suggests modification of some of Irene Hecht's figures. See also the important article by Bernard Bailyn, "Politics and Social Structure in Virginia," in Smith, ed., *Seventeenth-Century America*, pp. 90–115.

Bailyn's essay also provides significant interpretations of two levels of conflict in Bacon's Rebellion. This major event is the subject of conflicting interpretations by Thomas J. Wertenbaker and Wilcomb E. Washburn. Wertenbaker's more sympathetic views of Bacon are conveniently found in *The Torchbearer of the Revolution: The Story of Bacon's Rebellion and its Leader* (Princeton, 1940). Greater emphasis upon frontier problems and more sympathetic views of Sir William Berkeley are found in Washburn's *The Governor and the Rebel: A History of Bacon's Rebellion in Virginia* (Chapel Hill, 1957). More information on the identification of participants in the rebellion is included in Washburn's "Bacon's Rebellion, 1676–1677" (Ph.D. diss., Harvard University, 1955), pp. 665–85. Warren M. Billings has added "The Causes of Bacon's Rebellion: Some Suggestions," *Va. Mag. Hist. & Biog.*, 78 (October 1970), pp. 409–35. T. H. Breen argues with limited evidence for class conflict in Bacon's Rebellion in an article reprinted in Breen, ed., *Shaping Southern Society: The Colonial Experience* (New York, 1976), pp. 116–34.

Richard L. Morton's excellent narrative of *Colonial Virginia*, 2 vols. (Chapel Hill, 1960) is a valuable source with judicious interpretations for the full period of this study. Other useful secondary works for a frontier study include Thomas P. Abernethy, "The First Transmontane Advance," *Humanistic Studies in Honor of John Calvin Metcalf* (Charlottesville, 1941), pp. 120–38; Abernethy, *Three Virginia Frontiers* (Baton Rouge, 1940); Louis K. Koontz, *The Virginia Frontier, 1754–1763* (Baltimore, 1925); F. B. Kegley, *Kegley's Virginia Frontier: The Beginning of the Southwest, The Roanoke of Colonial Days, 1740–1783* (Roanoke, 1938); James L. Bugg, Jr., "The French Huguenot Frontier Settlement of Manakin Town," *Va. Mag. Hist. & Biog.*, 61 (October 1953), pp. 359–94; Robert E. and B. Katherine Brown, *Virginia, 1705–1786: Democracy or Aristocracy?* (East Lansing, 1964); David Alan Williams, "Political Alignments in Colonial

Virginia, 1698–1750" (Ph.D. diss., Northwestern University, 1959); and the recent perceptive study in historical geography by Robert D. Mitchell, *Commercialism and Frontier: Perspectives on the Early Shenandoah Valley* (Charlottesville, 1977).

E. G. Swem served as editor of the 23 volumes published as the Jamestown 350th Anniversary Historical Booklets (Williamsburg, 1957). The volumes consulted most frequently for this study were volume 6, *The First Seventeen Years, Virginia, 1607–1624* by Charles E. Hatch, Jr.; volume 11, *Virginia Architecture in the Seventeenth Century* by Henry C. Forman; volume 12, *Mother Earth: Land Grants in Virginia, 1607–1699* by W. Stitt Robinson; volume 17, *Indians in Seventeenth-Century Virginia* by Ben C. McCary; and volume 20, *Tobacco in Colonial Virginia: "The Sovereign Remedy"* by Melvin Herndon.

Other more extensive studies also contribute to interpretations of economic development. They include Philip A. Bruce, *Economic History of Virginia in the Seventeenth Century*, 2 vols. (New York, 1896); Manning C. Voorhis, "The Land Grant Policy of Colonial Virginia, 1607–1774" (Ph.D. diss., University of Virginia, 1940); Voorhis, "Crown versus Council in the Virginia Land Policy," *William and Mary Quarterly*, 3d series, 3 (October 1946), pp. 499–514; Edward Graham Roberts, "The Roads of Virginia, 1607–1840" (Ph.D. diss., University of Virginia, 1950); and Parke Rouse, *The Great Wagon Road from Philadelphia to the South*, vol. 11 of America Trail Series (New York, 1973).

Maryland

Maryland has been successful not only in bringing into the Hall of Records in Annapolis the county records for its colonial history, but has also published the best set of colonial records for the southern colonies. These are found in the on-going series of *The Archives of Maryland*, edited by William H. Browne et al. (Baltimore, 1883–) and now containing over 60 volumes. They include records of laws, legislative actions of the Assembly with its Lower and Upper Houses, executive and judicial decisions of the Council and Provincial Court (both including the members of the Upper House of the Assembly). There are also many court records, giving a rare glimpse of court leet and court baron at St. Clement's Manor (vol. 53). Other executive actions of special interest to the frontier are the volumes of the correspondence of Governor Horatio Sharpe (vol. 6,9,14), governor from 1753 to 1771.

Contemporary documents and accounts are found in Clayton C. Hall, ed., *Narratives of Early Maryland, 1633–1684* (Jameson, ed., *Original Narratives of Early American History*, New York, 1910). Lawrence C. Wroth has a valuable section on Maryland imprints in *History of Printing in Colonial Maryland, 1686–1776* (Baltimore, 1922). For Maryland and other American colonies, contemporary accounts are available in the American Antiquarian Society's Early American Imprints produced by the Readex Microprint Corporation from the list in Charles Evans et al., ed., *American Bibliography: A Chronological Dictionary of all Books, Pamphlets, and Periodical Publications Printed in the United States, 1639–1820*, 14 vols. (Chicago, 1903–59). *The Maryland Gazette* (Annapolis) provides information for the periods from 1726 to 1734 and from 1745 for the remainder of the period of this study.

Maryland is still lacking a satisfactory general history by current canons of scholarship. For the colonial period the histories cited under general works still provide the best source, particularly the studies of Charles M. Andrews and Wesley F. Craven. Additional information can be gleaned from John L. Bozman, *The History of Maryland from its First Settlement in 1633 to the Restoration in 1660* (Baltimore, 1837); James McSherry, *History of Maryland from its First Settlement in 1634 to the Year 1848* (Baltimore, 1849); John T. Scharf, *History of Maryland from the Earliest Period to the Present Day*, 3 vols. (Baltimore, 1879); William H. Browne, *Maryland: The History of a Palatinate* (Boston, 1884); Bernard C. Steiner, *Beginnings of Maryland, 1631–1639* (Baltimore, 1903); Steiner, *Maryland during the English Civil Wars*, 2 vols. (Baltimore, 1906–7); Steiner, *Maryland under the Commonwealth: A Chronicle of the Years*

1649–1658 (Baltimore, 1911); and Newton D. Mereness, *Maryland as a Proprietary Province* (New York, 1901). Mereness has the most satisfactory study from this group with an analytical approach.

More specialized works include essential information for a frontier study. Edward B. Mathews, *The Counties of Maryland, their Origin, Boundaries, and Election Districts* (Baltimore, 1907) gives basic facts on county formations. Clarence P. Gould's works are still useful, including *The Land System in Maryland, 1720–1765* (Johns Hopkins University Studies in Historical and Political Science, series 31, no. 1, Baltimore, 1913); *Money and Transportation in Maryland, 1720–1765* (Johns Hopkins University Studies in Historical and Political Science, series 33, no. 1, Baltimore, 1915); and "The Economic Causes of the Rise of Baltimore," in *Essays in Colonial History Presented to Charles McLean Andrews by his Students* (New Haven, 1931). Vertrees J. Wyckoff has two contributions of interest: "The Sizes of Plantations in Seventeenth-Century Maryland," *Maryland Historical Magazine*, 32 (December 1937), pp. 331–39, and *Tobacco Regulation in Colonial Maryland* (Baltimore, 1936). Aubrey C. Land's excellent publications on the Dulanys are of special value because of the family's interest in western lands and expansion. They include "Genesis of a Colonial Fortune: Daniel Dulany of Maryland," *William and Mary Quarterly*, 3d series, 7 (April 1950), pp. 255–69; "A Land Speculator in the Opening of Western Maryland," *Md. Hist. Mag.*, 48 (September 1953), pp. 191–203; and *The Dulanys of Maryland* (Baltimore, 1955). The role of commerce and entrepreneurial activities is emphasized in a later study of Maryland's men of fortunes in Aubrey C. Land, "Economic Base and Social Structure: The Northern Chesapeake in the Eighteenth Century," *Journal of Economic History*, 25 (December 1965), pp. 639–54. Also helpful are articles by R. Bruce Harley, "Dr. Charles Carroll: Land Speculator, 1730–1755," *Md. Hist. Mag.*, 46 (June 1951), pp. 93–107; and William A. Reavis, "The Maryland Gentry and Social Mobility, 1637–1676," *William and Mary Quarterly*, 3d series, 14 (July 1957), pp. 418–28. Although extending beyond 1763 for much of its emphasis, the analytical study of Charles A. Barker, *The Background of the Revolution in Maryland* (New Haven, 1940) is incisive for the eighteenth century.

Recent research by a group of scholars using new data, quantification techniques, or interdisciplinary approaches is greatly expanding our knowledge of colonial Maryland. Most helpful for this study have been Russell R. Menard, "From Servant to Freeholder: Status Mobility and Property Accumulation in Seventeenth-Century Maryland," *William and Mary Quarterly*, 3d series, 30 (January 1973), pp. 37–64; Lorena S. Walsh, "Servitude and Opportunity in Charles County, Maryland, 1658–1705," in Aubrey C. Land, Lois G. Carr, and Edward C. Papenfuse, eds., *Law, Society, and Politics in Early Maryland* (Baltimore, 1977); and Lois G. Carr and David W. Jordan, *Maryland's Revolution of Governmemt, 1689–1692* (Ithaca, 1974).

A number of general studies already cited examine both Virginia and Maryland, and a limited number of specialized works analyze the two Chesapeake colonies in terms of their economic and political similarities and differences. The three following volumes are of special value: Avery O. Craven, *Soil Exhaustion as a Factor in the Agricultural History of Virginia and Maryland, 1606–1860* (Urbana, 1926); Cyrus H. Karraker, *The Seventeenth-Century Sheriff: A Comparative Study of the Sheriff in England and the Chesapeake Colonies, 1607–1689* (Chapel Hill, 1930); and Arthur P. Middleton, *Tobacco Coast: A Maritime History of Chesapeake Bay in the Colonial Era* (Newport News, Virginia, 1952).

Carolinas

The two Carolinas of today were for a few decades under the same political organization, yet most of their historical records quickly focus on one. North Carolina now has the better set of published colonial records; South Carolina has a superb collection of unpublished documents in its Department of Archives and History that provides an opportunity for one of the outstanding projects of colonial history.

The most valuable documentary source for colonial North Carolina is William L. Saunders, ed., *The Colonial Records of North Carolina*, 10 vols. (Raleigh, 1886–90). Other documentary or contemporary sources provide some assistance, including William K. Boyd, ed., *Some Eighteenth Century Tracts Concerning North Carolina* (Raleigh, 1927); Mattie E. E. Parker, ed., *North Carolina Charters and Constitutions 1578–1698* (Raleigh, 1963); for both colonies, Alexander S. Salley, ed., *Narratives of Early Carolina, 1650–1708* (Jameson, ed., *Original Narratives of Early American History*, New York, 1911); John Lawson, *A New Voyage to Carolina* [1709], ed. Hugh T. Lefler (Chapel Hill, 1967); "Autobiography of Col. William Few of Georgia," *Magazine of American History*, 7 (November 1881), pp. 343–58; and William K. Boyd, ed., *William Byrd's Histories of the Dividing Line betwixt Virginia and North Carolina* (Raleigh, 1929).

A basic documentary source for South Carolina, although limited in availability, is the Public Records of South Carolina consisting of 36 volumes of transcripts made from the British Public Record Office for the period from 1663 to 1782. The first five volumes have been printed in facsimile (Columbia, 1928–47); the others are available at the Department of Archives and History, Columbia. Although still not completed, part of the journals of the lower house have been printed in Alexander S. Salley, ed., *Journal of the Commons House of Assembly, 1692–1735*, 21 vols. (Columbia, 1907–46), and in the on-going excellent editions of J. H. Easterby et al., eds., *The Colonial Records of South Carolina, Series I: The Journals of the Commons House of Assembly, 1736–1750*, 10 vols. (1951–). Other very useful sources include two by Alexander S. Salley, ed., *Journal of the Grand Council of South Carolina, 1671–1680, 1691–1692*, 2 vols. (Columbia, 1907), and *Commissions and Instructions from the Lords Proprietors of Carolina to Public Officials of South Carolina, 1685–1715* (Columbia, 1916); Langdon Cheves, ed., *The Shaftesbury Papers and Other Records relating to Carolina* (Collections of the South Carolina Historical Society, 5, Charleston, 1897); and Thomas Cooper and David J. McCord, eds., *The Statutes at Large of South Carolina*, 10 vols. (Columbia, 1836–41). Three volumes of Indian Books are of particular value and are well edited by W. L. McDowell as *Series II of Colonial Records of South Carolina: Journals of the Commissioners of the Indian Trade, September 20, 1710–August 29, 1718* (Columbia, 1955); *Documents Relating to Indian Affairs, May 21, 1750–August 7, 1754* (Columbia, 1958); and *Documents Relating to Indian Affairs, 1754–1765* (Columbia, 1970). Two other collections should be mentioned: B. R. Carroll, ed., *Historical Collections of South Carolina*, 2 vols. (New York, 1836); and Chapman J. Milling, ed., *Colonial South Carolina: Two Contemporary Descriptions* (Columbia, 1951), containing two accounts with valuable insights by James Glen and George Milligen. The *South Carolina Gazette* (Charles Town) extends from 1732 to 1776 and has frequent references to frontier events.

Secondary sources for North Carolina contain both old and new scholarship that contributes to this study. D. L. Corbitt provides convenient references for *The Formation of North Carolina Counties, 1663–1943* (Raleigh, 1950). Of some value are the older histories by Samuel A. Ashe, *History of North Carolina*, 2 vols. (Greensboro, 1908–25); and several volumes by R. D. W. Connor, especially *History of North Carolina*, volume 1, *The Colonial and Revolutionary Periods, 1584–1783* (Chicago, 1919), and *Race Elements in the White Population of North Carolina* (Raleigh, 1920). The best single volume for the state's history is Hugh T. Lefler and Albert R. Newsome, *The History of a Southern State: North Carolina*, 3d ed. (Chapel Hill, 1973). More detailed for the colonial period is Hugh T. Lefler and William S. Powell, *Colonial North Carolina: A History* (Milton M. Klein and Jacob E. Cooke, eds., *A History of the American Colonies in Thirteen Volumes*, New York, 1973). Harry Roy Merrens has one of the most valuable studies of recent scholarship, *Colonial North Carolina in the Eighteenth Century: A Study in Historical Geography* (Chapel Hill, 1964). Robert W. Ramsey makes excellent use of local records in identifying the sources of population for the area between the Yadkin and Catawba rivers in *Carolina Cradle: Settlement of the Northwest Carolina Frontier, 1747–1762* (Chapel Hill, 1964). The early chapters of Hugh T. Lefler and Paul Wager, eds., *Orange County,*

1752–1952 (Chapel Hill, 1953), provide important information, although not documented as a bicentennial project for the county. Desmond Clarke, using records both in Great Britain and the United States, gives a scholarly analysis of the interest in frontier expansion of *Arthur Dobbs, Esquire, 1689–1765, Surveyor-General of Ireland, Prospector and Governor of North Carolina* (Chapel Hill, 1957). Paul M. McCain examines the local institution of *The County Court in North Carolina before 1750* (Durham, 1954).

Secondary sources for South Carolina include two of the most valuable works for the study of the southern colonial frontier: Verner W. Crane, *The Southern Frontier, 1670–1732* (1928; reprint, Ann Arbor, 1956), and Robert L. Meriwether, *The Expansion of South Carolina, 1729–1765* (Kingsport, Tenn., 1940). Crane's exhaustive research and bold interpretations cover primarily the South Carolina frontier, although valuable insights are also included for relations with other English colonies and with the Spanish and French in the Southeast. Meriwether's meticulous examination of land grants and plats provides the foundation for this excellent study of eighteenth-century frontier townships and the back country of the 1750s and 1760s. General histories may also be consulted. Edward McGrady's *History of South Carolina under the Proprietary Government, 1670–1719* (New York, 1901) needs some corrections. William Roy Smith's *South Carolina as a Royal Province, 1719–1776* (New York, 1903) emphasizes constitutional issues and development of governmental institutions. Louise F. Brown helps explain the colonial interests of *The First Earl of Shaftesbury* (New York, 1933). More comprehensive and still of value are the works of David D. Wallace, *The History of South Carolina*, 3 vols. with a 4th consisting of biographies (New York, 1934), and his one-volume edition of *South Carolina: A Short History, 1520–1948* (Chapel Hill, 1951). The most recent political analysis that is an indispensable source is M. Eugene Sirmans, *Colonial South Carolina: A Political History, 1663–1763* (Chapel Hill, 1966). His early death in 1965 before completing all final details of the study required the editorial assistance of Wesley F. Craven and James M. Smith.

Other more specialized volumes contribute to this study. Two older secondary works include valuable primary material. William J. Rivers, *A Sketch of the History of South Carolina to the Close of the Proprietary Government by the Revolution of 1719* (1856; reprint, Spartanburg, 1972) contains documents in the Appendix not found elsewhere; Alexander S. Salley, *The History of Orangeburg County, South Carolina, from its First Settlement to the Close of the Revolutionary War* (Orangeburg, 1898) prints the valuable church records kept by the Giessendanners. Converse D. Clowse has completed a useful traditional economic history in *Economic Beginnings in Colonial South Carolina, 1670–1730* (Columbia, 1971). Peter H. Wood provides a modern analysis of blacks to 1739 in *Black Majority: Negroes in Colonial South Carolina from 1670 through the Stono Rebellion* (New York, 1974). James S. Maag provides new views in "Cattle Raising in Colonial South Carolina" (M. A. thesis, University of Kansas, 1964). Two doctoral dissertations have provided information on governors heavily involved in frontier activities: Mary F. Carter, "James Glen, Governor of South Carolina: A Study in British Administrative Policies" (Ph.D. diss., University of California, Los Angeles, 1951), and Clarence J. Attig, "William Henry Lyttelton: A Study in Colonial Administration" (Ph.D. diss., University of Nebraska, 1958).

Georgia

The shorter period of history from 1732 to 1763 for Georgia requires a less extensive listing of references for the young colony. Other sources are included in the subsequent section on the Spanish whose activities threatened the security of the Georgia colony.

The most valuable published primary material is Allen D. Candler and Lucian L. Knight, eds., *The Colonial Records of the State of Georgia*, 26 vols. (Atlanta, 1904–16). Other helpful references are in the on-going *Collections of the Georgia Historical Society*, 15 vols. (Savannah, 1840–).

The critical role of the Earl of Egmont during Georgia's early years can be followed in the *Diary of Viscount Percival, Afterwards First Earl of Egmont, 1730–1749*, 3 vols. (London, 1920–3); and in Robert G. McPherson, ed., *The Journal of the Earl of Egmont, 1732–1738: Abstract of the Trustees Proceedings for Establishing the Colony of Georgia, 1732–1738* (Athens, 1962). Additional contemporary accounts are available through the skillful editing of E. Merton Coulter of the three following volumes: *The Journal of Peter Gordon, 1732–1735* (Athens, 1963); and two journals of William Stephens, secretary of Georgia from 1737 to 1750 and president from 1741 to 1751, *The Journal of William Stephens, 1741–1743* (Athens, 1958), and *The Journal of William Stephens, 1743–1745* (Athens, 1959). Information about the serious factionalism in early Georgia is provided in Patrick Tailfer et al., *A True and Historical Narrative of the Colony of Georgia in America from the First Settlement thereof until the Present Period . . . 1741*, ed. Clarence L. Ver Steeg (Athens, 1960).

Early histories of Georgia may still be consulted for the first few decades of Georgia's frontier experience. Among the most useful are the Reverend Alexander Hewatt, *Historical Account of the Rise and Progress of the Colonies of South Carolina and Georgia* (1779; reprint, Spartanburg, 1962); William B. Stevens, *History of Georgia*, 2 vols. (1847, 1859; reprint, Savannah, 1972); and Charles C. Jones, Jr., *The History of Georgia*, 2 vols. (1883; reprint, Spartanburg, 1965).

The two most valuable single-volume histories are by E. Merton Coulter and Kenneth Coleman. The first nine chapters of Coulter's *A Short History of Georgia* (Chapel Hill, 1933) cover the period to 1763. Coleman's *Colonial Georgia: A History* (Klein and Cooke, eds., *A History of the American Colonies in Thirteen Volumes*, New York, 1976) provides a more detailed study and has an excellent up-to-date bibliographical essay on selected works.

Other specialized studies of value are P. A. Strobel, *The Salzburgers and their Descendants* (1855; reprint, Athens, 1953), chauvinistic and needs some corrections; W. W. Abbot, *The Royal Governors of Georgia, 1754–1775* (Chapel Hill, 1959); Albert B. Saye, *New Viewpoints in Georgia History* (Athens, 1943); Trevor R. Reese, *Colonial Georgia: A Study in British Imperial Policy in the Eighteenth Century* (Athens, 1963), based primarily upon official records in England; H. B. Fant, "The Labor Policy of the Trustees for Establishing the Colony of Georgia in America," *Ga. Hist. Quar.*, 16 (March 1932), pp. 1–16; M. T. McKinstry, "Silk Culture in the Colony of Georgia," ibid., 14 (September 1930), pp. 225–35; and Harold E. Davis, *The Fledgling Province: Social and Cultural Life in Colonial Georgia, 1733–1776* (Chapel Hill, 1976), a recent synthesis of traditional social history with an excellent bibliographical essay. For further details on the key role of Oglethorpe in early Georgia, the biographies of Amos A. Ettinger, *James Edward Oglethorpe: Imperial Idealist* (Oxford, 1936) and Leslie F. Church, *Oglethorpe: A Study of Philanthropy in England and Georgia* (London, 1932), are now supplemented by Phinizy Spalding, *Oglethorpe in America* (Chicago, 1977). Spalding commends Oglethorpe for his skill in Indian negotiations but is critical of his administrative shortcomings and his relationship with other trustees.

The Spanish

For an examination of the role of the Spanish in the Anglo-Spanish conflict on the southern frontier, some knowledge is needed of the organization of the Spanish empire in America. Volumes that help explain this subject are Charles Gibson, *Spain in America* (Commager and Morris, eds., *The New American Nation Series*, New York, 1966); C. H. Haring, *The Spanish Empire in America* (New York, 1947); and Lewis Hanke, *The Spanish Struggle for Justice in the Conquest of America* (1949; reprint, Boston, 1965). John F. Bannon has added *The Spanish Borderlands Frontier, 1513–1821* (Ray A. Billington, ed., *Histories of the American Frontier*, Albuquerque, 1974). The diplomatic aspects of the role of Spain may be examined in Max

Savelle, *The Origins of American Diplomacy: The International History of Angloamerica, 1492–1763* (New York, 1967), and Max Savelle, *Empires to Nations: Expansion in America, 1713–1824* (vol. 5 of *Europe and the World in the Age of Expansion*, Minneapolis, 1974). A fresh look at Spain's role with substantial use of Spanish sources is J. Leitch Wright, Jr., *Anglo-Spanish Rivalry in North America* (Athens, 1971).

Excellent studies focusing more directly on Georgia are Herbert E. Bolton and Mary Ross, *The Debatable Land: A Sketch of the Anglo-Spanish Contest for the Georgia Country* (1925; reprint, New York, 1968); John Tate Lanning, *The Spanish Missions of Georgia* (Chapel Hill, 1935); John Tate Lanning, *The Diplomatic History of Georgia: A Study of the Epoch of Jenkins' Ear* (Chapel Hill, 1936); Trevor R. Reese, "Georgia in Anglo-Spanish Diplomacy, 1736–1739," *William and Mary Quarterly*, 3d series, 15 (April 1958), pp. 168–90; and Reese's previously cited volume on *Colonial Georgia*. Other studies bringing the English efforts into perspective along with military activities include Kenneth Coleman, "The Southern Frontier: Georgia's Founding and the Expansion of South Carolina,;; *Ga. Hist. Quar.*, 56 (Summer 1972), pp. 163–74; Charles W. Arnade, *The Siege of St. Augustine in 1702* (Athens, 1959); Arnade, "The English Invasion of Spanish Florida, 1700–1706," *Florida Historical Quarterly*, 41 (July 1962), pp. 29–37; and Larry E. Ivers, *British Drums on the Southern Frontier: The Military Colonization of Georgia, 1733–1749* (Chapel Hill, 1974).

The military activities of both the Spanish and English can be examined in published primary works. Valuable among these are John T. Lanning, ed., *The St. Augustine Expedition of 1740: A Report to the South Carolina General Assembly* (Columbia, 1954); *Letters of Montiano, Siege of St. Augustine* (Collections of the Georgia Historical Society, vol. 7, part 1, Savannah, 1909); and *The Spanish Official Account of the Attack on the Colony of Georgia, in America, and of its Defeat on St. Simons Island by General James Oglethorpe* (Collections of the Georgia Historical Society, vol 7, part 3, Savannah, 1913).

The French

The organization and administration of French colonies in North America can be examined in Clarence W. Alvord, *The Illinois Country, 1673–1818* (Springfield, 1920); and in two studies that use French sources extensively and that vigorously present French dimensions by W. J. Eccles, *France in America* (Commager and Morris, eds., *The New American Nation Series*, New York, 1972), and *The Canadian Frontier, 1534–1760* (Ray A. Billington, ed., *Histories of the American Frontier*, Albuquerque, 1974).

For the overall view of the Anglo-French conflict culminating in the English victory in the eighteenth century, two multivolume studies may be examined. Francis Parkman describes in his excellent literary style but pro-English and pro-Protestant position the wars of the eighteenth century in his *Half-Century of Conflict*, 2 vols. (Boston, 1892), and *Montcalm and Wolfe*, 2 vols. (Boston, 1884). For a critique of Parkman, see W. J. Eccles, "The History of New France According to Francis Parkman," *William and Mary Quarterly*, 3d series, 18 (April 1961), pp. 163–75. Lawrence H. Gipson presents an imperial view and is also sympathetic to the English; vols. 4–8 of *The British Empire Before the American Revolution* cover the Anglo-French struggle to 1763.

The military aspects of the Anglo-French wars are examined in Stanley M. Pargellis, *Lord Loudoun in North America* (New Haven, 1933). Pargellis' views on "Braddock's Defeat," *American Historical Review*, 41 (January 1936), pp. 253–69, criticizing Braddock and his staff for not using effectively the approved tactics of the time, have been modified in such works as Paul E. Kopperman, *Braddock at the Monongahela* (Pittsburgh, 1977), which puts more blame on the average British soldier. Douglas Southall Freeman, *George Washington: A Biography*, 7 vols. (New York, 1948–57) analyzes in great detail the Monongahela campaign in vols. 1–2 and also differs from Pargellis in his emphasis upon the failure of Braddock to adjust to New World conditions and make better use of frontier style fighting and of American troops. Two brief studies using mainly English sources include Hays Baker-Crothers, *Virginia and the French and Indian War* (Chicago, 1928), and Howard H. Peckham, *The Colonial Wars, 1689–1762* (Chicago, 1964). A more detailed view is in Douglas E. Leach, *Arms for Empire: A Military History of the British Colonies in North America, 1607–1763* (New York, 1973). Chester R. Young has utilized data quantification in "The Effects of the French and Indian War on Civilian Life in the Frontier Countries of Virginia, 1754–1763" (Ph.D. diss., Vanderbilt University, 1969).

Contemporary accounts that have been useful include volumes from the *Illinois Historical Collection:* vol. 27, Theodore C. Pease, ed., *Anglo-French Boundary Disputes in the West, 1749–1763* (Springfield, 1936), and vol. 29, Theodore C. Pease and Ernestine Jenison, eds., *Illinois on the Eve of the Seven Years' War, 1747–1755* (Springfield, 1940). Also helpful are Stanley M. Pargellis, ed., *Military Affairs in North America, 1748–1765: Selected Documents from the Cumberland Papers in Windsor Castle* (New York, 1936); and Winthrop Sargent, ed., *The History of an Expedition Against Fort Du Quesne, in 1755* (Philadelphia, 1855).

Western Expansion and Indian Affairs

Records of the explorations and discoveries during the last half of the seventeenth century may be profitably examined in Clarence W. Alvord and Lee Bidgood, eds., *The First Exploration of the Trans-Allegheny Region by the Virginians* (Cleveland, 1912), and William P. Cumming, ed., *The Discoveries of John Lederer* (Charlottesville, 1958).

Land speculation, the fur trade, and Indian affairs frequently overlapped as both the national states of Europe and local colonists grasped opportunities for expansion and profit. The early chapters of Thomas P. Abernethy, *Western Lands and the American Revolution* (New York, 1937) cover activities on the southern colonial frontier. Clarence W. Alvord, *The Mississippi Valley in British Politics,* 2 vols. (Cleveland, 1917) and Jack M. Sosin, *Whitehall and the Wilderness: The Middle West in British Colonial Policy, 1760–1775* (Lincoln, Nebraska, 1961) examine British policy for the frontier. The activities of land companies and individual negotiators are analyzed in Kenneth P. Bailey, *The Ohio Company of Virginia and the Westward Movement, 1748–1792* (Glendale, Ca., 1939); Alfred P. James, *The Ohio Company: Its Inner History* (Pittsburgh, 1959); Albert T. Volwiler, *George Croghan and the Westward Movement, 1741–1782* (Cleveland, 1926); Nicholas B. Wainwright, *George Croghan: Wilderness Diplomat* (Chapel Hill, 1959); and Kenneth P. Bailey, *Christopher Gist: Colonial Frontiersman, Explorer, and Indian Agent* (Hamden, Conn., 1976). Published contemporary records for the Ohio Company are available in Kenneth P. Bailey, ed., *The Ohio Company Papers, 1753–1817: Being Primarily Papers of the "Suffering Traders" of Pennsylvania* (Arcata, Ca., [1947]); and Lois Mulkearn, ed., *George Mercer Papers Relating to the Ohio Company of Virginia* (Pittsburgh, 1954).

Two published bibliographies provide a summary of major works on the colonial fur trade: Stuart Cuthbertson and John C. Ewers, *A Preliminary Bibliography on the American Fur Trade* (St. Louis, 1939), and Joseph R. Donnelly, *A Tentative Bibliography for the Colonial Fur Trade in the American Colonies, 1608–1800* (St. Louis, 1947). Paul C. Phillips provides an overall view of *The Fur Trade,* 2 vols. (Norman, Oklahoma, 1961), but it needs corrections for the early period. William Byrd I and II, for example, are confused in I, 172; and Nathaniel Bacon, who died during the rebellion of 1676, is still alive in 1680, I, 178.

Other studies focus upon Indian-white relations in addition to the ethnohistorical publications cited earlier. Virginia's experience has attracted several scholars. Wesley F. Craven has published "Indian Policy in Early Virginia," *William and Mary Quarterly,* 3d series, 1 (January 1944), pp. 65–82 and a chapter on Indians in *White, Red, and Black: The Seventeenth-Century Virginian* (Charlottesville, 1971). W. Stitt Robinson defines the legal status of the natives and their role in Cherokee trade in three articles: "The Legal Status of the Indian in Colonial

Virginia," *Va. Mag. Hist & Biog.*, 61 (July 1953), pp. 247–59; "Tributary Indians in Colonial Virginia," ibid., 67 (January 1959), pp. 49–64; and "Virginia and the Cherokees: Indian Policy from Spotswood to Dinwiddie," in Darrett B. Rutman, ed., *The Old Dominion: Essays for Thomas Perkins Abernethy* (Charlottesville, 1964), pp. 21–40. The first major Indian attack of 1622 has been examined by William S. Powell in "Aftermath of the Massacre: The First Indian War, 1622–1632," *Va. Mag. Hist. & Biog.*, 66 (January 1958), pp. 44–75; and by Alden T. Vaughan, " 'Expulsion of the Savages': English Policy and the Virginia Massacre of 1622," *William and Mary Quarterly*, 3d series, 35 (January 1978), pp. 57–84. Gary B. Nash takes a broader look in "The Image of the Indian in the Southern Colonial Mind," *William and Mary Quarterly*, 3d series, 29 (April 1972), pp. 197–230. W. Neil Franklin's "The Indian Trade of Colonial Virginia" (Ph.D. diss., Princeton University, 1928) was followed by two articles of special interest for this study: "Virginia and the Cherokee Indian Trade, 1673–1752," *East Tennessee Historical Society's Publications*, no. 4 (January 1932), pp. 3–21 and "Virginia and the Cherokee Indian Trade, 1753–1775," ibid., no. 5 (January 1933), pp. 22–38.

For other southern colonies, Verner W. Crane's *Southern Frontier* gives great emphasis to Indian affairs in South Carolina, while John P. Corry, *Indian Affairs in Georgia, 1732–1756* (Philadelphia, 1936) provides the greatest detail for Georgia. E. Merton Coulter evaluates the intriguing role of "Mary Musgrove, 'Queen of the Creeks': A Chapter of Early Georgia Troubles," *Ga. Hist. Quar.*, 11 (March 1927), pp. 1–30. Knox Mellon, Jr., throws new light on the sensational career of a reformer from Europe in two articles: "Christian Priber's Cherokee 'Kingdom of Paradise,' " *Ga. Hist. Quar.*, 57 (Fall 1973), pp. 319–31, and "Christian Priber and the Jesuit Myth," *So. Car. Hist. Mag.*, 61 (April 1960), pp. 75–81. David H. Corkran includes the Indian point of view in his *Cherokee Frontier: Conflict and Survival, 1740–1762* (Norman, 1962), and *The Creek Frontier, 1540–1783* (Norman, 1967). Wilbur R. Jacobs demonstrates the importance of rewards in *Diplomacy and Indian Gifts: Anglo-French Rivalry Along the Ohio and Northwest Frontiers, 1748–1763* (Stanford, 1950). Helen L. Shaw's *British Administration of the Southern Indians, 1756–1783* (Bryn Mawr, 1931) is superseded for the colonial period by the thoroughly researched volume of John R. Alden, *John Stuart and the Southern Colonial Frontier: A Study of Indian Relations, War, Trade, and Land Problems in the Southern Wilderness, 1754–1775* (Ann Arbor, 1944).

Valuable contemporary sources include a commentary in the form of letters about the expedition against the Tuscarora Indians in North Carolina in "Journal of John Barnwell," *Va. Mag. Hist. & Biog.*, 5 (April 1898), pp. 391–402 and 6 (July 1898), pp. 42–55; reprinted in *So. Car. Hist. Gen. Mag.*, 9 (January 1908), pp. 30–54. A conference with the major southern tribes at the end of the French and Indian War is recorded in *Journal of the Congress of the Four Southern Governors, and the Superintendent of That District, with the Five Nations of Indians, at Augusta, 1763* (Charles Town, 1764).

Education and Religion

Background for religion and education may be obtained from general studies relating to more than one colony. Useful among these are Edwin S. Gaustad, *A Religious History of America* (New York, 1966); Gaustad, *Historical Atlas of Religion in America* (New York, 1962); William W. Sweet, *Religion in Colonial America* (New York, 1942); Bernard Bailyn, *Education in the Forming of American Society: Needs and Opportunities for Study* (Chapel Hill, 1960); Lawrence A. Cremin, *American Education: The Colonial Experience, 1607–1783* (New York, 1970); and Edgar W. Knight, *Public Education in the South* (Chapel Hill, 1922). The three volumes of Richard Beale Davis, *Intellectual Life in the Colonial South, 1585–1763*, were not available from the University of Tennessee Press in time to contribute to this study.

Among the many secondary books and articles on religious groups or religion in a specific area, the following have been of value for a frontier study: George M. Brydon, *Virginia's Mother*

Church and the Political Conditions under which it Grew, 1607–1814, 2 vols. (Richmond and Philadelphia, 1947, 1952); John T. Ellis, *Catholics in Colonial America* (Baltimore, 1965); Ernest T. Thompson, *Presbyterians in the South,* vol. 1, 1607–1861 (Richmond, 1963); Benjamin F. Riley, *A History of the Baptists in the Southern States East of the Mississippi* (Philadelphia, 1898); Jacob J. Sessler, *Communal Pietism among Early American Moravians* (vol. 8 of American Religion Series, New York, 1933); Adelaide L. Fries, *The Moravians in Georgia, 1735–1740* (Raleigh, 1905); Sarah M. Lemmon, "The Genesis of the Protestant Episcopal Diocese of North Carolina, 1701–1823," *North Carolina Historical Review,* 28 (October 1951), pp. 426–62; Wesley M. Gewehr, *The Great Awakening in Virginia, 1740–1790* (Durham, 1930); George W. Pilcher, *Samuel Davies: Apostle of Dissent in Colonial Virginia* (Knoxville, 1971); David T. Morgan, Jr., "The Great Awakening in North Carolina, 1740–1775," *N. C. Hist. Rev.,* 45 (July 1968), pp. 264–83; Morgan, Jr., "The Consequences of George Whitefield's Ministry in the Carolinas and Georgia, 1739–1740," *Ga. Hist. Quar.,* 55 (Spring 1971), pp. 62–82; Morgan, Jr., "George Whitefield and the Great Awakening in the Carolinas and Georgia, 1739–1740," ibid., 54 (Winter 1970), pp. 517–39; and H. Warren Gardner, "The Dissenting Sects on the Southern Colonial Frontier, 1720–1770" (Ph.D. diss., University of Kansas, 1969).

Education was often closely related to religion, particularly in efforts reaching out to minority groups. Helpful in the study of various educational activities are the following: C. F. Pascoe, *Two Hundred Years of the S. P. G.,* 2 vols. (London, 1901); Henry P. Thompson, *Into All Lands: The History of the Society for the Propagation of the Gospel in Foreign Parts, 1701–1950* (London, 1951); Bernard C. Steiner, *History of Education in Maryland,* United States Bureau of Education, Circular of Information No. 2, 1894 (Washington, 1894); W. Stitt Robinson, "Indian Education and Missions in Colonial Virginia," *Journal of Southern History,* 18 (May 1952), pp. 152–68; Robert H. Land, "Henrico and Its College," *William and Mary College Quarterly Historical Magazine,* 2d series, 18 (October 1938), pp. 453–98; Bernard C. Steiner, "A Pioneer in Negro Education," *Independent,* 51 (August 24, 1899), pp. 2287–90; Frank J. Klingberg, *An Appraisal of the Negro in Colonial South Carolina* (Washington, 1941); and the more recent but skimpy coverage of the colonial period by Henry A. Bullock, *A History of Negro Education in the South from 1619 to the Present* (Cambridge, Mass., 1967).

Primary sources that have valuable accounts are Records of the Society for the Propagation of the Gospel in Foregin Parts, The Journals, 1701–1850, Microfilm; W. S. Perry, ed., *Historical Collections Relating to the American Colonial Church,* 5 vols. (Hartford, 1870–78); Frank J. Klingberg, ed., *Carolina Chronicle: The Papers of Commissary Gideon Johnston, 1707–1716* (Berkeley, 1946); Klingberg, ed., *The Carolina Chronicle of Dr. Francis Le Jau, 1706–1717* (Berkeley, 1956); Theodore G. Tappert and John W. Doberstein, trans., *The Journals of Henry Melchoir Muhlenberg,* 3 vols. (Philadelphia, 1942–58); and Samuel Davies, *Sermons on Important Subjects* (New York, 1849). For an excellent description of the primary material available both in German and English about German immigrants to Georgia and the role of Johann Martin Bolzius, see Harold E. Davis, *The Fledgling Province: Social and Cultural Life in Colonial Georgia, 1733–1776* (Chapel Hill, 1976), pp. 265–6. Volumes 1–2 are excellent in Adelaide L. Fries et al., eds., *Records of the Moravians in North Carolina,* 11 vols. (1922–69). Volume 1 has relevant material in Edgar W. Knight, ed., *A Documentary History of Education in the South before 1860,* 5 vols. (Chapel Hill, 1949–53).

Index

Agriculture, 112; definition of corn and grain, 250; fencing requirements in Virginia and Maryland, 46–7; in Georgia, 182–3; marking of cattle and hogs, 47; in Maryland, 23, 44–7, 153–5; in North Carolina, 96–7, 179–80; in South Carolina, 89, 92–3, 165–70 *passim*, 174–6; in Virginia, 18, 20, 23, 44–7, 145. *See also* Tobacco, Viniculture

Amelia, S.C. frontier township, 165, 168

Apalache Indians, 106, 119, 140, 257; defeated by James Moore, 99–100; description of, 99; in Yamassee War, 113

Argall, Captain Samuel, 12, 14

Arthur, Gabriel: western expedition of, 57

Asiento, 189, 190, 200, 201; continued by Treaty of Seville, 1729, 186; in Treaty of Utrecht, 1713, 185; English to relinquish, 1750, 202

Atkin, Edmund, Superintendent of Indian Affairs in the South, 213, 224

Augusta, Ga., 104, 115, 169, 222; founded in 1735, 186; results of Conference, 1763, 224

Barnwell, John ("Tuscarora Jack"), 112, 120, 162, 185; construction of Fort King George (Altamaha Fort), 186; in Tuscarora War, 109; journal of expedition, 258; report to Board of Trade, 115, 140; warns of French threat, 119

Bacon, Nathaniel, Jr.: attacks Indians in Bacon's Rebellion, 64–5; conflicting interpretations of, 254; leader of Bacon's Rebellion, 61–7; sketch of, 61

Bacon's Rebellion, 61–7, 68, 69; reforms of, 66–7

Belfast (Londonborough), S.C. frontier township, 173, 263

Berkeley, Sir William, 48, 49, 51, 96; administration of North Carolina, 79–80; and Bacon's Rebellion, 61–7; arrives in Virginia as governor, 40; proprietor of Carolina, 78; supports western explorations, 56

Blainville, Céloron de: asserts French claims to Ohio River, 204–5

Bloody Marsh, Battle of: in War of Jenkins' Ear, 199–200

Bolzius, Rev. John Martin, 182–3, 231

Boone, Daniel: education of, 237

Boonesborough, S. C. frontier township, 173

Bourbon Family Compact: Second, 1743, 200; Third, 1761, 222

Braddock, Gen. Edward, 215, 247, 267; conflicting interpretations of expedition of, 210–1, 267, 282–3; defeat of, 210, 214, 215, 216; plans for campaign against French, 208–9

Bray, Rev. Dr. Thomas, 180

Byrd, William I, 126, 144; influence on Bacon, 64; plantation of, attacked by Indians, 62; promotes colonization, 125; sketch of, 58, 60–1; supports Bacon, 67

Byrd, William II, 133, 136, 142, 144; comment on Indian trade, 60; interest in iron mines, 127–8; pessimistic about Indian education, 242; promoter of western settlements, 145–6; writings of, 145–6

Byrd, William III: commander of expedition in Cherokee War, 220–2

Calendar, Gregorian, xiii

Carroll, Dr. Charles: land speculation of, 151, 154

Carroll, Charles, of Annapolis: land speculation of, 151, 154

Catawba Indians, 56, 60, 102, 110, 117, 128, 132, 165, 169, 192, 216; aid from, 219, 220; at Augusta Conference, 224; description of, 76; in Yamassee War, 113, 115; sought as allies against French, 209–14

Charles Town, S. C., 75, 78, 86, 89, 90, 94, 97, 110, 128, 163, 165, 175, 177, 190, 191, 192, 193, 194, 221; Cherokee delegation in, 219–20; Creek chiefs visit, 118; descriptions of, 83, 88; exports from, 174; French and Spanish attack on, 100; in Yamassee War, 113, 114; Negro school in, 243–4; trade routes from, 102, 104; trial of Weberites in, 236

Cherokee Indians, 57, 60, 76, 97, 100, 107, 110, 115, 117, 119, 128, 132, 169, 196, 198, 202, 225; at Augusta Conference, 224; critical role in Yamassee War, 113; description of, 76, 78, 192; influence of Christian Priber on, 195; linguistic classification of, 2;

Immigration: analysis of South Carolina middle and back country, 173–4; first Negroes to Virginia, 30–1; French Huguenots, 41, 42, 78–9, 88–9, 92, 124, 125–7, 144, 173, 241, 247; from West Indies, 80–1; Germans, viii, 87, 124, 128, 138, 146–9, 153, 155, 169, 171, 176, 177, 181, 226, 228–36 *passim*, 240, 246, 247; German-Swiss, 127, 168–9, 171; promotion of, 173, 176–7; Salzburgers, 181–3, 231, 235; Scots, 83, 88, 181, 183–4, 186, 198, 200, 220; Scots-Irish, viii, 124, 146–9, 155, 165, 166, 167, 173, 176, 177, 181, 222, 226, 228, 231, 246; Swiss, 107, 145–6, 148, 167–8, 170, 176, 181, 229; Welsh, 148, 166–7, 181. *See also* Religion

Indentured servants, 15, 31–2, 57, 83, 96, 114, 128, 153, 181, 246, 253; as apprentices, 239; social mobility in Maryland, 51–3

Indian education and missions, 20, 26–8, 130–4, 240–3, 244; sponsored by S. P. G., 180, 227; comments by William Byrd II on, 242; comments by Governor Dinwiddie on, 242; encouraged by legislature of Virginia, 18; proposed college in Virginia, 27–8; school at Irene in Georgia, 242; Spanish missions, 79, 81; supported by Boyle fund in Virginia, 241

Indians: at Williamsburg ceremonies, 121; building of boats, 6; culture areas of, 2–3; diverse roles of, 6; division of labor, 4; dress of, 2, 34, 121; houses of, 3–5, 34; linguistic classifications of, 2; marks of chiefs, 3; map of tribes in mid-seventeenth century, 77; map of tribes on deerskin, 105; political organization of, 2, 4; problem of estimates of population, 257; racial classification of, 2; social organization of, 2, 4. *See also* names of tribes, confederacies, and individual Indians

Indian relations: allies, 9, 23–5, 84, 188, 209–14; in Anglo-Spanish conflict, 190–7; bounties for scalps, 214; in plans of Board of Trade, 140–1; tributary, 24, 25, 50–1, 55, 61, 63, 68, 69, 114, 130, 131, 190, 209; tributary or settlement Indians, 84–5, 104, 110; treaties and agreements, 25, 42, 50, 55, 63, 68, 129–31, 188–9, 193, 194, 205, 224; wars, 28–30, 48–50, 64–5, 87, 107–10, 112–5, 217–22

Indian slavery, 32, 64, 84, 86, 87, 93, 96, 100, 104, 107, 241, 257

Indian trade, 25–6, 90, 93, 97; abuses in, and the Yamassee War, 112; and Bacon's Rebellion, 61, 63; and exploration, 54–61; description of white traders, 104, 106–7; factories, 117–8, mixed public and private, 118; monopolies of, 86–7, 117–8, 120, 131–4, 191, 224; payment for Cherokee burdeners in, 102; routes, 101–4; shortage of French goods in, 224; value of trade goods in, 100–2. *See also* Intercolonial relations

Intercolonial relations, viii, xii; in Cherokee War, 217–22; in Queen Anne's War, 124; in Tuscarora War, 108–10; in Yamassee War, 113–5; Glen-Dinwiddie rivalry over Indian allies, 209–13; Georgia rivalry with South Carolina over Indian trade, 191–2; South Carolina conflict with Virginia over Indian trade, 104, 128–9, 247

Iroquois confederacy (Five Nations, Six Nations), 76, 107, 110, 210; agreements at Logstown, 205–6; along Lake Erie, 204; in Treaty of Utrecht, 106; intercolonial conference in 1754 with, 207; linguistic classification of, 2; negotiations by Maryland and Virginia with, 70; raids in Virginia and Maryland by, 69

Jamestown, Va., 12, 14, 29, 33, 44, 57, 156; capital moved from, 121; characteristics of, 7; church tower at, 19; fire destroys fort at, 9; first Assembly in, 17; first permanent English settlement at, 1; glass house at, 21; in Bacon's Rebellion, 65; Indians in area of, 3, 4; James Fort reconstructed at, 10; spared in Indian massacre of 1622, 28; temporarily abandoned in 1610, 9

Jeffreys, Col. Herbert, 65; treaty with Indians 1677, 68–9

Jenkins, Capt. Robert: and War of Jenkins' Ear, 189

Johnson, Gov. Sir Nathaniel, 99, 104, 106

Johnson, Gov. Robert, 173; township plans of, 162–3, 186

King George's War, 158, 200, 201, 204

Kingston, S. C. frontier township, 165, 166, 170

King William's War, 70, 72, 73, 98, 122

Knights of the Golden Horseshoe, 132–3, 138, 142, 147

Lambert, Thomas: improves tobacco, 21

Land policy, xii, 159–60, 245–6; British concepts of land tenure, 6–7; British ground rent, 153; in Maryland, 36, 41–2, 151, 153–5; in North Carolina, 79–81, 82, 83, 84, 85, 256; in South Carolina, 80, 81, 82, 83, 84, 85, 171, 256; in Virginia, 6–7, 12–5, 17, 50–1, 127, 134–8, 141–2, 246; of Georgia trustees, 181, 246. *See also* Headrights, Land speculation, Quitrents

Land speculation, viii; and land companies in Virginia, 158–61; challenge to French by speculators, 158–61; in Maryland, 150–4; in South Carolina, 165, 171; in Virginia,

Percival, John, Earl of Egmont, 180
Percy, George: description of Virginia in 1607, 8–9
Pickawillany: Anglo-French conflict over, 204–5
Piscataway Indians, 4; linguistic classification of, 34; population of, 34; removal of, 124
Pocahontas, 49, 83; marriage of, and assimilation, 25, 29; visit to England, 27
Pollock, Thomas: in Tuscarora War, 110
Powhatan, 25, 27; death of, 28; policy relative to the colony of Virginia, 29; political authority of, 4; tribute system of, 24
Powhatan confederacy, 28, 48–50, 85, 125; and nature of alliances, 24; description of, 4; linguistic classification of, 2; population of, 23
Priber, Christian Gottlieb: advocates communistic society for Cherokee, 195; contemporary descriptions of, 194–5
Protestant Association, Md., 72
Purry, Jean Pierre, 229; promoter of immigrant colonization, 167–8
Purrysburg, S. C. frontier township, 165, 167–8, 170, 174, 176; ethnic groups in, 229

Queen Anne's War, 106, 124, 139; allies in, 98; military attacks in, 100
Queensboro, S. C. frontier township, 165, 166, 167, 174
Quitrents, 141–2, 159, 160; in England and America, 7; in Maryland, 36, 38, 151; in North Carolina, 80–1; in South Carolina, 114, 163, 166, 168; in Virginia, 38, 109, 134, 137, 140, 146. *See also* Land policy

Raleigh, Sir Walter, xi, 1, 20; expeditions of, 75
Randolph, Edward: report on Virginia land policy, 134–6
Rangers: in Maryland, 68–9, 70, 72, 124, 125; in South Carolina, 115, 117, 220, 222; in Virginia, 68–9, 70, 72, 122, 129
Religion: Anglicans, 40, 88, 89, 92, 107, 126–7, 165, 169, 180, 226, 227, 228, 229, 230, 231, 239, 247, 257; Baptists, 116, 227, 231, 235; Catholics, 40, 79, 88, 127; Dunkards, 231–2; extremes of, on frontier, 235–6; French Huguenots, 41, 42, 78–9, 88–9, 92, 124, 125–7, 144, 173, 241, 247; German Reformed, 227, 229, 231, 240; Great Awakening, 230, 235; Lutherans, 92, 146, 177, 182–3, 227, 229, 231, 240; Moravians, 148, 177, 232–4, 235, 240, 242, 248, 261; north-south cultural ties, 230–1; Presbyterians, 92, 146, 165, 169, 173, 227, 228, 229, 230, 231, 239, 240, 244, 247, 248; Puritans, 40–1, 42; Quakers, 41–2, 107, 166, 231; rights of dissenters, 227–9; role of Bishop of Quebec in

French administration, 203; toleration in Maryland, 40; Weberites in South Carolina, 235–6. *See also* Immigration, Indian education and missions, S. P. G.
Rolfe, John, 49; improves tobacco, 21, marriage to Pocahontas, 25

St. Augustine, Fla., 88, 100, 112, 118, 119, 140, 188; and Negro slaves, 190; attacked by English, 98; attacked by Oglethorpe, 1740, 198–9; Creeks visit, 193; in War of Jenkins' Ear, 197–200; population of, 1749, 202; Spanish settlement of, 79
St. Mary's, Md., 37, 40–2, 72, 73; capital moved to Annapolis, 122; conjectural drawing of, 35; description of, 34
Sánchez, Francisco del Moral, 188
Sandys, Sir Edwin, 14, 27, 30
Sandys, George, 20, 29
Savannah, Ga.: settlement of, 181
Saxe Gotha, S. C. frontier township, 165, 169, 170, 235
Sectionalism, vii; and addition of new counties in Virginia, 156; and location of capital in Virginia, 156–7; and tobacco inspection in Virginia, 157; in Bacon's Rebellion, 65–7; in South Carolina, 90, 92; nature of, 247
Seneca Indians, 2, 62, 70, 114. *See also* Iroquois confederacy
Severn, battle of, 41
Shaftesbury, 1st Earl of. *See* Cooper, Anthony Ashley
Sharpe, Gov. Horatio: and Maryland frontier after Braddock's defeat, 215
Shawnee Indians, 57, 87, 204; linguistic classification of, 2; Sandy Creek expedition against, 212
Silk production, 18, 20, 45–6, 92–3, 183
Six Nations of Indians. *See* Iroquois confederacy
Smith, Captain John, 25; description of Indians by, 4; leadership of, 9
Smith, Sir Thomas, 13, 14
S. P. G. (Society for the Propagation of the Gospel in Foreign Parts), 180, 229, 240–4 *passim*; founded in 1701, 227; description of religious needs in southern colonies by, 227
South Carolina: act for regulation of Indian trade, 1707, 104; act restricting Indian trade, 1711, 129; administration of Indian trade, 1716–51, 191; agriculture in, 89, 92–3, 165–70 *passim*, 174–6; church and state, 226; competition with Virginia over Indian trade, 104, 128–9, 247; description of education in, 236; Dinwiddie-Glen controversy over Indian allies for Braddock, 209–13; evolution of government, 90, 92; geography of, 75, 163; Indians in, 76, 78;